STRUCTURING

SPACES

POETICS OF ORALITY AND LITERACY

John Miles Foley, series editor

STRUCTURING

SPACES

ORAL

POETICS

AND

ARCHITECTURE

IN EARLY

MEDIEVAL

ENGLAND

Lori Ann Garner

UNIVERSITY OF NOTRE DAME PRESS
NOTRE DAME, INDIANA

Manufactured in the United States of America

Library of Congress Cataloging-in-Publication Data

Garner, Lori Ann.
  Structuring spaces : oral poetics and architecture in early medieval England /
Lori Ann Garner.
      p.   cm.
  Includes bibliographical references and index.
  ISBN-13: 978-0-268-02980-7 (pbk. : alk. paper)
  ISBN-10: 0-268-02980-6 (pbk. : alk. paper)
  1. English poetry—Middle English, 1100–1500—History and criticism.
2. Architecture in literature.   3. Architecture and literature.   I. Title.
  PR317.A73G37   2011
  821.9'09357—dc22

                                                        2010052719

FOR SCOTT

CONTENTS

FIGURES

PREFACE AND
ACKNOWLEDGMENTS

In his oft-quoted "The Monsters and the Critics," J. R. R. Tolkien employs an extended allegory of architecture to describe the state of Anglo-Saxon scholarship in 1936:

> A man inherited a field in which was an accumulation of old stone, part of an older hall. Of the old stone some had already been used in building the house in which he actually lived, not far from the old house of his fathers. Of the rest he took some and built a tower. . . . From the top of that tower the man had been able to look out upon the sea. (11)

Tolkien's metaphor is no less meaningful today and seems an especially appropriate way to open an examination of Anglo-Saxon architectural and poetic traditions. Like the buildings and depictions of buildings that the following chapters explore, many of the most productive and insightful studies of Anglo-Saxon poetry and oral traditions alike have employed valuable "old stone" excavated from many and varied academic disciplines.

Tolkien, of course, was not alone in using architectural imagery to explain textual works or vice versa. Connections between literature and architecture are all around us. We can speak of "narrative architecture," "semantic architecture," and "grammatical architecture" and even read "architextural" interpretations of buildings as well as books.[1] Such metaphorical usages point toward important connections between and among these various art forms, many of which are explored in the opening chapter; however, my main emphasis in this volume is Anglo-Saxon architecture in a more literal sense. The chapters that follow examine actual buildings: Anglo-Saxon houses and halls, ancient Roman ruins, stone and wooden churches—in short, the real-world spaces that literally structured the Anglo-Saxon built environment and that informed the poetry that we still read today. Such buildings play prominent roles in the surviving Anglo-Saxon poetic corpus, and understanding the traditional associations underlying architectural descriptions can go far in aiding our interpretations of not only these poems but also verse composed well into the post-Conquest period that relied in part on this earlier architectural poetics.

The correspondences between buildings on the Anglo-Saxon landscape and their fictionalized counterparts are far from straightforward, however. The twentieth century saw the excavation of tremendous amounts of archaeological evidence from the Anglo-Saxon period and almost as many attempts to link these findings with surviving Old English poetry. Connections were initially pursued, however, largely to help date the poems and/or the archaeological remains, to "prove" the reality of such texts as *Beowulf,* or to otherwise confirm or deny hypotheses regarding the Anglo-Saxon world. The dangers of overstating such correlations have been amply noted, especially with regard to *Beowulf.*[2] Yet when it comes to especially problematic or ambiguous passages involving architectural description or metaphor, there is more work to be done to find alternative approaches to address the interrelationships between Anglo-Saxon poetry and archaeology. This book seeks to move beyond direct parallels and to extrapolate idiomatic and traditional meanings invested in poetic depictions of architecture, depictions that often seem at odds with archaeological realities.

The idiomatic, extralexical meaning of architectural description put forth here is certainly not limited to medieval England. In our twenty-first-century world, we speak of academics who live in "ivory towers" and admire women who rise through corporate "glass ceilings." But even though ivory towers certainly can exist[3] and architects such as Fay Jones are well known for their work with glass ceilings and walls, the less literal meanings of such idioms are quite clear to us. Thus even those who may never have seen an actual ceiling made of glass can nonetheless grasp the implications of the phrase. In these and other similar expressions, the idiomatic truths supersede the literal. Even in those instances when the literal and metaphorical merge, we readily recognize the symbolism involved, as in the "Breaking Barriers" event at Mills College in 2008. During the newly named Lorry I. Lokey Graduate School of Business's celebration of its history of preparing women for leadership, a female student "climbed a ladder and broke a six-foot by 12-foot glass ceiling made from Hollywood-style breakaway glass."[4] Despite the obviousness of this gesture's reliance on verbal idiom for us today, it can be all too easy to default to highly literal interpretations when reading architectural descriptions in the poetry of the Anglo-Saxons, whose traditional idiom often differs greatly from our own.

The problem here is that the intervening centuries have made idiomatic meanings that would doubtless have been quite clear for medieval audiences far less readily apparent to modern readers. With older texts deriving from oral traditions that can no longer be observed, the traditional associations are often difficult to discern. Even the connection of such works to any living oral tradition is sometimes debated. The most productive analyses have therefore approached medieval (and other oral-derived) works as points along a continuum. Following this model, I see no need either to posit a "purely" oral model or to deny the importance of literary influences; instead, in this volume I merely intend to demonstrate that in Anglo-Saxon times, as today, buildings lay at the heart of many integral facets of life and that understanding traditional architectonics of various kinds of structures from the period can enhance our interpretation of Old English oral-derived texts that made use of them.

A number of insightful studies have examined specific traditional associations of particular buildings or of individual phrases within isolated poems. My aim here is to expand the scope of such inquiry by examining depictions of buildings across the body of Anglo-Saxon poetry and tracing larger patterns of phraseology and imagery that emerge throughout the Old English corpus and that persist even well into the Middle English period. Architectural descriptions and references appear not only in the well-known cases of *Beowulf* and *The Ruin* but also in maxims, riddles, elegies, hagiographies, and even charms. Because of their universality, such buildings provide a productive lens through which to view many Anglo-Saxon cultural ideals and values. Toward these ends, the present study draws on scholarship from art history, archaeology, anthropology, and architecture, as well as the great wealth of studies addressing the literature itself. Among the most significant influences, however, is the vast body of works on oral traditions, which has developed over the years in important and unexpected ways. Albert Lord and Milman Parry's original oral-formulaic theory, which initially demonstrated an analogous relationship between Homeric and South Slavic epic, opened the door to exploration of features shared by oral traditions and oral-derived texts from numerous cultures. From this foundation, the field has been expanded by many scholars who have increased our understanding not only of the composition but also of the transmission and reception of oral traditional verbal art in countless cultural traditions.[5] Studies in medieval English literature have been especially rich, and I am greatly indebted to the many scholars whose work is cited in the chapters that follow—in Tolkien's words, "the learned and revered masters from whom we humbly derive" (13).

At a more personal level, I also owe a huge debt to the generosity of numerous institutions and individuals who have graciously supported and assisted my work on this project. From the outset, I must make the qualification that all errors remain entirely my own. I take some comfort in Seth Lerer's compellingly argued claim that, from medieval times to modern, error has been a defining mode of identity in the history of scholarship, that we all "live, in the academy, by blunder" (*Error and the Academic Self* 2). I am grateful to the National Endowment for the Humanities for a summer stipend that funded research during June and July 2006.[6] The University of Illinois Research Board was also generous in providing funds for travel and equipment for the accompanying photographs. The libraries and staff at the following institutions provided access to a vast wealth of relevant resources: Princeton University, the University of Illinois at Urbana-Champaign, and Rhodes College.

I greatly appreciate the helpful feedback I received when presenting work related to this project at the 2002 Modern Language Association meeting (Old English Division), 2004 and 2009 Midwest Modern Language Association meetings, and the 2007 Illinois Medieval Association conference. Portions of chapters 2, 3, and 6 appeared in earlier forms in

Essays in Medieval Studies, Parergon, and *Clio: A Journal of Literature, History, and the History of Philosophy.* I am grateful for helpful ideas received during these journals' review processes and for their permission to publish portions of this work here.

Though I did not of course realize what role this turn of events was to play at the time, I owe many thanks to librarian Frances Chen (*in me - moriam*), who, after I completed my graduate degree from the University of Missouri in 2000, hired me to work in Princeton University's Architecture Library while my husband completed his own program at Princeton. It was here that the seeds of this project began to form in my mind. For assistance at much later stages, I owe thanks to Charlie Wright for useful comments on and bibliographic suggestions for chapters 1, 2, and 4. Thanks also to Heather Maring for helpful comments on chapters 4 and 5, as well as for hours of enjoyable discussion of Old English literature. Thanks to David Mason, Durham County Archaeologist, for sharing his knowledge of Binchester Roman Fort and its relationship to St. John's Saxon Church at Escomb, and to Mary Wright, lifelong member of St. Peter's Parish Church in Heysham, for sharing her knowledge of St. Peter's Church and St. Patrick's Chapel. Thanks also to Julie Woodhouse for permission to print her photograph of the Carn Euny fogou.

Among the many other friends and colleagues who, directly and indirectly, have helped see this book to fulfillment, the following deserve special mention: Mark Amodio, Rob Barrett, Martin Camargo, Anne-Marie Foley, Melissa Free, Larry Guinn (*in memoriam*), Betsy Hearne, Anna Ivy, Kara Laughlin, Amy Mohr, Scott Newstok, Elizabeth Oyler, Kenan Padgett, David Riner, Julia Saville, Renée Trilling, Julia Walker, Kirstin Wilcox, and Gillen Wood. I owe special thanks to Andrea Lively for her lifelong friendship, for her convincingly genuine interest in Anglo-Saxon architecture, which offers little practical value in her own field of health sciences, and, perhaps most of all, for her ready willingness to drive on the left side of the road so that I could take the photographs for this volume.

It has been a true pleasure and privilege to work with Barbara Hanrahan, director of the University of Notre Dame Press. She has been closely involved with this project almost from its inception, and I will always be grateful for her confidence in me and in the ideas underlying this book.

It has been a privilege to work with Rebecca DeBoer, Margaret Gloster, Wendy McMillen, and all those who helped see this book through publication. I especially want to thank Sheila Berg for her careful and thorough copyediting of my manuscript. I am also hugely indebted to the anonymous readers who provided invaluable comments and suggestions for revision, which I have done my best here to incorporate. Especially deserving of my thanks is John Miles Foley, "gleaw modes cræfta," mentor and friend for more than fifteen years. Through his encouragement and his example, he has inspired all of my work in Old English and in oral tradition. I am proud and honored that this book appears in his series.

And now for those closest. Though he is (at least I think) quite a few years away from reading this book, I want to thank my son, Nathaniel, whose love, imagination, and laughter keep me going every single day. At the age of five, Nathaniel made a drawing of Grendel with three arms, one as a spare. I keep it framed on my desk as a reminder that there will always be new ways to think about these ancient stories. Last, and most important, is Scott Garner, who must be thanked twice. First, as my closest colleague and collaborator, he has my everlasting gratitude for helping me sort through ideas at every phase, for offering his assistance with Latin texts, for teaching seven courses in oral tradition with me, all of which led to numerous insightful discussions relevant to this project, and for painstakingly proofreading almost every draft that the manuscript underwent. As my husband and partner in all things, Scott deserves even more thanks for his unwavering support and belief in me during every stage of my work on this book. His academic and professional expertise made it far better than it could have been otherwise, and his loving encouragement sustained me through its fruition. It is with much love and admiration that I dedicate this book, imperfect as it is, to him.

PART I

TOWARD

AN

ARCHITECTURAL

ORAL

POETICS

CHAPTER ONE

ORAL TRADITION AND VERNACULAR ARCHITECTURE

Sum mæg wrætlice   weorc ahycgan
heahtimbra gehwæs;   hond bið gelæred,
wis ond gewealden,   swa bið wyrhtan ryht,
sele asettan,   con he sidne ræced
fæste gefegan   wiþ færdryrum.
Sum mid hondum mæg   hearpan gretan,
ah he gleobeames   gearobrygda list. . . .

———

[A certain one is able to wondrously plan the making of all high
timbers; his hand is trained, wise and skillful, as is right for the
worker, to establish a hall; he knows how to securely join the wide
building against sudden downfall. A certain one is able to greet the
harp with hands; he possesses the cleverness of quick movements
on the joy-wood. . . .]

Gifts of Men 44–50[1]

If proverbial wisdom encapsulates widely held cultural truths, then the
commentary on builders and harpists in the Old English *Gifts of Men*
has much insight to offer modern readers regarding Anglo-Saxon conceptions of architecture and song and the relationship of these two art
forms to one another. The *Gifts of Men* catalogues approximately thirty

3

skills[2]—hunting, swimming, fighting, singing, sailing, riding, learning, writing, and many more, each distinguished as a valued "gift" from God—in seemingly random patterns of order and inclusion. What these otherwise disparate skills do have in common, though, is the unambiguous respect of the poet; all are *sundorgiefe,* "gifts apart," worthy of utmost admiration,[3] and especially prominent among the itemized crafts are those related to performance and architectonics, themes to which the poet returns repeatedly. Most of the poem's gifts are treated only one time each, often in as little as a single half-line; skills in oral or musical performance, however, receive 9 of the relatively brief poem's 113 lines, and skills in architectural prowess receive 7,[4] suggesting a heightened awareness of the value of these particular art forms.[5]

While the poem's typical Anglo-Saxon paratactic style ultimately leaves to its audience the task of discerning the actual relationships of these crafts to one another, the immediate juxtaposition of musical performance to architecture in lines 44–50 invites further speculation. In addition to the privilege of extended treatment, both of these gifts are presented as performative in nature. The portrayal of building syntactically parallels that of a harpist's performance, and, most notably, the mental planning of such building is depicted as concurrent with the act of physical execution. Rather than an architect designing a structure to be built later by others possessing gifts of construction, design and execution are instead presented as complementary aspects of a single gift. The craftsman able to plan *(ahycgan)* a building possesses hands that are "gelæred, wis ond gewealden" ["trained, wise and skillful"] (45–46), and thus it is said to be "wyrhtan ryht, sele asettan" ["right for the worker, to build a hall"] (46–47).[6] Such a combination of planning and building is striking because the overarching concern of this poem lies in its isolation of the various gifts scattered by God among men, leading us to expect that skills would be stratified to the extent that they were conceived of as being separable.

The conflation of architectural design and execution in the builder's gift is then immediately followed by a similar description of the harpist's craft. At a very basic level, the builder's hands constructing with wooden timbers *(timbra)* are paralleled by the harpist's hands striking his instrument—also made of wood *(beam).* Further, both crafts are characterized by interrelated physical skill and mental knowledge, traits that in each case are linked explicitly in the craftsman's hands. Like the builder's "wise" *(wis)* hands, the harpist's hands have physical dexterity resulting from mental acuity, *list*. The physical skill required for artistic production and the mental knowledge necessary for composition could have been presented separately by the poet, as occurs in other works of a similar nature,[7] but here they are put forth as being inextricable. In building as in music and poetry, planning and production occur together in time and space, gnomic wisdom here demonstrating a fundamental conception of architecture, not as preconceived plans leading to the subsequent creation of static artifacts, but as dynamic and responsive acts of composition in performance.[8]

The juxtaposition of and parallels between these arts are especially noteworthy as they are included in the format of a catalogue, a form characterized by lists or inventories but providing "a more comprehensive exposition of its subject" and suggesting "the interrelations among the various aspects of the subject" (Howe, *Old English Catalogue* 21). As Nicholas Howe observes for the *Gifts of Men* and catalogue poetry more generally, even an "accidental" arrangement of items in a given list can nonetheless be "suggestive" (111). As wisdom poetry, catalogues such as the *Gifts of Men* can be understood to present truths and organizational logic that would be most conventional and thus most obvious to an Anglo-Saxon audience. As we shall see, this didactic wisdom conveyed through the similar portrayals of performers and builders is also corroborated by less obvious connections found throughout the poetic corpus more widely.

The linking of verbal and material art forms through their performative aspects has profound and far-reaching implications for the reading of Old English poetry today. The present study argues that throughout the corpus of Old English poetry the skills of the builder and the poet intersect in many complex and often unexpected ways, with their respective crafts drawing demonstrably from many of the same traditionally encoded motifs and images. Through patterns of repeated use, building characteristics—as well as the phraseology used to describe these characteristics in verse—develop powerful associative meanings for verbal and material craftsmen, as well as for their respective audiences. Such connections are neither simple nor straightforward and require careful attention to historical, social, linguistic, and generic contexts alike. First, then, let us turn to an exploration of what constitutes "architecture" on the Anglo-Saxon landscape and in Old English verse.

DEFINING THE BUILT ENVIRONMENT

Even the scant survivals from the Anglo-Saxon architectural landscape give us some small sense of the varied structures that would have informed poetic descriptions of built space and their reception by Anglo-Saxon audiences. Prehistoric underground dwellings can still be found in Cornwall and along England's northern borders. Later, four hundred years of Roman rule left an impressive legacy on the landscape, and the Anglo-Saxons inherited much from this period both in building materials and in inspiration for the literary imagination. The Anglo-Saxons themselves built primarily from wood, though they used stone to a limited extent, especially in ecclesiastical structures later in the period. They incorporated into their buildings elements from Scandinavian, Celtic, Roman, and other traditions, often synthesizing features from multiple styles. They also often built these structures on Roman and Celtic sites and sometimes reused Roman stones, making it impossible to pin down any monolithic Anglo-Saxon style or to separate that which is unequivocally Anglo-Saxon from the rest of the surrounding landscape.[9] The fluid and evolving sense of space that resulted in Anglo-Saxon building practice is in turn often reflected in the Old English poetic vocabulary itself.

As is true for many cognitive categories, the Anglo-Saxons did not have a term equivalent to our concept of architecture for denoting built space.[10] This lack of correspondence is not surprising given that the word *architecture* itself developed in the very different cultural context of the seventeenth century from *architect,* a term that had the elite sense of "master builder" for more than a hundred years before any more general sense of building applied.[11] In contrast to this primary historical sense of "architecture," which implicitly focuses our attention on artist and product, Anglo-Saxon terms related to building tended to emphasize neither the individual designer nor the individual structure but rather the function to which built space was put and how such spaces were perceived, a conception of space much closer to the performative model seen in the *Gifts of Men.* Old English *burh* is a very common and widely encompassing term applied to built constructions and is among the closest equivalents to modern senses of "architecture";[12] however, *burh*'s multivalence reflects a distinctively Anglo-Saxon sense of space and demonstrates the need for a more expansive and reception-oriented model of "architecture" than the modern English vocabulary readily provides.

Burh's primary sense is that of an individual structure, "fortified enclosure" or "fortified dwelling," with a secondary and more generalized sense of a "fortified town" or "city."[13] As is typical with Old English vocabulary, greater specificity under this very general rubric is obtained largely through compounding, with *burh* occurring far more frequently in compounds than in isolation.[14] While *burh* compounds can and do delimit certain aspects of meaning such as function or location, these compounds, like *burh* itself, are ambiguous as to whether their specific referents are individual structures, building complexes, or even entire cities. *Burh-bot*, for instance, can refer to the maintenance of an individual "fortification" or to an entire "town"; likewise, *burh-weg* can mean either a general city road or a road leading to an individual building.[15]

Despite the vast range of meaning, what all concepts associated with *burh* share is a notion of built space in relation to its physical environment.[16] However, that space need be neither permanent nor detached from natural objects or materials, conditions that are commonly assumed in modern conceptions of architecture. While *burh* does unequivocally denote manipulation of materials in construction for human use (or for the use of personified objects, as in the case of some Exeter Book riddles),[17] the term does not exclude natural elements that interact with or function as built space, and *burh* can be used in reference to earthen mounds surrounding a city or hills on which cities and buildings are built.[18] The modern term *architecture*, of course, can also have broader senses overlapping with those here described for *burh* in the Anglo-Saxon period, but to most productively apply it to Anglo-Saxon practice a broadened awareness and a shift in emphasis are needed.

Another difficulty in understanding Anglo-Saxon building processes is that, as the example of *burh* illustrates, description of Old English architecture, especially in poetry, is most often characterized by a potentially frustrating lack of specificity. Even the most descriptive architectural terms frequently have numerous referents, conflating nature, buildings, and even human emotions[19] without maintaining clear-cut delineation.[20]

Terms for the buildings themselves follow similar patterns, *sele* referring to a modest "house," a grander "hall," or simply a generic "dwelling," and *ræced* likewise denoting structures as varied as "house," "hall," or "palace."[21] Further, in Old English poetry terms applied to buildings do not always differentiate natural from man-made structures, nor do they distinguish permanent from temporary. Such ranges of meaning in many descriptive words are certainly familiar to speakers of modern English as well, but it is generally the *only* type of description we are given during this period, with no "truly detailed descriptions" appearing until the twelfth century (Pickles 11). Indeed, "relatively few words among the many for dwelling and dwelling places seem clearly to relate to concrete structures" (Grundy and Roberts 102). The multivalence and ambiguity of architecturally descriptive terminology in Old English verse impede in many ways our modern ability to mentally process the verbal images provided, but often what we lose in visual detail we may gain in associative meaning. Or, as Lynne Grundy and Jane Roberts have put it, Old English poetic vocabulary, "notoriously opaque in reference," is "connotative rather than narrowly denotative" (102).

In the end, though this study is devoted to representations of "architecture," it also investigates a great number of structures that might seem architecturally ephemeral by some definitions. Accordingly, this exploration of Anglo-Saxon architecture as represented in surviving poetry examines built spaces and their descriptions sharing common phraseology and important associative meanings regardless of their position within conventional classification schemes or sometimes anachronistic categories. Across the spectrum of Old English poetry, ancient ruins, temporary military tents, Christian churches, heroic halls, and even nests or fox holes are described through common modes of poetic expression, often necessitating a shift in widely accepted cognitive categories for modern-day readers. The present study seeks to explore these imagined spaces and their real-world counterparts on the Anglo-Saxon landscape through a dual focus on architectonics and traditional verse. But in order to fine-tune this perspective, we will first turn to the theoretical frameworks that offer especially helpful methodologies for this type of analysis, specifically, those approaches found within the widely divergent fields of vernacular architecture and oral theory.

ANGLO-SAXON VERNACULAR ARCHITECTURE

Since Old English poetry does not sharply delineate among most kinds of built spaces, analysis of its architectural description requires an equally flexible conception of architecture in general, and here we can draw extensively from relevant work in vernacular architecture, a field interested in the "ethnographic" quality of buildings (Carter and Cromley xviii) and thus in keeping with the more performative model of building evidenced in the *Gifts of Men* and elsewhere in Old English poetry. With origins dating to the nineteenth century, studies in vernacular architecture have been characterized by a highly productive disciplinary inclusiveness. As a field of inquiry, it has both influenced and been influenced by theories and methodologies from not only architecture and architectural history but also folklore, anthropology, sociology, cultural geography, material culture, women's studies, archaeology, urban studies, and social history. In the United States in particular, the impact of vernacular architecture has been especially strong, affecting not only analytical studies but choices in design, preservation, policy planning, and curriculum development across the country.[22] The field's characteristic inclusivity extends to its subject matter as well, with studies in vernacular architecture addressing "individual buildings, assemblages of such buildings, and entire architectural landscapes" (Carter and Cromley xiv). As the name "vernacular" implies, the field seeks to understand each building tradition in its own cultural terms, and it is this open-ended and tradition-specific perspective that pertains most directly to this study.[23] As Camille Wells explained in *Perspectives in Vernacular Architecture II,* vernacular architecture denotes "less a *kind* of building than an *approach* to looking at buildings" (4; original emphasis).[24] Though models of vernacular architecture have been most notable in North American research and have seen very little direct application in medieval studies, the present work seeks to demonstrate not only the validity but also the necessity, of employing parallel approaches in understanding both the actual and the imagined spaces of Anglo-Saxon England.

It is important to note from the outset that neither the broader field of vernacular architecture nor my application to Anglo-Saxon buildings is limited to the study of "rustic" structures divorced from what might be considered high style or elite constructions.[25] Such delineation would be lethal to any comprehensive treatment of Anglo-Saxon building practices and perceptions for a number of reasons, not the least of which is that the very nature of the surviving archaeological and poetic record would seem automatically to privilege the less "ordinary." The buildings that survive to the present day are made almost exclusively of stone, a costlier building material and one associated more closely with Latin learning than with Germanic tradition. Likewise, the textual evidence that survives from the period deals much more with grand Anglo-Saxon halls than with "everyday" dwellings.[26] Perhaps most important, any such division based on perceived commonness or lack of refinement risks creating classifications inapplicable to architecture, as depictions in surviving Old English verse not uncommonly employ similar phraseology to describe structures as divergent as a king's hall, a modest church, an underground prison, or, for that matter, an earthen grave. The more fluid parameters of vernacular architecture also encourage and validate the study of "important and overlooked properties of impermanent architecture—structures designed for immediate and usually transitory functions" (Wells, "Introduction" 6).[27] This kind of expansion of what might typically be understood as architecture is very important in the present study, which treats impermanent architecture, such as camp tents and the elusive "burgeteld" in *Judith*, alongside more permanent halls and dwellings.

The chapters that follow thus avoid classification on aesthetic or functional grounds and instead examine the spectrum of architectural description on its own terms as it presents itself in the surviving manuscripts and against the context of the built environment as experienced during the Anglo-Saxon period, a goal well served by approaches from vernacular architecture. Characterized by "an aversion to define," a "growing reluctance to embark on classificatory schemes," and a "permissive approach" (Carter and Herman, "Introduction" 3), the field of vernacular architecture not only allows for but also is actually defined by an emergent and dynamic process of inquiry. In keeping with this concept of vernacular architecture, I am not interested in demarcating elite from common, manmade from natural, temporary from permanent, or even Anglo-Saxon from non-Anglo-Saxon but rather in examining the range of built spaces depicted in Old English poetry in relation to one another, to the larger built environment, and to their poetic and traditional contexts.

OLD ENGLISH ORAL POETICS

This book works from the premise that the built landscape and contemporary verse were produced alongside and informed by many of the same social, political, and cultural factors, and it examines the implications of these and related connections. An examination of built space across the spectrum of Old English poetry shows how the complex and dynamic nature of Anglo-Saxon cultural identity emerges powerfully through built and imagined spaces alike. However, the correspondences are far from tidy, one-to-one representations. Old English poetry includes references to numerous buildings whose architectural features would never have existed together on the actual landscape and, in some cases, that would have been structural impossibilities. Old English poetry also gives specific architectural description to imagined spaces altogether outside the human realm. It includes architectural metaphors that do not work at a strictly literal level. And buildings appear in translated works that depart radically from the sources they adapt. While a fluid concept of architecture—one that encompasses everything within the built environment as it was perceived in the Anglo-Saxon world, however far removed such structures might be from modern and conventional concepts of architecture—allows us to see connections across a wider range of built space, it takes us only part of the way toward understanding how descriptions of space function within Old English poetry in particular. How do we interpret repeated phraseology across the body of poetic architectural description? How do we account for seeming mistakes and inconsistencies in the use of poetic architectural imagery? For these questions, it is important to look beyond archaeological evidence and architectural possibilities and view poetic architectural description from the perspective of the surrounding oral traditional context.

Architectural description as it is present in Old English verse relies equally on the physical reality of the architectural landscape and on an oral poetics that invests such descriptions with associative meanings, a phenomenon that is perhaps most apparent at points where architectural description seems to diverge from physical and material realities of the period. By "oral poetics," I refer to the "powerful, supple, and highly associative expressive economy" that "enables poets efficiently to bring worlds of traditional meaning(s) to their narratives by deploying a vast array of compositional devices, some as small and highly tradition specific as a single lexeme or phrase and others as large and widely shared among discrete traditions as story patterns" (Amodio, *Writing the Oral Tradition* xvi).[28] There is no need here to posit an unambiguously oral provenance for any of the works discussed, especially given the complex relationships linking oral and literate cultures of the Anglo-Saxon period in what has been discussed productively in terms of an "oral-literate nexus" where the interplay between the Latin and the vernacular resulted in a "diglossic character of life in medieval England" with many types and degrees of literacy contributing to Anglo-Saxon textual culture (Amodio, *Writing the Oral Tradition* 15). Individuals in such a society used oral traditions and literary texts in a range of complex and often interrelated ways, and it would be irresponsible to reduce this reality to a simplistic process of evolution from a pure oral state to a literate one. Rather, the two modes of communication can be seen as working together and alongside one another in dynamic and ever-changing ways.[29]

"Oral" as it appears in this work thus necessarily refers to the "oral-influenced," "oral-derived," or "oral-connected" natures of texts produced in an era of newly emerging literacy, that is, works of verbal art that "employ the idiom of oral tradition and assume an audience fluent in that idiom" (Foley, *Homer's Traditional Art* xiv). The analysis offered here follows the line of thinking that "at some early point, verse in Old English was oral. From the time that Old English was first written, however, composition of verse in writing may be defined as 'literate' but only in a seriously restricted sense" (O'Brien O'Keeffe, *Visible Song* ix). It would be mistaken to project onto the Anglo-Saxons notions of twentieth- and twenty-first-century literacy, and the most productive discussions of Old English literature have instead allowed for the likelihood of numerous transitional states between the polarized extremes of pure "orality" and pure "literacy."[30] During a state of what Katherine O'Brien O'Keeffe has termed "transitional literacy," Old English poets—as well as scribes and translators—continued to operate according to the modes of an oral traditional society, and, as a result, the written poetry that we have exhibits many features of a "residual orality" (*Visible Song* x). In turn, as John Miles Foley has persuasively argued, any text employing such features "promotes—and its readership continues—a tradition of reception"

(*Singer of Tales in Performance* 137). The present work examines this oral-derived nature of Old English poetry—and its reciprocal tradition of reception—specifically as manifest in poetic depictions of architecture.

Because so little can be said with any certainty about the oral composition of Old English verse, this work concentrates more directly on aspects of reception, specifically, how audiences contemporary with the poetry being produced—audiences aware of and familiar with an ambient oral tradition—would have been likely to receive and interpret architectural phraseology and imagery in poetic contexts. My method throughout this study has been to work outward from individual lexemes, phrases, and clusters of images that are repeated in various architectural descriptions with an eye toward narrative and associative contexts that are shared across recurrent usages. The goal of this approach is to come to a clearer understanding of a given verbal unit's "traditional referentiality," what Foley defines as "the resonance between the singular moment and the traditional context" (*Homer's Traditional Art* 23). Through traditional referentiality, "value-added phrases, scenes, and other patterns resonate in a network of signification, with the singular instance dwarfed—but implicitly informed—by the whole" (23). Awareness of this traditional referentiality puts us in a much better position to adopt the role of "audience" in this complex and reciprocal exchange between verbal performance and interpretation.

This concept of traditional referentiality can be extended to architecture through its pertinence to spatial concerns. In oral tradition studies, the physicality of poetic space has been addressed through the concept of a "performance arena," a phrase Foley has used to designate "the 'place' that performer/author and audience go to compose and receive a given work" (*Homer's Traditional Art* 23).[31] In a living oral tradition, such a space would most likely constitute a shared location, a physical connection between performer and audience that cannot be assumed with a printed text. Though the dynamic is in obvious ways a very different one, "there is no wholesale dislocation when the performance arena changes from a 'real' site to a rhetorically induced forum in a text. The performer-audience relationship is no longer face-to-face, but it rhetorically recalls the same arena because it mirrors the same event" (Foley, *Singer of Tales in Performance* 23).[32]

This performance model, with its implication of shared space, underscores the reciprocal relationship between performer and audience.[33] The audience, through repeated experience within a given performance arena, can recognize and interpret traditional referentiality that is often otherwise elusive. In the case of Old English poetry, the often uncontextualized formulas and themes repeated throughout the body of verse suggest audiences who share an understanding of an idiomatic language, a language whose meanings are not always readily discernible to modern readers but that are likely nonetheless to have been highly resonant for readers and listeners contemporary with the poetry's production. Similarly, architectural spaces can be defined not only by actions that happen within them and by their features of construction but also by the connotative power that helps to determine the way they are experienced. These concepts of built space and oral poetics overlap when we consider that the poet describing *physical* space must also and necessarily enter a specialized *poetic* space, one that relies equally on audience familiarity with verbal and architectural art forms.

In extending relevant concepts from oral theory beyond the verbal realm, I argue that Anglo-Saxon architecture and Old English poetry share a common vernacular and that these connections were likely to have been recognized and appreciated by contemporary audiences. The concept of tradition put forth here is not a monolithic one, however. The complex interface of orality and literacy during the medieval period is characterized by many and varied cultural traditions exerting influence on the production of texts and buildings alike.[34] Even during the rise of vernacular literacy, early medieval composition and reception were highly dynamic processes, neither confined by the rigidity of a fixed text nor limited to any single cultural ideology.

MORE THAN A METAPHOR: TOWARD AN ANGLO-SAXON ARCHITECTURAL POETICS

Archaeological and textual evidence indicates that Anglo-Saxon architecture operated according to parallel principles, existing neither as the visions of single, solitary individuals nor as slavish copies. Much like the poetry of the time period, the architecture of early medieval England demonstrates a powerful syncretism of cultural traditions, innovation within limits, and reliance on traditional associations. Like the Old English poetry that seamlessly and unapologetically merges Germanic and Christian traditions,[35] many surviving Anglo-Saxon churches employ what today would be seen as inconsistent architectural styles and methods from various sources.[36] The church of St. John's at Escomb (fig. 20) follows the basic plan of Anglo-Saxon buildings but does so with stones excavated from Roman ruins;[37] the more elaborate monastery at Reculver at Kent incorporates Roman stones into its structure and does so within the walls of the original Roman site. As Eric Fernie has noted, the "buildings erected by and for the Anglo-Saxons" cannot be easily grouped together as representing a single, independent style (*Architecture of the Anglo-Saxons* 10). Anglo-Saxon audiences of the poems would have been accustomed to syntheses of traditions and familiar with the buildings that were constructed on similar principles. What remains is for us to better understand the precise nature of these implied connections.

But while the specific connections between architectural and poetic arts that underlie the present study have not before been fully explored, metaphors equating oral poetry and architecture are long-standing, appearing frequently in studies of both oral poetry and vernacular architecture.[38] Keith Bosley's explanation of oral composition as it relates to the Finnish *Kalevala* includes a vivid architectural metaphor: "A bard's repertoire can be compared with what one uses to build a garden wall—bricks, mortar, and a length of string to guide the builder. The bricks are the 'formulas'. . . . [T]hey may be whole or half bricks, chunks of stone, pebbles, flints, shards. The mortar is the bard's powers of invention: here, where the bricks are regular, only a thin layer is needed; there more is needed, in which to set the awkward pieces" (xxvi). Such metaphors have had a long history in oral-formulaic theory, with Albert Lord frequently discuss - ing the units of meaning employed in oral composition in architectural terms, as he described the process of laying a "foundation" (78), "building" a theme (92), and adding to a formulaic composition with "ornamental" motifs (89). And applying the metaphor to Old English formulaic verse more specifically, Robert Payson Creed refers to words and phrases in *Beowulf*'s prosody as "the building blocks of the poet's composition"

("How" 215). These metaphors, however, tend to focus on the compositional aspect of oral performance and are in this sense potentially limiting. Therefore, in an effort to shift scholarly focus away from composition toward transmission, reception, and the dynamic exchange between performer and audience, Foley offers the metaphor of language as a replacement for architectural imagery in describing the register of South Slavic traditional verse when he writes, "Precisely because it is a language, and not a handy compositional kit of readymade building blocks, the *guslar*'s performance style is subject to expectable avenues of differentiation one encounters with any language" ("Performance of Homeric Epic"). In other words, nuanced meanings are created through subtle manipulation of formulaic phraseology, and thus repeated formulas and themes are never *merely* building blocks.

Neither, of course, are actual architectural structures themselves simple accumulations of similar building blocks in the material world. As those utilizing built space employ and encounter specific materials and features across a range of social contexts, patterns of form and function inevitably emerge; thus, over time, certain types of structures become invested with powerful connotative meanings in specific cultural contexts. And just as scholars of oral tradition have turned to building metaphors to convey the functionality and economy of orally composed verse, those working with architecture repeatedly choose metaphors of poetry and oral tradition to convey the more aesthetic and creative aspects of building with traditional materials. Henry Glassie, for instance, counters notions of the mundane in vernacular architecture by observing that "buildings, like poems and rituals, realize culture" (*Vernacular Architecture* 17). Jean Baudrillard also observes that "at some point, architecture is like poetry" (Baudrillard and Nouvel 66). And James Warfield's 2005 exhibition at the University of Illinois featuring stone vernacular architecture from various regions of the world exemplified these cross-disciplinary connections in its very title: *Stone Poems*.[39] Further, the interchangeability of architecture and verbal art as referent and analogical equivalent—or, more precisely, the metaphor's tenor and vehicle—indicates that the parallels are not purely superficial. Such metaphors are frequently employed because they are effective, and this effectiveness exists because the underlying connections between the two art forms are indeed real and tangible.[40]

As the above examples illustrate, metaphors linking oral and oral-connected poetry with architecture can be employed in myriad ways. But the connections explored in the present study are best reflected in R. M. Liuzza's more nuanced architectural metaphor to explain *Beowulf*'s complex position "between song and text": "Like an Anglo-Saxon church made from the salvaged stones of a Roman temple, the structure of *Beowulf* may reveal complex layers of source and context; built perhaps by many hands over many years but according to an ancient plan and with a single purpose, it is unified by use and time rather than pre-formed design" (*Beowulf* 31). I seek here to explore the underlying connections that give this and related metaphors such force and to examine the wider implications for our reading of Anglo-Saxon architecture as it is depicted in Old English poetry. By taking advantage of developments in vernacular architecture, oral theory, and medieval studies more widely, a reexamination of architecture in Anglo-Saxon poetry through a more comprehensive and thoroughly contextualized approach becomes possible. *Beowulf*'s Heorot, of course, has been previously and quite extensively examined for architectural and archaeological accuracy,[41] as has the structure described in *The Ruin*.[42] Less attention, however, has been paid to the prisons in *Juliana* and *Andreas*, *Judith*'s "burgeteld," the "feldhus" of the *Exodus*, or the elaborately described architecture of hell in *Christ and Satan*. Important, too, are architectural metaphors in such poems as *Christ I*, a charm against wens, and the maxims. These images cross boundaries of religion, function, and genre; taken together, though, they give us a more complete picture of how buildings were perceived and used to create meaning in Old English poetic contexts.

Chapter 2 thus begins my investigation by examining the traditional associations inherent in building materials used and seen by the Anglo-Saxons, that is, the actual wood, stone, and earth. Particular attention is given here to such connotations as found in the epic *Beowulf* both because it exhibits a large variety of architectural structures and because it has previously received by far the greatest attention in terms of its architectural descriptions' correspondence to the archaeological record. Central to this chapter's argument is that Heorot's idealized descriptions establish a correspondence between *comitatus* ideals of heroism and specific building features (most notably, timber construction, height, elevated location, prominent gables, and arched structures), connections that are then evoked—and sometimes subverted—in subsequent architectural descriptions within the poem. From the famous wooden hall of Heorot to the subterranean abode of Grendel's kin beneath the mere to the stone and earth construction of the dragon's lair and even to Beowulf's memorial monument, *Beowulf* employs numerous architectural images to evoke important traditional associations for Anglo-Saxon audiences, which can in turn help us understand elements in the description of other structures in such generically divergent poems as *The Ruin, Christ,* and *Andreas.*

Chapter 3 then focuses exclusively on depictions of structures even further removed from the actual Anglo-Saxon landscape, especially those found in poems translated or adapted from known Greek and Latin sources. Buildings as varied as dedicated prisons, biblical tents and pavilions, the architectural structures of hell, and legendary temples appear frequently across a wide range of texts and genres, including the Old English *Andreas, Judith, Daniel, Christ, Elene, Genesis, Exodus,* and *Juliana,* and these structures that were drawn from other cultures and traditions often posed interesting challenges for translators. Examining thematic and phraseological patterns in the adaptation of foreign or otherwise unfamiliar buildings can help us understand more precisely how Anglo-Saxon poets recast built spaces into the oral traditional register and also how given images might be best interpreted, not solely in a literal sense, but in terms of their connotative and associative meanings. The treatment of these more unusual structures thus often provides helpful insights into Anglo-Saxon perceptions of various building types and in turn also aids our interpretation of the poems as a whole.

Chapter 4 continues the inquiry by exploring the metonymic meanings underlying a number of figurative uses of architecture in Old English poetry, including an extended and highly technical metaphor in the first of the *Advent Lyrics (Christ I)* of Christ as the cornerstone, the formation of the bird's dwelling in *The Phoenix,* the many architectural metaphors in the Exeter Book riddles, and even a healing charm against *wens*[43] that demands a swelling to shrink "as muck in a wall." Across this diversity in terms of genre is a unity in architectural expression, and examining these and other figurative images in light of actual architectural practices and in the context of more literal poetic architectural description puts us in a much better position to understand precisely what architectural metaphors and similes are implying about the subjects with which built structures are compared.

Chapter 5 looks more closely at the role of architectural description in interpreting the past and negotiating multiple layers of cultural history as well as personal memory. The body of poems in the Exeter Book manuscript known collectively as "elegies" draws especially heavily on architectural imagery with their numerous descriptions of life in idealized Anglo-Saxon halls as well as ruminations on the former glories of ancient stone ruins. A number of cruxes in interpretation of these poems result from seeming inconsistencies between poetic descriptions (sometimes highly technical) and archaeological evidence. During the past century, for instance, lack of archaeological correspondences with the highly technical descriptions in *The Ruin* have led scholars to place the described ruins in such divergent locations as Bath, Babylon, Hadrian's Wall, and Chester, none of these locations entirely satisfactory from an archaeological perspective. Adding to such speculation the perspective of the surrounding oral tradition, however, explains apparent contradictions in this poem as well as images in other elegies, such as the wall in *The Wanderer,* the "earth-hall" of *The Wife's Lament,* and even elegiac passages embedded in longer narrative works such as *Beowulf.*

Chapter 6 is the first of two chapters that explore continuations and developments of building practices beyond the Anglo-Saxon period into post-Conquest England, examining first the programmatic replacement of Anglo-Saxon spaces with Anglo-Norman cathedrals and castles, then the subtle persistence of Anglo-Saxon architectural practices in the midst of such radical changes, and finally the implications of the emergent Norman architecture on early Middle English verse still to some extent reliant on Old English oral poetics, with special attention given to the verse *Brut.* Extending this discussion of dual oral and literate influences on the production of verse, chapter 7 examines poetic architectural description found in later Middle English narrative verse, specifically, *King Horn, Havelok the Dane, Sir Orfeo,* and *Sir Gawain and the Green Knight.* Just as Anglo-Norman builders continued to employ certain methods of Anglo-Saxon construction in their work, these later medieval texts all share thematic and, to a lesser extent, phraseological modes of description with Old English poetry in their depictions of built space. The pervasiveness of traditional architectural and poetic features during a time of such marked changes attests to the continuing resonance of Old English oral poetics amid numerous other architectural and literary influences during the Anglo-Norman period. Thus it is that, to various degrees and in different ways, architectural descriptions in these works serve to negotiate complex issues of social class, to develop characterization of buildings' inhabitants, and to subtly shape audience response to narrative events. Finally, a brief afterword explores ways modern audiences encounter actual and fictionalized Anglo-Saxon spaces, both in surviving parish churches scattered across England and in modern media disseminated to a global audience. Special attention is given to those specific architectural features that were charged with associative meaning in Anglo-Saxon times and that continue to resonate even today.

Included in this book is a collection of images presenting pre-Anglo-Saxon structures that helped inspire the Old English poetic imagination, surviving churches built by the Anglo-Saxons themselves, modern reconstructions of Anglo-Saxon architecture based on archaeological excavations, representations of architecture in Anglo-Saxon sculpture, and later medieval structures that demonstrate a persistence of Anglo-Saxon architectural aesthetics into the post-Conquest period. Individually, these images illustrate numerous points throughout the text. But taken together, they provide a visual overview of the Anglo-Saxon architectural landscape and its later developments, providing a visual context that brings us at least somewhat closer to the experience of an Anglo-Saxon audience and enables us to more productively understand and interpret architectural imagery in surviving verse. Let us now begin with the Anglo-Saxon buildings themselves and the meanings with which Old English oral traditions invested them.

CHAPTER TWO

FROM STRUCTURE TO MEANING IN OLD ENGLISH VERSE

Probably the most well known architectural work in all of Old English poetry is Heorot, Hrothgar's renowned hall. Just as in the *Gifts of Men*, the passage describing the building of Heorot juxtaposes the crafts of builder and poet. As Edward Irving has observed, "That the first act undertaken in the newly constructed hall is the song by the scop about God's creation of the world is extraordinarily appropriate" (*Reading* 89). The collocation of the etymologically related *scop* (poet) and *scippan* (to create) in the initial descriptions of Heorot establish important connections between architectonics and oral performance from the very outset.[1] Hrothgar "*scop* him Heort naman" ["created the name Heorot for it"] (78), songs "*scopes*" ["of the singer/creator"] are heard in celebration (90), and the song sung is of the world's creator who "life ac *gesceop*" ["created life for all"] (97). In each case the act of creation—whether of architecture, poetry, or nature itself—is a dynamic, performative pro - cess. Yet although *Beowulf* repeatedly and consistently establishes Heorot as a space appropriate for and integral to the poem's heroic action, the details with which it does so operate more through idiomatic and associative meaning than through illustration, in effect conveying the *sense* of its grandeur rather than the totality of its physical representation. In the famous passage of its creation (67–83), audiences are told that Hrothgar, king of the Danes, planned and successfully built the "greatest of hall dwellings" ["healærna mæst" (78)],[2] a structure that took many men to construct and decorate, "manigre mægþe geond þisne middan geard" ["many tribes throughout this middle-earth"] (75). Its fame having spread widely through oral/aural transmission, Heorot was intended to be greater than "children of men had ever heard," "yldo bearn æfre gefrunon" (70), and its attainment of this status is confirmed by the speaker who "widely heard" of its grandeur, "ic wide gefrægn" (74). However, in the seventeen lines devoted to the description of its origins, we are given only two actual physical details, and these are quite vague: the hall is "heah" ["high"] (82) and "horngeap" ["wide-gabled"] (82). Over the course of the poem, we are provided a few additional features, but the level of detail always remains insufficient to construct much more than the most basic mental image of the hall: Heorot is constructed of wood (307, 1317); it is built on an elevated site (285); it is bright (997) and adorned with gold (994, 1800) and has massive doors with iron hinges (998).

Far from a complete image, these few characteristics leave readers with substantial gaps to fill, what Wolfgang Iser has called "gaps of indeterminacy" ("Indeterminacy" 11 ff.). With the responsibility of supplementing the scant details provided, the audience becomes in effect a co-creator of the work. In *Immanent Art: From Structure to Meaning in Traditional Oral Epic,* Foley has compellingly demonstrated that oral traditional texts—whether oral-derived or unambiguously oral—imply "an audience with the background to perform certain interpretive tasks" (47). In order to perform such tasks, an audience experiencing an oral or oral-derived work of verbal art must to some extent share with the work's creator a degree of familiarity with the associative and connotative meanings underlying the use of particular phraseology or imagery, in short, a work's traditional context. Because the analysis of Old English verse that follows relies especially heavily on this concept of an implied reader able to interpret from within a context of widely understood traditional signals, I quote Foley's discussion of this phenomenon at some length.

> If the reader views the text through a cognitive lens fundamentally similar to that employed in its making, the work will take shape as a more or less faithful realization of textual potential, given expectable sorts of variation. If, on the other hand, one insists on using cognitive categories foreign to its making (and thus disabling to its faithful construal), one necessarily stands to falsify the process and, in effect, to 'read the wrong work.' ... The reader

who seeks to interpret a given performance or version of a work with fidelity must be able to manage the cognitive categories in which it is transmitted, to hear the associative meaning inherent in the structural units of phrase and narrative. This level of fluency of course demands some knowledge of the tradition to which the performance or version necessarily refers and from which it derives its meaning. In the case of nonliving oral traditions, this knowledge will necessarily be even more incomplete, but even a partial awareness of referentiality is better than none. (*Immanent Art* 54–55)

In the case of Heorot and similar architectural images, a "fluency" in Old English oral poetics would thus enable an audience to understand the traditional referentiality that infuses a given phrase with meaning beyond the purely lexical. But an audience must also be "fluent" in the architectural register of the period in order to understand not only what types of architecture are referenced by the text but also what meanings and values are most closely associated with particular building types and features. In this dynamic process of transmission and reception, the "gaps of indeterminacy" created by incomplete depictions of Heorot and other such structures—those "aspects of the text that call for the reader's active invention (and intervention) in solving the problems they pose" (Foley, *Immanent Art* 41)—imply a reciprocal relationship between poet and audience and a mutual understanding of cultural idiom.[3] An audience that shares with the poet the same cognitive categories for architectural works and the conventional language for describing them is consequently in the best position to complete and understand otherwise cryptic images such as those in the description of Heorot. The poet's implied audience(s), contemporary with the production of the poem, almost certainly would have interpreted within such idiomatic and cultural contexts, where modern-day audiences must work much harder to reconstruct idiomatic meanings in interpreting verbal cues. Thus an awareness of this wider traditional referentiality is imperative for our understanding of the text's extralexical significance, especially when we are faced with the seemingly vague and sometimes self-contradictory images presented in the architectural description of Old English verse.

THE LOG CABIN AS AN EXAMPLE OF ARCHITECTURAL
TRADITIONAL REFERENTIALITY

To illustrate how an architectural form and its verbal counterpart can become invested with this kind of traditional referentiality, let me turn briefly to an example that contemporary readers, especially in the United States, are likely to recognize more readily, the log cabin. As an architectural form, the log cabin—that is, a "cabin of notched logs set horizontally to form the walls" (Weslager 53)—has a long and complicated history in the United States, with tools and domestic housing techniques brought by Swedish, Finnish, German, and Scotch Irish immigrants from the eighteenth century onward.[4] The subsequent proliferation of the log cabin in North America, however, is inadequate to explain the set of ideals that over time has come to be associated with this architectural structure, including integrity, perseverance, humility, and preindustrial simplicity.

In the United States, especially in the midwestern region, there is a strong connection between the log cabin and the era of Abraham Lincoln. So powerful is the log cabin's association with Lincoln that tourist sites go to great lengths to feature log cabins with even the most indirect connection to Lincoln. Enshrined in a memorial building at the Abraham Lincoln Birthplace National Historic Site in Hogdenville, Kentucky, is not the actual birthplace of Lincoln but a nineteenth-century log cabin *symbolic* of the one-bedroom cabin in which Lincoln was believed to have been born. At nearby Knob Creek tourists can visit a log cabin that *may* have belonged to the *neighbors* of Lincoln. The Abraham Lincoln Presidential Library and Museum in Springfield, Illinois, includes a *replica* of the one-room cabin in which Lincoln was born, and the Pioneer Memorial State Park features a restored log cabin where Lincoln's parents were supposedly married in 1806. The namesake of the Lincoln Log Cabin State Historic Site in Lerna, Illinois, is a home of Thomas and Sarah Bush Lincoln, Abraham Lincoln's father and stepmother. During the period in which Thomas and Sarah Bush Lincoln resided in this cabin, Abraham Lincoln himself was living in Springfield—in a *frame* house he owned from 1844 to 1861, *not* a log cabin. Although Abraham Lincoln would have been only a visitor to this cabin, the traditional force of the log cabin and its implied ideals supersede more direct connections to Lincoln's actual life.

Many American children grow up visiting these and other log cabin tourist sites,[5] constructing play cabins from toy Lincoln Logs, and reading Lincoln biographies such as *Log Cabin President* (Woods) and *From Log Cabin to White House* (North), all of which simultaneously reinforce idealized images of log cabin and president alike. The question remains, though, as to how a structure such as the log cabin can come to be invested with such widely understood traditional meanings. As great a figure as he is in American history, Lincoln is not the source of all positive associations with the log cabin. Traditions can seldom be explained so simply. Even though the earliest colonists built frame homes and many settlers, especially farther west where trees were more scarce, made sod homes, the log cabin became early on a symbol of the American frontier. And the president whose campaign first molded this image of the log cabin as symbol of distinctly American ideals was not Abraham Lincoln but William Henry Harrison. The famous "log cabin campaign" that ultimately led to Harrison's election as president in 1840 began in response to a slur claiming that Harrison was more suited to his log cabin than to the White House.[6] The Harrison campaign immediately embraced the notion, following up on then-nascent associations between log cabins and the country's founding fathers. During and following the Harrison campaign, the log cabin theme spread across the country, appearing not only on campaign buttons and memorabilia but also on paper weights, bookends, almanacs, quilts, umbrella heads, and countless other items (Weslager 270). From this point on the manufacture of log cabin merchandise became a commonplace in American culture. Americans were repeatedly exposed to the phrase "log cabin" and to images of the log cabin in particular in highly idealized contexts. Although the log cabin had obtained positive associations prior to this election, it was through the Harrison campaign that the log cabin "clinched its place as a symbol of America and all but dislodged other early dwellings from the national memory" (Van Dine 133). During this period, history was to some extent reimagined visually as well, with the pilgrims of Plymouth—who actually built and lived in frame houses—now being depicted in log cabins. Harold R. Shurtleff has argued that historical "log-cabin illustrations have undoubtedly done more to spread the myth than all the writings of historians put together" (194). Among the most influential were popular pictures of an all–log cabin Plymouth that came out around 1887 and were used to illustrate textbooks and decorate picture postcards, and, later, the illustrated *Pageant of America,* published in 1925 with a wide circulation in schools, which depicted a log cabin Jamestown. As these and other examples show, the symbolic power that the log cabin holds is in many ways largely independent of the actual architectural record.[7]

The connotative power of the log cabin belongs not only to actual log cabins and illustrations of log cabins but also to the verbal collocation "log cabin." The phrase "log cabin," distinct to the United States and first attested in the eighteenth century, is as charged as the structure itself.[8] Saying that Lincoln was born in a one-room house of trimmed unhewn timber simply does not have the same rhetorical force. The verbal designation of such a structure as a "log cabin" is more emotionally resonant for many audiences than "log house," "wooden cottage," or any other such terminology not because it is more descriptive but because over time American culture has developed powerful associative values with this particular wording. Songs commemorating the log cabin, such as "The Rough Log Cabin," initially sung as part of the campaign promoting Harrison, illustrate the connection between the phrasing "log cabin" and a particular set of ideals (quoted in Weslager 272):

> I love the rough log cabin
> It tells of olden time
> When a hardy and an honest class
> Of freemen in their prime
> First left their father's peaceful home
> Where all was joy and rest
> With axes on their shoulders
> And sallied for the West.

Like the structure itself, the phrase "log cabin" taps into a complex set of ideals associated with frontier life—perseverance, hardiness, honesty, humility, preindustrial simplicity—ideals reinforced through song, architecture, and material culture. The connections are deceptively simple to many because they are so deeply engrained, but in actuality the relationship between the cabin, presidents such as Lincoln and Harrison, and the associated ideals is so complex that even the most detailed architectural descriptions could never fully capture the connotative essence of the phrase "log cabin."

As it stands today, "the log cabin has survived and indeed flourishes as an expression of indigenous American architecture" (Weslager xxv). Imagine, however, that a thousand years from now all nineteenth-century log cabins (and their twentieth- and twenty-first-century reconstructions) have disintegrated. Nothing remains of them except perhaps changed composition in the soil where their foundations once stood. Imagine too that the textual record has been radically depleted, including information on the Harrison campaign, certain details of Lincoln's childhood, and the building techniques of early American immigrants. Without sufficient exposure to the log cabin as verbal and visual symbol, would someone coming across the lyrics to "The Rough Log Cabin," an empty bottle of Log Cabin syrup, or a reference to a log cabin in a randomly preserved Lincoln biography be likely to have any real sense of the larger implications, of the traditional force behind "log cabin" as image and as phrase? The seemingly obvious connection that a native midwesterner might make between Lincolnian ideals and small houses constructed of unhewn horizontal timbers would undoubtedly be far less intuitive to audiences outside of twentieth- and twenty-first-century American culture. This scenario brings us much closer to the current relationship that we ourselves maintain with Anglo-Saxon architecture such as that described with respect to Heorot.

What constitutes "log cabin" in the minds of many Americans is not inherent in the phrase, in images of the structure, or even in the structure itself. Rather, it is through repeated exposure to images of and references to log cabins in association with particular values that many Americans develop the cognitive category "log cabin," a phrase that connotes far more than its literal sense might convey. So powerful are the positive associations between Lincoln and log cabins that Lincolnian ideals can be conveyed through the mere image of a log cabin, even if Lincoln himself is never mentioned explicitly. Likewise, a reference to Lincoln's birth can summon the image of a log cabin, even if the setting is not explicitly identified as such. For those without repeated exposure to conventional log cabin imagery (verbal as well as material), any text or structure implicitly referencing such connections would be at least somewhat depleted of meaning. Such gaps between image and implied audience must be filled through an awareness of the log cabin's "traditional referentiality."[9] The process of transmission is complex, however, for though the log cabin as symbol both strengthened and was strengthened by the positive associations with Lincoln, the connection, as we have seen, is not one that can be attributed unequivocally to any specific individual or individuals. Lincoln's connection to the log cabin built on the associative value of the Harrison campaign, which in turn built on the (largely false) notion that America's founding fathers lived in New England log cabins. As a phrase and as a structure, the symbol of the log cabin developed as most oral traditions do, through consistent patterns of transmission and reception, gaining linguistic and iconic currency through repeated use in specific, though complex, cultural and social contexts.[10]

The claim that log cabins and references to log cabins evoke a particular ethos neither presupposes a homogeneous audience nor assumes that all components of a given audience will receive and interpret log cabin imagery in exactly the same way. For those deeply schooled in American political history, such imagery might evoke associations with Harrison's log cabin campaign; midwesterners inundated with stories of Lincoln would be more likely to recall his birthplace and the corresponding set of Lincolnian ideals; and, for many, associations may entail only a vague sense of America's frontier past. Further, even members of an audience who share the same basic understanding of the log cabin's implied values can have a wide range of responses. Some may embrace the frontier ideals in their entirety, while others might reject them as sentimental, rustic, or naive. Still others might choose to complicate the notion, pointing out that not everyone who was born in a log cabin shares the same values and that Abraham Lincoln himself moved into a frame house as soon as he was financially able to do so. Any appropriate response, however, whether positive or negative, requires at least some rudimentary understanding of ideals in log cabin imagery implicit in the larger tradition of American culture. The arguments that follow assume an equally diverse set of responses to a shared understanding of Anglo-Saxon architectural imagery and iconography.

IMPLICATIONS FOR EARLY MEDIEVAL VERBAL
AND MATERIAL ARTS

Anglo-Saxon halls are of course far removed from the log cabin in many obvious ways. Where there exists an extensive textual record through which we can trace the origins and development of the log cabin both as a phrase deeply invested with positive meaning and as an architectural symbol, Anglo-Saxon records provide relatively little in the way of histori- cal context. While we are at less than a two-hundred-year remove from the earliest designation of structures as "log cabins," we are separated by over a thousand years from the earliest Anglo-Saxon halls. And while the associations implicit in log cabin imagery are so familiar to most of us as to render thorough explication entirely unnecessary, traditional conno- tations embedded in Anglo-Saxon hall imagery are far more easily lost on modern-day readers. Although the log cabin and the Anglo-Saxon hall are arguably related in possible Scandinavian origins of timber construc- tion, the associative meanings are vastly different. In fact, it is in part the rustic qualities associated with log cabins and wood construction more generally that make it especially difficult for some modern readers to see the grander associations of timber construction with which Anglo-Saxons invested their wooden buildings and poetic depictions thereof. The par- allels lie instead in the ways that an awareness of traditional referentiality enables audiences to interpret verbal and architectural cues whose nu- ances might be lost to those outside these respective traditions. Just as "log cabin" has acquired powerful extralexical meanings in American oral and textual traditions, the phraseology and imagery employed in descriptions of such structures as Heorot would assuredly have had strong resonances with Anglo-Saxons repeatedly exposed to traditional language and archi- tectural imagery. Modern audiences are so far removed, however, that once-obvious meanings are inevitably more opaque. Without sharing the poets' fluency in the traditional idiom, we are left at times with what seem to be vague and largely meaningless architectural details.

However, Ruth Waterhouse convincingly argues that what to modern audiences might seem a lack of visual detail is due to a different aesthet- ics and differing conceptions of space. Addressing *Beowulf* specifically, she observes that any "attempt to make an organic whole of the scattered details about Heorot is a twentieth-century type of preoccupation, which would have been alien to the open-ended conception of spatiality and spatial form encoded by the poet, where the context in which each detail is given changes the focus each time, and it is not always possible to fit them together" (95–96). Further, "if the poem were performed orally for an Anglo-Saxon audience, then such building up of the setting would demand a retentive memory; and a reader would need to search back and forth to find the relevant references" (95). Waterhouse speaks thus in terms not of reading but of "decoding" poetic texts, noting that Anglo-Saxon concepts of space require active audience participation in conceptualizing and contextualizing the minimal details provided. In architectural representation, verbal and visual "formulas" can reveal complex and sometimes enigmatic relationships with the materials they depict, operating sometimes in tandem with and sometimes against physical "reality."

It is important to note from the outset that this model does not assume a homogeneous audience. As with the log cabin in American culture, the architectural features associated with a hall such as Heorot, for instance, could achieve varying degrees of specificity in terms of audience response but always within the general framework of heroic ideals. For some, timber construction might have been associated with specific halls of specific leaders, yet for others the associations with heroic society may have been much more general in nature. Some may have accepted the positive associations with which the tradition invested wood construction but then put images of wood to new Christian allegorical uses, and still others could have rejected wood, with its associations of heroic Germanic culture, favoring instead the stone construction associated with Romano-Christian culture. Indeed, *all* of these various "readings" of architecture have been evidenced in the Anglo-Saxon textual record, as is more fully discussed in the chapters that follow.[11] Nevertheless, each of these responses, however different they might be from one another, requires an awareness of implied associations with wooden construction and verbal imagery within a larger tradition, associations that would have developed through repeated use on the part of artisans and poets as well as through repeated exposure on the part of their contemporary audiences.

Our analysis here seeks, then, to accomplish two goals: (1) to better understand what images poetic description might have brought to mind for audiences familiar with Anglo-Saxon architecture and verse and (2) to uncover the associations likely to have been evoked by those few details provided in surviving poetry, details that are made all the more salient and prominent by their scarcity. The first of these goals can be accomplished through surveys of architectural and archaeological evidence surrounding the Anglo-Saxon architectural landscape; the second must be attained for the most part by discerning the traditional referentiality activated by particular phrases and by the building features themselves. At a verbal level, each repeated usage of a given phrase in a particular context serves to strengthen associations, over time creating a tradition of associative meaning that deepens with each repeated use. In architecture, tradition can likewise develop from consistent patterns of use, as a given feature is repeatedly used in similar social or structural contexts. Still, in those cases where verbal formulaic descriptions overlap with actual architectural features, we cannot say with any certainty which came first, the idealized depiction in oral tradition or the actual feature in construction. Even in the well-attested case of the log cabin, an unambiguous chain of events is impossible to reconstruct with complete accuracy. It is enough to say that the two traditions—architectural and verbal—serve to validate and reinforce one another and that our reception can be substantially enhanced through an understanding of both. Exploration of surviving textual and material evidence suggests that in fact Anglo-Saxon builders, artists, poets, and scribes of the period all employed a shared "language" of architectural form that was used to transmit similar meanings.

Because of the diversity of its landscapes and structures and its more extensive treatment of architectural detail relative to other surviving poetry, *Beowulf* provides a point of comparison for a wide range of poems reliant on architectural imagery, such as the elegiac *Ruin,* the heroic *Andreas,* and the religious *Christ and Satan.* The epic thus provides a constructive starting point for discussing Anglo-Saxon poetic representations of architecture, allowing me to delay more extensive treatment of other poems and genres until later chapters. However, a crucial first step to understanding the traditional language employed in descriptions of buildings in Old English poetry and the imagined spaces that such descriptions are likely to have evoked in the minds of contemporary audiences is to examine actual construction methods employed by Anglo-Saxon builders and the aesthetic principles governing their choices.[12]

THE ART OF ANGLO-SAXON CONSTRUCTION

Anglo-Saxon architecture is characterized by extreme flexibility and diversity. The Saxon walls at St. Mary's, Sompting, are made from the region's native stone (fig. 14); St. Andrew's, Greensted, from vertical timbers (fig. 17); St. John's, Escomb, from reused cut Roman stones (figs. 20 and 21); and All Saints Church, Earls Barton, from rubble decorated with stone pilasters (figs. 2 and 22). Across this great diversity in building materials and forms, however, certain aesthetic principles consistently emerge, a number of which transcend purely practical and geographic considerations. And several of these recurrent architectural tendencies correspond closely to those features that are mentioned most explicitly and repeatedly in poetic architectural description: construction from wood (or stonework employing timber prototypes), high walls relative to building width, elevated building sites, rounded and arched openings and decorative features, and gabled roofs and ceilings. These features are also attested in Scandinavian analogues, further indicating a long-standing Germanic architectural aesthetic.

Anglo-Saxon attitudes reflected in the textual record and building techniques discernible from archaeological evidence indicate that the tendency to construct from wood rather than stone resulted from choice rather than necessity. Unfortunately, only one Anglo-Saxon wooden structure survives to the present day, the nave of St. Andrew's Church at Greensted, but even this single structure gives us some insight into the carpentry skills required for timber construction.[13] The original walls consist of split oak logs, a technique that Håkon Christie, Olaf Olsen, and H. M. Taylor explain would have "resulted in a great variation of texture, with a vivid play of light and shade" (97). The planks are arranged side by side and joined together through an elaborate tongue-and-groove technique in which "tongues are let into the spaces formed by the grooves of adjacent planks" (Christie, Olsen, and Taylor 97). This technique served to keep the planks from slipping out of line and to protect the wall against inclement weather. The planks were then also beveled at the top on the exterior sides to fit into a wall plate (fig. 17). Christie, Olsen, and Taylor explain that the technique "must have been intended for the technical purpose of providing a sound joint between the plank and the wall plate, but this technical reason was clearly utilized for decorative purposes" (97).

As we will later see, these dual practical and aesthetic functions of wood construction are also evident in Anglo-Saxon oral poetics.

With a wealth of stone churches surviving but only one wooden structure still intact, the extant evidence of timber construction can be quite misleading. By 1972 P. V. Addyman had noted the excavation of over 150 sites of timber buildings. While carpentry techniques varied widely, the use of wood across England, even in areas with plenty of available stone from Roman sites, demonstrates wood's cultural and architectural importance. Excavations at Dorchester show evidence of half-timbered buildings on unmortared stone, and excavations at West Stow reveal innovations in wooden construction that vary considerably from European counterparts, indicating that the use of wood was not merely a mindless exercise in imitation, but a genuine preference.

The succession of halls at Yeavering also suggests that the Anglo-Saxons constantly sought improvements of design in their construction of halls, and wood continued to be the material of choice. An early hall at Yeavering[14] was aisled with narrow end rooms, planked floors, and heavy outer walls of posts in palisade construction set in continuous trenches.[15] A later hall on the same site reveals new types of construction, still with wood but now including massive buttress posts, which were eight feet deep and inclined inward with the internal partitions producing two end rooms. This hall, 80 feet by 50 feet, shares similarities with buildings at Chalton, Hampshire, suggesting a "distinctive and wide-spread architectural tradition" (Addyman). Philip Rahtz's excavation at Cheddar has likewise shown that such wooden halls were constructed late into the Anglo-Saxon period and that methods continued to change and adapt in a dynamic and varied tradition. Like oral traditions that vary in some ways from one performance to the next while consistently retaining certain defining features, these halls exhibited multiforms across time and space but always within traditionally accepted limits.[16] One constant amid numerous variations was this use of wood.

Analogous traditions of wood building attest to not only the presence but also the importance and value of timber construction in and around England and illustrate possibilities of design beyond the mere dimensions and floor plans deduced from the holes left in the soil from upright timber posts. The simplicity of the floor plans that can be reconstructed from these postholes are potentially misleading, as examples of wooden structures surviving in Scandinavian countries can illustrate. Nigel Kerr and Mary Kerr note that the often-simple floor plans of Scandinavian stave churches, for instance, do not adequately reflect the elaborate structures in their three-dimensional forms (*Anglo-Saxon Architecture* 58). Medieval Norwegian stave churches were built with vertical posts, as evidence indicates was also true for Anglo-Saxon construction. Above a simple rectangular base there are sometimes several tiers of sloped roofs and walling with elaborate carvings in the woodwork at every level. This is not at all to say that Anglo-Saxon architecture shared these specific features with Norwegian stave churches but only to point to the many possibilities for early medieval wood construction that might not be discernible from postholes. Archaeological and literary parallels in Ireland and Northumbria also point to more imaginative possibilities of wood construction and decoration within and surrounding Anglo-Saxon England. Catherine Karkov argues that for both areas "decoration of wooden architecture was not only greater in degree than has previously been assumed, but also . . . played a more active role within society than that with which it has previously been credited" ("Decoration of Early Wooden Architecture" 40). Even the Romans used wood more frequently than surviving structures would suggest. As Guy de la Bédoyère explains, timber "played a vital part in Romano-British building," and a number of structures "may have had stone footings but timber superstructures" (*Architecture* 20).

In addition to these analogues that demonstrate elaborately conceived and skillfully articulated timber buildings in and around England, comparative evidence from Germany and Denmark further points to a widespread, long-standing, and highly valued Germanic heritage of wooden buildings. Excavations of Saxon villages such as those of War - endorf or Elisenhof in Germany have revealed long-houses that share a number of features with the long, rectangular halls of both Anglo-Saxon archaeology and Old English poetry.[17] And, like the Anglo-Saxon halls, these long-houses seem to have served as the center of social life. With regard to *Beowulf* in particular, much recent attention has focused on parallels with archaeological evidence at Lejre, a town on the island of Zealand in East Denmark, where a timber hall 154 feet long and 25 feet wide at its midpoint was built sometime around the sixth century.[18] With parallels in German, Danish, Norwegian, Irish, and even Romano-British architecture, we need not establish a linear chain of influence in order to appreciate the significance and value of timber in England's early medieval construction and the importance that timber would most assuredly have had in the minds of Anglo-Saxon audiences.

Offering yet another interpretive lens, experimental archaeology has yielded important insights into the building process itself and further demonstrates the tremendous investments of time and resources involved in Anglo-Saxon timber construction. Among the most recent and well-documented reconstruction projects is the village at Bede's World in Jarrow. This program selected buildings from settlement sites formerly excavated in Northumbria "in its heyday" and employed in the building "only the tools and techniques known to have been used at the time" (Fowler and Mills 116). To date, the largest reconstructed hall on the site models that of the excavation of a mid-seventh-century settlement of Thirlings (fig. 19). Even the reconstruction of this rather modest hall of 40 feet by 20 feet (in contrast with a royal hall at Yeavering of 80 feet by 46 feet) demonstrates the substantial human and natural resources required. The project took three years (1994–97) and

> consumed about 30 tons of green, fifty-sixty-year-old oak of the correct diameter for the main structural timbers; substantial quantities of willow, hazel and birch for the wattle paneling . . . ; about 25 tons of local boulder clay, straw and water for the daub; slaked line, water, brick-dust (for coloring) and boiled linseed oil (waterproofing) for the lime-wash. For the roof, seventy ash poles from Suffolk were interwoven with hazel rods from Cumbria; and eighteen hundred bundles of reed from Tayside in eastern Scotland were used for thatch. (Fowler and Mills 120)

Although wood and reed were in greater abundance and in closer proximity to building sites in the Anglo-Saxon period, the project nonetheless led to a much greater appreciation of the woodworking skills of Anglo-Saxon artisans and the lengths to which they went to continue the tradition of timber construction.

Even construction features involving no wood reveal its continuing value, as decorative patterns in stone were often made to *look* like wood by Anglo-Saxon masons. Such "skeuomorphs," which involve "a design feature, no longer functional in itself, that refers back to an avatar that was functional at an earlier time," visibly testify to the "social or psychological necessity for innovation to be tempered by replication" (Hayles 16).[19] A number of such skeuomorphs in Anglo-Saxon art and architecture attest to the pervasive attachment to wood, even in structures in which stone had become the more dominant construction material. Karkov argues that stone hogback monuments, such as that on the Franks Casket, are possibly skeuomorphs of wooden structures. Some have suggested that the long and short stripwork[20] decorating the tower of the eleventh-century All Saints Church at Earls Barton in Northamptonshire (fig. 2) was designed to imitate contemporary wooden structures.[21] Wooden exemplars have also been posited for the shallow, concentric grooves carved into the semicircular arched stone at St. Patrick's Chapel, Heysham (fig. 31), likely "in imitation of faceplate-turning done on the wood lathe" (Rodwell 174).[22] An Anglo-Saxon stone church at Barnack features "both pierced scroll decoration and slotted openings exactly like those still to be found in medieval boards in belfry openings" (174). Letha Smenton argues that the "long and short work" characterizing Anglo-Saxon quoining in many stone churches "is probably an attempt of the mason . . . to imitate timber posts by laying stones end on end" (10). And columns in the crypt at Repton also appear to be copies of wooden prototypes (fig. 10), as Rodwell explains: "The coarse, barley-sugar twist with a raised rib seen on the Repton column shafts has been laboriously cut in emulation of spiral wood turning (an advanced technique involving considerably more skill than plain turning)" (173).

It would be misleading, however, to say that wood served strictly an ornamental or a symbolic function. Warwick Rodwell's study of the design of surviving Anglo-Saxon churches—which were constructed primarily from stone—shows that "there was considerably more structural and other functional timberwork in the early churches than has perhaps hitherto been appreciated" (171). Exploration inside the tower of St. Mary's at Sompting has revealed elaborate and unexpected wood construction inside the visible stone exterior, demonstrating a continuing reliance on wood even after it had ceased to be the preferred medium for church construction (fig. 14).[23] Though this helmed roof is the only one of its kind to survive intact, there is strong evidence for others of similar construction, such as at St. Bene't's Church in Cambridge (Kerr and Kerr, *Anglo-Saxon Sites* 183). Like Sompting, the Barton-upon-Humber tower also evidences a "substitution of timber in places where it would not be noticed," something that would be "unthinkable to a true mason" (Rodwell 174) but a natural choice for carpenters valuing woodwork.

Rodwell explains that the use of lacing (a method of bracing in which timbers are placed behind and around other supports) and the presence of additional large timbers within stone walls suggests "a mistrust of the cohesive strength of rubble masonry" (172). Further, "a number of architectural features in stone which have load-bearing functions can be seen as direct copies of timber prototypes" (172). In some cases, the employment of carpentry methods in stone construction led to structural weakness. The double-belfry window openings characteristic of Anglo-Saxon stone masonry, for instance, "apply shearing forces to the through-stone which must have resulted in many failures and consequent collapses" (172),[24] although the same technique performed with wood, much lighter and more flexible, would have produced a highly satisfactory and stable construction. In addition, some non-load-bearing features that have only decorative function in stone structures "can immediately be appreciated as integral components of a framed structure" if we imagine a translation into timber (173). The previously discussed pilaster strips on the tower at Earls Barton (fig. 2) and similar strips at Barton-upon-Humber, for example, can be seen as "an imitation of a form of lap joint used by carpenters for bracing a vertical post" (173).[25] The persistent employment of carpentry methods by Anglo-Saxon stonemasons attests to the faith builders continued to have in timber construction techniques and also demonstrates the reluctance to part with wood even when stone became the preferred medium for church construction.

In wood (and later stone) construction, a number of aesthetic principles consistently emerge, most notably height of structures and elevation of building sites. Archaeological evidence of long-deteriorated wood structures suggests that ceilings in Anglo-Saxon timber halls were quite high; for instance, the largest of the three cauldrons discovered at Sutton Hoo would have required 14 feet to extend its chainwork to its full length (Evans). A ninth-century hall in Cheddar shows evidence of inside supports sloping inward, indicating that the structure was likely high enough for an upper floor. The preference for height is also evident in surviving churches. H. M. Taylor and Joan Taylor note that doorways "are both tall in an absolute sense and also exceptionally tall in proportion to their width" (817). A doorway at Bradford-on-Avon, for instance, has a height four times its width, 8 feet 5 inches by 2 feet 1 inch. The church as a whole (fig. 3) also reflects a preference for height, as dimensions provided by Taylor and Taylor indicate: "The chancel arch is only 3 ft 6 in wide and no less than 9 ft 9 in tall" (87). The wall of the nave is 25 feet 3 inches, so tall that during its use as a school and lodging quarters the building was divided into three floors. Such "disproportionate" ratios are common in Anglo-Saxon construction. The walls of St. Peter-on-the-Wall at Bradwell-on-Sea (fig. 5), for instance, are an impressive 24 feet high.[26] The tendency to build in prominent and elevated locations is also a clear pattern in Anglo-Saxon construction, with structures like St. Patrick's Church, Hey-sham (fig. 31), built on a high rocky ledge 40 to 50 feet above sea level overlooking the Morecambe Bay, and All Saints Church positioned high on a hill in the center of Earls Barton, visible for miles even today from the motorway. The strategic reasons for building in high locations make the choice itself unremarkable, and the Anglo-Saxons are certainly not unique in this practice, but, as I discuss later, *fictionalized* buildings are said to be constructed on high ground even when other militarily advantageous features are omitted. Beyond, and likely because of, the obvious security and visibility offered by such a location, elevated architectural sites in the textual and poetic record connote an inherent nobility and positive aura that transcend sheer military advantage.

Anglo-Saxon architectural practices, in constructions of stone as well as wood, are further characterized by a tendency toward curved and rounded structures. In their three-volume, comprehensive treatment of surviving Anglo-Saxon architecture, Taylor and Taylor note a number of patterns among an otherwise diverse collection of buildings, including a preference for curves: "Like most other Anglo-Saxon openings, windows are predominantly round-headed" (844). Doorways also were "most often round-headed" (8). Further, this roundness is often emphasized with frames and decorative detail. The west doorway of the tower at Earls Barton (fig. 22), for instance, has a round-headed doorway, and the entire doorway is framed by a massive curved stone with decorative curved designs on either impost.[27] The windows on the south wall of St. Paul's chancel at Jarrow all have round heads, which "are cut from single stones, shaped to a curve both below and above" (341). One of these heads frames a rounded slab pierced with a circular opening, an oddity that Taylor and Taylor attribute to a lack of a large enough piece of glass (fig. 23).[28] Even without the necessary glass for the window opening that seems to have been planned, the builders took great care to accentuate curves of the small piece of glass and of the surrounding stone slab used to fill out the space. The decorative blind arcading (range of arches attached to a wall, not freestanding) on St. Laurence Church at Bradford-on-Avon (fig. 3) also illustrates the Anglo-Saxon preference for curved structures.

Archaeological evidence also shows that many timber halls were not built according to a purely rectilinear plan. The ninth-century hall at Cheddar had bow-sided walls, broadest at the building's center and tapering at either side. Additional bow-sided structures are attested in Hamwih (Southampton) (Fernie, *Architecture of the Anglo-Saxons* 21) and have a long-standing tradition in Viking settlements such as Lindholm Høje and Fyrkat in Denmark and Trelleborg in Sweden as well as in later settlements in Warendorf, Germany, and Dorestad in the Netherlands (21). The halls at Lejre also followed this plan, "bowed slightly outward in the middle" (Niles et al. 196).

Roofs, incredibly important in poetic renderings of architecture, are rare in surviving architecture, but what survives of the archaeological record indicates that the poetry's preoccupation with gables[29] reflects the period's general architectural aesthetic, in which they were another prominent architectural feature. St. Mary's Church at Sompting, a rare example of a surviving Anglo-Saxon roof, features four gables on its famous "Rhenish helm" (fig. 14). Gables—in combination with height and rounded openings—are also pronounced in the representation of a building on the base of a ninth-century cross-shaft in St. Peter's churchyard at Heysham, Lancashire (fig. 15).[30] In this minimalist rendering of what some believe represented the home of Lazarus and others interpret as depicting the three Marys at Christ's resurrection, a roof with widely protruding gables rests atop a building quite high in relation to its width. Above the rounded doorway are two levels of curved windows through which faces appear. A stylized house depicted on a hogback tombstone from Brompton likewise features a wide (and arched) gabled roof.[31] And, again, Scandinavian analogues lend support to a wider-ranging Germanic tradition of buildings with prominent and often multiple gables, one that encompasses both the Anglo-Saxon tradition in which *Beowulf* was written and the Scandinavian culture in which it is set.

The textual record supplements but also complicates the picture provided by archaeological evidence, suggesting sometimes conflicting associations with timber during a time when stone was becoming increasingly important, especially in church construction. For Bede, for instance, wood was sometimes associated with the Irish church and with lesser methods of construction. Bede claims that the church at Lindisfarne was constructed "after the Irish method, not of stone but of hewn oak," and that the church at York, first "hastily built of wood," was replaced later by "a greater and more magnificent church of stone."[32] One of the primary issues involved in the reconstruction of built spaces at Bede's World in Jarrow, discussed above, is the contrast between "stone-rich ecclesiastical centers" and timber buildings of "the early medieval secular world" (Fowler and Mills 116). The growing preference for stone in religious contexts, especially in the late Anglo-Saxon period, is also evident in architectural illustrations in Harley 603, an illustrated text that follows the Utrecht Psalter. Depictions of buildings in this manuscript generally tend toward stone, even when ostensibly copying timber images from the eleventh-century psalter.[33]

In contrast, an extended architectural metaphor in the preface to Alfred's version of Augustine's soliloquies demonstrates strongly positive associations with wood and timber construction more generally:

> Gaderode me þonne kigclas and stuþansceaftas, and lohsceaf-
> tas and hylfa to ælcum þara tola þe ic mid wircan cuðe, and boh -
> timbru and bolttimbru and to ælcum þara weorca þe ic wyrcan
> cuðe, þa wlitegostan treowo be þam dele ðe ic aberan meihte. . . .
> Forþam ic lære ælcne ðara þe maga si and manigne wæn hæbbe,
> þæt he menige to þam ilcan wuda þar ic ðas stuðansceaftas cearf,
> fetige hym þar ma, and gefeðrige hys wænas mid fegrum gerdum,
> þat he mage windan manigne smicerne wah, and manig ænlic hus
> settan, and fegerne tun timbrian, and þær murge and softe mid

mæge oneardian ægðer ge wintras ge sumeras, swa swa ic nu ne gyt ne dyde. . . . [34]

———

[I gathered for myself then staves and studs, and bars and handles, and for each of those tools that I knew how to work with, and curved timbers and straight timbers, and for each of those works which I knew how to build, the fairest trees as far as I was able to bear them. . . . Therefore, I advise anyone who is strong and who has many wagons to [go to] the same wood where I cut these posts, fetch himself there more, and load his wagons with fair branches, so that he might wind (construct by weaving or interlocking) many beautiful walls, and establish excellent house(s), and build a fair estate, and there dwell happily and comfortably both in the winter as in summer—such as I have not yet done. . . .]

In this metaphor Alfred "has used Augustinian wood to build his own textual edifice, freely shaping his source material to create a new vernacular building, far beyond what we might consider to constitute the act of translation" (Harbus 725).[35] While the image is a common trope in classical rhetoric and the metaphor itself conveys the value placed on Christian Latin texts, Alfred's particular employment of it in this preface also reflects a familiarity with Anglo-Saxon building practices and vernacular architectural aesthetics, with its careful attention to specific tools, particular types of timbers, and the method of "winding" timber walls. As Keynes and Lapidge note of his translation of Gregory, Alfred's work was often "directed to the holders of ecclesiastical office, but his words are frequently couched in terms that would be equally applicable to the holders of secular office" (124), and the metaphor in this preface would likely have had a satisfying meaning for lay as well as clerical audiences. Alfred's preface reflects the same inextricably linked processes of planning and construction seen in the *Gifts of Men* (see chap. 1) and implies that wood is an appropriate building material even for a king. Alfred's wood has inherent value and beauty, both in the forest and in its final construction, and the building made from this wood is one that provides security, warmth, and protection. Unlike the hastily built wooden churches described by Bede, Alfred's metaphorical timber constructions are to be not only admired but also emulated.[36] For Alfred, wood, metaphorically at least, is a building material appropriate for kings, and buildings constructed from timber are sources of security, beauty, and joy.

This more positive sense is much closer to that depicted in the period's vernacular, which Alfred himself did so much to cultivate. While prose texts, such as the previous example from Bede, include a wider range of associations with timber construction, positive as well as negative, Old English verse tends to be more conservative in its consistently positive treatment of wooden buildings. Within the Old English poetic register, the most unambiguously positive material for building is not stone but wood, a phenomenon that invites further exploration regarding the particular associative value of wood for both poets and their implied audiences. The Old English language itself suggests that wooden structures were not viewed as inferior to stone, though twentieth-century scholarship might suggest otherwise. The generic verb *timbr(i)an*, "to build," is, of course, related to the word *timber*. And the Old English account of Genesis even suggests that wood constitutes the architecture of heaven by employing the term *heofontimber* (*Genesis A*, l.146). Even if we understand *timber* as a generalized term applicable to all building materials, the regular employment of the term gives us no reason to view wood as inferior to stone. With these observations in mind, let us turn now to the images of architecture employed in Old English poetry, with specific emphasis on *Beowulf* itself.

TIMBER CONSTRUCTION AND HEOROT

As mentioned earlier, *Beowulf*'s depiction of Heorot, in a fashion typical of Old English poetic architectural description more generally, provides only a very few specific visual details. To say the least, "Old English literature is not very forthcoming on the specifics of hall construction and layout" (Pollington 68). Viewed in the context of the surrounding poetic and cultural tradition, however, what might at first appear to be a lack of descriptive language[37] can ultimately lead to a more precise understanding of the associative values connected with those few architectural features provided and of how these same features might be more thoroughly and productively understood in the poetic corpus more widely and even in prose works, such as Alfred's preface to the *Soliloquies*. Extensive physical details would in many ways be extraneous for an audience already familiar with Anglo-Saxon construction methods, though alternate functions also existed for architectural description. And for audiences aware of traditional connotations in the language, physical details doubtless produced visual images that were much more than an aggregate of isolated features. Instead of merely enabling imaginative visualization, those few architectural features provided also served to evoke particular associations through a process similar in many ways to that of the log cabin's associations with frontier ideals. In a reciprocal exchange between poem and audience, architecturally descriptive language can thus serve to highlight traditionally resonant features that are valued for the ideals they connote.

Because it exemplifies both the realities and the traditional referentiality of hall construction and because numerous features in its description are found across multiple genres of Old English verse, Heorot provides an excellent introduction to poetic architectural imagery.[38] A number of the features discussed in the building of Heorot are repeated in passages scattered throughout the text, features that find parallels in the period's architectural practices: wood, building height, elevated location, curved and arched structures, and prominent gables. Both in combination and in isolation, these characteristics invest the poetry's buildings with positive valence. More specifically, examination of these features in their narrative contexts shows a close correspondence between this combination of architectural traits and the cluster of ideals associated with the Germanic *comitatus*.[39]

Just as timber construction was the dominant material in actual Anglo-Saxon hall construction, the main fabric of Heorot is wood. Although its material would not be in question for Anglo-Saxon audiences—since Anglo-Saxon secular halls (like halls in the Germanic tradition more widely) were indeed made of wood—Heorot's timber construction is still explicitly stated twice: when it is described as a "sæl timbred" ["timbered hall"] (307) and later when the "healwudu dynede" ["hall wood resounded"] (1317). Also in keeping with the architectural aesthetics seen in real-world construction, the poem repeatedly references Heorot in terms of its admirable height. Grendel approaches Heorot, the "hean huses" ["high house"] (116), and later seeks men "in sele þam hean" ["in the high hall"] (713). Like Hrothgar in Heorot, Hygelac is also said to dwell in a heroic hall characterized by its height: "Bold wæs betlic, bregorof cyning, / hea healle" ["The house was splendid, the ruler a brave king in the high hall"] (1925–26). Attention is further drawn to the height of Heorot by multiple references to its roof, as when Beowulf leads the Geats "under Heorotes hrof" ["under Heorot's roof"] (403) or when Hrothgar looks up at Grendel's arm toward the "stepne hrof" ["steep roof"] (926). In addition, the roof receives the special distinction of being unscathed even after Grendel's wrath. Although the walls suffered great damage and must be made "goldfah" ["gold-adorned"] (994) once again and even the hinges *(heorras)* of the great doors come apart, the roof, the building's highest point, survives intact and offers continuing protection for its inhabitants: "hrof ana genæs / ealles ansund" ["the roof alone endured all sound"] (999–1000).

Not only is the idealized hall tall, a "hean hus" (116), but it also sits on an elevated location, yet another way that Heorot is aligned with the architectural ideals seen in actual construction. When the coast guard admits the Geats, the hall is described as positioned "on heahstede husa selest" ["on a high place, the best of houses"] (285). Later, following Beowulf's defeat of Grendel, retainers congregated at "sele þam hean" ["the high hall"] (919). Other halls in the poem are similarly marked as having been built on elevated locations. In the Finn episode, for instance, warriors retreat to "hamas ond heaburh" ["homes and high town"] (1127). Hygelac's hall, also much revered, has a geographic location correspondingly high, near the seawall on a cliff, "ham wunað ... sæwealle neah" (1923–24).

Given the attention to height, it is not surprising that the uppermost parts of the hall are those most frequently singled out for attention. In keeping with this emphasis, the roof's gables are referenced twice, the hall described as "horngeap" (82) at its creation and the building itself later referred to as a "hornreced" (704). Again exhibiting architectural ideals evidenced in Anglo-Saxon architecture (timber as well as stone), Heorot, like many buildings of heroic significance in Old English verse, is described as rounded or arched,[40] most frequently with the term *geap*, which in *Beowulf* has connotations of both height and roundness: "curved," "vaulted," or "spacious" (Fulk, Bjork, and Niles 383). At the point of its creation, it is said to be "heah ond horngeap" ["high and with wide/curved gables"] (82). Grendel's shoulder and arm hang from the "geapne hrof" ["curved/ wide roof"] (836); the warriors celebrate and rest in Heorot, "geap ond goldfah" ["curved/wide and gold-adorned"] (1800). As noted above, Anglo-Saxon halls such as that at Cheddar and numerous Scandinavian analogues attest to rounded, bow-sided walls rather than linear rectangular forms.[41] Thus the specific features of Heorot most frequently provided and stressed throughout the poem—its height, its elevated location, its gables, and its arched structures—serve to reflect and perhaps reinforce many of the aesthetic principles followed by Anglo-Saxon carpenters and masons. The question remains, though, what specific meanings such features were likely to have had for audiences contemporary with the poetry's production.

As a point of comparison, surviving illustrations of Anglo-Saxon architecture in the visual arts only selectively convey the reality of Anglo-Saxon construction. M. O. H. Carver notes that in Anglo-Saxon artistic renderings "representative accounts of particular buildings" are rare ("Contemporary Artifacts" 120). Nonetheless, the choices made in architectural representation reveal a different kind of reality, one based largely in the associative meanings transmitted through certain images, the "image vocabulary" of the larger cultural tradition. For instance, comparison of images in the Harley 603 manuscript against those in the Utrecht Psalter (from which the Harley images were ostensibly copied) shows that the Harley illustrators frequently provided stone buildings where the Utrecht Psalter had wood, a choice with deep implications: "it is the stone church which is evoked, but account should also be taken of the Roman ruins which dominated early medieval scenery, and with which, no doubt, the illuminator of a Latin text may have felt himself specially connected" (125). In a pattern not unlike that operating in much oral-traditional literature, such representations of architecture in Anglo-Saxon art thus "combine aspects of credible realism with many of the more schematic formulae employed in the thousands of other images over which there can never be any independent control" (119).

The process of reading the seemingly sketchy descriptions in Old English poetry is thus not comparable to viewing a photograph or a realistic portrait but closer to the way one might approach the more selective and stylized artwork of manuscript illustrations or even coins and buttons. As Leslie Webster has observed, in such small spaces provided by dress accessories or coins, a "visual language" (21) is at work, with images that are "highly elliptical" (13). Like Carver's notion of an "image vocabulary" ("Contemporary" 118), the metaphors employed by Webster of a "visual language," a "traditional grammar of Anglo-Saxon style," and the "cognitive skills needed to *read*" (21; emphasis mine) Anglo-Saxon small-scale art all point toward potential connections with verbal art, and indeed parallel methodologies are highly useful for "decoding" the many compressed verbal descriptions of architecture that we see in Old English verse.

Therefore, in order to understand the fuller meanings of the architectural details of Heorot, we must look beyond mere physical attributes and turn to the social values with which particular building features—or collocations of features—are encoded by the surrounding tradition. The description of Heorot's physical characteristics in fact are in many ways subordinated to the social activities taking place therein, with the poem relying on the implied audience's traditional awareness to provide the building with architectural significance. In the passage describing its creation and throughout the poem, Hrothgar's hall is described largely in terms of what goes on inside rather than according to its purely physical characteristics: it is a *medoærn* ["mead-dwelling"] (69), a *folcstede* ["people-place"] (76), a *beahsele beorhta* ["bright ring hall"] (1177). Such terms and phrases tell us much more about the associative meanings of architectural form than the architectural record alone is able to provide. In its description, Heorot's physical characteristics are inextricably linked with the social functions of the hall and Germanic heroic ideals more broadly. In a discussion of core elements associated with the Anglo-Saxon hall, Kathryn Hume reminds us that Old English poems celebrate not simply the hall as a building but also the social system associated with it, namely, gift-giving, loyalty, and *wynn* or joy (66, 68)—all features brought out in this description of Heorot. In Heorot, Hrothgar "distributed rings" and there was "treasure at the feast": "beagas dælde, / sinc æt symle" (lines 80–81). The building is also referred to as a "guðsele" ["war hall"] (443), a "drihtsele" ["retainer's hall"] (485), and a "winsele" ["wine hall"] (695). The text indicates that Heorot's fame among all peoples as a place of order and security is far more important for an audience to understand than are its exact proportions.[42]

The positive valence of the hall is at times conveyed explicitly but at other points implied through traditionally resonant architectural features, such as prominent gables. For instance, during the description of Heorot's creation, when the poem first asserts its status as the greatest of all halls, gables are mentioned in conjunction with the building's impressive height, "heah ond horngeap" (82).[43] And at the narrative moment when Beowulf establishes himself as a lone hero, the only one guarding Heorot who does not sleep, the hall is described as a "hornreced" (703). Here and elsewhere in Old English verse, heroic actions are preceded by descriptions of the built spaces associated with these actions as "horned" or gabled. When Andreas is being called upon to perform heroic acts in saving Matthew and rescuing those imprisoned within Mermedonian walls, for instance, the ship on which he sails is marked as a "hornscipe" (270), and the Mermedonian buildings he first encounters are "hornsalu" (1158). (On Mermedonian architecture, see further chapter 3.) Likewise, the hall of the *Finnsburh Fragment* is not just once but twice referenced as having "hornas" (2), immediately prior to a heroic call to arms. The fragment opens with the statement that "hornas byrnað næfre" ["the gables never burn"] (1), followed by a speech in which the king wakes his men to the threat of attack and again specifically refers to the hall's gables: "ne ðis ne dagað eastan, ne her draca ne fleogeð, / ne her ðisse healle *hornas* ne byrnað; / ac her forþ berað" ["This is not the dawn from the east, nor do dragons fly here, nor do the hall gables burn; but they bear forth here"] (3–5). The gables here metonymically reference the entire hall, which is not burning but is under threat from attackers. The warriors are then told to "habbað eowre linda, hicgeaþ on ellen, / winnað on orde, wesað on mode!" ["Have your linden shields, intend brave deeds, contend in the front of the fight; be brave!"] (11–12). At the moment when the hall is most in need of defense, the single feature provided is the presence of gables, indicating that gables are a defining architectural feature of a hall and also a poetic symbol of corresponding heroism for the poet's implied audience. Like the hall in the *Finnsburh Fragment*, Heorot is referred to as gabled precisely when the heroism of its inhabitants is most needed: "Sceotend swæfon, / þa þæt hornreced healdan scoldon, /

ealle buton anum" ["The warriors slept, those who should have held the gabled hall, all but one"] (703–5). In each case gables are closely linked to the anticipation of heroic action.

In fact, many of the building's relatively few physical characteristics seem to serve largely to suggest a place where such significant events may occur, often in formulaic and traditional terms. As noted above, Saxon builders went to great lengths to employ timber construction methods even in stone buildings, to prize roofs with prominent and often multiple gables, to emphasize rounded structures even when it would have been more practical to do otherwise, to build high walls and doors relative to building width, and to build these high structures in prominent and elevated locations. This particular combination of features is likewise idealized in verse, where curved, high arches help mark *Beowulf*'s Heorot as the "husa selest," a phrase repeated no fewer than four times (146, 285, 658, 935). The combination of features explicitly attributed to Heorot, while insufficient for complete visualization, are those chosen to demonstrate Heorot's inherent greatness, presumably because this particular combination of features would have been most resonant for the poem's implied audience. Across the poetry, these features are also those most closely associated with the ethos of heroism that pervades the poem: specifically, the *comitatus* involving the lord and his band of retainers, the glory and feasting of the mead-hall, courage in battle, public boasts of bravery, gift-giving and receiving of treasure, loyalty between lords and retainers, and the desire for immortal glory. As the log cabin is able to evoke a loosely configured but culturally powerful set of pioneer ideals, architectural imagery of the hall provided Anglo-Saxon poets and artisans with an efficient and powerful way to index the ideals of the *comitatus*.

Such issues of indexed meaning are also important in those passages that pose logical inconsistencies or that have no viable real-world counterparts. The presence of gold in the construction of Heorot's walls, for instance, is architecturally incongruous with surviving evidence of actual halls but nonetheless consistent with the heroic ideals conveyed through the architectural imagery. Beowulf and his men arrive and are struck by the "goldfah" ["gold-adorned"] hall (308); the hall in general is said to be gilded, "fætum fahne" (716), and the roof is singled out as "gold fahne" ["gold adorned"] (927). Because gold "has positive valence when appropriated for social purposes, negative when hoarded" (John Hill 260), the architecture itself serves as social commentary, implicitly reinforcing social norms.[44] The decorative gold on the communal hall thus stands in contrast to the dragon's hoarded gold later in the poem.

Architecturally anachronistic, the image is nonetheless perfectly consistent in its traditional referentiality. As in many places throughout the poem, combinations of features that do not reflect architectural reality demonstrate consistency at a traditional level, and the very departure from the norm serves to draw attention to those features that accentuate the building's heroic significance. Just as the *comitatus* ideal "is not intended to reflect an actual cultural praxis" (Amodio, *Writing* 49), the architectural features attributed to buildings in which such ideals are practiced need not reflect actual Anglo-Saxon building methods to offer a satisfying and traditionally appropriate interpretation. Noting that "the hall's golden ornamentation is one of its salient features," John Niles explains that the particular combination of realistic and fantastical features attributed to Heorot invite audiences "to envision the hall as distinguished from ordinary buildings" by its "almost supernaturally golden radiance. At once we see it in its true nature, as pertaining to the real world as augmented by imagination" (Niles et al. 172).

Indeed, it is often in the incongruities that we can most readily discern traditional meanings. Without the structural limitations of actual physical materials, the poet was free to combine materials in ways that could not be rendered into visual images and that lacked any viable real-world counterparts on the Anglo-Saxon architectural landscape. A poet could depict a gold roof, as that on Heorot, thus investing the building with heroic nobility without worrying about whether gold could weather the elements or be supported structurally by the timbers. A building's height need not be limited by an adequate supply of timber on surrounding lands. And, as I demonstrate in later chapters, poetic buildings can be simultaneously invested with features of wooden as well as stone construction without having to conform to any laws of physics. The example of Heorot, whose description is sparse but otherwise relatively unproblematic in its logical consistency, has provided us with those features most closely associated with heroic ideals.

While descriptions of Heorot certainly exploit the traditional referentiality of numerous idealized architectural features, the preceding discussion of *Beowulf* is not intended to suggest that this epic represents an unambiguous expression of traditional oral poetics, either in its architectural representation or in its portrayal of the Anglo-Saxon heroic code. On the contrary, as Mark Amodio convincingly argues in *Writing the Oral Tradition*, although *Beowulf* has in fact received much attention in oral tradition studies, it is actually not the most traditional or conventional in its employment of traditional themes or phraseology. The *Beowulf*-poet employs but "ultimately subverts" the *comitatus* ideal, which partially breaks down during the fight with the dragon when Beowulf's retainers flee at the first sight of the dragon and when Beowulf himself "fractures the ideal's foundation" in telling his companions that the fight "Nis ... eower sið" ["is not your undertaking"] (2532b). While the *comitatus* ideal "figures integrally in *Beowulf,*" the poet "significantly altars its contours and in doing so probes some of the fundamental tensions that arise when a heroic ideal collides with human nature" (51). This tension and fracturing involving the heroic code is paralleled and even foreshadowed in architectural imagery from Heorot's earliest description. The fulfillment of Heorot as the literal embodiment of heroic ideals is conveyed visually through its explicit description as high (in terms of both its construction and its location), gabled, arched, and wooden. Then projected onto this idealized image is the very real susceptibility to fire threatening the actual wooden buildings in Anglo-Saxon times. Similarly, the gabled Heorot is portrayed as in need of, and worthy of, protection; but only one, Beowulf, lives up to the appropriate ideals of heroic conduct. In contrast, the men in Finnsburh, who are also called upon to protect a hall explicitly referenced as gabled, ultimately fail in their endeavors but rise to the challenge and fight to the death, more effectively fulfilling the expectations of heroism.

In the building as in the narrative events themselves, *Beowulf*'s "encroaching sense of the tragic limitations of the heroic life does not negate its recognition and celebration of its beauty and value" (Liuzza, *Beowulf* 39). Liuzza's statement of *Beowulf*'s ideals as "precious but precarious, noble but impossible" (39), applies equally well to the hall in which Beowulf's heroic ideals are first realized. Heorot is presented as the epitome of heroic buildings, even as the ideals and the buildings alike are ultimately held up as unsustainable. The relationship of architectural description to the ideals expressed through the narrative action is apparent not only in Heorot but in the poem's subsequent architectural settings as well.

STONE AND THE MERE

Whereas Heorot is clearly aligned with the human world and can be readily understood as an architectural space, the poem's later dominant settings are characterized by more fluid boundaries between the human and nonhuman spheres and, correspondingly, between built space and the natural environment.[45] Klaeber noted early on the problems posed by the mere's description at a literal level and the combination of features attributed to the mere "without regard for absolute consistency" (Klaeber, lst ed. 176). More recently, Niles has observed that "archaeological parallels can be cited to the dragon's barrow and to many other features of *Beowulf* as well, but the place that is home to the Grendel creatures can scarcely be thought of as modeled on any part of the natural world" (Niles et al. 218).[46] The impossible space inhabited by Grendel's mother is surrounded by cliffs, lies beneath the water, and is overhung with trees—clearly, it would seem, more a phenomenon of nature than of architectural planning. At the same time, however, this space is also portrayed in terms of a built space; it is referred to as a hall, *sele*, no fewer than three times (1513, 1515, 2139), complete with flooring, *flet* (1540), and walls from which precious objects are displayed (1662). As with Heorot, we are given very few concrete details regarding the mere's physical characteristics. Those few specific features we are given, as problematic as they might be for constructing a coherent visual image, nonetheless provide a poetically fitting architectural space for the events that follow. "Decoding," to use Ruth Waterhouse's term, the mere's architectural details reveals a built space that is both traditionally appropriate for its inhabitants and fitting for Beowulf's heroic actions that take place therein, as inconsistent as these contradictory elements might be at a purely literal level.

The description of the mere is horrific to be sure—descending into unknown depths, shrouded in fog and mist, impenetrable to light, and eerily encompassing both fire and water—in many ways much like Anglo-Saxon portrayals of hell.[47] At the same time, however, some of these very features are parallel with features isolated for description of Anglo-Saxon halls, thus inviting audiences to consider the events taking place within the mere in terms of the Anglo-Saxon heroic, and human, code of conduct. Heorot's description centered on elements that were valued in Anglo-Saxon architectural aesthetics and thus helped mark that fictional construction as the greatest of all halls for audiences sharing in this aesthetic. In the mere, we are shown a physical space that is at once visually distinct from but parallel to that of the Anglo-Saxon hall in its utilization and subsequent subversion of wood, height, elevated location, and arched spaces. Where Heorot's greatest threat—because of its wood construction—is fire, the mere, though overhung with wooden branches, is dominated by stone and withstands "fyr on flode" ["fire on the water"] (1366). Where Heorot is a high building constructed on an elevated space that is visible from great distances, the mere "under næssa genipu niþer gewiteð, / flod under foldan" ["goes deep under dark cliffs, water under the earth"] (1360–61), its cliffs descending rather than ascending and its construction visible to no one above the water's surface. And where Heorot's roof features broad, well-built wooden gables, the mere is overshadowed by arched wood in a more ominous form, "hrinde bearwas, / wudu wyrtum fæst" ["frosty branches, wood held fast in its roots"] (1363–64).[48]

The presence of wood is mentioned numerous times in relation to the entrance of the mere's space. Hrothgar says of the space that "wudu wyrtum fæst wæter oferhelmað" ["wood held fast overhangs the water"] (1364); Beowulf assures Hrothgar that Grendel's mother will not escape into the "fyrgenholt" ["mountain wood"] (1393); and the first details provided when Beowulf first arrives are the "fyrgenbeamas" ["mountain beams"] (1414), "wynleasne wudu" ["joyless wood"] (1416).[49] Such references serve to evoke Anglo-Saxon hall ideals only to subvert and distort them. Throughout this episode the mere's horrific composite of the architectural features most often attributed to halls in which heroic deeds take place architecturally reflects the subversion of heroic ideals practiced by Grendel and his mother. An eerie subversion of the timbers in the hall, the mere's wood is arched because it is bound to the earth, and this bowed wood towers not above a structure high overhead but over one that plunges deep, deep below. Such repeated references to wood— specifically, arched wood above what is explicitly described as a "hrof-sele" ["roofed hall"] (1515) later in the poem—metonymically evoke the context of the wooden Anglo-Saxon halls even as other architectural features effectively subvert it through a distorted and horrific composite of the architectural features most closely tied to *comitatus* ideals. The "fyrgen-beamas" hang not over a wooden hall but over "harne stan" ["gray stone"] (1414–15). This juxtaposition of wood and stone creates a poetic and architectural tension between the order of the hall and the chaos of the unfamiliar, a contrast that only intensifies as the episode progresses. The designation "harne stan" offers an early indicator that description of the space operates at more than a purely literal level, the phrase itself a powerful example of traditional referentiality in poetic architectural description.[50]

The particular collocation reaches beyond the simple description of a structure as gray and formulaically marks the mere as an architectural space inhabited by unnatural and formidable enemies, indicating what Michael Swisher has described as "a boundary between the known, familiar world of human activity and the frightening realm of monsters, the supernatural and unusual adventure" (133). This phrase, used for the entrances of not only Grendel's mere but also the dragon's lair (1415, 2744), appears also in the embedded story of Sigemund, where we again see the phrase marking the boundary through which the hero must pass (887–89): "He under harne stan, / æþelingas bearn, ana geneðde / frecne dæde" ["Under the gray stone, he ventured alone, the son of a prince, on the daring deed"]. In *Andreas* also, the hero must pass through "harne stan" (841) before freeing Matthew and other prisoners from the city of cannibals. An audience attuned to traditional markers would likely recognize the architectural imagery and be on alert for the ensuing supernatural conflict, which eventually manifests itself in the form of a demon in Andreas's cell.[51] As Swisher demonstrates, "the hero who sees this marker is forewarned and if he treads further, he does so with the knowledge that a normal struggle with an earthly foe must not be expected" (133). While evidenced primarily in secular verse narratives, "harne stan" operates in a similar way in Blickling Homily XVI. In this portion of the homily Paul, being shown the underworld by the archangel Michael, sees above the waters a "harne stan," under which sea monsters and other evil spirits are said to dwell. Here, as in the poetry, the phrase marks a boundary between the human and the supernatural, suggesting an idiom that transcends purely poetic contexts.[52]

While the particular collocation of "harne stan" specifically denotes imminent danger, stone even without the demarcation of "harne" carries a certain inherent tension. Native Germanic construction was of timber, stone being instead the dominant material of ruins left on the landscape from the period of Roman occupation. At a basic level, stone characterized the construction of outsiders, neither inherently good nor bad, impressive but categorically "other." Phrases such as "enta geweorc" ["work of giants"] applied to stone ruins suggest that ancient Roman walls and other stone structures scattered across the landscape were both impressive and mystifying to many Anglo-Saxons.[53] The highly charged phrase *enta geweorc* is applied not only to architectural structures such as the crumbling walls in *The Ruin* or *The Wanderer,* the dragon's pillars in *Beowulf,* and even the ruins outside of Mermedonia through which Andreas is dragged (see further chap. 3 below) but also to smaller objects of great power and significance, such as the hilt of the sword that Beowulf gives to Hrothgar.[54] As Foley has explained, "what these usages share . . . is not the particular circumstances in which they appear, or any literal relationship to giants and their works, but rather the idiomatic value of retrojection into the deep past" (*Singer* 199). The material legacies of this "deep past," poetically marked as "enta geweorc," are awe-inspiring, to be sure, but in a way that is at the same time removed from distinctly Germanic traditions.

The incertitude toward stone by Anglo-Saxon builders indicated by the extensive internal woodwork in such stone structures as the tower of Sompting (fig. 14) is also exhibited in surviving poetry. For instance, when recounting the miseries he endured for the sons of men in *Christ,* Christ explains that as a baby he was made to lay on stone: "læg ic on heardum stane" ["I lay on hard stone"] (1424). "Stane" here is not the alliterating element, indicating that the material was a choice independent of metrical concerns. The hard stone serves here to indicate Christ's isolation and hardship, his separation from the known and the familiar. In similar fashion, the stone of the mere serves to heighten Beowulf's separation from the known world of the heroic hall and his isolation in the solitary fight against Grendel's mother. As a stone anti-hall beneath an arched timber roof, the space of the mere is at once evocative of Anglo-Saxon architectural practice and decidedly foreign, the presentation of architectural space anticipating the subversion of heroic battle that soon follows.

Further down in the murky depths, the tension created by architectural description continues. The bottom of the fen is initially described simply as "ground" ["grund," 1394]. During combat, however, the "ground" becomes the floor of a built space, more closely paralleling the description of the hall; Grendel's mother carries Beowulf "to her court" ["to hofe sinum," 1507], and she twice falls to the "floor" ["on flet," 1540, 1568]. The hall terminology continues as Beowulf drags Grendel's head "on flet" (1647).[55] Though *flet* can be translated more generally as "floor" or even "ground," the usages in *Beowulf* refer almost exclusively to floors of halls or, through synecdoche, the halls themselves.[56] Heorot itself is referenced as a "flet/te" no fewer than four times (1025, 1036, 1647, 2017). Hygelac's hall (1976), Offa's hall (1949), the Heathobards' hall (2034, 2054) all receive similar terminology. While the sense of "ground" is most logical in the immediate narrative context of the mere, the preponderance of its usage as "floor" or "hall" in the poem overall has the effect of evoking this second sense. Thus the term's multivalence allows audiences to retain a sense of the mere as a subterranean natural phenomenon (with a "ground") while at the same time marking even this most hostile space as one in which heroic events can occur (with the "floor" of a hall).

Grendel and his mother are further placed in the context of heroic ideals, even as they subvert them, as "dwellers of a house" ["huses hyrdas," 1666]. Their home has "walls" from which they hang precious treasures, just as Beowulf and his men do in the corresponding Heorot. The word chosen to describe the walls, however, embodies the ambiguity of the space itself. The sword hangs from a "wage" rather than a "weall." *Wag* or *wæg* can be used to refer to walls of buildings but also frequently refers to the "walls" of water in high waves.[57] Both meanings are evoked here, as a sword could only hang from a wall in the former sense, while the underwater nature of the cave makes the latter sense equally appropriate. The connection between man-made and natural space is further developed in Wealtheow's claim that Beowulf will be known throughout "windgeard, weallas" ["wind-dwelling, walls"] (1224). All of nature here is seen in terms of a walled space large enough to be home to the winds themselves.

The conflation of natural and built space and the subversion of heroic architectural conventions all help anticipate the paradoxical nature of the battle with Grendel's mother, who is simultaneously a human(oid)

opponent participating in a heroic battle and a monster from the supernatural realm. When Beowulf first enters the architectural space of Grendel's mother, he is described as a "gist" ["guest," "stranger"] (1522) just as
Grendel was described as a "gæst" upon entering Heorot.[58] Within the
realm of the mere, Grendel's mother is a "merewif mihtig" ["mighty mere-
woman"] (1519), and Beowulf now, as Grendel was before, is the intruding
party. The ambiguous nature of the space is reflected in its architectural
description: it is an ominous "niðsele" ["hall of conflict"] (1513) and, just
two lines later, a protective "hrofsele" ["roofed hall"] (1515). Though it is
the residence of Grendel and his kin, an "ælwihta eard" ["abode of monsters"] (1500), the architectural space itself is not inherently evil.[59]

On the contrary, the structure works to aid Beowulf (a phenomenon we see in *Andreas* as well, when the prison's column becomes a hero's
companion).[60] In much the same way that the heroic Wiglaf fends off
the dragon while Beowulf strikes, the *hrofsele* (variously translated "hall-
roofing" [Heaney] or "roofed-hall" [Jack 119; Gordon 31]) aids Beowulf
in holding off the force of the waters, allowing him to achieve victory
against Grendel's mother (1512–16):

>   . . . Ða se eorl ongeat
> þæt he [in] niðsele   nathwylcum wæs,
> þær him nænig wæter   wihte ne scepede,
> ne him for hrofsele   hrinan ne mehte
> færgripe flodes. . . .
>
> ———
>
> [Then the earl found that he was in some kind of hostile hall, where
> no water in any way touched him, nor could the sudden clutch of the
> flood come near him because of the roofed hall. . . .]

Simultaneously hostile and protective, the "hall" itself is at this point
clearly aligned with neither protagonist nor antagonist. When Beowulf
later recounts these events, the abode of Grendel's mother is described
as a "guðsele" ["battle-hall"] (2139), the same compound used to describe
the Geats' dwelling earlier in the poem (443).

The wood at the mere's entrance helps evoke the heroic context of the
Anglo-Saxon hall, while the stone just below underscores its otherness.

Wood was the dominant material for Germanic, Anglo-Saxon construction, whereas stone, while employed in later Anglo-Saxon architecture—most notably churches—belonged to outside architectural traditions. The poetic tradition in part reflects this architectural reality, with stone conveying a sense of otherness, an unknown quantity that can ultimately be either positive or negative. As I discuss later, stone can mark the world of monsters and dragons (or, in the case of *Andreas,* cannibals and demons),[61] or it can mark the work and space of ancient and skilled giants (as in *The Ruin*) or even God himself (as in *Advent Lyric I*). Where the features of wood construction in combination with arches, height, and gables can slot architectural spaces such as in *Beowulf* as inherently positive, elements of stone construction convey a sense of awe but simultaneous uncertainty, and Anglo-Saxon poets and scribes took full advantage of the sometimes conflicting associations embedded in this complex tradition of architectural poetics. To complicate the issue still further, the domain of the dragon includes not only stone but also earth, creating an even more ambiguous space, blurring the boundaries between the natural and the man-made, the earthly and the supernatural, the heroic and the horrific.

EARTH AND THE DRAGON'S LAIR

Like the mere, the dragon's lair conflates different types of architectural elements to create an image that is simultaneously unrealistic in physical terms and highly resonant in poetic ones. The barrow's description, like that of the mere, draws attention to those specific features that align it with, or define it against, the architectural ideals of an Anglo-Saxon hall—its construction materials (wood vs. stone), height, elevation of location, roof construction, and arches. The barrow is explicitly referenced as a hall, not a timber hall, but an "eorðsele" (2515). Wood is prominent in the dragon episode, not as the dragon's dwelling, but as the target of his disastrous flames. The hoard guarded by the dragon is marked explicitly as high, in a "heaum" ["high"] (2212) mound. The structure is also characterized as arched, supported with "stanbogan" ["stone arches"] (2718). But rather than with a gabled roof, this space is constructed beneath an "inwithrof" ["evil roof"] (3123).

The juxtaposition of features associated with heroism (e.g., arches and height) and features that depart from or even subvert these same conventions of heroic architecture (e.g., its "harne stan" and "inwithrof") reflects an understanding of built space as neither inherently positive nor negative but as invested with ideals from other generations of inhabitants. The tendency to appropriate sacred spaces of former peoples is evident in Anglo-Saxon building practices, such as St. Pancras Church at Canterbury built on the ruins of a pre-Christian temple (Kerr and Kerr, *Anglo-Saxon Sites* 190). Materials, too, could be reused, as were the Roman stones employed in the construction of St. John's Anglo-Saxon church at Escomb (see figs. 20 and 21). The poetic space of the dragon's lair follows similar patterns of appropriation, as it is first chosen and built by "æðelan cynnes" ["a race of nobles"] (2234), stocked by the last survivor of this people (2244–45), occupied by the dragon for "þreohund wintra" ["three hundred winters"] (2278), and ultimately reappropriated as the location of Beowulf's funeral monument.

As is true of other architectural spaces in the poem, the barrow's description is closely tied to the values and ideals of its inhabitants. And because the inhabitants of the space change over time as the barrow undergoes a continual process of appropriation and reappropriation, the attributed architectural features reflect these layers of occupation, thus at an architectural level conflating what Irving has referred to as the worlds of *humanitas* and *draconitas* (*Rereading* Beowulf 100–101). The retrospective account of the Last Survivor refers to the structure as new, occupying a prized location high above the water (2241–43):

> ... Beorh eall gearo
> wunode on wonge   wæteryðum neah,
> niwe be næsse,   nearocræftum fæst.

———

[The barrow, all ready, stood on the ground near the sea waves by the headland, newly made, held fast with difficult powers.]

Connections between the structure and heroic ideals are then made explicit in the speech of the Last Survivor, which laments ways of life highly specific to the Anglo-Saxon hall: the "seledream" ["hall joy"] (2252), the hawk flying through the hall ["ne god hafoc/geond sæl swingeð,"

2263–64], the sound of horses on the courtyard ["se swifta mearh/ burh-stede beateð," 2264–65]. The Last Survivor's speech in effect dedicates the space as a heroic one, and the structure is appropriately stocked with treasures of heroes who have passed.

In the period contemporary with *Beowulf*, however, the space is occupied by the dragon. This same structure, now aged, is most frequently referred to as a "hlæw" (e.g., 2296) or "beorg," and the dragon's epithets connect him closely to this later manifestation of the structure: he is the "beorges hyrde" ["protector of the barrow"] (2304), "beorges weard" ["guardian of the barrow"] (2524). The portion of the narrative depicting this period, when the occupancy is furthest removed from Anglo-Saxon heroic ideals, invests the structure with features decidedly foreign to hall construction. Not only does the dragon dwell in a structure devoid of wood, but the flames he spews seek out and destroy timber dwellings. As the poem observes in the description of Heorot's very construction, the greatest threat of all to the native wooden architecture is fire, a threat realized when the dragon departs from his stone landscape ["stonc ða æfter stane"] (2288) to burn the wooden homes of men: "Ða se gæst ongan gledum spiwan, / beorht hofu bærnan" ["began to spew forth flames, to burn the bright dwellings"] (2312–13). Even Beowulf's home, "bolda selest" ["best of buildings"] (2326), is said to melt under the surges of the dragon's fire. Beowulf's choice of shield before this battle reinforces the limitations of wood (2337–41):

> Heht him þa gewyrcean   wigendra hleo
> eall irenne,   eorla dryhten,
> wigbord wrætlic;   wisse he gearwe
> þæt him holtwudu   he(lpan) ne meahte,
> lind wið lige.

> ———

> [Then the protector of warriors, the lord of earls, ordered an iron shield, a splendid war shield, to be made for him; he knew well that a wood shield would not be able to help him, linden wood against fire.]

Although the shield of course is not an architectural structure, the tensions between the heroic ideals associated with wood and its inherent vulnerability to fire nonetheless echo the anticipation of Heorot's burning early in the poem. The treatment of wood in the final third of the poem marks the dragon's realm's complete separation from an Anglo-Saxon heroic code of conduct and at the same time points toward the limitations of wood in real-world construction. Once again, the heroic ideals of the *comitatus* are closely linked with architectural representation. Architectural embodiments of ideals associated with the *comitatus*, the timber halls of Beowulf's kingdom—tall, elevated, arched, and gabled— fall at precisely the same moment when the *comitatus* itself begins to break down. A cup has been stolen, and soon Beowulf's men will abandon him. The narrative's treatment of architecture powerfully illustrates how significant yet fragile the hall and its accompanying social system truly are.

In many ways the opposite of the architecture characterizing Beowulf's sphere, the dragon's barrow is described as stone. As discussed above, stone in both Anglo-Saxon architecture and poetic architectural description fairly consistently denotes a non-native quality, although the connotations can be either positive or negative. The first direct reference to the dragon's barrow marks the structure as stone with no specifically negative connotations, perhaps even somewhat positive: "stanbeorh stear(c)ne" ["strong stone barrow"] (2213).[62] The danger of its inhabitant is only later indicated architecturally through the space's description as "harne stan," when Beowulf asks Wiglaf to go to the hoard "under the gray stone" ["under harne stan"] (2744), the "harne stan" of this structure aligning it with such spaces as Grendel's mere, the city of the Mermedonian cannibals of *Andreas,* and even the underworld itself as portrayed in the Blickling Homilies. Unlike each of these other instances, however, when the "harne stan" precedes the entrance of a dangerous and supernatural foe, the reference to the "harne stan" of the dragon's lair appears long after we are aware of the danger and fatal consequences, when Beowulf lies dying from the dragon's attack. The architectural description here does not warn us of impending danger but rather reminds us that Beowulf's death was not caused by any ordinary foe but by a supernatural and monstrous enemy against whom even the most valiant effort would prove insufficient. More than simply providing the hue of the stone, the phrase here helps exonerate the dying but no less honorable Beowulf.

This theme of death that pervades the final portion of the poem is further conveyed in the dominant material of the poem's final architectural space: earth. Its earthen construction is underscored more than any other feature, and explicit references to earth appear at every point in the structure's history—in its description as it is mourned by the Last Survivor, in descriptions of its occupation by the dragon, and in its final appropriation as Beowulf's final resting place. What all of the poem's many references to earth have in common is a close connection with death. When the cup is first stolen from the dragon's hoard, we are told that the treasures were stored here in an "eorðse(le)"[63] (2232) by warriors long dead: "Ealle hie deað fornam/ærran mælum" ["Death took them all in earlier times"] (2236–37). When the dragon enters the human realm and appropriates it as his own, the forts of this outside world are also referred to as earthen structures, with the dragon described here as having "eorðweard ðone / gledum forgrunden" ["destroyed with flames the earthen stronghold" (lit., "earth-guard")] (2334–35). Finally, at the moment when Beowulf fully realizes his own mortality, the image of the earth hall is again evoked. A certain nostalgia accompanies this last reference to the earth hall, one that uses "reced" instead of the more typical "sele" (2715–19):

> ... Ða se æðeling giong,
> þæt he bi wealle, wishycgende,
> gesæt on sesse; seah on enta geweorc,
> hu ða stanbogan stapulum fæste
> ece eorðreced innan healde.

> ———

> [Then the prince, wise-minded, went so that he could sit in a seat by the wall; he saw in the work of giants how the earth hall was held fast inside with the stone arches.]

The cluster of disparate architectural images ascribed to the barrow in this poignant description parallels and comments on the psychological and emotional complexity of this point in the narrative. The dragon's dwelling of *Beowulf* is marked as "enta geweorc" ["work of giants"] (2717), evoking the space's pre-dragon and awe-inspiring origins. We are also told of the structure's "stanbogan" ["stone arches"] (2718), stone, as we have seen, being outside the architectural world of the *comitatus* but the arches ("bogan") simultaneously reflecting the aesthetic seen in the heroic architecture of the poetry's timber halls. As with other "eorð" compounds, the compound "eorðreced" ["earth hall"] has more ominous associations, not only in the immediate events of the narrative, but also in Beowulf's final remembrances. Beowulf, himself near death inside an earthen structure, recounts how Ongentheow retreated from Hygelac's forces "under eorðweall" ["under the earth wall"] (2957). After valiant and heroic feats, Ongentheow is defeated: "ða gebeah cyning, / folces hyrde, wæs in feorh dropen" ["then the king fell, the guardian of people was mortally wounded"] (2980–81). The compound appears again when Wiglaf describes how he went "under eorðweall" (3090) to gather treasure to carry before the dying Beowulf. It would be easy to assume that Wiglaf's only parallel here is between Hygelac and Beowulf, yet this would be to oversimplify, since the phrase "under eorðweall" links Beowulf not with Hygelac, as we might expect, but with the fallen Ongentheow, whose death is portrayed as heroic despite his position as Hygelac's enemy. Both Ongentheow and Beowulf have fallen heroically and taken refuge "by the wall." Much more than a mere description of physical surroundings, "under eorðweall" serves to connect Beowulf with other fallen heroes.

Like Beowulf's death, the dragon's death is marked by his presence in an earthen structure: "wæs ða deaðe fæst, / hæfde eorðscrafa ende genyttod" ["He was then held fast by death; he had enjoyed the earth-cave for the last time"] (3045–46). Long a refuge to be enjoyed, the earth-cave is now the dragon's captor in death. Viewed in isolation, each "eorð" compound suggests merely a possible building material or natural structure, but taken together these "eorð" compounds, so prevalent throughout the final third of *Beowulf,* reveal a pattern of death and refuge. Such associations are reinforced by *eorð* compounds outside of *Beowulf,* most explicitly in the lesser-known poem *The Grave* (15): "Ladlic is þet eorðhus" ["Loathsome is that earth-house"]. Christ's tomb is referenced three times as an "eorðærne" in *The Descent into Hell* (3, 12, 19), and the "eorðsele" of *The Wife's Lament* provides additional evidence of the associations with exile and death. That the compound does not appear in prose would suggest that its meaning resides largely in poetic terms.[64]

Collectively these instances provide important context for those references to earthen architecture where associations with death are less readily apparent. The "þreotteoða secg" ["thirteenth man"] (2406) guides Beowulf's men "to ðæs ðe he eorðsele anne wisse, / hlæw under hrusan holmwylme neh, / yðgewinne" ["to where he alone knew the one earth hall to be, the barrow under the ground near the surging sea, tossing waves"] (2609–11). At 2410 the structure is referred to as an "eorðsele" ["earth hall"] when Beowulf and his men are led to the dragon's home, and when Beowulf demands that the dragon abandon the barrow, the structure is once again described as an "eorðsele" (2515). An awareness of the associations of the earth hall makes this scene even more ominous than we might otherwise perceive. The warriors are not simply being led to a structure that happens to be constructed of earth, but to a death anticipated in powerful traditional architectural description. All of these usages indicate that at the point in time when Beowulf and Wiglaf encounter it, the earth-and-stone structure of the dragon's abode is one that foreshadows death and exile. And it is death that leads us to the poem's final architectural structure.

SYNTHESIS: BEOWULF'S MEMORIAL MONUMENT

The poem's conclusion brings us to construction of another kind, Beowulf's pyre and his final memorial. As with other descriptive passages, the details are selective and few. Despite its obvious functional differences, the description of Beowulf's memorial shares a number of key features with the prized Anglo-Saxon halls, underscoring Beowulf's heroism even in death through well-chosen architectural detail.[65] The location's elevation above the water is emphasized when the dragon is thrown "ofer weallclif" ["over the wall cliff"] (3132), and this high space is then heroically reappropriated when Beowulf's body is carried to the headland "Hrones Næsse" (3136). The Geats then prepare an "ad on eorðan" ["pyre on the earth"] (3138) for Beowulf's body, itself a "banhus" ["bone house"] (3147), a compound inviting us to think even of Beowulf's body in terms of architectural space. The pyre's construction of wood is made explicit twice, when "boldagendra" ["dwelling owners"] (3112) are ordered to bring "bælwudu" ["firewood" (specifically, for a funeral pyre)] (3112) and when the "wudurec" ["wood smoke"] (3144) floats upward. As with the halls inhabited by Beowulf in life, height is one of the few

characteristics stressed in the sparse description of his memorial constructed after the pyre has burned. It was built, "betimbredon" (3159),
"heah ond brad" ["high and broad"], as a "beadurofes becn" ["battle-bold
beacon"] (3158, 3160). The location itself is on high ground. It has walls,
"wealle" (3161), for protecting treasure. Unlike the hall, however, it is partially earth, a barrow on a promontory, "hlæw on h(o)e" (3157).[66] Built
of wood and earth and filled with treasure from the stone ruins, these
final built monuments tie together several of the poem's architectural
themes. Wood is heroic but also vulnerable to fire; stone is awe-inspiring
but sometimes threatening; earth suggests a space for refuge but also
death. All are key components in the architectural world of Old English
poetry and serve to symbolize the world of *Beowulf* in its totality.

PART II

THE

ARCHITECTURAL

LANDSCAPE

OF

OLD

ENGLISH

VERSE

CHAPTER

THREE

THE ROLE OF ARCHITECTURE IN VERSE TRANSLATIONS

Many architectural spaces are, in a way, themselves translations, as space is utilized, abandoned, appropriated, and reappropriated in continuous cycles of use. The exact nature of these transitions, however, is often less clear. The Escomb Church visitor's guide claims that St. John's Anglo-Saxon church (fig. 20) "is built largely from Roman stones foraged from Binchester" (Whitehead and Whitehead 4), an assertion seen in a wide range of studies in Romano-British and Anglo-Saxon architecture.[1] The likely reality, however, is far from simple. The stones of Escomb Church are unquestionably Roman, some of them still bearing Roman inscriptions and markings (fig. 21).[2] But the specific source of the stone is far from being as certain as most literature on the subject would suggest. Roman pottery has been found at Escomb, leaving open the possibility that there was a source of masonry much closer and more accessible than that at Binchester, more than three miles away. While the Anglo-Saxons could have transported Roman stone for building over such a distance, it is far less likely that they would have transported pottery shards and other household items from Binchester. And despite the popularity of the Binchester theory, more probable hypotheses exist for the stone's provenance, including a possible Roman building on or near the site of the church itself or the superstructure of a Roman bridge downstream from the fort at Binchester.[3] But the idea of Binchester as the specific source remains appealing largely because we can *see* it today. Although much of the site remains underground, the basic outline of the fort has

been identified, and visitors can view a small portion that has been excavated, including a well-preserved hypocaust system (fig. 7). So the stones
of the Saxon church (fig. 20) could have come from Binchester. But they
could also have come from sites still buried underground, sites that have
vanished entirely, or, perhaps even more likely, a combination of several
sites.[4] The syncretic nature of building practices is paralleled in the production of Old English verse.

Whereas chapter 2 examined associations with materials and building types that could have been witnessed firsthand by the Anglo-Saxons,
here I explore the choices poets made to describe buildings that would
have been less familiar in the typical Anglo-Saxon experience,[5] focusing especially on points of departure from architectural description in
"source" texts and the ways that Anglo-Saxon poets draw from multiple architectural and poetic conventions to convey such spaces. The
Mermedonian and Roman prisons in *Andreas* and *Juliana,* the Babylo -
nian and Hebrew tents in *Judith* and *Exodus,* and the Hebrew and early
Christian temples in such texts as *Daniel* and *Elene* are all translated and
adapted from non-Anglo-Saxon sources. Nonetheless, all evince features that would have resonated strongly with Anglo-Saxon audiences.
Just as the Roman stones used in the construction of Escomb Church
cannot be traced with absolute certainty to any single Roman site, the
ultimate sources of such works as *Juliana* and *Andreas*—and the buildings described in them—can seldom be unequivocally determined, with
these works likely having been influenced by multiple sources, both oral
and written, both Anglo-Saxon and classical.[6] Thus it is that in referring to such works as *Andreas, Judith, Exodus, Genesis,* or *Juliana* as
"translations," we necessarily refer to the "indexed" or "traditional" concept of translation, one with a "notion of a target language that offers its
own highly developed repertoire of expressive possibilities" (Foley, *Singer*
187).[7] In building and poetry alike sources were used with much fluidity:
the Anglo-Saxons borrowed what they needed but made the new structures and poems entirely their own. And much like the buried and vanished Roman sites that often provided Anglo-Saxon building materials,
the oral tradition often leaves little trace but nonetheless played an important, if today obscured, role in the "construction" of Old English verse
translations.

PRISONS

While there are numerous prisons in Old English hagiographic verse, it is Andreas's and Matthew's Mermedonian prison, a structure that dominates the architectural world of the Old English *Andreas,* that receives the greatest attention in terms of its architectural features and can thus serve well as a primary point of departure here. As discussed in chapter 1, when confronted with foreign verbal images, audiences are likely to fill in gaps of indeterminacy with images from lived experience and to invest unfamiliar images with associative meanings based on similar phraseology encountered in other poetic contexts. My strategy here is thus twofold, offering first an exploration of the *Andreas* prison in light of real-world imprisonment practices likely to have been most familiar to contemporary Anglo-Saxon audiences and then examining the specific phraseology applied to this prison in the context of similar phraseology employed in the poetry more widely. With an understanding of how Anglo-Saxons were likely to have conceived of "prison" alongside an awareness of the traditional referentiality of terms applied to literary prisons, we can thus gain sharper insights into the associative meanings embedded in prison imagery appearing across a range of poetic works, including not only *Andreas* but also *Juliana, Elene, Genesis A* and *B, Christ,* Riddle 50, *Christ and Satan,* and even *Beowulf.*

As is discussed at more length below, the prison of the Old English *Andreas* follows Greek and Latin analogues—most notably, the Greek *Praxeis Andreou kai Mattheia* (Acts of Andrew and Matthew)[8]—in being an architectural structure devoted specifically to imprisonment substantial enough in size to house hundreds of prisoners. A logical first question is what precisely an Anglo-Saxon audience might have envisioned when presented with a visual image so far removed in time and space from the Anglo-Saxon world. Archaeology provides little help for us here, with surviving Anglo-Saxon architecture lacking any evidence of prisons, large or small. The lack is telling and suggests that the massive prison of *Andreas* would indeed have been a foreign concept for most early medieval English audiences. Early law codes offer more context and lend additional support to the idea that "prison" would have denoted something very different to Anglo-Saxon audiences than it might have to earlier audiences

of Greek and Latin analogues from which it was likely adapted and different still from what today's readers are likely to envision after centuries of
dedicated prisons.

The earliest explicit reference to prison in Anglo-Saxon England occurs in a law of Alfred that dates to the late ninth century, and it does
not assume the existence of structures designed specifically for imprisonment.[9] The law states that anyone who failed to fulfill a lawful oath or
pledge must

> selle mid eaðmedum his wæpn 7 his æhta his freondum to gehal-
> danne 7 beo feowertig nihta on carcerne on cyninges tune, ðrowige
> ðær swa biscep him scrife, 7 his mægas hine feden, gif he self mete
> næbbe. Gif he mægas næbbe oððe þone mete næbbe, fede cyninges
> gerefa hine. Gif hine mon togenedan scyle, 7 he elles nylle, gif hine
> mon gebinde, þolige his wæpna 7 his ierfes. (1.2–4)

> ————

> [humbly give his weapons and possessions to his friends to keep,
> and remain 40 days in prison at a royal manor, and undergo there
> whatever [sentence] the bishop prescribes for him; and his rela-
> tives shall feed him if he himself has no food. If he has no relatives,
> and [if he] has not the [necessary] food, the king's reeve shall pro-
> vide him with it. If he will not submit unless force is used against
> him, [i.e.,] if he has to be bound, he shall forfeit his weapons and
> property.][10]

From this early passage, we see that while Alfred assumed the presence
of a "carcerne," he was most likely not envisioning a structure built exclusively for detainment or one that could accommodate the more than
two hundred men and women who inhabited the Mermedonian prison
of the *Praxeis* (1035–40). Rather, anyone detained should stay in the king's
residence, or "tun."[11] The law also indicates that confinement was a lesser
punishment, whereas for the Mermedonians it was a cruel and gruesome
precursor to murder during which victims were blinded and tortured as
they awaited certain death.[12] Under the laws of Alfred, imprisonment was
required for breaking an oath, and punishment for more substantial or violent crimes involved fines or, less frequently, exile. Prison sentences were
treated very seriously in the laws, however, and escape potentially resulted

in exile from the community and excommunication from the church: "Gif he losige, sie he afliemed 7 sie amænsumod of eallum Cristes ciricum" ["If he succeeds in making his escape, he shall be banished, and excommunicated from all the churches of Christ"] (1.7).[13]

Churches were also granted the authority to hold fugitives, providing additional spaces for detention but still not indicating architectural spaces specifically for imprisonment. While the church could ostensibly be a place of sanctuary for fugitives for up to seven days, the system was nonetheless punitive, as church authorities were ordered to ensure that "during this time no food is given to him" ["him mon on ðam fierse mete ne selle"]. The church also had the power to hold fugitives for the same period as the punishment in the law prescribed:

> Gif he self his wæpno his gefan utrǣcan wille, gehealden hi hine
> xxx nihta 7 hie hine his mǣgum gebodien. (5.3)
>
> ———
>
> [If he himself is willing to hand over his weapons to his enemies,
> they shall hold him in their power for thirty days; and they shall
> send formal notice of his position to his kinsmen.][14]

The law implies, however, that many churches were not equipped to serve as such an asylum and that alternate arrangements were sometimes necessary.

> Gif hiwan hiora cirican maran ðearfe hǣbben, healde hine mon
> on oþrum ærne, 7 ðæt nǣbbe ðon ma dura þonne sio cirice. (5.1)
>
> ———
>
> [If the community have so great need of their church, he shall be
> kept in another building, and this shall not have more doors than
> the church.][15]

Phrasing of the laws further suggests that imprisonment could also mean physical confinement, as in stocks, outside the confines of any specific architectural space.[16]

The laws of Æthelstan continued to include references to imprisonment but still did not suggest the presence of structures dedicated to this purpose. Under the laws of Æthelstan, anyone accused of causing death by means of witchcraft was subject to "cxx nihta on carcerne" ["120 nights in prison"] (6.1),[17] in addition to fines and other penalties. Like Alfred's, Æthelstan's laws indicate that imprisonment was used for custody and punishment of lesser crimes, a very different sense of imprisonment from that found in *Andreas* and other Old English verse hagiography. Rather than the torturous precursor to violent death seen in *Andreas,* imprisonment was the punishment assigned for children under fifteen years of age whose crimes might otherwise warrant execution or for prisoners who willingly cooperate with authorities: "gif he þonne on hand gan wille, þonne do hine man on carcern" ["if he will give himself up he shall be put in prison"] (12.1).[18] Also like Alfred's, Æthelstan's law made contingencies for instances in which prisons were unavailable, again indicating that prisons as such were not standard architectural institutions.

> Oððe gif he in carcern ne cume, 7 man nan næbbe, þæt hi hine niman be his fullan were on borh, þæt he æfre ma ælces yfeles geswice. (12.2)
>
> ———
>
> [If he is not put in prison, none being available, they [his relatives] shall stand surety for him, to the full amount of his wergeld, that he shall desist for evermore from every form of crime.][19]

The laws therefore indicate that dedicated prisons were a fairly late development, that they were used sparingly (sometimes serving more as refuge than punishment), and that the facilities and circumstances for imprisonment were not at all fixed.

In fact, imprisonment in England does not emerge as an institution until at least the twelfth century (Pugh 1). R. B. Pugh explains that "once private jurisdictions begin to emerge, and this was perhaps in the eighth century, some kind of 'prison' may be presumed to exist" but notes that "'prison' is a comprehensive term" that could refer to multiple forms of confinement and was most often "not endured for long" (1). A more recent study of imprisonment in England and Wales likewise asserts that "some means of detention becomes necessary as soon as disputes over wrongs come to be settled in any but the most immediate and brutal fashion" but that "detention before trial does not, of course imply an organised or extensive system of purpose-built gaols throughout the countryside, for a man may be held for this purpose in a house, under guard, in stocks or simply bound by ropes" (Harding et al. 3). Lisi Oliver argues that two of Wihtred's laws calling for "freo hals" [lit., "free neck"] in lieu of "healsfang" [lit., "neck capture"] refer to fines in place of captivity (171), suggesting that captivity was an option, although less preferable and less common. Penalties such as execution, exile, or mutilation all offered "much simpler" and "less expensive" methods of punishment for crime (Harding et al. 7). Internal evidence in the poetry also indicates the absence of dedicated prisons in Anglo-Saxon culture. The "ræpingas" ["prisoners," "criminals"] of Riddle 52[20] are taken not to a specially designated structure but beneath the roof of a hall, "under hrof sales" (Riddle 52, 1–2).[21]

Linguistic evidence also argues against dedicated prisons during the Anglo-Saxon period. The borrowed terms used in both the laws and the poetry indicate that the concept of prison itself was foreign and a late historical development. *Carcern* or *carcærn*, deriving from Latin *carcer* ("prison") and compounded with *ærn* or *ern* ("place," Bosworth), makes its first appearance in the late ninth century (Pugh 1). As C. P. Biggam observes, a common reason to borrow a term for building descriptions is that the technology or structure is also borrowed (114), and, though the prison is referred to repeatedly in *Andreas*, the term *carcern* itself is employed only ten times.[22] Because the concept of a structure built specifically for imprisonment was apparently a foreign one, more often the Mermedonian prison is referred to with native terms that convey *characteristics* of the prison rather than denoting a specialized type of architectural structure. These terms include "hearmlocan" ["chamber of harm"] (95, 1029), "hleoleasan wic" ["comfortless"] (131), "heolstorlocan" ["dark chamber"] (144, 1005—unique to *Andreas*), "morðorcofa" ["evil chamber"] (1004), "gnornhofa" ["house of sadness"] (1008, 1043), "clustor - cleofa" ["locked chamber"/"prison cell"][23] (1021), "hlinscuwan" ["darkness of confinement"] (1071), "hlinræced" ["grated building"] (1463), "dung" (or "ding") ["prison"] (1270), "neadcofan" ["prison"; lit., "chamber of extremity"] (1309), "dimme ræced" ["dark building"] (1308), "wic unsyfre" ["unclean place"] (1310), and the simple "sele" (1311). Since these features have limited or no precedent in source texts and since they cannot have been drawn from experience with Anglo-Saxon buildings, the connotative meanings of these phrases in the wider context of Old English poetry become even more important for the poem's interpretation. By looking at these terms collectively, we can more fully ascertain the traditional referentiality of these features in isolation and in combination and thus gain a better sense of how audiences contemporary with the poetry's production might have understood "prison."

Consistent with the notion that the concept of a dedicated prison was foreign is the relatively high frequency of unique or highly unusual compounds, new terms being created to accommodate new concepts. *Nead-cofa* is a *hapax legomenon* in *Andreas,* though similar in form to *morðor-cofa* (1004). *Cofa* has the sense of "room" or "chamber" but can also refer to "cave" or "den" *(DOE),* thus simultaneously characterizing the space as underground and man-made, both of which fit the sense of the poem. *Gnornhof* is also unique to *Andreas,* occurring twice in this poem and nowhere else. Other terms are adapted from more familiar general concepts. Brooks notes, for instance, that *ding* should be understood as a form of *dung,* meaning "chamber" more generally and thus here "prison cell" (108 n.).[24] Likewise, *sele,* generally meaning "hall" (see chap. 1 above), is applied at line 1311, a choice that has a powerful effect at this point in the narrative both in its departure from the *Praxeis* and in its contrast with the preponderance of negative imagery applied to this space. The *Praxeis* states that "when evening came, they led him again into the prison, bound his hands behind, and constrained him again until the morrow. And the Devil appeared with seven demons whom the blessed one had cast out of the surrounding country, and after they entered into the prison, they stood before him, wishing to kill him" (trans. Boenig, *Acts* 18). The Old English adaptation greatly expands on the description of the prison *and* the description of the demon himself:

> se halga wæs   to **hofe** læded
> . . . in þæt **dimme ræced**;
> sceal þonne in **neadcofan**   nihtlange fyrst
> wærfæst wunian   **wic unsyfre.**
> þa com seofona sum   to **sele** geongan. (1307–14)

> [the holy one was led to the **house** . . . into that **dim hall**; he had to dwell faithful then in the **house of constraint**, the **dirty dwelling**, all night long. Then came one of seven to go to the **hall**.]

The references to buildings in boldface above are all unprecedented in the Greek text, and, as discussed below, all have connotative meaning in the wider context of Old English verse. The particular combination of terms referring to the prison at this point in the narrative—immediately prior to Andreas's encounter with the demon—serves to simultaneously intensify the hostility of the space and subtly suggest its heroic potential. The effect is thus to heighten the heroism of the poem's protagonist by amplifying the formidability of Andreas's foe and situating the battle in a traditionally appropriate architectural space for heroic battle. The first three lines of this descriptive passage establish the prison as dark *[dimme]*, confining *[nead]*, and unclean *[unsyfre]*, all fairly logical negative characteristics but features added to the Old English adaptation and thus presumably of special importance to the Old English poet. While all of these traits are appropriate, *unsyfre* has special connotative importance in the Old English poetic idiom. At a literal level *unsyfre* simply means "unclean," but examination of its usages indicates much darker connotations. Of the four instances of "unsyfre" ["unclean"] in Old English poetry, two refer to buildings. Like *Andreas*'s prison, the metaphorical building representing the human body in *Christ* is also described as "unsyfre": "For hwan þu þæt selegescot / þæt ic me swæs on þe / gehalgode, hus to wynne, / þurh firenlustas, fule synne, / unsyfre bismite sylfes willum?" ["Why, through your wicked lusts, foul sins, have you filthily defiled of your own will that tabernacle/lodging-place, a house of joy, which I consecrated in you for myself?"] (*Christ* 1480). Both usages are associated with spaces that are not merely physically unclean but that have moral implications as well; that is, the spaces are used for depravity.

Immediately after a series of terms establishing the physical and moral corruption of the space, the passage surprisingly refers to the prison as a "sele" ["hall"], thus superimposing the ethos of the Anglo-Saxon hall onto this otherwise grim scene. Employment of "sele" instead of the more logical "carcern" at this point not only allows for alliteration with "seofan" (a word that does correspond to the Greek text) but also helps activate the register of heroic ideals by setting the action in the space most closely associated with the *comitatus*.[25] Having established the heroic context of the verbal battle soon to ensue between the demon and Andreas through the use of "sele," the poem goes on to elaborate on characteristics of the demon, showing him to be a much more ghastly foe than that presented in the *Praxeis,* the Old English poem's closest analogue. (Characteristics unprecedented in the Greek text are in boldface.)

atol æglæca,   yfela gemyndig,
morðres manfrea   myrce gescyrded,
deoful **deaðreow**   duguðum bereafod. (1312–14)

___

[the horrible monster, mindful of evil, the lord of malice and murder shrouded in murk, the Devil **deadly cruel** robbed of his host.]

Thus just as the building in which the demon confronts Andreas is characterized as more unclean, dim, dark, and constraining than the corresponding building in the Greek, the Old English demon is associated more explicitly with evil, malice, and murder than his Greek counterpart. The architectural features of the prison thus align the space at this point in the narrative with the demon rather than Andreas. The amplified horror of the demon thus reinforced by the grimness of the built space serves to heighten Andreas's own heroism when he emerges victorious in the "sele" in spite of such formidable foes and spaces.

But though the conceptualization of the space helps anticipate Andreas's heroic performance against the demon, the terminology applied to the built space—specifically *clustorcleofan* ["prison-cell"][26]—indicates that Andreas is not acting entirely alone. *Clustorcleofan* is another compound unique to *Andreas* and one that shares close associations with other prison descriptions, connections that help us further interpret the prison space in its narrative and traditional contexts. An examination of the word *clustor* in the corpus of Old English verse shows that in the poetry more widely the detail of being locked, or "clustor," consistently applies to prisons or doors entered by supernatural means. As Satan plans his escape from hell in the Old English *Genesis,* he considers how he might pass "þurh þas clustro" ["through this bar/gate"] (416)[27] and soon after sends his messenger, who effectively does so with the aid of a helmet that makes him invisible. In *Juliana* also we see "clustre" associated with imprisonment, and again the locked doors are inexplicably opened when the "clustre carcernes duru" ["locked prison doors"] (236) are entered by the demon. In *Advent Lyric IV* (see chap. 4) the "clustor" doors (314) keep mankind out of paradise rather than in prison. As in the other instances, however, the locks can be lifted only by supernatural means, in this case the power of God himself. And in *The Descent into Hell* doors marked specifically as "clustor" (40) open only with the aid of supernatural aid from the "cyning" ["king"] (40), "godes sylfes" ["God's own self"] (52). The contexts of these other doors indicated as locked with the term *clustor* help situate the *hapax* "clustorcleofan" and point us toward its connotative meaning. The usage in *Andreas* coincides not with the entrance of a supernatural god or demon but that of a man, Andreas, who enters Matthew's cell. He does so, however, only with the assistance of God. By marking the structure as "clustor" at this point in the narrative, the poet indicates that the doors were not opened with Andreas's own human strength but through the miraculous intervention of Christ. It should be kept in mind also that given the semantic range of *clustor*, which includes "cloister" and "cell" as well as the more general "prison" or "enclosure," the term may have brought to mind for Anglo-Saxon audiences additional types of captivity, such as imprisonment in cages, which Pugh explains was likely prior to Edward I (347). More important than the specific nature of the structure as a whole is the correspondence in verse between doors or buildings marked as *clustor* and entrance/exit by means of supernatural elements.

These locked prison doors, or "carcernes duru" ["prison doors"] (1075), of *Andreas* are further described as "hamera geweorc" ["work of hammers"], a phrase also applied to prison doors in *Juliana:* "Ða wæs mid clustre carcernes duru / behliden, homra geweorc" ["The prison doors were closed, fastened with bolts, the work of hammers"] (236–37).[28] In both cases this phrase effectively subverts the much more common and traditionally charged formula, "enta geweorc" ["work of giants"], with all its associations of ancient worth, in order to emphasize the lowly status of these doors, not the ancient work of giants that suggests connections with an awe-inspiring past, but the man-made work of hammers, void of the empowerment formulaically vested in objects of traditional value.[29] In other words, the phrase "work of hammers" operates at an idiomatic level in opposition to "work of giants," distancing objects marked as such from works of ancient worth rather than simply meaning that the items are literally made with hammers.

As such embellishments to the descriptions of prisons would suggest, prisons in general assume greater prominence in such texts as *Juliana* and *Andreas* than in analogues. Where other architectural structures mentioned in source texts go nameless in the Old English adaptations—the "praetorium" ["palace"] (13) to which Juliana is taken in the *Acta Sanctorum* (BHL), for instance, is reduced to a "domsetle" ["judgment seat"] (530), rather than a prominent building realized in its entirety[30]—prisons in Old English verse adaptations—most notably *Andreas* and *Juliana*— tend to be referenced more frequently than in their analogues and with more descriptive phraseology. Significantly, the Old English supplies highly specialized compounds where corresponding points in probable Latin exemplars employ more generic phraseology. The *Acta Sanctorum* (BHL) typically refers to Juliana's prison with the predictable "carcer": "Iterum jussit ligamen per femora ejus mitti, et sic eam in carcerem recipi" ["Next he (Eleusius) ordered her to be bound by her legs and thus taken to prison"] (4). Likewise, another version of *Passio S. Iulianae* (BNF lat. 10861) also employs "carcer" at this point: "Iterum iussit legamen per femora eius mitti, et sic eam in carcere praecipi" (Lapidge, "Cyne - wulf" 158).[31]

The Old English *Andreas* and *Juliana*, however, tend to supply more value-laden terms when discussing their respective prisons. *Juliana* employs "carcer" only twice (233, 236). Both posited sources of the Juliana story (BHL 4522 and BNF lat. 10861) make far fewer explicit references to the prison and tend to use "carcer" when they do.[32] In contrast, Juliana's Old English prison is invested with numerous characteristics that convey the structure's physical characteristics as well as the deeply troubled state of the structure's inhabitants; it is an "engan hofe" ["narrow house"[33]] (532), a "nydclafan"[lit., "chamber of need/trouble"] (240),[34] and a "hlin-ræced" ["grated building"/"prison"] (243). *Andreas*'s two "hlin compounds" serve as examples of terms referring to the prison that are unprecedented in the *Praxeis* and conveying far more than their strictly lexical meanings would indicate.[35] *Hlinræced* and *hlinscua*[36] cast the structure as one of confinement, tumult, and darkness but, within the poetic idiom, also help to anticipate heroic action.

In both *Juliana* and *Andreas* the compounds are applied to prisons precisely at moments when the poems' respective heroes demonstrate their greatest strength. When God enters the prison to comfort Andreas, the building is described as a "hlinræced" (1463). And just before a demon, significantly disguised as an angel of God, speaks to Juliana, her prison is likewise described as a "hlinræced" (243). The lack of correspondence here with either proposed source text points toward the poet's careful choice in including the detail. The *Acta Sanctorum* (BHL 4522)[37] does not make any explicit reference to the prison at this point in the narrative, moving directly from Juliana's prayer to the demon's entrance: "Et dum finisset orationem apparuit ei dæmon, nomine Belial, in figura angeli" ["When she had finished the prayer, a demon called Belial appeared to her in angel's form"] (6). The connection is also absent in the version of *Passio S. Iulianae* edited by Michael Lapidge (BNF lat. 10861), with the corresponding section in this text stating simply, "Tunc Belial daemon ueniens in figura angeli [242–4], dixit ad eam" (159). Adding a connection between prison and hell, common in Old English verse (see further below), the Latin "dæmon" corresponds to a "helle hæftling" ["hell captive"] (246).[38]

In these and other ways, architectural imagery acquires extralexical meaning in the Old English adaptations that reflect the traditional referentiality of repeated lexemes and phrases. As with *hlinræced,* shared contexts of use are evident in the employment of the *hlinscuwa* (also *hlinscua*) compound as well. In *Andreas* the Mermedonian warriors discover that Andreas has released the prisoners who earlier had suffered grievously "under hlinscuwan" ["under the dark prison"] (1071). Using the same phraseology, the demon, speaking with Juliana, concedes that he has been defeated by Juliana "under hlinscua" (544). Both usages occur at the precise points when the poems' respective protagonists are proved victorious.

Another group of specialized compounds relating to prisons in *Andreas* with parallels in other hagiographic verse involves the word *locan.* The form *locan* does not itself seem to be especially marked, appearing more than seventy-five times in the corpus of Old English texts (approxi - mately fifty times in verse), with the lexeme *loc* referring generally to an "enclosure" or "stronghold." The collocation of the dative *locan* with "under," however, is limited specifically to poetry and does seem to acquire a more specialized referentiality within the traditional register. It occurs no fewer than fourteen times, and the vast majority of these involve prison or confinement,[39] with its most frequent employment in *Andreas* itself where the referent is assuredly a prison in its first five usages:

God speaks to Matthew "under hearmlocan" ["under/in the harmful/evil stronghold"] (95),[40] Matthew waits "under heolstorlocan" ["dark enclosure"] (144), and Andreas is ordered by God to go to Matthew "under burhlocan" ["enclosed stronghold"] (940). Andreas arrives to find Matthew "under heolstorlocan" ["dark enclosure"] (1005), and Andreas leads the innocent prisoners from "under burglocan" (1029). The final occurrence of the "under (x-) locan" phraseology, though, is somewhat more ambiguous. After Andreas has left the prison and gone out into the city, "Gewat him þa Andreas inn on ceastre" (1058), he then sees a column and sits beside it, waiting for the next chain of events:

> þanon basnode   under burhlocan
> hwæt him guðweorca   gifeðe wurde. (1065–66)
>
> ———
>
> [there he waited *under burhlocan* what battle-deeds would be granted him.]

Boenig translates *burhlocan* here as "jail," in keeping with earlier usages of the phrase at lines 5 and 939, though Brooks argues that the meaning is more general, offering "city enclosure." Taken together, however, the usages of "under (x-) locan" indicate a specialized and idiomatic meaning for this phraseological system that evokes the context of confinement without necessarily requiring the physical building of (or even a particularized lexeme indicating) a prison.

Examination of the "under (x-) locan" system outside of *Andreas* reinforces this pattern. Two instances appear in *Elene*, one unambiguously evoking the prison context. When Elene has Judas pushed into a pit to convince him to speak, he is described as "*under hearmlocan*   hungre ge - þreatod / clommum beclungen" ["in an enclosure of harm, threatened by hunger, bound with fetters"] (695–96). The detail of bondage and the phrase "under hearmlocan" are unprecedented in the Latin *Acta Sanctorum* in which Helena ordered him to be cast into a pit and guarded by jailors for seven days (8). Christ's tomb is also described with the same formulaic system, suggesting the temporary confinement of the body prior to the Resurrection: "þreo niht siððan / in byrgenne bidende wæs / *under þeosterlocan*" ["For three nights afterwards he remained in his tomb, under the dark chamber"] (481). Like the earlier phrase, "under þeosterlocan" has no parallel in the Latin text, where Christ was simply "buried" (6). Rather than derive from a biblical source, the phraseology operates within a distinctly Old English poetic idiom. By referencing a tomb for the dead in terms of a prison for the living, the phraseology very subtly anticipates the resurrection itself.

The usages of "under (x-) locan" in *Genesis* evoke similar contexts. When Satan and his followers are exiled from Heaven, they are described as "under hearmlocan" (91).[41] And in line 2539, Lot's escape occurs "under burhlocan" in Segor, the city that survived the destruction of Sodom and Gomorrah. In this case "captivity" is sought as a refuge. The reciprocal nature of prison and sanctuary evidenced in Old English verse is a natural corollary to a legal system in which buildings served multiple functions, "imprisonment" being captivity within a hall or church. The passage in which this particular phraseology occurs is a greatly expanded translation of the Latin Vulgate Genesis, suggesting that this portion of the narrative, including its architectural imagery, held special meaning for the Old English poet. As an "indexed" translation, the elaboration of the simple "Segor" in the Latin Vulgate (19.23) as "under burhlocan" helps translate the concept into the traditional idiom of Anglo-Saxon verse and mark Segor as a space for refuge, but a refuge with implications of forced captivity.

Another instance of a seemingly positive context for the "under (x-) locan" system is seen in *Beowulf*. Hygd is described as "wis" ["wise"], "þeah ðe wintra lyt / *under burhlocan* gebiden hæbbe" ["though she had endured few winters in the stronghold"] (1927–28). The passage explicitly links Hygd's wisdom to her being in the stronghold. The usage of "under (x-) locan," which has undertones of captivity, serves to heighten the absolute necessity of being in the enclosure, and perhaps her lack of choice as a woman. But the usage of "under burhlocan" can be seen as more than a commentary on this particular—and celebratory—narrative moment. In combination with Hygd's identification as "Hæreþes dohtor" (1929) and the immediate comparison with the ignoble Modþryð, we are reminded that Hygelac's hall is not her original home but that her presence in this hall is nonetheless necessary to being a noble woman. It is only in "Offan flet" ("Offa's hall") that Modþryð regains any degree of honor. The usage of "under burhlocan" in reference to Hygelac's hall also serves as a reminder that protective halls can become prisons when under threat;

just as Heorot was arguably a prison for its inhabitants during the night-time reign of Grendel, the "burhlocan" here will eventually become a place of necessary confinement and, during the dragon's flights, a place of security that ultimately fails.

In *Juliana* it is not a person but treasure that is held captive. Juliana rejects her suitor Heliseus (Eleusius), though he possessed "feohgestreon / under hordlocan" ["treasure in the hoard-container"] (42–43). This phraseology indicates that the treasure itself is not negative but casts grave doubts as to the integrity of the current owner, Eleusius, who hoards rather than shares his treasures. In the Anglo-Saxon social system, treasure is of course to be distributed among loyal retainers, not hoarded. The connotations of this and other formulaic systems are often lost in translations, which are not usually able to convey such indexed meanings. Such terms as "treasure-chest" and "coffer"[42] capture a meaning appropriate for the narrative context, but the larger idiomatic associations of the "under (x-) locan" system remain untranslated. As with the earlier traditionally charged phrases, this instance does not have a parallel in proposed source texts. While Eleusius is described as a powerful man, an "amicus imperatoris" ["friend of the emperor"] (1.1) in the *Acta Sanctorum* (BHL), the specific mentions of treasure in *Juliana* are innovations in the Anglo-Saxon adaptation.[43]

Yet another innovative usage of the system occurs in *Christ*.[44] Here, as in *Genesis*, the formula is employed to suggest not so much captivity as a way to keep unwanted evils *out:* "Forþon we fæste sculon wið þam færscyte / symle wærlice wearde healdan, / þy læs se attres ord in gebuge, / biter bordgelac, under banlocan, / feonda færsearo" ["Therefore we must always firmly and carefully guard against a sudden shot, lest the venomous point, the bitter weapon, the sudden artifice, pierce into the bone chamber"] (766–70). The choice here of "banlocan," especially in collocation with "under," metaphorically transforms the body into a stronghold and protection against the evils of the world. Although no literal prisoners are held inside, the implications of suffering and endurance inside the body remain.[45]

What emerges from the collection of prison references in *Andreas* is a cluster of images and motifs neither precedented in possible Latin sources nor attested in Anglo-Saxon archaeology. Prisons are dark ("he-

olstor," "dimme"), filled with sadness and suffering ("hearm," "hleoleasan," "gnorn"), unclean ("unsyfre"), locked ("clustro") and accompanied
by evil, whether inside the prison confines (as in *Andreas* or *Juliana*) or
outside (as in *Genesis*). From our modern perspective at least, such images are perhaps logical for any depiction of prison. But for the Anglo-
Saxons—without the physical reality of dedicated prisons—the choices
of phraseology must be seen in a different context. For instance, the prisons of poetry are dark, but because churches and residences were used for
confinement, "prisons" would be no darker than these same structures
would be in their more ordinary employment. In fact, prior to Edward I
prisoners were likely kept in yards—presumably in sunlight—due to
lack of space (Pugh 347). Thus while darkness might at first seem to indicate a specific and specialized interior space, it belongs instead to a traditional collocation of images associated with confinement. Here, as elsewhere, the phraseology employed suggests traditional rather than purely
literal meanings. The terms for prisons discussed above and the architectural details ascribed to them reflect little of Anglo-Saxon legal practices
but provide much insight into the idea complex associated with prisons
in Old English verse.

THE ARCHITECTURE OF HELL

In terms of its phraseology, the architecture of prisons as rendered in Old
English verse is closely related to the architecture of hell, which—not entirely unlike the dedicated prisons of *Juliana* and *Andreas*—would be a
surprising sight on the Anglo-Saxon landscape. The compound *morðor-
cofa* ["murder-chamber"] (1004) is unique to *Andreas,* appearing as a reference to the city prison. A related architectural *morðor* compound, however, is employed with similar connotations in *Elene*'s description of hell
as a *morðorhofe* (1303), which renders the afterworld of the most wicked
with the same terminology employed in *Andreas* for earthly prisons:

> . . .   Bið se þridda dæl
> awyrgede womsceaðan,   in þæs wylmes grund,
> lease leodhatan,   lige befæsted
> þurh ærgewyrht,   arleasra sceolu,

in gleda gripe.   Gode no syððan
of ðam **morðorhofe**   in gemynd cumað. . . . (1298–1304)

[The third portion, cursed evil-doers, false tyrants, in the bottom
of the surge shall be held fast in the fire through earlier works,
a multitude of lawless ones in the grasp of flames. They shall not
come afterwards into the mind of God from the murder-house. . . .]

Together with "morðorhofe," the phrases "gleda gripe" ["grasp of flames"]
and "lige befæsted" ["fast in fire"] suggest a hell characterized by the
bondage, confinement, and murderous associations seen previously in
depictions of earthly prisons. Although there are certainly references to
hell in extant Latin versions of such texts as *Juliana* and *Elene,* many such
details ascribed to hell in corresponding Old English adaptations are absent from source texts, suggesting an independent Anglo-Saxon concept
of hell, one that frequently overlaps with prison imagery.

Another feature shared by architectural depictions of hell and prison
in Old English verse is the potential of the space (hell or prison) to serve
as refuge or sanctuary. As we saw earlier in Lot's story in the Old English
Genesis, the line between refuge and prison is quite blurry, a natural development given that actual prisons as discussed in Old English laws could
be utilized for multiple purposes. Whether serving as punishment or refuge, prisons and hell in Old English verse are unambiguously characterized by grief, suffering, and necessary confinement. Though it may seem
counterintuitive to view hell as a refuge, in *Juliana,* for instance, hell is explicitly described as the demon's refuge: "þe wearð helle seað / niþer ge-
dolfen,   þær þu nydbysig / fore oferhygdum   eard gesohtes" ["Then the
pit of hell was dug beneath you; there, suffering for your arrogance, you
sought a dwelling place"] (422–24). This notion that an otherwise safe
structure can become a prison or that a prison can alternately be a place of
refuge is consistent with the Anglo-Saxon practice of converting spaces
such as churches and residences into prisons, and accounts of hell—
described in terms of prison—naturally follow similar patterns.

That hell was in fact visualized by some Anglo-Saxon poets as an architectural space, complete with walls and doors, is evidenced especially
clearly in *The Descent into Hell.* Following the resurrection, Christ enters

hell triumphantly to "helle weallas / forbrecan" ["break the walls of hell"] (34–35), and at his presence "þa locu feallan" ["the locks fell"] (39). With Christ's coming, the "helle duru" ["doors of hell"] (53) now "hædre scinan" ["shine brightly"] (53) where before they were "bilocen" ["locked"] (54) and "beþeahte mid þystre" ["covered with darkness"] (55). The doors are again referenced as hell's inhabitants are described as "beofiende / under helle dorum" ["trembling behind hell's doors"] (86–87) and "in bendum" ["in bonds"] (88). The hell of *Genesis B* is also equipped with doors (447) and forged iron (383). The Mermedonian prison in *Andreas* has "hlindura" (993), with "hlin" generally understood as "latticed" or "grated,"[46] a feature that might seem innocuous enough, but this reference to latticed or grated doors appears only once elsewhere in the corpus of Old English writings, in the description of hell in *The Whale* (78), when the whale's jaws, or the doors of hell ("helle hlinduru"), snap shut on the wicked at the poem's conclusion.[47] Although doors would presumably have been a common feature in all types of architecture, they do not often get special mention in verse architectural description. In fictionalized spaces, doors are especially prominent in poetic descriptions of prisons and hell, and similar phraseology is employed to characterize both. Like "hlinduru," the employment of "behliden" in the *Juliana* passage suggests a close connection between the architecture of hell and prison, as this word is also used in reference to hell's doors in *Elene*, "behliden helle duru" (1229). While the literal meaning of "behliden" (or "beliden") is simply "closed," the connotations are much more stark given that this participial form survives only in these specific references to the doors of prison or hell, the doors of hell being referenced more frequently than any of its other structural features. Hell as depicted in *Christ and Satan*, for instance, has dragons guarding the "helle duru" (97), and "helldora" (447) are blocked for *Genesis B*'s Satan.[48] As these examples indicate, doors typically receive special mention in poetry only when there is a threat from outside or within, most frequently in the contexts of hell or prisons. Thus, while the presence of doors as an architectural feature is of course not noteworthy in itself, the explicit mention of the doors is connotatively potent in idiomatically marking danger.

An additional characteristic of hell as described in *Genesis* involves the iron that characterizes its space. References to iron are common enough in descriptions of weaponry, but the detail of iron as an architectural feature has much darker connotations.[49] Wright has convincingly argued that the Celtic motif of the "Iron House" was familiar to Anglo-Saxon scribes and one used specifically in the description of hell in the Old English "The Devil's Account of the Next World."[50] The Celtic motif, preserved in the Irish tales *Mesca Ulad* ("The Intoxication of the Ulstermen") and *Orgain Denna Ríg* ("The Destruction of Dinn Ríg"), as well as in the Welsh tale *Branwen* from the *Mabinogion*, involves an "iron house or chamber" "specially constructed, to be fired when the enemies have been lured within by the offer of food and drink" (201), whereupon the iron house is then "secured by an iron chain fixed to a pillar" (201) and filled with fuel, leading to the ultimate incineration of the enemies now trapped inside. As Wright argues, "There were certainly sufficient contacts between the Celtic, Anglo-Saxon, and Norse cultures for oral transmission of literary motifs to have taken place" (206), and the motif is one that "lent itself easily to an infernal context" (204). While *Genesis* clearly does not use the Iron House motif as such, it does seem to exploit established traditional connections between infernal imprisonment and iron architectural space in conveying Satan's plight. In his confinement in hell, Satan laments in *Genesis B* that he is surrounded by iron bonds: "licgað me ymbe irenbenda / rideð racentan sal" ["around me lie iron bonds, the chain of the fetter is on me"] (371–72);[51] "Licgað me ymbe / heardes irenes hate geslægene / grindlas greate" ["Great bars of hard iron, forged in heat, lie around me"] (382–84). Bondage, especially as expressed in the phrase "bendum fæstne," is a typical feature of prisons as well as hell. Matthew is bound in prison "bendum fæstne" (183), as is Andreas at a later point (1356). Likewise, as Juliana drags the devil to his imprisonment, he is "bendum fæstne" (535), and the "ræpingas" of Riddle 50 are also "bendum fæstra" (7). But the iron in *Genesis* is twice said to lie around, *ymbe*, Satan, suggesting that iron not only binds the prisoner but also defines his surrounding space.

That "irenbendum" likely refers to architectural features (in addition to Satan's own bonds) is reinforced by the fact that the only other references to "irenbendum" in Old English verse are in descriptions of an architectural structure, Heorot. Like hell in the verse *Genesis*, Heorot is described as being braced with "irenbendum." Situational parallels in the two narratives accompanying the usage of this compound point to shared extralexical meaning in the usages. In both instances, the "iren-bendum" help define a space in which inhabitants suffer excruciating torment, in Heorot at the hands of Grendel and in hell at the hands of God. Also in both cases, the bonds marked as "irenbenda"/"irenbendum" are ultimately broken, in *Beowulf* from the outside by Grendel and in *Genesis* from within by a "godes andsaca" ["adversary of God"] (442).[52] Significantly, the detail of the iron bands, associated elsewhere with un-endurable torment, is first provided for Heorot precisely at the point when the hall is under greatest threat, during the battle between Beowulf and Grendel.

> Þa wæs wundor micel   þæt se winsele
> wiðhæfde heaþodeorum,   þæt he on hrusan ne feol,
> fæger foldbold;   ac he þæs fæste wæs
> innan ond utan   **irenbendum**
> searoþoncum besmiþod.

> [Then it was a great wonder that the wine hall withstood the bold warriors, that it did not fall to the ground, the fair earth-building; but it was too firmly braced inside and out with **iron bands** made with cunning thoughts.] (771–75)

The use of *irenbendum* at this point helps convey that under Grendel's terrorizing reign, Heorot's inhabitants were essentially prisoners in their own hall enduring hellish torments. But, as in several other related struc-tures described in Old English verse, the imprisoning bonds also had the capacity for protection, ultimately surviving the battle between Grendel and Beowulf. The protection afforded by the iron fastenings is empha-sized during the cleansing of Heorot, which is said to be firm within its iron bonds, "eal inneweard irenbendum fæst" (998). By relying on this web of associations in descriptions of imprisonment (in hell or on earth), the poet of *Beowulf* is thus able to characterize Grendel's ravages as truly hellish for Hrothgar's people. When under attack a protective hall can quickly become a prison, a transformation even more easily achieved since in the Anglo-Saxon world prisons *were* usually buildings such as halls or churches that were more typically employed for other purposes. And it is not surprising that a distinct pattern should also emerge in which prisons and hell share significant architectural features and corresponding traditional associations as spaces of torment. Awareness of this idea complex can thus enhance our understanding of passages that apply the phraseology typical of prisons to other structures by providing the more complete associative context that likely would have been experienced by Anglo-Saxon audiences.

TENTS AND PAVILIONS

Like the hells and prisons that Anglo-Saxon verse adapted into the poetic idiom, tents, pavilions, and related structures of biblical narrative are also frequently rendered in traditionally appropriate, if sometimes architecturally incongruous, language. Especially fraught with extra-lexical meaning are the terms *burgeteld* (in *Judith*), *træf* (in *Judith, Beowulf,* and *Andreas*), and *feldhus* (in *Exodus*), all of which at various points are used in reference to tents. Tents might initially seem outside the purview of architectural space for modern readers, but Old English poetry makes explicit connections between tents and more permanent built spaces such as halls and temples that require us to rethink conventional categories.

The tent in *Judith* is by far the most prominent in Old English narrative verse. Though referred to throughout as a "geteld" or "træf," terms generally rendered "tent," Holofernes' residence as it is described in the Old English *Judith* has strong connections with the Anglo-Saxon hall. As Katherine Hume has aptly observed, Holofernes' rule evokes and subverts the typical associations of the Anglo-Saxon hall inside his military tent.[53] He is described as a "burga ealdor" ["leader of strongholds"] (*Judith* 58) but a corrupt one; there is drinking at mead-benches, but Holofernes' men are "*ofer*drencte" (31; emphasis mine); Holofernes is surrounded by retainers, but his *comitatus* serve as "weagesiðas" ["slaughter-companions"] (16) rather than heroes. The events of Holofernes' residence can thus be understood as activities of an "anti-hall" (Hume, "Concept" 73). The men are described in terms of a hall as "*flet*sittendum" [lit., "hall-sitters"] (19, 33) and "*benc*sittende" ["bench-sitters"] (27; emphasis mine),[54] but the structure itself—the antithesis of a heroic hall—is not described as a "sele" or "ræced" but instead as a "træf" (43, 255, 268) or "burgeteld" (57, 248, 276). The only *sele* compound in the text describes not Holofernes' worldly residence in the poem but hell, when we are told he will likely never leave the "wyrm*sele*" ["worm-hall"] (119) after he dies. Instead of visiting the leader in his hall, Judith is said to leave her own "gysterne" ["guest-house"] (40) to see Holofernes in his "træf" (43). Thus the poem presents a physical structure very different (and less monumental) from a hall but superimposes onto that structure a subverted depiction of hall life. Understanding connotations of the specific terms *geteld* and *træf* can fill gaps left by the architectural disparity.

While "geteld" and "træf" both refer to Holofernes' residence and translations of Old English verse typically translate *burgeteld* and *træf* as synonyms,[55] the two have different contexts of employment in Old English verse. *Burgeteld,* "geteld" meaning "tent,"[56] is the closer of the two in rendering the sense of the Latin Vulgate, the generally acknowledged source of the Old English poem *(Liberi).* The corresponding architectural structure to Holofernes' tent in the Latin Vulgate is most often referred to as "thesauri" ["storage places"] (e.g., 12.1) and "tabernaculum" ["tent"] (e.g., 12.4). *Geteld* does not appear in uncompounded form in surviving verse, though it is very common in the prose, suggesting an attempt on the part of the translator/scribe to provide a more literal translation in *burgeteld* rather than rely on the phraseology more typical of architecture in poetic descriptions. The *geteld* portion of the compound has a fairly wide semantic range, with possibilities including "tent," "pavilion," "tabernacle," "tent," and "cover" (Bosworth). In *Judith's* context of a military campaign, the "tent" or "pavilion" meanings are most likely.

Before moving into extralexical meanings of *geteld,* it is important to establish what the term might have evoked at a literal level for Anglo-Saxon audiences. As limited as surviving evidence for Anglo-Saxon halls has been, far less exists for such temporary structures as military tents. Numerous productive and insightful projects reconstructing halls have been led by established archaeologists, but some of the most earnest efforts to determine specific physical characteristics of the "geteld" have actually been undertaken by reenactment groups interested in early military strategies. In fact, despite the relative lack of scholarly interest in the subject, popular interest is so high that various Web sites offer instructions and plans for making such tents, giving a better sense of the extensive resources required for tents of the scale appearing in Anglo-Saxon manuscripts.[57] A reconstructed Anglo-Saxon tent is even available in a 15-millimeter miniature version for collectors. In addition to references in literature, there are numerous illustrations of the "getelds" in manuscripts, the most well known being those in the Utrecht Psalter and the Harley Psalter. But even the reenactment groups recognize the scarcity of archaeological evidence and the inherent limitations of pictorial images. Though Mark Harrison notes that "tents are illustrated in several 10th- and 11th-century Anglo-Saxon manuscripts," he also observes that such illustrations are likely "based on Continental sources, and seem to be conventional depictions rather than drawings from life" (25).[58] The images do, however, give us a sense of the possibilities in the Anglo-Saxon imagination and an idea of what structures may have come to mind at references to the "geteld" in *Judith*. And, more important, the nuances of meaning behind even subtle departures from actual practice can become more readily discernible.

It seems that these tents were, at least in idealized form, quite substantial. The scale of people beside tents in the illustration accompanying Psalm 27 of the Harley Psalter, for instance, suggests substantial measurements. Reconstruction attempts have demonstrated that such a scale is possible but have required substantial resources: a ground length of 22 feet 4 inches, 136 by 60 feet of fabric, and a wooden ridge pole of 16 feet, raised to a height of 8 feet.[59] As discussed in chapter 2, architectural illustrations in the Harley manuscript frequently display a distinctly Anglo-Saxon aes - thetic, though it is commonly believed that they are based on similar representations in the Carolingian Utrecht Psalter.[60] Height was of course valued greatly in this aesthetic, and though the tent in the Utrecht Psalter (Psalm 119) is no higher than shoulder level in relation to the warriors in the picture, the otherwise similar tent in the Harley Psalter (Psalm 27) towers to more than twice the height of the illustration's warriors. If the poetic imagination of Anglo-Saxon audiences paralleled that of the period's illustrators, Holofernes' "geteld" could have been visualized as quite a grand structure indeed. The addition of *bur* (which can mean "bower," "chamber," "apartment," "storehouse," "cottage," or "dwelling") to the compound adds to the building's proportions. Though the exact nature of difference between an unqualified *geteld* and the compound *burgeteld* is not completely recoverable, the usage in *Judith* indicates a dwelling more permanent than "geteld" alone might suggest.

The alternate term employed in the poem for the tent, *træf*, reinforces the notion of a more permanent and monumental architectural space. Where *geteld* refers fairly unambiguously to tent, *træf* (or *traf*) can mean "tent" or "pavilion" but can also have the broader meaning "building" or "dwelling."[61] Unlike "geteld," which appears over three hundred times in Old English prose, "træf"/"traf" is relatively rare, occurring only a handful of times and primarily in the poetry. Though modern translations frequently translate both *burgeteld* and *træf* as "tent," the terms' usages in Old English verse convey markedly different connotations.[62] Rather than temporary tents, the *trafu* in *Andreas*, for instance, are described as stone and tile-adorned and thus help constitute an impressive and seemingly permanent aspect of the Mermedonian skyline (840): "Beorgas steape, / hleoðu hlifodon, ymbe harne stan / tigelfagan trafu, torras stodon, / windige weallas" ["Steep hills, cliffs rose up; around the gray stone tile-adorned *trafu*, towers stood, windy walls"] (840–43). That the *trafu* are adorned with tile and composed of stone indicates a more durable structure than a tent, and the association with the cannibalistic Mermedonians provides the term with distinctly negative associations. The negativity is then reinforced through a *traf* compound by description of Mermedonian "helltrafum" (1691).[63] The only other architectural space in surviving Old English poetry designated as "trafum"—the *hær-trafum* of *Beowulf*—are likewise negatively portrayed:

> Hwilum hie geheton   æt *hær*gtrafum
> wigweorþunga,   wordum bædon
> þæt him gastbona   geoce gefremede
> wið þeodþreaum (175–78)

> [At times at *hærgtrafum* they promised idol worship/sacrifice, asked with words that the soul-slayer might bring about help against the people's misery.][64]

Like the actions of Holofernes in *Judith* and of the Mermedonians in *Andreas*, these activities in *Beowulf* occur outside what is socially acceptable in the poem's social context and also outside the *physical* context of the more familiar, and positive, Anglo-Saxon hall.

Though buildings marked as "træf" in Old English verse are architecturally very distinct from one another—a military tent in *Judith*, tall buildings on the skyline in *Andreas*, and cultic spaces in *Beowulf*—buildings designated as *trafum* share negative connotations, and the usage of the lexeme and its compounds serves to distance the inhabitants of *trafum* from the ideals of the poems' heroic protagonists.[65] Literal renderings of *træf* in *Judith* are insufficient to convey this negativity, and translations of *træfe þam hean* as "lofty tent" or "towering tent" may even evoke quite positive associations for speakers of modern English.[66] In the end the precise natures of *træf* and *burgeteld* are largely ambiguous, but the broader archaeological and poetic contexts suggest that the building inhabited by Holofernes as rendered by the *Judith*-poet was conceived as a military tent but one beyond the realm of actual experience. Through the word *burgeteld*, the poet conveys a space monumental enough to warrant implicit contrast with the ethos of Anglo-Saxon halls, and the usage of *træf*, while architecturally ambiguous, casts the space clearly at odds with the values of the poem's Judeo-Christian heroine.

Like these referents denoting the overall structure, more specific features attributed to Holofernes' architectural domain reinforce the image of the space as the antithesis of the heroic hall. The fairly lengthy description of Holofernes' residence as Judith approaches includes several such features:

> Þær wæs eallgylden
> fleohnet fæger   7 ymbe þæs folctogan
> bed ahongen,   þæt se bealofulla
> mihte wlitan þurh,   wigena baldor,
> on æghwylcne   þe ðær inne com
> hæleða bearna,   7 on hyne nænig
> monna cynnes,   nymðe se modiga hwæne
> niðe rofra   him þe near hete
> rinca to rune gegangan. . . . (46–54)

[There was a fair curtain all golden hung round the leader's couch, so that the evil man, the prince of warriors, could look through on each of the sons of men who entered there, and no man on him, unless the proud man ordered one of his mighty warriors to draw nearer him to hold council. . . .]

The introductory *fleohnet*—a compound unique to *Judith*, except for two occurrences in glosses[67]—is a translation of the Latin *conopeo,* but the details of the tent are greatly altered in the Old English version. The corresponding description in the Latin Vulgate states that "videns itaque Holofernem Iudith sedentem in conopeo quod erat ex purpura et auro et zmaragdo et lapidibus pretiosis intextum" ["Judith saw Holofernes as he sat there with a canopy over him, a canopy of purple, with gold and emeralds and other precious stones worked into it"] (10.19). The specific visual details of the emeralds and stones are thus reduced to the simple adjective *eallgylden* ["all golden"], and, in typical Anglo-Saxon poetic fashion, the poet instead fills out the scene in a way that gives us more information about Holofernes himself and the negativity of the situation than about the structure's specific physical details. The one-way see-through net is not represented in the Latin text, and the innovation clearly links the dwelling with the culpability of Holofernes by conveying his voyeuristic nature. In contrast to the openness of idealized halls, the traditionally appropriate space for public oaths and displays of valor, the architectural features of the tent render it a space for clandestine secrecy; even Holofernes' own men—his *comitatus*—are unknowledgeable about the actions in his dwelling. These dual images of a structure both heroically adorned and dangerously negative are then later encapsulated in its description as a "wlitegan træfe" ["beautiful *træfe*"] (255), which suggests a structure at once beautiful and hostile, stable and temporary.

Even following Holofernes' death, the description of his architectural space departs from its source in conveying a more permanent structure than a "tent." Holofernes' head rolls across a "flore" ["floor"] (111), whereas in the Latin Vulgate, Holofernes' attendants discover his body lying only on the ground, "super terram" (14.14). The idea of the earth or ground is reinforced in the Latin text when Vagao announces

that "enim Holofernis iacet *in terra* et caput ipsius non est in illo" ["Holofernes lies *on the earth* and there is no head on his body"] (14.16). The
semantic range of Latin *terra* does not include "floor," being limited to
"ground" or "earth"; the dominant meaning for Old English *flor*, however,
is the floor of a building.[68] Like the Old English poet's choice of "træf,"
"flor" offers an adequate translation of *terra* but leaves open the possibility of a far more substantial structure, enhancing its architectural and
narrative significance. Holofernes' dwelling thus evokes a number of potentially contradictory images. The presence of "bencsittende" suggests
benches of the sort found in Anglo-Saxon halls; "burgeteld" suggests a
temporary tent, while "træf" and the presence of a "flor" indicate a more
stable, imposing structure. And such innovations in *Judith* as the compounds *burgeteld* and *fleohnet* point toward a uniqueness in the structures
being translated, unfamiliar concepts requiring innovative vocabulary.
The effect of this language in visual terms is potentially confusing, but
in the poetic tradition the phraseology employed in *Judith* allows us to
maintain an image of the temporary tent while infusing the structure with
the solidity and significance worthy of the Anglo-Saxon heroism displayed in Judith's slaying of Holofernes.[69]

    While Holofernes' tent is unquestionably a negatively charged space,
it is the phraseology that makes it so, not its status as a tent in particular.
The *feldhus,* also translatable as "tent," in *Exodus* (85, 133, 223) is portrayed
in the Old English adaptation as an architectural wonder of the most
positive kind. As "burgeteld" is a compound that occurs only in the context of *Judith* to render a structure outside Anglo-Saxon experience, "feldhus" is a compound unique to *Exodus* and employed in describing foreign structures deriving from biblical texts. Two of the three instances
of "feldhus" are more or less unremarkable, referring to tents of nomadic
people as would be expected. *Feldhus* occurs in reference to the "wic"
["dwelling place"/"camp"] at 133,[70] and its final usage in *Exodus* occurs
at 223, where the men "flotan feldhusum" ["moved with tents"].[71] It is an
earlier appearance in the work, however, that raises the most questions in
"its departure from the bare account of the book of Exodus" (Irving, *Old
English* Exodus 73). Not only does it deviate from the biblical narrative,
which makes no mention of a tent, but it employs a term elsewhere in the
poem used to denote a structure made by men in reference to a structure

made by God. The "feldhus" here renames the cloud, or sail ("segl"), sent
by God to protect the people from the sun:[72]

>   hæfde witig god
> sunnan siðfæt   segle ofertolden,
> swa þa mæstrapas   men ne cuðon,
> ne ða seglrode   geseon meahton,
> eorðbuende   ealle cræfte,
> hu afæstnod wæs   feldhusa mæst. (80–85)

> [The wise God had covered the course of the sun with a sail,
> even though the men did not know the mast-ropes, nor could
> earth-dwelling ones see the sail-yards, nor understand how that
> greatest of *feldhusa* was fastened.]

The projection of sea imagery onto a narrative of a desert people has been
much commented on, and Nicholas Howe has convincingly argued that
this potentially problematic conflation of the sail and tent in the desert
setting allows the poet to incorporate elements of the Anglo-Saxon migration across the ocean into biblical history, thus creating a link between the
exiled Israelites and the Germanic tribes who first migrated to England.
The cloud—both sail and tent—is thereby described through "an evocative range of images that could contain the experience of both peoples"
(*Migration* 99). In addition, the combination of seemingly unlikely images could also speak to the "Viking practice of netting their ships at night"
(*Migration* 97). The Gokstad ship, for instance, had tent frames (Kendrick,
History of the Vikings 24), and Old Norse sagas also include descriptions of
tented ships.

It is through the resulting syncresis of Germanic architectural practice and biblical tradition that the description of the cloud as a built structure affirms the integrity of Germanic tradition by implicitly equating native building practice with the designs of God. And although heavenly
sails would seem to fall outside the periphery of architecture as such, the
poet repeatedly describes the sail in terms of built space, inviting associations with architectural spaces. As with *burgeteld,* the innovative compound *feldhus,* not seen outside of *Exodus,* indicates that the poet, very

logically, envisioned this divinely sent structure as one different from those that could be described by more usual terms, such as *geteld* or *hus* alone, but the features attributed to the structure are nonetheless far less abstract than those of the Vulgate and Hebrew texts. The Old English cloud is described as a sail framed with a "bælc," a *hapax* translated as "covering" but cognate with the Germanic *gebälk*, "beams" or "timber of a house."[73] The Old English version further reinforces the notion of the cloud as a built structure by asserting that the Israelites were unable to see how this shielding "tent," or "feldhus," was fastened and built. They could see only the two pillars, or "beamas," that led the way. The *bælc* corresponds to the beam extending the length of Anglo-Saxon tents and serves to familiarize an otherwise foreign image. The divine sails are said to have "hlifedon," "towered" above (89), reinforcing the notion of the cloud as a built structure and adhering to the Anglo-Saxon preferences for height.

The description of the cloud as a sail and tent is unprecedented in the Latin Vulgate account of Exodus, but this image is immediately followed by a description of two *beamas,* beams, that do correspond to Exodus 13:21–22. In the Latin Vulgate:

> Dominus autem praecedebat eos ad ostendendam viam per diem in columna nubis et per noctem in columna ignis ut dux esset itineris utroque tempore numquam defuit columna nubis per diem nec columna ignis per noctem coram populo.
>
> ———
>
> [The Lord then preceded them to show the way by day in a column of cloud, and by night in a column of fire so that he might be their guide at both times. The column of cloud never failed in the day, nor the column of fire at night before the people.]

The Old English version, however, while clearly using the Latin Vulgate as a source, differs markedly in the autonomy given to the pillars and in having the two pillars work in tandem—in a *comitatus* relationship in service to the Holy Ghost—rather than alternating day and night:

> Him beforan foran   fyr ond wolcen
> in beorhtrodor,   beamas twegen,

þara æghwæðer   efngedælde
heahþegnunga   Haliges Gastes
deormodra sið   dagum ond nihtum. (93–97)

———

[Before them went fire and cloud in the bright sky, two beams,
which were equally high in their service of the Holy Ghost,
in the journey of the brave ones during days and nights.]

The Latin text makes it abundantly clear that the columns acted separately, one at night and the other by day, yet the Old English depicts two pillars leading together, performing the service of thanes ("þegnunga") alongside the Israelites on their journey. If we look at the image from an architectural perspective, it makes more sense. Prior to their departure, we are told that "seledreams" ["hall-joys"] passed away (36). The image of the constructed cloud as a "feldhus" with "bælk" preceded by wooden timbers or "beams" follows approximately fifty lines later, providing an alternative to the hall for the exiled people, much as the Seafarer found joys at sea in the absence of his former hall. Superimposed onto the source text of fire and cloud pillars is an image of two vertical timbers, beams, reminiscent of Germanic hall construction—timbers that, much like Andreas's column in the prison, work directly with the poem's protagonists in a *comitatus*-like relationship as they together seek refuge in their exile, a "wicsteal." The use of *feldhus* to describe the cloud immediately prior to this passage is much in keeping with this architectural image.

In addition to linking Israelite and Germanic experience through a pairing of the unlikely metaphors of sail and tent, the development of the *feldhus* image at this point anticipates the usages of the more ordinary tents used by the nomadic people later in the poem, when the Israelites spread tents for their camps, "flotan feldhusum" (133, 223). By referring to both God's construction (the cloud) and the dwelling places of the traveling Israelites (tents) with the same term—*feldhus*—the Old English *Exodus*-poet ennobles the entire journey through a shared sense of divine and human built space. In the Old English indexed translation, to use Foley's term, God's miraculous intervention here becomes a part of the Germanic experience. The tents that the Israelites inhabit thus offer a divinely ordained surrogate for the *sele* left behind and are linked with God's architectural creation through shared phraseology.

TEMPLES

Like tents and prisons, temples in Old English poetry tend to be used to activate a set of traditional associations more than to call to mind specific physical details based on architectural reality. Though this is certainly true for many if not most vocabulary items, it is important to note from the outset of this discussion that modern English *temple* has connotations somewhat different from *tempel* as used in Old English verse. Bosworth offers "temple" as the modern English equivalent for a number of Old English terms, including *alh, eahl,*[74] *ealhstede,*[75] *bold* (secondary definition), *cyrice, hearh, hearge, hof, heall,* and *hus.* Like much Old English architectural terminology, most of these terms have a broader semantic range than "temple" might suggest; the more general meaning of *alh* is "sheltering place," and *heall,* of course, more generally refers to a secular "hall." Thomas Markey's study of Germanic terms for "temple" and "cult" also shows that Old English had numerous native vocabulary items referring to "enclosed 'temple' worship" or "open-air rites" (365), most notably "hof," "hearg," "alh," and "wih."[76] Without such a range of synonyms in modern English, "temple" becomes the default translation for a vast range of terms, and because modern English dictionaries, editions, and translations use the term *temple* quite freely and in ways different from Old English poetic contexts, it takes a closer look to see what the specific Old English term *templ/tempel* as employed specifically in Old English poetry was likely to have meant for Anglo-Saxon audiences.[77]

To some extent, *tempel* and *ciric* ["temple" and "church"] can be understood as synonymous terms. The paratactic construction in *Andreas* describing the building erected near the poem's conclusion has them syntactically parallel: "þa se modiga het, / cyninges cræftiga, *ciricean* ge - timbran, / gerwan godes *tempel,* þær sio geogoð aras / þurh fæder fulwiht ond se flod onsprang" ["Then the spirited one, the king's craftsman, commanded a *church* be built, God's *temple* be prepared, where the youth had arisen through the Father's baptism and the flood had sprung up"] (1632–35; emphasis mine). The usages of "tempel" in the poetry, however, indicate that temples, like the prisons, tents, and pavilions discussed above, denoted structures that belonged to something outside the field of any direct experience and thus evocative of a strong sense of otherness, whereas "churches" more typically indicate buildings much more familiar to the implied audience. The Old English charms, for instance, which offer practical instructions and assume the presence of *actual* structures, direct readers to *churches* rather than temples: "And bere siþþan ða turf to circean, and mæssepreost asinge feower mæssan ofer þan turfon" ["And then afterwards, carry the turf to church, and a mass-priest sing four masses over the turf"] (Dobbie, Metrical Charm 1, 14). An expecting mother is told to "ga þonne to cyrican" ["go then to church"] (Metrical Charm 6, 13) to help bring her child to term. The *Anglo-Saxon Chronicle* includes an account of an attack on the Abbey of St. Mary in Glastonbury, and, again, when this actual building is being referenced, the term employed is *church:* "sume urnon in to cyrcean" ["some ran into the church"] (quoted in Pickles 228).[78]

While "temple" is often the modern English term employed to translate structures with non-Christian and often negative associations, Old English poets themselves tended to reserve the word *tempel* for contexts that were both positive and removed from everyday Anglo-Saxon life.[79] Of the twenty-three instances of "templ" or "tempel" in Old English poetry, none are compounded, and all refer to Judeo-Christian structures rather than native Germanic buildings. *Exodus* refers to the "tempel gode" (391), *Daniel* includes the "tempel" of Solomon (60, 710), and in *Andreas* Christ speaks in a "tempel" (667),[80] while Andreas also commands that a "godes tempel" ["temple of God"] (1634) be built. Numerous references to temples in Christian contexts occur in *Christ* (186, 206, 495, 707, 1138), and further specific references to "godes temple" appear in *Guthlac A* and *B* (490, 1002, 1113, 1149) and in *Elene* (1057, 1021), all unambiguously positive.[81] With these patterns in mind, let us turn to structures in *Andreas, Daniel,* and *Exodus* that are described in some detail and that are explicitly referred to as "temples" in Old English verse.

In *Andreas* the poem's hero recounts a story of Christ speaking in a temple, clearly a highly significant space both architecturally and poetically. Though it is designated as a "tempel" (667), we are told that people frequently came to this "meðelstede" ["meeting place"] (658) and those coming to see Christ there are described in terms appropriate to the hall, "sottre selerædend" ["wise hall counselors"] (659). Christ and his followers are then described as going

þær getimbred wæs   tempel dryhtnes,
heah ond horngeap,   hæleðum gefrege,
wuldre gewlitegod. (667–69)

———

[where a *temple* of the lord was built, high and wide-gabled,
known among heroes, wondrously adorned.]

At this "getimbred" (which can be rendered generically as "built" but
is also evocative of native timber construction) temple, Christ is derided
by those present, and when he departs it is once again referred to as a
"meeting place": "þa se þeoden gewat þegna heape / fram þam meðelstede" ["Then the prince departed with his troop of thanes from the meeting place"] (696–97). Where the Greek text seems to distance Christ and
his followers by referring to the structure as a "temple of the Gentiles"
(Boenig, *Acts* 8), the Old English poem embraces it by giving it the status
of "meðelstede," a term reserved for heroic dwellings, such as that of the
legendary Hengest and Finn (*Beowulf* 1082). When Christ returns a second time, the structure is again referred to as a "temple":

Syþþan eft gewat   oðre siðe
getrume mycle,   þæt he in temple gestod,
wuldres aldor.   Wordhleoðor astag
geond heahræced (706–9)

———

[Afterwards, the lord of glory went back another time with great
strength so that he stood in the temple. Loud words raised
throughout the high hall.]

The semantic marker "temple" denotes a building whose grandeur extends beyond the parameters of daily life, whereas the designation as a
"heahræced" casts the building in familiar and highly positive terms. As
discussed in chapter 2, the physical details of this temple as high and
gabled, not present in the Greek and more commonly associated with
Anglo-Saxon halls, serve to align the building itself with a heroic Christ
and to mark the structure as a place where events of great significance
will occur. The evidence from surviving Anglo-Saxon poetry indicates that

the phrase "heah ond horngeap"—which, like the Heysham cross-shaft (fig. 15; see further chap. 2), combines height, gables, and arches—carried powerful associations in the poetry. The phrase in *Beowulf* precedes the conflict between Beowulf and Grendel in Heorot. Exactly the same phrase is employed here in the heroic hagiography *Andreas* to describe a temple in which Christ spoke (668) and seems to serve a similar connotative function, establishing the building as a location worthy of heroic battle. Specifically, the new church is described this way in anticipation of a verbal confrontation between Jesus Christ and the chief priest, who is filled with "inwitðanc" ["evil-thought"] (670). Though the temple in *Andreas* would presumably have been physically quite different from Heorot, important associations are shared, and the phrase "high and wide-gabled" helps index both as buildings where agonistic events of great significance take place.

The Old English poet again goes far beyond the depiction in the Greek text in describing the angels on the walls of the structure, drawing special attention to the way in which they were carved:

> Swylce he wrætlice   wundor agræfene,
> anlicnesse   engla sinra
> geseh, sigora frea,   on seles wage,
> on twa healfe   torhte gefrætwed,
> wlitige geworhte. (712–16)
>
> ———
>
> [So he, lord of victories, saw on the wall of the hall on two sides marvelous things carved, likenesses of his angels, brightly decorated, beautifully made.]

The building thus identified as a space of great import and the wall's adornment established as nobly made, the miracle now takes place. The stones descend from the wall at Christ's command and speak. Again greatly embellishing the description found in the *Praxeis,* the poet gives further praise to the stone, including the descriptors "bremestan" ["re - nowned stone"] (718) and "frod fyrngeweorc" ["wise ancient work"] (737). Characterized by the poet as wise, famous, and ancient, the stone acquires a much greater role than in the Greek text. More than a mere conduit for a miracle, the Old English stone becomes a noble ally of Christ the hero, accomplishing deeds known "geond þæt side sel" ["through-out the wide hall"] (762). Like the column in Andreas's prison, the stone in Christ's temple is given a prescience of its own and helps activate the traditional context of the Anglo-Saxon hall.

In *Daniel* also we see a great structure described as both temple and hall. The Chaldean soldiers are said to have "tempel strudon, / Salomanes seld" ["destroyed the temple, the hall of Solomon"] (710–11). As with Christ's temple in *Andreas,* this combination of Solomon's temple as both "temple" and "hall" places the building in dual contexts. As a "temple," it evokes an otherness and a greatness beyond anything in daily life. As a "hall," however, its significance is made immediately present and relevant. In contrast to the poem's heroes, the enemy Chaldeans meet in an "ealh-stede" (673). Unlike the more positively charged "meðelstede," which is used to describe Christ's temple above, "ealhstede" (as well as "ealh" and "alh" in isolation) is associated with pre-Christian ritual (Markey 365). The compound also appears in *Andreas,* where associations with non-Christian practice are explicit as the Mermedonians are said to have aban-doned "diofolgild, / ealde ealhstedas" ["devil worship, old *ealhstedas*"] (1641–42). In *Daniel* the traditionally freighted language of the poem in-dicates that the Chaldeans and their buildings were actually once heroic. The "mæst and mærost" ["greatest and most renowned"] warriors for a time find "protection under walls" ["under wealla hleo"] (690). Their pro-tection "wealle belocene" ["enclosed in the wall"] (695) ceased, however, when Belshazzar provoked God ["godes frasade"] (694). The *Dictionary of Old English* provides two meanings for the *ealhstede* compound, either "a heathen temple" (*Andreas* 1638) or more generally a "city," with the refer-ences in *Daniel* (671, 686) provided specifically as examples of the more generalized meaning. While the sense of "city" is appropriate in the narra-tive context, the sense of "heathen temple" also seems idiomatically ap-propriate and relevant for describing the space of the Chaldeans.

Solomon's temple also makes an appearance in *Exodus,* again em-ploying terminology that marks its distance from the Anglo-Saxon world even as it becomes vested with the architectural traits most prized by the Anglo-Saxons:

> þær eft se snottra   sunu Dauides,
> wuldorfæst cyning,   witgan larum

getimbrede   tempel gode,
alh haligne,   eorðcyninga
se wisesta   on woruldrice,
heahst and haligost,   hæleðum gefrægost,
mæst and mærost,   þara þe manna bearn,
fira æfter foldan,   folmum geworhte. (389–96)

———

[And there, afterwards, the son of David, the most glorious king,
the wisest of all earth-kings in the world-kingdom, according
to the teaching of the prophets, built a temple for God, a holy place,
the holiest and highest and most well-known among men, the
greatest and most splendid of all that the sons of men have built
upon the earth.][82]

Interestingly, this building is also described as an "alh," a term that, as
noted earlier, is closely associated with pre-Christian worship (Markey
365) and has negative connotations in *Daniel* (673) and *Andreas* (1642).
This "alh" of *Exodus*, however, is "haligne" ["holy"] and a "tempel gode"
["a good temple"]. Such usage seems to explicitly contrast the typical
"ealh" with a new and "haligne" "ealh," appropriating the terminology
and situating it in a new and positive religious context in a pattern similar to the physical appropriation of actual ancient spaces themselves. As
discussed above, the appropriation of ancient spaces and building materials for new, Christian functions was typical in Anglo-Saxon building
practices and parallels what we find in poetic architectural depiction
more generally.[83] Solomon's "tempel" is built on the site of the positively
charged "meðelstede" (397),[84] and it is described with more superlatives
than perhaps any other architectural structure in Old English poetry. It
is not just high; it is the "highest" ["heahst"] (394). Embodying the best
of all known structures, including pre-Christian ones, it is "holigost,"
"mæst," "mærost." Its distance from the Anglo-Saxon world is marked
by its status as "temple" rather than "church," and this distance seems to
be underscored with the use of "alh." It is this very distance, however,
that allows Solomon's temple to take on characteristics superseding any
structure in the known and familiar world. Such nuanced and connotative meanings are difficult to convey with modern English terminology,
with "tempel" denoting a positive and typically Judeo-Christian space in

the Anglo-Saxon poetic idiom and "ealh" referring specifically to "heathen" space, both most often receiving the ambiguous and somewhat misleading rendering "temple" in modern English.

ARCHITECTURE AND URBAN LANDSCAPE IN *ANDREAS*

To this point I have been examining various types of structures in isolation. But to close this chapter, I would like to employ the methodology from vernacular architecture offered in chapter 1 regarding landscape and bring several structural images from *Andreas* together with their surrounding landscape in order to demonstrate through a brief overview how a better understanding of such architectural imagery can affect and positively inform our reading of this poem's larger urban space across the poem in its entirety. In *Andreas* the city of Mermedonia provides much more than a mere setting. Andreas is of course sent by God to Mermedonia to help release Matthew from cruel imprisonment. While there, Andreas frees not only Matthew but also hundreds of other prisoners who were likely to be tortured and perhaps even eaten by their captors. Later, Andreas himself is imprisoned, tortured, and dragged through the city's streets before he debates a demon in the city's underground prison and eventually, through divine intervention, brings about a flood that ends the threat of the Mermedonians and ultimately leads to the conversion of the city's inhabitants. But despite the fact that the city of Mermedonia is shown to be inhabited by cannibals and serves largely as a prison for the poem's two key protagonists, depictions of this city and its architectural structures employ not only predictable negative imagery but also certain phraseology and descriptive language applied to unambiguously positive contexts elsewhere in Old English verse. What follows is a more comprehensive treatment of how these spaces are presented in relation to one another, specifically, in the built spaces constituting Mermedonia, to create a sense of urban space. Perhaps more clearly than in any other surviving verse translation, the architecture and architectural imagery of *Andreas* are expanded from known exemplars in ways demonstrably consistent with the Old English poetic practices more generally, and the poem's numerous architectural descriptions as well as its frequent meta -

phorical allusions to other buildings provide important insights into the roles buildings and architectural imagery played throughout Anglo-Saxon oral poetics.

One of the issues complicating the depiction of Mermedonia in the Old English verse adaptation of *Andreas* is the city's enigmatic location. Though some early versions of the story associate this city of cannibals with actual locations such as Scythia or Myrmecium, the story's geographic setting generally remains elusive.[85] To complicate the matter further, the Old English verse *Andreas* departs from prose versions of the story in portraying Mermedonia as an island (lines 15, 25). Kenneth Brooks argues that *igland* (line 15) is not meant in a literal sense here: "The meaning is not 'island', but 'land beyond the water.' "[86] But the usage of *igland* can also be explained in terms of Anglo-Saxon experience, as Krapp has done: "to the insular Anglo-Saxons all foreign lands must have been 'waterlands,' " and "in this poetical sense the word also carried with it the connotation of remoteness," in effect intensifying the isolation of Mermedonia and its inhabitants from the world of Matthew and Andreas (Krapp 78). The Old English poet is thus translating not simply a narrative, but a legendary landscape whose actual geographic location is less important than its psychological distance from the audience's sphere of experience. As noted at several points above, the architectural imagery as presented in *Andreas* departs at numerous points from classical analogues and speaks instead to Anglo-Saxon expectations, reflecting in part the architectural reality of early medieval England while drawing also from an oral poetics surrounding buildings and architectural terms evidenced in Old English poetry more widely.[87] What emerges is a distinctly Anglo-Saxon understanding of Mermedonian urban space, one more consistent with the architectural and poetic traditions that would have been most familiar to its original audiences.

On the surface Mermedonia as Andreas first encounters it appears to be a positive, awe-inspiring city. Before he arrives on its shores, we are told twice that the city is "mæran byrig" ["a renowned city"] (40), a phrase referring to heroic and valued buildings and spaces in such poems as *Elene* (863), *The Phoenix* (633), and *Christ and Satan* (622). The city is also said to sit high on a hill where it is visible from a great distance—the kind of location that was highly valued in Anglo-Saxon poetry and construction alike. The opening line of *Maxims II,* for instance, tells us that cities should be seen from afar, "ceastra beoð feorran gesyne" (1). And the Anglo-Saxons themselves tended to construct tall buildings in high spaces, as discussed in chapter 2. St. Peter's Anglo-Saxon chapel at Bradwell-on-Sea (fig. 5), the ruins of St. Patrick's Chapel at Heysham in Lancashire (fig. 31), and St. Mary's Saxon church built onto the Roman lighthouse at Dover Castle are just a few examples of Anglo-Saxon sites surviving to the present day that were built on elevated locations above the water, the very kind of space on which the buildings of Mermedonia are said to have been built. The strategic advantage of building on elevated locations is obvious and certainly not unique among the Anglo-Saxons. What is interesting here is that this prized location is in this case attributed to a largely fictionalized space, one where actual military advantage need not apply, and moreover to a city known for its inhabitants' ghastly and ignoble deeds.

From his ship, Andreas sees before him on high cliffs tile-adorned buildings, high towers, steep walls, nothing so far that on the surface denotes danger:

> Onwoc þa wiges heard,   wang sceawode,
> fore burggeatum.   Beorgas steape,
> hleoðu hlifodon,   ymbe harne stan
> tigelfagan trafu,   torras stodon,
> windige wealles.   þa se wisa oncneow
> þæt he Marmedonia   mægðe hæfde
> siðe gesohte. . . . (839–45)

> ———

> [Then the one hardened in battle awoke, saw the plain before the city-gate. Steep hills, slopes rose up; around the gray stone tile-adorned temples, towers stood, windy walls. Then the wise one knew that he had found on his journey the tribe of Mermedonians. . . .]

However, through the traditional phraseology explored previously, the poet tells his audience, nonetheless, to expect the worst. The phrase "harne stan" [lit., "gray stone"] seems harmless enough at a literal level, but, as discussed in chapter 2, its traditional uses as evidenced in the poetry more widely reach beyond the simple description of a structure as gray. Elsewhere in Old English verse, and even in the prose Blickling Homilies, the phrase marks an architectural space through which a hero must pass prior to a battle with a superhuman foe, "a boundary between the known, familiar world of human activity and the frightening realm of monsters, the supernatural, and unusual adventure" (Swisher 133).[88] While in the case of *Andreas* the battle at this point in the narrative is not imminent and the nature of the foe is not immediately discernible, the presence of the "gray stone" nonetheless marks the boundary through which Andreas, the hero, must pass before entering into a battle with unknown foes, who will in this case turn out to be cannibals and, later, an actual demon. An audience familiar with Old English idioms and attuned to traditional markers, whether clergy or lay, would very likely recognize the import of this architectural imagery and be on alert for the ensuing supernatural conflict.

In addition to "harne stan," the Mermedonian skyline includes tile-adorned "trafu." "Trafu," like "harne stan," on the surface provides a neutral description of structures. And in their ornamentation, they are reminiscent of such positive structures as the tile-adorned towers of the elegiac poem *The Ruin*. Accordingly, Brooks's edition (like several others) glosses *trafum* with the neutral term "buildings" (167).[89] But if we look at the second occurrence of "traf" in *Andreas* we see that it is used in conjunction with hell, as the people turn away from "helltrafum" (1689), a pattern also followed in *Beowulf* and *Judith*, as discussed above.[90] In each case the activities that occur in "trafum" fall outside the bounds of social acceptability. At a literal level, *trafum* may have evoked images from experience with the Anglo-Saxon landscape. Stone temples left by Romans are still evident on the British landscape, such as the *mithraeum* (temple dedicated to Mithras) at Carrawburh (fig. 13), the temple of Antenociticus at Benwell also along Hadrian's Wall, and a first-century Roman temple at Colchester.[91] The Romano-Celtic temple unearthed at Bath and other such spaces could have provided a visual context for Anglo-Saxon audiences encountering descriptions of Mermedonian temples. Evidence of a Germanic cultic temple located at Yeavering (Hope-Taylor 278) suggests still further possibilities of visual frameworks. Traditional phraseology, however, invests the Mermedonian structure with a meaning beyond that of any particular visual image. Although the immediate narrative situation in *Andreas* does not suggest anything especially negative about this space, the usages in Old English poetry more widely indicate that negative activities and a context of otherness would very likely have been foregrounded for the audience by this usage of *trafum*.

Across the poem we see other predominantly negative architectural imagery, such as the dark, dirty prison discussed previously and the rugged stone streets through which Andreas is dragged. However, embedded in these descriptions are hints of a heroic potential waiting to be reclaimed, as noted in the usage of *sele* in reference to prison. Andreas, for instance, is pulled "æfter dunscræfum, / ymb stanhleoðo stærcedfer-þþe" ["through dark caves, the stout-hearted one around rocky slopes"] (1232–33), "dunscræfum" calling to mind the "eorðscræf" of the dragon's barrow in *Beowulf* (3046) or the "eorðscræfe" said to conceal a long-dead warrior in *The Wanderer* (84), both sites of death but heroic death. And while the "stanhleoðo" is evocative of the ominous "stanhlið" of the Grendel mere (1409) or the distant "stanhlið" occupied by the exiled lover in *The Wife's Lament* (line 48; see also chap. 5), these same city streets also feature "enta ærgeweorc, innan burgum, / stræte stanfage" (1235–36), where the variation of the "enta geweorc" formula suggests an ancient worth predating the occupation of the cannibalistic Mermedonians.

We might also be surprised to find part of the otherwise ominous and dank Mermedonian prison actually aiding the hero and bringing *Andreas* to its miraculous conclusion. Significantly, the poem's use of architecture varies radically from the *Praxeis*. In the Greek text Andreas "saw a pillar standing and an alabaster statue lying on the pillar."[92] Where the Greek text asserts that Andreas asked the water to come through the mouth of the statue on the pillar, the Old English *Andreas* has the water coming from the base *(stapol)* of the column itself. Explanations can be found both in the architecture of the time period and in the oral tradition. Animals carved at the top of imposts and capitals do appear on occasion, such as the beast carved on an arch in St. Bene't's Church, Cambridge, or the snake on the capital of St. James, Selham (fig. 11). However, as Mary Kerr and Nigel Kerr have noted, the designs of Anglo-Saxon imposts and capitals were, in general, very simple. Capitals such as those in the crypt at Repton, Derbyshire (fig. 10), were likely much more common, and elaborate sculptures of the type indicated in the Greek text would have been extremely rare in Anglo-Saxon England.[93] Perhaps more significantly, however, buildings and other important objects in Old English poetic tradition have an inherent power, and the intermediary role of the anthropomorphized statue becomes unnecessary. The speaking cross that serves as Christ's comrade in *Dream of the Rood* and the countless objects speaking in the Exeter Book riddles provide more than sufficient evidence for a tradition of sentient and highly powerful objects that can aid heroes in battle.

Despite the prison's otherwise ominous features, the powerful, magical nature of the prison's "sweras unlytle" ["great pillars"] (1493) that Andreas observes is indicated early in the passage by their status as "enta geweorc" ["work of giants"] (1495), a phrase completely unprecedented in the Greek text, as Foley has noted. This formula is applied not only to architectural structures such as the crumbling walls in *The Ruin* and the dragon's pillars in *Beowulf* but also to smaller objects of great power and significance, such as the hilt of the sword that Beowulf gives to Hrothgar. As Foley explains, "What these usages share . . . is not the particular circumstances in which they appear, or any literal relationship to giants and their works, but rather the idiomatic value of retrojection into the deep past" (*Singer* 199).

Traditional associations also help explain what would otherwise pose a logical problem of the prison in the description of the pillar that aids Andreas. The pillar is said to be "storme bedrifene" ["beaten upon by storm"] (1494), another phrase unprecedented in the Greek text and one that makes little sense at a literal level since the prison is inside. The usage, however, makes perfect sense idiomatically: just as Heorot's endurance of flames and battles anticipates the building's role in the events that later take place within its walls, the assertion of the pillar's endur-ance of storms serves to separate it from the otherwise decidedly unheroic prison and prepares us for its significant role in bringing about the flood that will end the terror of the Mermedonians.

When Andreas brings about the conversion of the Mermedonians, the latent greatness inherent in the urban space at large finally becomes fully realized as the poem closes with a description of the urban space very different from that of its opening. After the construction of Andreas's

Christian temple, we immediately see a change in the language employed to describe the city of Mermedonia more widely, one that draws less from imagery of stone ruins and heathen temples but relies instead on imagery more typical of the Anglo-Saxon hall. Mermedonia is now described as a "goldburg" ["gold-city"] (1655), filled with "seledream" ["hall-joy"] (1656), "beorht beagselu" ["bright ring-halls"] (1657), "salu sinchroden" ["richly adorned halls"] (1673), and "sincgestreon" ["precious treasure"] (1656)—all elements commonly found within the halls of Anglo-Saxon heroic verse. By the poem's close we have unambiguously positive language, with increasing imagery of heroic Anglo-Saxon halls, to describe the city and the architectural structures within it.

Early in the poem we are presented with a Mermedonia that is awe-inspiring but also fraught with potential danger. Within the city we see isolated structures—columns, pillars, stone ruins—that seem to have an inherent power and the potential for greatness. Andreas utilizes this inherent power in isolated structures such as the prison pillar, thus realizing the heroic potential of the city as a whole, and the conversion of the city's people from cannibalistic heathens to saintly Christians is thus marked by a shift in the descriptions of Mermedonia from a "renowned city" of potential greatness to one of unequivocal heroism. As Hugh Magennis has noted, in such compounds as *winburh* and *medoburh,* "the social connotations of the hall, as expressed in the drinking images, are extended to the stronghold/city as a whole" (42). The city itself enters a "transformed state after the conversion" (175). By recognizing and interpreting the traditional idioms embedded in the description of these Mermedonian spaces, we are able to complete the signifying loop begun by the poet and see the city as much more than a setting for heroic action. A reading of traditional cues reveals the city as an independently functioning entity, distinct from, though certainly connected to, its fallen inhabitants and its newly arrived hero. The poem's narrative progression develops not only Andreas's fulfillment as a hero and the conversion of the Mermedonians but also the actualization of Mermedonia itself as a positively charged, and unambiguously heroic, urban space.

The imagined prisons, pavilions, temples, and landscapes are in many ways far removed from the Anglo-Saxon landscape; nonetheless, Anglo-Saxon verse never veers far in architectural description from traditional points of reference. Descriptive terms and phrases, more than providing clues for visualization, often help direct audience response through traditional associations. The structures inhabited in these translated and adapted texts are largely imagined spaces and, as such, frequently push the boundaries of physical possibility. More than mere translations of architectural description, however, these passages convey much about Anglo-Saxon notions of built space, and in these imagined spaces we see a powerful nexus of multiple cultural and religious traditions. Pushing such boundaries even further are the many architectural metaphors and analogies permeating Anglo-Saxon verse. This type of architectural language is the focus of the next chapter.

CHAPTER

FOUR

The power of metaphor is perhaps nowhere more evident than in the Old English charms, which frequently employ incantations and rituals that rely on metaphorical associations. An example involving buildings in particular is seen in the metrical charm against a wen (Metrical Charm 12), in which the wen's swelling is described in terms of the building process. The wen is first ordered not to build: "her ne scealt þu timbrien" ["here you must not build"] (2), and a corresponding architectural metaphor is also employed in the portion of the incantation calling for a reduction of the swelling as the wen is told to "scring þu alswa scerne awage"[1] ["shrink as muck in a wall"] (9). This comparison seems to refer to the wattle and daub technique of building, in which mud or clay (the daub) is plastered over branches or thin laths (wattles). This method is sometimes used to provide a filling between the vertical beams of timber-frame houses (Fleming, Honour, and Pevsner 476), and as it dries the daub shrinks dramatically. Susan Mills notes that "daubing the walls" for a reconstructed Anglo-Saxon timber building in Jarrow showed that "even with the best mixture . . . , there was substantial shrinkage and cracking which fluctuated according to the weather conditions" (71). After extensive experimentation with "various proportions of clay, straw and water," the team concluded that most likely "the maintenance of the lime-washed daub in a sound condition was an annual task on these buildings" (71). Even with an improved method of construction and maintenance, shrinkage and cracking are still readily apparent to visitors of the reconstructed hall (fig. 18).

Archaeological evidence and attempts at Anglo-Saxon reconstructions thus suggest that the shrinkage of daub would have been a familiar sight relevant to the performance of this charm. The shrinkage was constant and dramatic, making it an apt metaphor for the desired reduction of the wen. But acting as much more than a simple metaphor with one-to-one correspondences, the charm requires us to understand Anglo-Saxon traditions and building practices in order to perceive its full significance. As Foley has argued, oral traditions often rely heavily on metony-mic meaning, a complex process in which "a text or version is enriched by an unspoken context that dwarfs the textual artifact, in which the experience is filled out—and made traditional—by what the conventionality attracts to itself from that context" (*Immanent Art* 8). In the case of the wen charm and in architectural metaphors throughout Old English poetry, metaphor and metonymy provide multiple layers of such traditionally encoded meaning.[2]

Where the previous chapters have examined depictions of buildings that were literal, at least in their narrative contexts, the pages that follow explore the explicitly metaphorical uses of architectural images within the body of Old English poetry. In a wide range of genres—saints' lives, riddles, biblical translations, elegies, and maxims, as well as more explicit allegories—architecture plays an important role in conveying key concepts and associations. Understanding these associations requires us to examine architectural metaphors in the dual contexts of archaeology and literature, since the metaphors that survive in the poetry are rich with associative meanings embedded in actual building materials, ornament, and design.[3]

Comparison of Old English adaptations with Latin analogues frequently reveals a tendency toward more concrete imagery, a "fondness for realistic detail" (Renoir, "*Judith* and the Limits of Poetry" 146).[4] As seen in chapter 2, Old English poets working from Latin or Greek source material often condensed and omitted substantial sections of narrative, choosing instead to focus on fewer elements in greater detail. Architectural metaphors are among those elements most frequently retained and expanded in indexed translations. Metaphors of buildings and building processes in such adaptations as *Christ I, Juliana, Exodus,* and *The Phoenix* demonstrate a reliance on Latin source texts as well as a rich stock of traditional phraseology reflective of the Anglo-Saxon material world.

Oral-derived texts, even those also influenced by and produced within highly literate cultures, thus require us to read from multiple perspectives. In discussing oral-derived Homeric texts, Richard Martin cautions against reading as "a closed set of tropes, balanced against or connected to one another, but appreciated fully only in retrospect, not at the moment of performance but in the leisure of reading" (143). "The dominant mode of close (and closed) reading," he says, directs readers "away from the full implications of oral poetics" (143).

The dominant reading for many architectural metaphors embedded in Old English religious texts has also often involved study of tropes in the larger context of medieval Christian literature. Ruth Wehlau is one who takes a productive alternate view; while freely acknowledging the debt of Old English architectural imagery to patristic literature (17), she observes that architectural metaphors—especially metaphors of creation—include "an element that does not exist in the patristic and biblical analogues; they describe the building of Creation as if it was specially made for people" (20). *Cædmon's Hymn,* for instance, presents God as creating a home for earth dwellers: "He ærest sceop eorðan bearnum / heofon to hrofe, halig scyppend" ["He, the holy shaper, first created heaven as a roof for the children of earth"] (5–6),[5] and the *scyppend* in the scop's song of creation in *Beowulf* sets the sun and moon in the sky specifically "leohte landbuendum" ["as light for land-dwellers"] (95). For these and many other such metaphors, a "marriage" of rhetorical and thematic approaches allows us to consider "both the local immediate affective strategies at work and the wider-reaching thematic purposes" (Martin 144).[6]

As Martin's analysis suggests, there are in fact subtle but significant differences between the use of metaphor within an oral poetic system and the use of metaphor as a more rhetorical and literary trope, as studies with living oral traditions have effectively demonstrated. In his insightful study of metaphor in folk song across a range of cultures, Barre Toelken observes that "although all metaphors pull the abstract into palpable range, vernacular folk metaphors usually do so by using images drawn from a rich supply of customary ideas that the participants already share" (*Morning Dew* 34). Like the vernacular songs discussed by Toelken, Anglo-Saxon poetry was composed within an oral poetics in which the "rich supply of customary images" could be relied on for their conventional referential meanings in order to create multivalent and highly nuanced variations in metaphorical and narrative description alike.[7] Focusing on architectural metaphor more specifically, Wehlau notes a connection between orality and architectural metaphor in Old English verse: "Since oral style is more paratactic than the style of written poetry, Old English architectural metaphors of Creation reflect the paratactic style of the poetry by emphasizing the element of joining in architectural structure, rather than a more hierarchical 'architectonic' structure. Just as oral poetry itself places less emphasis on overall structure and more on connections, so Old English poetry views the construction of the cosmos as a binding together" (39). Old English architectural metaphors thus make more direct connections between real-world experiences and their metaphorical counterparts. In the absence of a living tradition in which to contextualize allegorical language, we nonetheless need to view medieval metaphors beyond the context of a closed network of texts. In the case of Anglo-Saxon architectural metaphor, there are to be sure numerous medieval literary tropes from which vernacular poets could and did draw, but a more cross-disciplinary approach can give a much broader understanding of Anglo-Saxon arts, where there is significant overlap between material and literary culture.[8]

CORNERSTONES AND KEYS: *ADVENT LYRICS I* AND *II*

The first *Advent Lyric* of *Christ I* provides one of the most fully developed architectural metaphors in Old English poetry, describing Christ as the *weallstan* ["wallstone"] (2) rejected by the builders.[9] And as the "head" or "headstone" ["heafod"] (4) of the building,[10] Christ joins walls and flint with firm bonds (6) in a structure visible from great distances (7–8). The roof and walls of this structure are in danger of decay and wait for Christ, who comes to restore the ruins to their former glory (11–14). Despite the poem's apparent attention to architectural and technical detail, so rare in Old English verse, the inherent contradictions in the description of this metaphorical building render attempts to reconstruct even the most basic image in physical reality frustratingly impossible. As Johanna Kramer has aptly observed, the "poetic trajectory results in a somewhat problematic assemblage of seemingly disjointed images" (90). The wallstone, for instance, holds an ambiguous placement at both the top (head) *and* bottom (cornerstone) of the structure; Christ is creator *and* repairer of the structure, in addition of course to being *part of* the building; and the structure itself, somewhat logically assumed to be a Christian temple given its religious purpose, shares phraseology more typically employed in poetic descriptions of secular Anglo-Saxon halls and ancient Roman ruins. The metaphor is in fact a highly charged one, and one that depends on traditional, and secular, architectural associations in the poetry more widely for its import.

The lyric's widely acknowledged source is the antiphon of the magnificat for December 22 (Allen and Calder, *Major Latin Texts* 70–71), a text brief enough to quote in its entirety: "O Rex gentium et desideratus earum, lapisque angularis qui facis utraque unum: veni, et salva hominem quem de limo formasti" ["O King of the Nations and the One they long for and the cornerstone; you who make both things one, come and save man whom you fashioned out of clay"] (Burlin, *Old English Advent* 58). Though the metaphor itself stems from a fairly direct translation of *lapis angularis,* the antiphon "lacks a sustained and encompassing architectural theme" (Kramer 92).

Many scholars have previously commented on the expansion of the metaphor from the presumed Latin source, observing that the "weallstan" of *Advent Lyric I* corresponds with the "lapis angularis" of the antiphon (e.g., Campbell, *Advent Lyrics* 12; Burlin, *Old English Advent* 58). It has also been noted that a building "was a frequent metaphor for Christ's Church, either temporal or eternal" (Campbell, *Advent Lyrics* 12). As a result of these metaphorical connections, the architectural imagery employed in the poem is assumed to depict a Christian church or temple. For instance, Robert Burlin takes it for granted that "the words *healle mærre* certainly suggest a temple or church" (*Old English Advent* 64),[11] and he asserts further that the poet's phrasing "clearly points to an interpretation of the figure as one for the founding of the universal church" (59). Burlin then goes on to seek parallels in descriptions of temples and religious structures employed in such Christian sources as the homilies of Ælfric (60–62), especially the building of Solomon's temple.[12] However, even though Latinate tropes and patristic literature clearly informed this poem as a whole in many important and undeniable ways, the poet is drawing from multiple traditions in expanding the imagery. Kramer, for instance, has compellingly demonstrated strong parallels between the seemingly inconsistent and problematic image of Christ as building *and* builder and an illustration in the Book of Kells, "The Temptation of Christ," that visually renders Christ as part (specifically the upper third) of a building. Kramer suggests that "the illustration is an iconographic attempt to express the same Christological paradoxes as Lyric I" and that the Kells artist "employs the architectural imagery of Christ as *lapis angularis* and relies on the viewers' recognition of its associated spatial symbolism" (99). In addition to such connections with insular visual art, the phraseology employed specifically in the architectural description involves a combination of images related to Anglo-Saxon halls and Roman ruins rather than the strictly limited frame of reference provided by temples or churches.[13] And while many have observed that the poet is working from a clear source in the antiphon and subtly employs the common trope in Christian literature of Christ as builder, what has been explored less fully is the poet's simultaneous participation in the poetic idiom of Anglo-Saxon oral tradition.

The combination of features in this extended metaphor share a great deal with architectural imagery elsewhere in the corpus of Anglo-Saxon poetry: materials of earth as well as wall-stone, a reference to kingship, and a variation of the "(x-) geweorc" phraseology discussed in previous chapters. Such collocations can be easily missed when examining the poem strictly in its Christian and Latinate contexts, even though the dominant reading of the *Advent Lyrics* has been through these non-Germanic filters. Burlin's edition, for instance, includes chapters devoted to "scriptural typology" (4–22) and "literary typology" (23–36), as well as indices of "biblical references" (191–92) and "patristic citations" (193–98). While such comparative contexts are enormously helpful in understanding the poem in the context of Christian literature, we risk missing the full significance of the metaphor by limiting parallels to explicitly religious works. If, on the other hand, we examine the first *Advent Lyric* through its connections with corresponding imagery from *The Ruin* and *Maxims II*,[14] another traditional and complementary perspective on the poem emerges.

As Foley has argued, reading oral and oral-derived texts requires us to "examine unexamined assumptions" (Foley, *How to Read* 40) and to change our "default reading" of texts (60). In the case of *Advent Lyric I,* this means rethinking the somewhat logical assumption that the metaphorical building described in the unambiguously Christian *Advent Lyric I* must be a Christian church. Shifting this rather natural "default" to allow for the possibility, even likelihood, that secular buildings also inform this complex metaphor opens up new and significant possibilities regarding the imagined spaces that the poem's descriptions might have conjured in the minds of Anglo-Saxon audiences and, even more important, the associations that such descriptions may activate when the poem is read in the register of secular, heroic verse.

Such a reading provides alternative (but not mutually exclusive) ways of understanding the poem's imagery and of reconciling a number of seeming ambiguities and contradictions embedded in the complex architectural metaphor. For instance, the *weallstan* compound at the center of *Advent Lyric I* is also employed in *The Ruin* and *Maxims II,* two works having little direct connection with Christian architecture. A distinct pattern emerges when we look at the architectural imagery across these three poems: the presence of a king, visibility from great distances, wallstone, variation of the (x-) geweorc formulaic system, and a connection to earth. The opening lines of *Maxims II* illustrate these connections in an especially compact image:

> **Cyning** sceal rice healdan.   Ceastra beoð **feorran gesyne,**
> orðanc **enta geweorc,**   þa þe on þysse **eorðan** syndon,
> wrætlic **weallstana** geweorc. (*Maxims II* 1–3)
>
> ——————
>
> [A king must rule. Cities are seen from far away, cunning work of giants, which are on this earth, wondrous work of wall-stones.]

While the telegraphic nature of maxims renders these elements in close proximity in *Maxims II,* similar connections are evident in all three poems discussed here. Each, for instance, clearly alludes to kingship in relation to the architectural structure being described. Damage to the manuscript makes the immediate narrative context unclear, but the phrase "þæt is cynelic þing" (48) in *The Ruin* nonetheless parallels the "cyninge" (1) of *Advent Lyric I* and the "cyning" of *Maxims I*. "Cyninge," which is the first word of the *Advent Lyric* fragment (though not the poem), derives from *rex* in the antiphon. But *Maxims II* and *The Ruin* indicate that core elements associated with a "cyning" are "wealstan" and a widely visible city, both of which are expanded on in *Advent Lyric I*. Further, the grouping of these images in the form of a maxim also demonstrates the presence of the traditional wisdom underlying this particular collocation of concepts.

The choice of "weallstan" to translate the Latin *lapis angularis* is especially significant. Ælfric translates *caput anguli* ["head of corner"][15] very differently from the *Advent Lyric* poet, rendering the phrase as "hyrn-stan" in his commentary, with *hyrne* meaning "horn," "corner," or "angle":[16] "Soðlice se sealm-sceop awrat be Criste, þæt he is se hyrn-stan þe gefegð þa twegen weallas togædere" ["Truly the psalmist wrote concerning Christ, that he is the corner-stone which joins the two walls together"] (60–61). The *weallstan/wealstan* compound employed in *Advent Lyric I*, however, appears only in verse and only in reference to secular structures rather than churches. It is typically translated simply as "stone for building," with no specific associations with corners or even angles (Bosworth). With such a broad semantic range, the compound is linked in a general rather than specific way and opens itself up to a different network of associations. The wall-stone now belongs not only to an abstract biblical text but also to a structure evocative of the cities and ruins on the Anglo-Saxon landscape and comparable to the wall-stone in such secular verse as *Maxims II* and *The Ruin*.

As with the structures depicted in these poems, the building described in *Advent Lyric I* is prized for its visibility. Like *Maxim II*'s strongholds that are "feorran gesyne" ["seen from far away"], Christ of *Advent Lyric I*, both "cyning" and allegorical "weallstan," belongs to a structure "þæt geond eorðbold . . . geall eagna gesihþe / wundrien to worlde wuldres ealdor" ["that throughout earthly mansions (or dwelling places), all those with eyes to see may wonder at the glory of the lord"].[17] The structures in all three poems also include explicit references to "earth." The speaker of *The Ruin* laments that "eorðgrap hafað / waldend wyrhtan" ["the earthgrip has the builders"] (6–7), the image of the earth reinforced with "heard gripe hrusan" ["earth in its hard grip"] in the following line (8). *Maxims II* speaks of the structures "þa þe on þysse eorðan syndon" ["which are on this earth"] (2). And the first *Advent Lyric* speaks of the wide walls visible "geond eorðbold" ["throughout earthly dwelling places"] (7).

A subtler parallel across the three poems is evident in the usage of the phraseology surrounding *weorc*. In *Maxims II* and *The Ruin*, the "wealstan" is described in highly traditional and formulaic terms as "enta geweorc" (*Maxims II* 2; *The Ruin* 2), "enta geweorc" being typically associated with ancient objects of great worth, as previously discussed. The structure of *Advent Lyric I*, however, is "þin *sylfes* weorc" ["the work of your self"; emphasis mine] (9), "self" here referring to Christ. The phrase seems prompted by both the direct address in the antiphon on which it is based and by the traditional idiom. Following the Latin antiphon, the poem speaks directly to the king (Latin *rex* / Old English *cyning*) and then goes on to shift the traditional "(x[genitive]-) weorc" phraseology to fit this second-person construct. The combined effect is a powerful one: having activated the web of associations in the "wealstan," the king, the visibility from far places, and reference to "earth," the poet of the *Advent Lyric* alters the traditional phrase "enta geweorc" to "sylfes weorc," making Christ himself the origin of the structure rather than the elusive giants of the traditional idiom.

Just as with the "enta geweorc" of *The Ruin*, the "sylfes weorc" of *Advent Lyric I* lies in need of repair, with the "brosnade burgseall" of *The Ruin* (28) paralleling the "gebrosnad" (13) structure of *Advent Lyric I*. By casting the message of the antiphon in terms of the Old English ruin motif, the significance of the metaphor of Christ as repairer is greatly heightened. There is no hope for the structure in *The Ruin* because both build - ers and potential repairers are gone forever: "Betend crungon / hergas to hrusan" ["The repairers fell, armies to the earth"] (28–29), and "Eorð - grap hafað / waldend wyrhtan forweorone, geleorene, / heardgripe hru- san" ["The earth-grasp, the hard grip of the ground, has the mighty build - ers, decayed, passed away"] (6–8). In contrast, the "cyninge" of *Advent Lyric I*—both builder and mender—is called on to restore the structure to its former glory: "þæt se cræftga cume ond se cyning sylfa, / ond þonne gebete" ["that the craftsman come and the king himself, and then re- store"] (12–13). Unlike the "gebræcon" ["broken"] wallstone (1) of *The Ruin*, the flint of *Advent Lyric I* is thus "unbræcne" ["unbroken"] (6). By evoking the cluster of images employed in elegiac and wisdom poetry, *Advent Lyric I* provides a context of ruin and absolute loss against which the emergence of Christ as ultimate repairer becomes far more forceful than a direct translation of the Latin antiphon would have conveyed.

In isolation, none of these images or phrases would seem especially noteworthy, but taken together *Maxims II, The Ruin,* and *Advent Lyric I*—a collection of poems disparate in terms of both genre and subject matter—draw from and reinforce the traditional referentiality underlying their shared phraseology and imagery. In each poem the references to kingship, earth, wall-stone, and work *[enta/sylfes]* together create a powerful image of a structure worthy of the greatest admiration and awe. By drawing on this cluster of images, the poet of *Advent Lyric I* is able to expand and recast a metaphor, already invested with much meaning in its Christian and liturgical context, into a highly charged traditional idiom. The resulting confluence of hall, religious, and ruin imagery in *Advent Lyric I* creates an architecturally ambiguous image but one that activates a potent, traditionally charged metaphor.

An awareness of how Anglo-Saxons interacted with their architecture can also help answer questions and address seeming inconsistencies in *Advent Lyric II,* which has been noted as continuing the architectural imagery of the first *Advent Lyric* (Burlin, *Old English Advent* 71) but somewhat enigmatically omitting the central image of the source antiphon, which opens "O Clavis David." The Old English poem has thus been criticized for leaving out this aspect of the metaphor, namely, Christ as "key."[18] The Old English lyric opens instead with emphasis on the lock:

Eala þu reccend, ond þu riht cyning,
se þe locan healdeð, lif ontyneð . . . (18–19)
———

[You ruler of all, and you rightful king,
who hold the lock, open life . . .]

If we restrict our comparisons only to religious texts, then the omission certainly is surprising. But if we look more closely at how keys were used by Anglo-Saxons and at how keys appear in their poetry, the poet's choice is quite logical. Locks, not keys, are the more significant items in Old

English poetry. The door to Heorot is protected not with lock and key but with "fyrbendum" ["iron bands"]. Archaeological evidence also points to doors locked from the inside with bars rather than opened with keys, a feature reproduced in reconstructed halls at both West Stow and Jarrow (figs. 16 and 19). The most prominent keys in Old English verse appear in the double entendre Riddle 44 and in Riddle 91,[19] but neither of these poems conveys the sense of solemnity evident in the second antiphon. Further, women in the upper classes were far more likely than men to be in charge of such household items as keys, as evidenced by the *Laws of King Cnut,* where a wife whose husband had brought stolen goods to the house was to be held as guilty only if the stolen items were kept in a location for which she had the keys.[20] Grave goods found in women's burial sites also indicate that keys were more typically seen as the possession of women.[21] Further, the women buried with keys tend not to be buried with jewelry (Fell 60),[22] indicating that those with keys were not nobility. Such evidence suggests that the key as symbol of kingship would be inappropriate on the basis not only of gender but also of class. For all these reasons, God as king—at least an Anglo-Saxon king—would therefore be unlikely to hold keys that were located primarily in the domain of female housekeepers. With this cultural context, the shift in emphasis from key to lock in this poem is quite logical.

Understanding such cultural and traditional contexts is essential for these and other architectural metaphors to work. Metaphor demands "the perception of two or more relatable concepts at once," thus setting up a "reflective ambiguity" (Toelken, *Dynamics* 33). Audiences are thus required to "register more than one level of meaning at a single moment" and have "the capacity to bring several 'loaded' referents together into a vivid articulation or dramatization that should need no decoding" (33). But metaphorical images based on multiple layers of meaning can often be highly ambiguous, especially when we are more than a millennium removed from the poet's immediate experience. Vernacular metaphors frequently involve more than simple one-to-one correspondences between "real" meaning and metaphorical equivalents. Instead, the greater significance is often embedded in connotations of imagery drawing from multiple registers: "To understand how ambiguous metaphors work we must look for frequency and consistency of occurrence, for coherent usage in repeated expressive environments, and for meaningful parallels and reverberations with other expressive genres in the same or very similar cultures" (Toelken, *Morning Dew* 17). By looking closely at the phraseology of the metaphor in *Advent Lyrics I* and *II* in the context of architectural imagery elsewhere in the poetry, we come to a fuller understanding of the "cultural assumptions" that we must understand in order to fully appreciate and comprehend vernacular metaphor as it is employed within religious verse. The Christ of *Advent Lyric I* encounters ruins beyond repair, ruins that in virtually any other poetic context would provoke nostalgia for a distant and irrecoverable past. However, Christ here not only repairs the building, but becomes the building's foundation and wall. The structure that emerges shares the phraseology used to describe Anglo-Saxon halls and, as such, greatly heightens the metaphorical message. The king who emerges in the second lyric guards the lock but does not hold the key, exactly as would be fitting in Anglo-Saxon society. The metaphors provide an image of godliness and kingship at once reflective of the Latin antiphons from which they derive and consistent with Anglo-Saxon cultural and poetic traditions.

FOUNDATIONS AND WALLS: *JULIANA*

The *Acta Sanctorum,* a posited source of the Old English *Juliana,*[23] includes an architectural metaphor near the climax of the narrative. In her final speech before she is beheaded, Juliana exhorts those present, including Christians newly converted by the narrative's preceding miracles, to "ædificate domos vestras super firmam petram, ne venientibus ventis validis disrumpamini" ["build your houses on firm rock, so you will not be shattered by the coming fierce winds"] (20).[24] But in the Old English this simple metaphor is then expanded to include actual directions for walls and foundation:

> . . . ge eower hus
> gefæstnige, þy læs hi ferblædum
> windas toweorpan. Weal sceal þy trumra
> strong wiþstondan storma scurum,
> leahtra gehygdum. Ge mid lufan sibbe,
> leohte geleafan, to þam lifgendan

stane stiðhydge   staþol fæstniað,
soðe treowe . . . (648–55)

[You must fasten your house lest the winds destroy it with their
sudden blasts. The strong walls must withstand more securely
showers of storms, thoughts of sin. You, with bonds of love,
with resoluteness, must fasten its foundation more firmly to
the living rock, with true faith . . .]

The choices both to retain the central elements of the architectural metaphor from a Latin source and to supplement them with more specific and
focused building imagery suggest that those features that are included
perhaps resonated more strongly with its Anglo-Saxon audience than
other, omitted, features.

The metaphor is apparently an important one, and the poet goes to
great lengths to make its meaning clear. Because the Anglo-Saxons typically did not build houses on stone foundations, the image likely required
more unpacking for it to be directly relevant in its new cultural setting.
For instance, where the "firm rock" that serves as the foundation in the
Latin text is given no further explication, the foundation *(staþol)* of the
Old English metaphor is described as "fastened" to stone. Unlike the possible Latin sources, the Old English *Juliana* is concerned about the integrity of the building as a whole rather than focusing strictly on the foundation. *Staþol* itself is not limited strictly to "foundation" but can refer
to any supporting structure—for instance, the columns in *Andreas*[25]—
and postholes and other archaeological evidence show that secular structures, including houses, were most typically built directly on the ground.
For Anglo-Saxons, the primary focus of the building process was the construction of sturdy walls rather than firm foundations. Consistent with
this mode of building, the Old English poem immediately follows the
original foundation metaphor with a discussion of the structure's walls:
"Weal sceal þy trumra / strong wiþstondan storma scurum / leahtra ge -
hygdum" ["The strong wall must withstand more securely showers of
storms, thoughts of sins"] (650–52). Expansion of this metaphor to include walls at this point also affords the additional advantage of associ -
ations with other strong walls in the poetic tradition, such as are manifest

in *The Ruin*'s famous "wrætlic" wallstone (1). Such connections would certainly not have been as easy to make through the isolated image of house foundations, which were rare in archeology and poetry alike.[26]

In addition, the paratactic structure of the clauses, typical of Old English verse and of oral traditional composition more generally,[27] makes some of the metaphorical referents even more explicit, as the storms threatening the building become metaphorically equivalent to thoughts of vice, the "leahtra gehygdum." But, once again, understanding the traditional associations of the building imagery can take us beyond a simple one-to-one correspondence. The specific phraseology used to translate the *firmam petram* ["firm rock"] of the original suggests a more powerful rock than a literal translation alone can convey, especially with the people being told to fasten foundations to living stone, "to þam lifgendan / stane stiðhydge staþol fæstniað." The dynamic power of stone, not just firm but also living, is also emphasized in *Andreas*, where the juxtaposition of terms here is closely paralleled in the description of the more literal living stone, which becomes a character itself. In this poem when the stone that leaps from the temple wall speaks at Christ's command, we see again the juxtaposition of *stan* and a similar *stið-* compound ("stiðhycgendum" instead of "stiðhydge" ["resolute"]): "wrætlic þuhte / stiðhycgendum stanes ongin" ["the action of the stone seemed wondrous to the resolute ones"] (740–41).[28] In both instances, the firmness of the stone seems to correspond to the mind-set of those being addressed, in *Juliana* to the resoluteness Juliana demands of her listeners and in *Andreas* to the more negative obstinacy of the temple priests. The adjective *firmam* applied to the rock in the *Acta Sanctorum* finds its equivalent in a character trait in the Old English *Juliana*, creating a subtle shift in emphasis from the stone itself to its effects. And this metaphor of the living stone that affects resolute people in *Juliana* finds a literal manifestation in the image evoked in *Andreas*, a connection underscored by similar phraseology.

WALLS OF THE SEA: *EXODUS*

As with the figurative buildings in *Juliana*, architectural metaphor in the Old English *Exodus* is also greatly expanded from the corresponding Latin

Vulgate version, a choice consistent with the tendency in Old English poetry to intensify comparisons and create vivid and immediate images. After the Vulgate's description of the parting of the Red Sea, the waters through which the Israelites pass are compared to a towering wall: "et ingressi sunt filii Israhel per medium maris sicci erat enim aqua quasi murus a dextra eorum et læva" ["And the Israelites went through the midst of the sea dry-shod, with its waters towering up like a wall to right and left"] (14.22). But the Old English version creates a far more complete image by adding both foundation and roof to the metaphorical walls. The parted waters are likened to walls, parting to reveal seafloors that become ancient foundations in the extended metaphor,[29] foundations never before seen by men:

> Yð up færeð,   ofstum wyrceð
> wæter wealfæsten.[30]   Wegas syndon dryge,
> haswe herestræta,   holm gerymed,
> ealde staðolas   þa ic ær ne gefrægn
> ofer middangeard   men geferan,
> fage feldas,   þa forð heonon
> in ece tid   yðe þeahton,
> sælde sægrundas. . . . (282–89)

> [The wave rises up; the water swiftly makes a rampart. The ways are dry, gray army-roads; the water opened up, old foundations which never have I heard over all the world for men to go, which henceforth,[31] in all times, the waves would have concealed, shining plains, sealed sea-grounds. . . .]

Further expanding the image, the poet then supplies the structure with stepped walls leading up to the roof:

> Syndon þa foreweallas   fægre gestepte,
> wrætlicu wægfaru,   oð wolcna hrof. (297–98)

> [The outer walls are fair and stepped, a wondrous wave-road, up to the roof of clouds.][32]

The Latin simile thus provides basic physical information about the water, which temporarily acquires the physical characteristics of a wall firm enough and high enough to pass by without danger, and, as important features of Anglo-Saxon construction, these qualities are retained in the Old English as well through the phrase "fægre gestepte," where the past participle of *stepan* ["step"], *stepte,* is difficult to translate idiomatically in modern English.[33] Nevertheless, when we look at the stepped ele-vations employed in Anglo-Saxon construction, such as the multilevel, quite literally "stepped," plinth on the chancel of St. Wystan's Church, Repton (fig. 24), we can see that the metaphor evokes quite literal associations with valued buildings and construction methods entrenched enough in Anglo-Saxon culture to be continued into the Norman period in such buildings as St. Margaret's, King's Lynn (fig. 25).

In addition, this passage in the Old English *Exodus* equating the waters with walls not only expands the image by adding a roof and foundation not present in the original but also turns the analogy from a simile into a direct metaphor.[34] Old English poets seem to have preferred metaphor for such comparisons, reserving side-by-side comparisons afforded by the simile for parallel situations (such as the famous lament of the grieving father compared with Beowulf's own situation).[35] The effect is to give an immediacy and intensity to the comparison, in which the vehicle and tenor are one and the same, rather than side by side. The waters of the Old English *Exodus* are not simply *like* walls as they are in the Latin rendering; rather, they *are* walls.

However, through its extended architectural parallel, the Old English *Exodus* provides more than physical characteristics for the water's structure, with the composer once again tapping into a complex network of associations that move beyond the details of mere construction. Specifically, the phrase "wolcna hrof" ["roof of clouds"] is evocative of a larger traditional context shared with other heroic poetry. For instance, when Holofernes' death is forecast in *Judith,* we are told that he will receive the kind of death that he inflicted when he "wunode under wolcna hrofe" ["lived under the roof of clouds"] (67). And in *Elene,* Constantine is promised that he will triumph when he sees a sign "ofer wolcna hrof" ["above the roof of clouds"] (88). In both instances, the phrase "wolcna hrof" is linked with assured victory for the protagonist and forecasts certain doom for the enemy. The walls in the Latin Exodus thus spark a series of highly associative architectural images that heighten the glory of the Israelites and promise a swift demise for the pursuing Egyptians, connotative meaning that would be missed by relying on the phrase's lexical meaning alone.[36]

"HUS GETIMBREÐ": THE PHOENIX

The poet of the Old English *Phoenix* also expands a metaphor of construction from a Latin source text. The first 380 lines are a relatively faithful adaptation of Lactantius's late classical Latin *Carmen de ave phoenice*, while the latter portion of the poem involves an explicitly Christian allegory not present in the Latin work.[37] The reworking of the source material both altered and increased the poem's metaphorical possibilities. Through employment of selective details from his source and additions of motifs in Christian thought, the poet reworks the source material and alters the poem's central metaphors,[38] a pattern especially evident in the construction of the phoenix's nest, from the first portion of the poem:

> on þam telgum   timbran onginneð,
> nest gearwian . . .
> . . .   þonne feor ond neah
> þa swetestan   somnað ond gædrað
> wyrta wynsume   ond wudubleda
> to þam eardstede,   æþelstenca gehwone,
> wyrta wynsumra . . .
> . . .   þær he sylf biereð
> in þæt treow innan   torhte frætwe;
> þær se wilda fugel   in þam westenne
> ofer heanne beam   hus getimbreð,
> wlitig ond wynsum . . . .

———

[in the branches, it begins to build, to make a nest. . . . Then far and near it gathers and collects the sweetest and most delightful of herbs and woodflowers to the dwelling. . . . There he himself bears the beautiful treasure to that tree; there the wild bird in the

waste builds a beautiful and delightful house over a high beam/
branch . . . .] (188–203)

The description of the nest's construction is modeled in part on a description of nest building in the Lactantius text:

> construit inde sibi seu nidum sive sepulcrum
> nam perit ut vivat se tamen ipsa creat
> colligit hinc succos et odores divite silva
> quos legit Assyrus quos opulentus Arabs.
>
> ———
>
> [The phoenix then builds herself a nest, or [rather] a tomb; for she
> dies in order to live, though it is she who begets herself. She gathers
> from the rich forest such juices and perfumes here as the Assyrian
> or the wealthy Arab selects.][39]

The description continues:

> cinama dehinc auramque procul spirantis amomi
> congerit et mixto balsama cum folio.
> non casiae mitis non olentis vimen achanti
> nec thuris lachrymae utraque pinguis abest
> his addit teneras nardi pubentis aristas
> et sociat myrrhae pascua grata nimis
> protinus in strato corpus mutabile nido
> vitalique toro membra quieta locat
>
> ———
>
> [Hence she heaps together cinnamon and the odour of the
> far-scented amomum, and balsams with mixed leaves. Neither
> the twig of the mild cassia nor of the fragrant acanthus is absent,
> nor the tears and rich drop of frankincense. To these she adds
> tender ears of flourishing spikenard, and joins the too pleasing
> pastures of myrrh. Immediately she places her body about to be
> changed on the strewed nest, and her quiet limbs on such a couch.]

As O'Donnell has noted, "even in the first half of the poem, where he is
still following Lactantius's original text, the Old English *Phoenix* poet

quite freely adapts and alters the details of his source to bring them into line with a Christian perception of the world," such as omitting the "most intractable references to pagan mythology and religion" (161). It should be added that many of the poet's adaptations also serve to bring the poem into line with Germanic tradition, notably in its selectivity of details in the building of the nest. The Latin poem explicitly links the nest with a tomb, juxtaposing the two structures but leaving the precise connection somewhat open-ended.[40] O'Donnell observes, however, that "the phoenix's nest is frequently referred to in the *Hexameron* and later examples of the Latin *Physiologus* tradition as a *theca*—a word that can be used for 'coffin' or 'sepulchre' in medieval Latin" (168). The Old English poem, on the other hand, conspicuously moves in the opposite direction, focusing on earthly rather than funerary associations. Where the Latin emphasizes the funeralistic nature of the structure, itemizing the ritual items of the nest in great detail, the Old English says only that the bird surrounded itself with "sacred odors and the noblest blossoms of earth" ["þa swetestan somnað ond gædrað wyrta wynsume"] (193–94). The Old English structure is a "hus getimbreð" ["built house"] (202) and an "eardstede" ["habitation"] (195), with *eard* possessing a fairly broad semantic range but always referring to earthly homes in which to live.[41] The poem thus emphasizes the living nature of the nest and its domesticity.

In places the phraseology moves us further still from explicitly funerary associations, with the nesting materials described in terms of heroic treasure. The plants and blossoms that were applied in funerary contexts in Lactantius's poem are described in the Old English rendering as "torhte frætwe" ["bright treasure"] (200), phraseology associated elsewhere in Old English verse both with living birds and with heroic architecture. For instance, the angel sculpture that descends from the temple walls at Christ's command in *Andreas* is similarly described as "torhte gefrætwed" (715). In *Judgment Day I*, heaven itself, a "bold" ["building"] (90) constructed by God, shares similar phraseology:

> þæt is sigedryhten þe þone sele **frætweð**,
> timbreð **torht**lice (92–93)

[That is the victorious lord who adorns the hall, builds it brightly.]

In Riddle 5 we see the feathers of a bird—most likely a swan—likewise described in terms of a hero's arming. The swan's "frætwe" ("trappings"/ "ornaments"; typically understood to refer to feathers) are specifically referenced as "torhte" (6–8).[42] In each case, this pairing of the lexemes *torht* and *fræt* occurs in conjunction with heroic beings and structures, and the attendant shift in emphasis from the funerary to the living in this particular description of the phoenix's nest thus anticipates the joyous renewal of the latter, explicitly Christian, portion of the poem, where the architectonic imagery will continue as Christ shines "heah ofer hro-fas" ["high over roofs"], good works are known throughout the "bliþan ham" ["happy home"] (599), and people dwell without sorrow in "þam wicum"["these dwelling places"] (611). By placing the phoenix's nest in a more heroic light, the poem connects the first portion more clearly with the second, drawing simultaneously from Christian motifs and Germanic heroic traditions. In conjunction with its portrayal of the phoenix as an armed and appropriately adorned hero, the elaboration of the bird's dwelling prior to its death helps anticipate the "wicum" to come after its rebirth, not funerary, but vibrant dwellings to be shared by all.

ARCHITECTURAL METAPHOR AND THE EXETER BOOK RIDDLES

Riddles are generally thought of as a "form of literary game" but also function as "a metaphoric disguise" (Williamson, *Old English Riddles* 26),[43] and throughout the riddles of the Exeter Book architectural im-agery looms large, in some cases as the referent of the metaphor—or tenor—but more often as the vehicle, the metaphorical object or lan-guage applied to that referent. Specifically, built structures seem to be the referent or solution only to Riddles 68 (lighthouse) and 17 (ship),[44] but, as a metaphorical vehicle, architectural imagery is employed to con-vey a much wider range of referents: objects in nature, such as a storm (1), egg (11), fox (13), sun and moon (27), iceberg (31), fish in water (81), and water itself (80); man-made objects, such as a battering ram (51), a weave and loom (54), a bible or book (65, 88), mead (25), music (29), a rake (32), and a beaker (61); or abstract concepts, such as creation (38) or the soul/body dichotomy (41). As I discuss below, architecture serves as a way to metaphorically project the unknown object into a familiar built space, thus reflecting the daily life and social realities of their audiences and their makers. As Foley observes, riddles "seek to understand the rhythms and recurrent destructiveness of natural phenomena, the meaning of religious objects and ideas in a rapidly changing environment, and other problems that seem mysterious or difficult to fully explain" ("How Genres Leak" 91). Throughout the large body of Old English riddles, architecture figures prominently in these explorations, thus giving us further important insights into the conceptual and architectural world of the Anglo-Saxons.

Riddles with Built Structures as Referents

Riddle 68.   The brief two lines that survive of Riddle 68 provide us with the most explicit architectural work—most likely a lighthouse—as a referent:

> þe swa wrætlice be wege stonde
> heah ond hleortorht hæleþum to nytte
>
> ───────
>
> [who stands so boldly by the way,[45] high and cheek-bright,[46]
> of use to men]

While others, most notably Krapp and Dobbie, have seen these lines as a continuation of the previous riddle, Pope argues that a folio is missing between the two riddle fragments, noting, among other features, the first-person verb form of *stonde* in Riddle 68 that contrasts with the third person employed throughout 67. But whether we see these lines as the conclusion to Riddle 67 or as a separate riddle in its own right, they undeniably echo language used to describe valued built structures elsewhere. The description "heah on hleortorht" (2) is reminiscent of the "heah ond horngeap" buildings in *Andreas* and *Beowulf* and the "heah horngestreon" (22) structure of *The Ruin* (see chap. 2). In each of these poems, height is valued in built structures and "hleortorht" personifies and animates the structure in a way consistent with the poetry more widely. The use of

"hæleþum," which means "heroes" as well as more generic "men," makes
the heroic context still more explicit. And if we accept the solution of
"lighthouse" preferred by Williamson, it is worth noting that there were
lighthouses towering above the landscape, such as the Roman lighthouse
that still stands at Dover (fig. 1), and these structures would certainly
have been "hæleþum to nytte" ["of use to heroes/men"] (2). Whatever the
exact nature of the structure, its phraseology clearly places it in a positive and heroic context.

Riddle 17. The even more ambiguous Riddle 17 also reflects elements
valued in built structures but has succeeded better at concealing its referent from modern readers.

Ic on siþe seah . ᚻᚱᚠ
ᚾ hygewloncne,   heafodbeorhtne,

swiftne ofer sælwong   swiþe þrægan.
Hæfde him on hrycge   hildeþryþe—

.ᛏᚠᛗ.   Nægledne rad

ᚠᚷᛗᛈ . . . .

———

[I saw SROH quickly, proud, head-bright, swift over the plain.
It had on its back a battle power, NOM. AGEW came on the nailed
creature. . . .]

Williamson follows the reading "ship," based on the use of runes in
the first two lines, transliterated as "SROH," which is in reverse "HORS,"
thus understood as a "ship" or "sea horse" (188–89).[47] This built structure is said to be "heafodbeorhtne" ["head-bright"] (2), "hygewloncne"
["proud"] (2), and "swiftne" ["swift"] (3), but the only specifically visual
detail we are given is that it is "nægledne" ["nailed"] (78). Evidence from
the Sutton Hoo ship burial indicates that Anglo-Saxon ships (like Viking
ships) were built with the "lower edge of each plank overlapping slightly
the upper edge of the plank below and riveted to it at frequent intervals by

clench-nails of iron, clenched on the inside over an iron washer, the rove"
(Green 49). In such a construction, the nails would be quite pronounced,
making this clue a significant and helpful one for audiences familiar
with ship construction. The descriptive term "nægledne" in the absence of
other identifiable features also suggests that an object being nailed (and
presumably wooden) would have been an especially salient feature to both
the riddler and the poem's Anglo-Saxon audiences,[48] with wooden structures being highly valued in both literary and architectural traditions.

The Use of Architectural Metaphor to Signify Natural Referents

Far more common than riddles of the type above, however, are those with
architectural imagery as the vehicle rather than the tenor, that is, riddles
that use architectural imagery to convey nonarchitectural solutions.

Riddle 1.   As Williamson observes, through riddles poets "celebrate in
human, poetic terms the nonhuman world about them" (*Old English
Riddles* 27). Time after time, this nonhuman world is described specifically in relation to the architectural world of men, with nonhuman,
even inanimate objects described in terms of their surrounding houses,
walls, and halls. The first-person speaker of Riddle 1, for instance, ravages ["reafige"] (6) homes ["folcsalo"] (5) and halls ["ræced"] (6). The
smoke is described as rising "ofer hrofum" ["over roofs"] (7). The effects
on wood, the primary building material of the Anglo-Saxons, are especially pronounced; the being shakes wood ["wudu hrere"] (8) and fells
trees or beams ["beamas fylle"] (9), and in later portions of the poem
the devastation wrought on buildings is even more explicit:

> ...   ac ic eþelstol
> hæleþa hrere;   hornsalu wagiað,
> wera wicstede,   weallas beofiað,
> steape ofer stiwitum. . . . (37–40)
>
> ———
>
> [But I shake the ancestral home of heroes; shake gabled halls,
> the dwellings of men; walls tremble, steep over stewards
> (or householders). . . .][49]

Notably, timber construction, height, steepness, and gables—four characteristics seen again and again as cherished and especially prominent in Old English heroic poetry—are all mentioned here. As discussed earlier, these features are closely associated with the Germanic *comitatus,* the riddle thus implying a threat not only to the buildings but also metonymically to the ideals on which heroic society rests.

The habitat of the being—generally understood as a storm in one of various forms on land or sea—is also described in terms of a building, a place of confinement, where the master "fæstne genearwað" ["confined fast"] the speaker.[50] The speaker here is in bonds ["bende ond clomme"] (45) but not necessarily in prison. Significantly, he travels *with* roof, floor, and wall: while wandering, the being is "holme gehrefed" ["roofed with water"] (10). In contrast to the high roofs emphasized in the world of men, this being seeks instead the lowest part of the metaphorical building, the "garsecges grund" ["floor (or ground) of the ocean"] (18). He drives water to shore against the wall, "wið wealle" (50). Both anthropomorphized and contextualized in a moving dwelling, the storm within his flint gray home ["flintgrægne"] (49) contrasts with and contends against the high and powerful wooden buildings on land. The wooden ["wudu"] (53) ships at sea likewise fight against the stone cliffs ["stanhleoþu"] (56). Awareness of the mostly positive, heroic associations with wood and the more ambiguous, often ominous associations with stone in the poetry more widely (see chap. 2) would no doubt have heightened the terror and conflict depicted in the poem.

Riddle 27. Riddle 27 depicts another type of contest, this time waged between the sun and the moon and, again, using images of built space to convey meaning. The moon, depicted as carrying stolen treasure (i.e., the sun's light) between its horns,[51] has no other desire at this point than to build a secure dwelling for herself:

Walde hyre on þære byrig   bur atimbran,
searwum asettan,   gif hit swa meahte. (5–6)

———

[She wished to build a bower for herself in the stronghold, establish it with skill, if it might be.]

The sun, however, snatches the treasure back, driving the moon away: "Nænig siþþan / wera gewiste þære wihte sið" ["No one afterwards knew where that creature traveled"] (13–14). For the purposes of the metaphor, the moon's desire to build is somewhat extraneous. The analogy works perfectly well without it, as an audience would need to know only of the moon's journey for the solution itself to make sense. The added detail of the moon's desire, however, heightens our sympathies with this seemingly exiled figure, who must now travel against its will to unknown destinations. The architectural aspect of the metaphor is continued with the sun's arrival from "ofer wealles hrof," literally, "over the roof of the wall," but often translated as "over the mountaintop" (Gordon 299; Bosworth 1174), in language appropriate to the solution but potentially limiting with respect to the building imagery as the roof and wall metonymically reference the whole of the man-made social system from which the moon has now been exiled. The two usages of *ham* in lines 4 and 9 further underscore the building imagery. Line 4 shows the moon wishing to go home ["ham"] (6) with light, but after the sun reclaims the treasure, the moon is *forced* to go home ["ham"] (9) but in darkness.[52] The riddle's images of built space thus guide our sympathies and responses as the poem's key characters leave, return to, build, and are exiled from their respective homes.

Riddle 80.   Though the manuscript is badly damaged, Riddle 80's solution as water is so far uncontested. As also in Riddle 81 and Riddle 1, water is here described in terms of a building, though unfortunately in a badly damaged portion of the text:[53] "Biþ stanum bestreþed, stormum [. . . .] / [. . .]len [. . .] timbred weall, . . ." ["It is strewn with stones, with storms . . . timbered wall . . ."] (44–45). While the exact phrasing is impossible to reconstruct, the assumption that these phrases refer in some way to the poem's speaker (water) seems highly likely. As such, the speaker has simultaneous status as "stanum bestreþed" and "timbred weall" (44–45), thus creating a powerful image of both the heroism of a timbered, most likely wooden,[54] wall and the endurance of a structure of stone. In an inversion of the more typical *wordhord,* the speaker here asks his audience to "hordword onhlid" ["reveal the treasure-word"] (54). Decoding the word-treasure here requires an understanding of the encoded associ-

Architectural Metaphor and Metonymy | 137

ations within the structure that serves as the metaphorical vehicle, stone and timbered walls.

Riddle 81.   In the relatively unambiguous Riddle 81 ("fish and river"), the speaker also describes himself in relation to a physical dwelling. The fish dwells in "min sele" ["my hall"] (1). In riddlic paradox, this hall moves swiftly even while the speaker is at rest, yet its resident remains always inside. The speaker cryptically explains, "ic him in wunige" ["I dwell in him"], and he says that he will die if separated from the dwelling: "gif wit unce gedælað me bið dead witod" (7). The choice of a hall, or *sele,* to metaphorically represent the water without which the fish will die speaks not only to the value of water to the fish but also to the importance of the hall to men. Interestingly, though the motifs of house and houseguest, speaker and silent companion, and two comrades bound on a journey in the opening lines all may be attributed to the influence of Symphosius, lines 3b–7, which include this hall reference, "are altogether new" (Williamson, *Old English Riddles* 374). The additional lines and the architectural imagery ground the metaphor within a more distinctly Anglo-Saxon worldview in which the hall and its inhabitant are seen as working together in a *comitatus* relationship.[55] In the context of the poetry more widely, the "sele" is a place of refuge and order, without which Anglo-Saxon culture could not survive. A society without a hall is by analogy a fish out of water.

Riddle 13.   The animal (usually solved as "fox")[56] of Riddle 13 dwells in a "wic" ["house," "dwelling-place"],[57] a metaphorical home complete with doors and window. The speaker dreads the time when a "gæste" will come "to durum minum" ["to my doors"] (10–11) and fears that he will stalk the family in their room, "geruman" (16). The speaker plans to tunnel "þurh steapne beorg" ["through the steep stronghold"] (18) and ultimately "þurh dunþyrel" ["through the hill hole"; lit., "hill-window"] (21). Where roofs and walls are frequently referenced in Old English verse depictions of buildings, references to windows are exceedingly rare. The poet thus seems to be going out of his way to develop the architectural metaphor through the reference to a "hill-window." After safely depositing her brood, the mother no longer fears the predator and goes to meet her foe in battle on a hilltop, a location also described in architectural terms, "hylles hrof" ["roof of a hill"] (27).

The riddle clearly establishes the image of an animal's subterranean lair, but even underground dwellings for humans would not have been unknown to the Anglo-Saxons, with elaborately built Iron Age fogous[58] scattered throughout Cornwall and souterrains to the north of England in Scotland.[59] *Fogou*, Cornish for cave, refers to any of numerous artificial underground passageways—many of which are still accessible today—built of dry walling and roofed with lintel stones. Though their specific purpose is unknown, these structures are usually in close proximity to prehistoric settlements and typically have more than one entryway. Such fogous as that found at Carn Euny (fig. 12) evoke a structure not unlike that of Riddle 13. This particular passage is 66 feet long, 33 feet of which are still covered today. In places the height of the passageway is over 5 feet, with a width of over 6 feet. This fogou also includes a passageway to a circular chamber 10 feet in height and averaging 15 feet in diameter, now unroofed but probably once domed (Clark 35–44). The Cornish fogou at Carn Euny is far from an anomaly; such underground structures also exist at Boscaswell, Halligey, Trewardreva, Chysauster, and other locations. Irish souterrains and Scottish earth houses further attest to the possibilities of underground dwellings. And though the riddle was unlikely meant to evoke a specific location, underground human dwellings paralleling the animal's den may not have been wholly unfamiliar to the Anglo-Saxons. That medieval persons found their way to these dwellings is evidenced by the fragments of pottery and sherds dated to the period (Clark 136, 145). With such built spaces on—or, more precisely, under—the landscape, the description in Riddle 13 is potentially appropriate not only for the riddle's tenor (animal in den) but also for the vehicle (mother in underground built home).

In addition, as with other poetic underground dwellings—such as the habitat of *The Wife's Lament* (see chap. 5) or even *Andreas*'s underground prison (see chap. 3)—the sense of danger within the underground refuge of this poem is palpable. Irving has noted that this riddle presents a potentially "non-heroic" but realistic moment of battle: "In this riddle we share the experience of being outmanned and cornered: you hide in your house from a fearsome enemy who intends to kill all your children; you fight desperately to save them, first by racing through underground tunnels and then at last by savagely attacking the invader" ("Heroic Experience" 202). It is precisely through the detailed description of the house—complete with doors and windows that provide barriers and escape paths for the speaker—that we are able to empathize with the speaker in the way that Irving describes. Through this imagery we can imagine ourselves inside and identify with the creature, "fighting any way we can for the survival of those we love" (204).

Riddles 11 and 25.   The chickens of Riddle 11 are also described in terms of their (human) dwellings. We are told "fell hongedon / sweotol ond gesyne on seles wæge / anra gehwylces" ["a robe, fine and well-seen, hung on the wall of the hall, one for each"] (3–5). The reference seems to be to the membranes of the eggshells. Williamson notes that "anyone who has seen the newly discarded 'house' of a young chick with its 'skin' hanging on the wall can attest to the accuracy of the description" (*Old English Riddles* 169).[60] Since we are in fact able to see an eggshell and attest to the description's accuracy, solving the riddle in the most natural way possible poses little challenge.

Even the honey of the bees in Riddle 25 (typically solved as "mead") is described in relation to its architecture, as buzzing wings bear the speaker "under hrofes hleo" ["under the protection of a roof"] (5). Here and in each of the riddles discussed above, man-made space becomes a way to explain and understand natural phenomena.[61] Riddles with referents in the (Anglo-Saxon) human world rather than the natural world can thus be more ambiguous for modern readers and more difficult to untangle.

The Use of Architectural Metaphor to Signify Man-Made Referents

Riddle 50.   As with the nature riddles, riddles with man-made objects as referents depend heavily on architectural metaphor, and objects are frequently described (or describe themselves) in relation to the buildings that they inhabit. Riddle 50, for instance, has been solved as "flail," "broom," "well buckets," or "yoke of oxen" (Williamson, *Old English Riddles* 295) and begins with two "ræpingas" ["criminals" or "prisoners"] being carried into a hall, "in ræced" (1). The image of the hall is then reinforced in the next line, as the two prisoners are bound together "under hrof sales" ["under the roof of a hall"] (2). As discussed in chapter 3, prisoners were more often held in residences (or churches) than in dedicated prisons, a fact that helps us appreciate the riddle at both levels more fully. The metaphor works precisely because actual Anglo-Saxon halls could be both spaces for housework (performed by such proposed solutions as buckets or brooms) and spaces for prisoners, "ræpingas."

Riddles Relying on the Positive Valence of Wood (51, 53, 54, 88).   In chapter 1 we saw heroic associations with wood throughout the body of Old English poetry, in halls such as the renowned Heorot as well as the wooden elements present in otherwise stone structures such as *The Ruin.* In Riddles 51, 53, 54, and 88, we see additional hall imagery and more specific references to wood and the social contexts referenced by this construction material. Although these four riddles do not describe architectural works themselves, they are nonetheless important for my analysis because they demonstrate that timber as a construction material was valued beyond purely architectural purposes and was closely associated with the ethos of the Anglo-Saxon hall. Not only are the wooden halls heroic in the context of the riddles, but numerous wooden objects employed in the hall and by its warriors are made to elicit sympathies, admiration, and wonder. Riddle 51, for instance, begins with a description of "on bearwe beam hlifian" ["in the forest, a tree towering"] (1). The tree is described in explicitly positive terms, "tanum torhtne" ["bright with branches"] (2), "wudu weaxende" ["blooming wood"] (3), and "on wynne" ["in joy"] (2). But when its savage ["aglachade"] (5) fate turns, it is slashed and wounded, with its head bound in chains. The object now becomes a warrior fighting alongside another warrior in a *comitatus* relationship: "Oft hy an yste strudon / hord ætgædre" ["Often they plunder the hoard together"] (10–11). And though the riddle's solution is ambiguous—"battering ram" being the most widely accepted solution and others including "spear" and "cross"—there is no questioning the poem's reverence and respect for wood, noble not only in the forest but also when serving even as an enslaved warrior for men.[62]

Riddle 53 is more problematic in terms of its solution, though uncertain proposals such as weapon chest, sword rack, and cross have been made. Again, however, the riddler's respect for wood is never in doubt. The speaker values the wood for its connection to the cross, which is described as a ladder, "hlædre," out of the "helwara burg" ["stronghold of hell"]. Next, the speaker openly praises the wood's composition:

> . . .   Ic þæs beames mæg
> eaþe for eorlum   æþelu secgan;
> þær wæs hlin ond acc   ond se hearda iw
> ond se fealwa holen (7–10)
>
> ———
>
> [I am able to say before men the lineage of this beam; there was maple and oak, hard yew and burnished holly]

The combination of woods listed is precisely the problem for modern readers. Williamson notes the "structural weakness of such a hybrid" (*Old English Riddles* 301), and the object would certainly be made structurally unsound by such a composite; however, the juxtaposition of multiple types of the esteemed wood would have strengthened the power it had poetically by linking the object with not just one but several valued construction materials. Modern readers have understandable difficulty rising to the speaker's challenge to "wordum secgan hu se wudu hatte" ["say in words how this wood is called"] (16), but we should have no trouble grasping the speaker's admiration for its composition.

As with Riddle 53, Riddle 54 juxtaposes the tree in its natural form to the wooden object in the hall. The solution accepted by Williamson, Krapp and Dobbie, and others is that of a weaver's web and loom. The "holt" ["wood"] (3) or "wudu" ["wood"] (5) describing the object in its form as a tool is contrasted with that of the tree in the lines that follow (9–10): "Treow wæs getenge   þam þær torhtan stod / leafum bihongen" ["A tree was near, which stood bright, hung with leaves"]. The speaker of Riddle 88 (often solved as "book") also connects the "tree in the wood" ["beam on holte"] (1) with a man-made object that seems to be parchment: "wifes sond / gold on geardum" ["message of woman / gold in dwellings"] (3–4). The voices speaking in these poems suggest that the tree is highly revered and that the tree in its natural form was never far from the minds of those who used man-made wooden implements.

Riddle 58.   Like other riddles we have seen, Riddle 58 employs the language of buildings in its contrast of the natural world to the human. The uncertain speaker of the riddle (possibly a reed pen or rune staff)[63] describes itself as being "sæwealle neah" ["near a seawall"] (1) in its "frumstaþole." Although "frumstaþole" (3) is typically translated as something like "first state" or "original place,"[64] its literal meaning, "first-foundation," allows the compound to operate in conjunction with the seawalls to help complete the visual image of this metaphorical space. This original seawall home is then contrasted with the speaker's habitation, the hall; this enigmatic object "speaks," mouthless, over the meadbenches of a hall, "ofer meodubence muðleas sprecan" (9). This riddle is sometimes read as part of *The Husband's Message,* which directly follows Riddle 58 in the Exeter Book manuscript. In this interpretation, the speaker of both is understood as a speaking rune staff. The speaker of Riddle 58 describes itself as having been "be sonde" ["by sand"] (1) and "æt merefaroþe" ["ocean stream"] (2), a logical origin for the speaker of *The Husband's Message,* who also travels across water "on ceolþele" ["on a ship deck"] (9) to deliver his message. The conflation of man-made and natural structures offers a solution for a crux in *The Husband's Message,* specifically, the ambiguity earlier in the poet at line 8, with the word "hofu" ["dwellings"]. Klinck notes that "over the high dwellings" "appears not to fit the nautical context" and suggests that "possibly a scribe mistook the rare 'hafu,' 'seas,' for the more common *hofu*" (201). Though many, such as Treharne (81), do emend to "hafu" and translate as "over the high seas," the emendation seems unnecessary given the frequent conflation of man-made and natural structures in Old English verse. For the poem's inanimate speaker, a traveling rune stick on a ship, the high seas would in fact be a dwelling, eliminating any semantic conflict. Given the much-noted connection of *The Husband's Message* to Riddle 58, the sea as metaphorical dwelling would not be at all far-fetched.

Another connection between the two poems lies in the hall imagery; where the speaker of Riddle 58 delivers messages "muðleas" ["mouthless"] across the mead benches of a hall, the speaker in *The Husband's Message* reminds its recipient of a former time "þenden git moston   on meoduburgum   / eard weardiagan,   an lond bugan" ["when you were allowed to dwell in mead fortresses, in a home, inhabit one land"] (17–18) with "se þisne beam agrof" ["the one who carved this wood"] (13).

Whether or not the speaker of Riddle 58 is the same as that of *The Husband's Message*, the speakers of both poems invite us to see their referents in human terms and accomplish their dual senses in part through the images of the man-made spaces that permeate these poems.

Riddle 32. Shifting our attention to the outside of man-made buildings, the speaker of Riddle 32 opens with a description of the riddlic "creature" ["wiht"] in relation to man-made buildings: "Ic wiht geseah in wera burgum" ["I saw a creature in/near houses of men"] (1). Further, it "wæþeð geond weallas" ["hunts around walls"].[65] The "wiht," solved by most editors as "rake," is anthropomorphized in terms of a hunting animal but placed physically in terms of a building, once again underscoring the importance of architecture in the riddling genre and in the poetry more widely. The speaker of Riddle 12 (solved by all major editors as "horn") likewise describes itself in terms of the building it inhabits, "wlitig on wage" ["beautiful on the wall"] (12). With details provided so selectively, the prominence of building references suggests the great significance that the features chosen for inclusion were likely to have had in the minds of poets and audiences alike.

Riddles 29 and 61. The haunting and beautiful musical instrument described in Riddle 29 (solved by most modern editors as "bagpipes")[66] is explicitly placed in the hall as well. First the speaker says that "ic seah sellic þing singan on ræcede" ["I saw a wonderful thing sing in the hall"] (3). Likewise the speaker of Riddle 61 ("beaker") makes two references to its physical location within a building, first indirectly through "seledreame" ["hall-joy," 1], a compound that is followed by a more explicit reference to its placement "on cofan" ["in a chamber"] (4). The two together contrast the communal life in the hall with the more intimate space "on cofan," where the speaker is held and kissed by men.[67] The two terms for buildings heighten the contrast around which the poem revolves as they provide crucial clues to the solution. Like the object described in Riddle 65, the riddles discussed here speak to us without mouths ["nænne muð hafað"] (6), yet they do speak. And to hear we must learn as much as possible about the rich and complex world of associations in which they were wrought.

Riddle 38. While tangible referents are far more common in the Old English riddles, in a small number the tenor is more abstract. Like the figurative expressions addressed by Toelken, some of the Anglo-Saxon riddles "bring up strong associations of value and response based on cultural correspondences and human experiences that relate a concrete pictorial image with its abstract referent" (*Morning Dew* 16). In the Old English riddles, the "concrete pictorial image" is often architectural in nature. The creator, "scyppend," of Riddle 38 rules specifically with columns, "wreð-stuþum," a rare usage in Old English poetry here most likely translating the "columnis" of Aldhelm's "Creatura."[68] Once this noble architectural space has been established as the ruler's, the "wraðscrafu" ["evil den"] (41) "under eorþan" ["under the earth"] (40) provides a clear contrast to the more glorious pillars early in the poem. These two compounds are rare, especially in the poetry, heightening the significance of the choices. The juxtaposition of the two similar-sounding (if not etymologically related) compounds *wreðstuþum* and *wraðscrafu* helps link the two realms above and below the earth described in this complex poem. Though the underground reference does have precedent in the Latin, the reference is very different in nature: "inferior terris" ["beneath the earth"] prompts the reference to an underground structure, but it is the Old English poet's specific lexical choices that highlight the underlying rhetoric through architectural imagery and contrast.

Of course, architectural metaphor is prominent not only in Old English verse, but in medieval culture more widely. David Cowling notes that in late medieval and early modern French literature, for instance, "developments in real architectural styles . . . are not reflected in descriptions of buildings in literary texts in any clearly demonstrable manner" (7). Instead, he argues, "writers exploited the symbolic significance and traditional resonances of buildings, using them to structure narratives and/or present knowledge in ordered form" (6–7). Such "allegorical architecture," he explains, "triggers a reading that draws on a range of commonly used metaphors to arrive at an interpretation whose complexity and sophistication may surprise" (1). In like manner, Old English poets exploit distinctly Anglo-Saxon "traditional resonances of buildings" through the extended metaphor of Christ as foundation and cornerstone in *Advent Lyric I,* the "wall" of water complete with roof and foundation in the Old English *Exodus,* the foundations Juliana encourages her listeners to build in their hearts, the building of the nest in *The Phoenix,* and the extensive use of architectural metaphor in the Exeter Book riddles. Even when such texts can be shown to derive from classical or biblical sources, their included architectural metaphors are clearly grounded in an Anglo-Saxon oral poetics and material culture, demonstrating a concept of built space that can be used to understand objects past and present and illuminate natural phenomena, man-made structures, and even intangible abstractions. These overlaps between past and present, natural and man-made are even more pronounced in the Old English elegies, the focal point of the next chapter.

APPENDIX: NUMBERING SYSTEM CORRESPONDENCES

To provide easy reference, the following list shows correspondences between Williamson's numbering system of the Exeter Book riddles and Krapp and Dobbie's earlier system. Except where noted below, Muir's edition of the *Exeter Anthology* (M) follows Krapp and Dobbie's numbering from *ASPR*.

$$W1 = KD1-3$$
$$W5 = KD7$$
$$W11 = KD13$$
$$W13 = KD15$$
$$W17 = KD19$$
$$W25 = KD27$$
$$W27 = KD29$$
$$W29 = KD31$$
$$W31 = KD33$$
$$W32 = KD34$$
$$W38 = KD40$$
$$W41 = KD43$$
$$W50 = KD52$$
$$W51 = KD53$$
$$W53 = KD55$$
$$W54 = KD56$$
$$W58 = KD60$$
$$W61 = KD63$$
$$W65 = KD67$$
$$W68 = KD70.5-6 = M70$$
$$W80 = KD84 = M83$$
$$W81 = KD85 = M84$$
$$W87 = KD91 = M90$$
$$W88 = KD92 = M91$$

CHAPTER FIVE

(RE)CONSTRUCTIONS OF MEMORY

A visitor to any single historic site on the British landscape is likely to encounter traces of numerous cultures and time periods more or less simultaneously. The architecture of Dover Castle, for example, witnesses the convergence of multiple historic periods: a Roman lighthouse (fig. 1) stands adjacent to St. Mary's Saxon church, beneath which lie wartime tunnels from the twentieth century. St. Wystan's Church at Repton, Derbyshire, features an Anglo-Saxon chancel and crypt (figs. 24 and 10), gravestones damaged during periods of Viking destruction, post-Conquest medieval walls and tower, and numerous additions and adaptations representing every point since. Moving through such multilayered spaces gives a perspective we do not always sense from reading architectural surveys that typically treat Roman, Saxon, and Norman archaeology as fairly discrete periods and styles. Perhaps even more than modern-day visitors, the Anglo-Saxons themselves encountered architecture as dynamic spaces that evidenced their complex and varied histories, with construction features testifying to a wide array of Celtic, Scandinavian, Roman, and Anglo-Saxon traditions. The poetry produced during this period did likewise, and Old English elegiac verse in particular includes some of the most detailed and multivalent architectural descriptions in Anglo-Saxon literature. In poetic description, as on the landscape, built space provided a powerful focal point for both personal and historical memory, and the poignancy and evocativeness of Old English elegy derive precisely from the conflux of multiple traditions, often within a single syncretic space. The speakers of *The Wanderer* and *The Ruin* meditating on past inhabitants of "eald enta geweorc" ["old work of giants"], the woman dwelling beneath an oak tree in *The Wife's Lament* recalling her personal trials, and the grieving father walking through an empty hall in *Beowulf,* for instance, all require us to make connections across time and through space and thus fully engage the varied cultural heritage of the Anglo-Saxon world, a heritage often conveyed through architectural diversity and, in many cases, ambiguity as well.

Previous chapters addressed concepts of history in more explicitly narrative contexts. This chapter offers a closer examination of lyric verse, specifically, the use of traditional architectonics in elegiac poems to direct emotional response to past and present events. It explores conceptions of history projected onto past generations through images of ancient ruins as well as personal histories that become localized through architectural imagery.

Such analysis necessitates an understanding of not only how the Anglo-Saxons conceived of earlier generations of Roman and Celtic inhabitants and the structures they left behind but also how modern readers have been conditioned to respond to verbal and material artifacts from these various points in time and how we see them in relation to one another. Ernst Gombrich explains that "all thinking is sorting, classifying" (301), and in order to understand the cognitive categories underlying the expressive Old English verse, it is first important to recognize how modern classification schemes for the analysis of this verse have been formulated and how assumptions inherent in these schemes inevitably affected subsequent readings. As shown in chapter 1, material and poetic arts in Anglo-Saxon culture manifest tremendous overlap, with verbal and nonverbal modes of expression tapping into many of the same cognitive constructs in producing and interpreting texts and visual arts alike. In contrast, disciplinary divisions in twentieth- and twenty-first-century academic contexts tend toward analytic categories that foreground points of difference.[1] The modern disconnect between material and verbal discourse thus leaves us with substantial interpretive gaps, with the result that modern classifications of poetic genre, building type, and historical period all potentially obscure meaning-laden connections in surviving Old English verse.

CLASSIFICATION AND MEMORY

Modern architectural classification schemes have done much to delineate features of the various building traditions in England's history but have also—if inadvertently—created categories that inevitably limit how we understand the equally important overlaps and intersections among these traditions. Just as with poetry, serious attention to Anglo-Saxon architecture began in earnest in the nineteenth century, and these early discussions of architecture made sharp delineations between the Roman and the Germanic, divisions that continue to the present day. As the terminology assigned to the architecture indicates, the "Romanesque" buildings of the Anglo-Norman period were understood as the continuation of earlier, pre-Germanic Roman construction, thus glossing over Germanic timber construction, which for the most part was seen as an entirely separate, and generally inferior, entity.

In medieval architecture, the groundbreaking work of Gerard Baldwin Brown did much to shape the categorical constructs employed in the emerging field. For Brown, one of the earliest scholars devoted to the study of the period, the lack of linear continuity in architectural traditions was an enormous source of frustration. Anglo-Saxon "work," he argued, "is wanting in consistency and system, and exhibits . . . an alternation of brilliant or at any rate promising achievement with crude and tentative production" (1). While he urged his readers to look at Anglo-Saxon architecture on its own terms rather than seek origins in European prototypes, he nonetheless diminished the relative value of native construction with his critiques of the "somewhat uncertain and even haphazard efforts" at this architecture and observed a "logical evolution" in the development of Norman work that is absent in the Anglo-Saxon period (4). The "ruthless conquerors," he claimed, "were quite fully conscious of the superiority of their own forms and methods, and the more important Saxon buildings fared badly at their hands, but at the same time in lesser buildings they took over into their own practice some of the Saxon arrangements and details" (5).

Following this early pattern, most treatments of Anglo-Saxon architecture—in academic studies as well as in practical guides and overviews—have continued this sharp division, leaving aside discussions of Romano-British works and focusing instead on Germanic origins and

Scandinavian parallels.[2] For instance, J. M. Richards characterizes Anglo-Saxon buildings as "the first intelligible buildings erected by the English for the English," since "the Roman buildings that preceded these were the product of an alien culture" (foreword). David Watkin's *English Architecture* makes similar choices in omitting Romano-British works, and even those studies that attempt a more comprehensive treatment of buildings on Britain's landscape treat works from different periods in separate chapters. Lucy Archer's clear and concise *Architecture in Britain and Ireland, 600–1500,* for example, devotes separate chapters and sections to the topics "Prehistoric Beginnings," "The Roman Legacy," and the "Saxon Period," with little if any discussion of possible crossovers.

Where nineteenth- and twentieth-century discussions of architecture tend to distance Anglo-Saxon building from the Roman world, analyses of Anglo-Saxon literary genre categories—which were developed somewhat earlier[3]—tend toward the opposite direction, emphasizing instead classical associations and affinities. In his work, *Illustrations of Anglo-Saxon Poetry,* W. D. Conybeare included an "Arranged Catalogue of All the Extant Relics of Anglo Saxon Poetry" (lxxvi–lxxxvi), the impact of which is not to be underestimated. This catalogue not only made editions of many poems widely available and provided lineation that made Anglo-Saxon prosodic structures more readily apparent; it also made the poetry more accessible by organizing it into a system of classification that was naturally indebted to other classification systems already in place based on categories of classical genres, such as hymns (lxxix), odes, and epitaphs (lxxx).[4]

However, both sets of models in this early scholarship address Anglo-Saxon literature and architecture through conceptions of time and space that are more ours than the Anglo-Saxons'. Looking backward to Latin and Greek for generic precursors to Old English literature seeks a linear chronology more typical of a literate than an oral traditional culture. Similarly, approaches in archaeology that sever Anglo-Saxon methods of building from those of Roman Britain deny the plurality inherent in the Anglo-Saxon world. Indeed, all such classification systems are potentially divisive, and in a severe critique of polarizing vocabulary in architectural studies—such as Western/non-Western, high-style/vernacular—Güslüm Baydar Nalbantoğlu sees that "there is no pure and virtuous space outside our present categories. The idea, then, is to accept the porousness and malleability of boundaries and identity categories and be aware of their strategic significance" (26). Accordingly, she works from the premise that "architecture, as an identity category, can only be defined in relation to an entire network of other identity categories" (20).

Over the years, conceptions of genre in folklore and literature scholarship have increasingly viewed verbal arts in terms of similar "networks," taking account of the variability and change inherent in the production of traditional art forms in order to allow for productive discussion across disciplinary and generic boundaries. In his 1976 study of folklore and genre, for instance, Dan Ben-Amos observed that when "folklore became a discipline, and its research assumed scientific garb, we took these existing terms and canonized them as scientific concepts. We transferred them from the context of 'natural langue' in which ambiguities, ambivalences, and multiplicity of meanings appear to reign, and attempted to consider them terms in the language of science whose meanings are clear and specific referents" (30). Johannes A. Huisman has further noted that the terminology of *genera* itself "grew out of the system of the biological sciences" (124), a development that has affected numerous fields within the humanities. But despite this growing awareness of our somewhat arbitrary categories and the fluidity of cultural and temporal categories, the initial lines that were drawn in the fields of Anglo-Saxon architecture and literature inevitably continue to inform perceptions of both buildings and poetry, with one of the many results being an exacerbation of the disciplinary distance between literature studies—which emphasizes classical heritage—and archaeological studies—which emphasizes the native.

In actuality, influences from multiple cultural traditions and across vast periods of time are quite visibly evident in the architecture of the period, as even a few examples can indicate. The *Anglo-Saxon Chronicle* tells us that Reculver was given to Bassa by King Egbert in 669 to build a church, though the site had had a long history of occupation prior to this grant. The ruined buildings of Roman shore forts "afforded a handy source of building materials" (Kerr and Kerr, *Anglo-Saxon Sites* 194), including Roman bricks, tile, and stone. With its Anglo-Saxon design and Roman materials, the new building thus began its life as an example of the cultural syncretism that pervades literary and architectural art of its period. The basic plan of the church was then extended in the eighth century with the addition of a western porch (Kerr and Kerr, *Anglo-Saxon Sites* 194), a development further illustrating the dynamic nature of ever-adapting building practices. Evidencing syncresis of another nature, the church of St. John at Escomb reflects a continuity from Celtic timber buildings (Kerr and Kerr, *Anglo-Saxon Sites* 36), in addition to its reuse of Roman work (36). (See chap. 3.) Focusing on the reuse of Roman materials specifically, Tim Eaton argues that in the construction of the church at Hexham, most likely built with Roman masonry, Wilfrid "was advertising a direct link between himself and the Romans that preceded him, thus promoting the idea that the Church was the natural successor to the power and authority of ancient Rome."[5] In each of these instances, we see meaningful and self-conscious usages of the past in contemporary construction practice.

As with the architecture of the period, a tendency to synthesize multiple traditions and to conflate various time periods is manifest within Old English verse also. Due in part to the tradition's dynamic and somewhat fluid nature, the poems themselves and the buildings depicted within them often defy easy modern classification. For instance, the genres of the poems in the Exeter Book, most often dated to the latter part of the tenth century, and no later than 1072,[6] have long been the subject of debate, in large part because, as discussed above, the generic boundaries being imposed by nineteenth- and early-twentieth-century scholars were not designed to reflect Anglo-Saxon poetic categories but were instead borrowed from studies of Greek and Roman poetry. The lack of titles in the manuscript combined with a lack of knowledge as to how and why the poems were composed and collected have made attempts at classification and analysis difficult tasks indeed.

Adopted from terminology applied to classical poetry, the term *elegy* itself has been especially problematic, despite its continued use for the seven or so poems from the Exeter Book categorized under this label.[7] As Klinck observes, "The poems considered here are not elegies in the Classical sense of compositions in elegiac metre ... nor in the tradition of the English pastoral elegies ... such as Milton's *Lycidas*" (11), and because of this inherent problem with the term, a number of scholars have variously redefined *elegy* specifically for application to Old English poetry. Among the most widely accepted definitions for some time has been Stan-ley Greenfield's: "a relatively short reflective or dramatic poem embodying a contrasting pattern of loss and consolation, ostensibly based upon a specific personal experience or observation, and expressing an attitude towards that experience" ("The Old English Elegies" 94). More recently, Klinck has offered a definition based on her analysis of the poetry as "a discourse arising from a powerful sense of absence, or separation from what is desired, expressed through characteristic words and themes, and shaping itself by echo and leitmotif into a poem that moves from disquiet to some kind of acceptance" (246).[8] But what is shared by these and all other mainstream definitions is an emphasis on reflection. And corresponding to this reflective tone is an acute awareness of space.

The *Seafarer,* for instance, has been the subject of great debate, receiving various generic designations such as "elegy, allegory, an ascetic journey of expiation (a *peregrinatio*), and a medieval planctus" (Foley, *Traditional Oral Epic* 19). The juxtaposition of traditional and nontraditional patterns, Foley observes, has led scholars to "accuse the *Seafarer* of inconsistency or mixed modes" (19),[9] but we would do better to see the poem instead as a "dynamic work of art" ("Genre(s) in the Making" 694), with its dynamism lying partially in its negotiation of various spaces: the hall the speaker has left behind, his new home on the sea, and his hoped for home with God. Through traditional language and imagery, as we shall see below, this collocation of spaces channels the speaker's meditations on his past as well as the contemplations of his future.

Wulf and Eadwacer, because of the ambiguous narrative context established in the poem, has also been read productively through multiple generic lenses, not only as an elegy, but also as a woman's song (Desmond), a riddle (Eliason), a wen charm (Fry), and a psychodramatic monologue (Mattox). Just as enigmatic are the spaces in which the narrative occurs, where isolation is described specifically in terms of physical space: "Wulf is on iege, ic on oþerre" ["Wulf is on one island; I on another"] (4). Even *The Wife's Lament,* which Greenfield has viewed as "the most pronouncedly elegiac poem" of the seven Exeter Book elegies ("Old English Elegies" 119), has drawn ample controversy as to its generic classification. Patricia Belanoff connects the poem with *Frauenlieder,* a genre of Germanic women's songs, popular rather than courtly (194).[10] Faye Walker-Pelkey, on the other hand, bases her interpretation on connections with the riddles in the Exeter Book and argues that *The Wife's Lament* is not a lament at all but a riddle. Such controversy points toward complexities in this poem that can best be dealt with by remaining open to multiple registers operating simultaneously within any given poem and "view[ing] each of these labels as apposite rather than as all inclusive" (Foley, *Traditional Oral Epic* 19). In its phraseology and content the poem suggests multiple generic registers and, with these registers, multiple architectural spaces.

This heightened importance of spatial concerns provides specific motivation, then, for understanding the buildings depicted in the Exeter Book elegies as more than simple exercises in ecphrasis. Instead, these poems bear witness to multiple building types erected at various periods in this area's complex history and provide us with some of the most detailed architectural descriptions that the poetry has to offer. As Nicholas Howe observes, "the most vivid descriptions of landscape in Old English poetry . . . are found in moments of extremity or crisis" ("Landscape" 108), and these are precisely the moments at the center of elegiac verse.

As discussed in chapter 1, Mary Carruthers's work with medieval memory has shown architectural space to be a common and productive mnemonic for storing information, a mental image of a physical inventory. Old English elegiac poetry shows that architectural space can serve a similar function with personal and communal memories as well. Buildings in the Old English elegies provide real-world spaces within which to situate and focus abstract concepts addressed in the elegies, such as life's transience and human grief. These physical spaces provide visual images within which to locate—and, in some cases, project—memories. Through traditional imagery and phraseology of various built structures, Anglo-Saxon poetry thus negotiates past, present, and future.

Of course the use of space to navigate memory is perhaps more readily apparent to us today in larger narrative contexts such as *Beowulf*, where elegiac motifs can be embedded and then more fully articulated than in most Old English lyric verse. For instance, the Lament of the Bereaved Father in *Beowulf* (2444–62), where the father moves throughout his hall contrasting the idealized space with its painful emptiness, provides an excellent example of how space localizes memory and emotion.[11] Here, the bereaved father mourns while wishing for an heir to be with him "burgum in innan" ["in the strongholds"] (2452), and he gazes with sorrow on his son's "bure" ["bower"] (2455), the "winsele westne, windge reste" ["deserted winehall, windy lodging"] (2456). As with many of the Exeter Book elegies, the significance of built space is at this point in the poem underscored by the explicit absence of music and joy in places where they should be found: "nis þær hearpan sweg, / gomen in geardum" ["there is no harp tune, joy in the yards"] (2458–59). The lament then goes on to observe the inappropriateness of the father's physical space for his current bereaved situation: "þuhte him eall to rum, / wongas ond wicstede" ["it all seemed to him too spacious, the fields and the dwellings"] (2461–62), and the scene closes with the father's departure to his own chamber: "Gewiteð þonne on sealman" ["He goes then to his chamber"] (2460).

The embedded lament thus provides an efficient way to order some of the many layers of memory and history in the poem and understand these events in relation to one another. Beowulf's speech draws on this exemplum in order to establish the helplessness of Hrethel after the loss of his son. Like the father whose son has been hanged for committing an offense against his king, Hrethel was unable to take revenge against the man who killed his own son, because the death was unintentionally caused by another son. In the exemplum, the father cannot violate the higher law of the king, and in Beowulf's story, Hrethel is bound by familial ties to his son who is also the murderer. The lament thus has an important function in the narrative in explaining Hrethel's situation, which in turn parallels Beowulf's own sense of helplessness in confronting the dragon. The elegiac register employed here evokes all the connotations of exile, and the hall through which the grieving father leads us provides a physical space within which to focus all of these layers of grief and loss. Although we do not have such a narrative context for the Exeter Book elegies, the use of architectural spaces to negotiate memory are evident nonetheless, most markedly in *The Ruin, The Wanderer,* and *The Wife's Lament.*

THE RUIN

The Ruin, a work discussed briefly in chapters 2 and 4, is the Old English poem that has by far been the most widely discussed in terms of its architecture. Although it is most often classified in the category of elegy, the architectural and traditional contexts supplied by other "nonelegiac" heroic poetry such as *Beowulf* and *Andreas* also often provide us with solutions to challenges posed by the poem for modern readers. The exact nature of the structure at the center of poem's description has been widely debated, each theory offering productive insights regarding the poem's associative meanings. In the discussion that follows, I first explore architectural contexts posited for the poem and gaps caused by disparities between the poem's description and any likely architectural reality. Next, I turn to an examination of phraseology employed in architectural description in relation to not only other poems classified as elegies but also the larger body of Old English verse. In numerous cases, architectural anomalies can be explained in terms of traditional referentiality, where associative meanings underlying specific architectural characteristics or descriptive phraseology supersede physical accuracy.

A prevailing view regarding the structure being described has been Roman Bath, a theory supported by Leslie (22–28) on the basis of the springs "hat on hreþre" ["hot in its bosom"] (41a) and the stream that "hate wearp / widan wylme" ["hotly gushed in wide surging"] (38b–39a).[12] For Leslie, the circular pool, or "hringmere" (45), likely refers to the cold plunge circular bath lying to the west of the site's rectangular Great Bath, with its natural hot water from springs below. The tiles in the poem correspond to "debris of tiled roofage" found during excavations of the Great Bath (Leslie 25) and now on display in the Roman Bath visitor's center.

Alternative suggestions for the structure include man-made baths along Hadrian's Wall, with supporters such as Stephen Herben arguing against the prevailing view that the hot baths of the poem must be natural and instead positing that the poet "could scarcely have missed the function of the caldarium at Chesters with its boiler and flues" (38). (See fig. 6.) In addition, he sees the "walanwirum wundrum togædre" ["wire strips wound together"] (20) as "a type of Roman construction illustrated by the bridge at Chollerford where the stones were bound together by long iron rods set in lead" (38), and "wigsteal" [lit., "war place" or "idol place"] (27),[13] he says, could refer to "a place of pagan worship," such as the temples dedicated to Mithra (fig. 13) at locations along the wall such as Carrawburh (39). Also countering the Bath theory, Gareth Dunleavy (113) has argued for Roman Chester as a location, the red sandstone eliciting the adjective "readfah" (10). The hot baths, he claims, refer to "surface springs, earthen pipes and hypocausts" of the ruined site (117).[14]

Whereas most investigations assume that *The Ruin* depicts some form of Roman architecture, R. I. Page has raised the possibility that the poem takes "its departure from an abandoned Anglo-Saxon stone complex, awaiting the robbers who would come to steal its materials for new construction" (23). The successive halls at Cheddar (see chap. 1) and evidence of extensive rebuilding at such villages as West Stow and Chalton suggest that Anglo-Saxon structures in disuse would indeed have been common sights on the landscape of the period. For Page, such building practices and the attendant ruins would have affected the poem's earliest interpretations regardless of whether the image was Roman or Saxon. Even if the structure being described is in fact Roman, Page suggests, the existence of contemporary stone ruins would give immediacy to the Anglo-Saxon's response to this "ancient dead city" in the poem.

But regardless of whether or not the architectural description in *The Ruin* was based directly on one or more of the more specific structures visible to the Anglo-Saxons, Klinck's observation that "the poem reads like an actual site" (61) is undeniable. And those structures that survive even to the present day provide us with particular architectural models that might have been evoked in the minds of *The Ruin*'s original audiences: the hot baths, or *burnsele* (21), in *The Ruin* may have reminded them of the waters of Roman sites such as Bath, the references to crumbling towers may have evinced images such as the towers along Hadrian's Wall or the Dover lighthouse (fig. 1), and listeners may have imagined ruins such as those found at Pevensey (fig. 26) when hearing or reading the description of crumbling stone walls. All verbal description, however, is inherently selective. What we can conclude is that the descriptive elements, though abundant, are not comprehensive, and those elements that are provided must individually have been especially salient for the poet or for the poem's anticipated audience. Whether describing a single and specific structure or collating features remembered from a range of locations, the details are traditionally encoded with values. More important, then, than discussing the images' sources themselves is understanding the particular connotative meanings that such images had for their audiences. What specific associations did audiences have with these various types of Roman and/or Anglo-Saxon architecture? As Klinck has observed in her recent edition of the elegies, "the abandoned Roman cities and forts which dotted the landscape must have made a powerful impression on the Anglo-Saxon mind, and they have found a place in the common stock of poetic formulas and themes" (62). It is therefore likely that an examination of traditional meanings activated by the poem's formulaic language can explain many features of *The Ruin* that have so far been unable to be accounted for by archaeological evidence alone.

It is of course *The Ruin*'s rare specificity in architectural detail that has led to the multiple conclusions about its probable real-world model.[15] We might consider the possibility, however, that the uncharacteristic specificity is significant for a very different reason: it underscores the otherness of the structure. The details of familiar buildings—even highly prized ones—need not be described and typically are not. An audience familiar with Anglo-Saxon architecture can envision the structures from scant details. In his observation that the world of Anglo-Saxon poetry is largely lacking architectural specificity, Earl Anderson observes an "association of the uncarpentered with oral tradition" along with a corresponding "awed regard for Roman ruins" ("Uncarpentered World" 60). There are alternatives to Anderson's assumption that the Anglo-Saxons considered such ruins "the products of a technologically superior culture" (69), however. Many of the details of *The Ruin* in fact speak to the tastes and values conveyed elsewhere in Anglo-Saxon poetry and art and are not reserved for Roman architecture. The structure is high, wide, bright, red, curved, and gabled—all features that conform to Anglo-Saxon aesthetics and poetic conventions more widely.

The most prominent features of the ruin involve its alleged height and size. The adjectives "stea[p]" ["high"] (11), "geap" ["wide"] (11), "bradan" ["broad"] (37), "wide" ["wide"] (25), and "heah" ["high"] (22) all characterize these ruins. As discussed in previous chapters, height and size were valued in Saxon and Roman architecture alike. Other adjectives provide more specific visual detail and more distinct traditional associations. For instance, the adjective *beorht* occurs no fewer than three times in the description, each time with unambiguously positive connotations: "beorht . . . burgræced" ["bright hall-dwelling"] (21), "beorhtan burg" ["bright city"] (37), and the "beorhtan bosme" ["bright bosom"] of the wall (40). As Dodwell notes, "the lustrous and the precious" were highly valued in Anglo-Saxon art (29). Like the "beorhtan beam" in *Elene* (1254), these ruins are viewed in highly positive, and largely native, terms. More explicit value judgments also abound, as the speaker imagines the "hygerof" ["stout-hearted"] (19) builders and their abilities to construct "wundrum" ["wondrously"] (20).

But even adjectives that seem at first glance to be less value-laden nonetheless convey associations likely to have resonated with Anglo-Saxon audiences. The "readfah" ["red-stained"] stones perhaps correspond to Roman walls in Chester as Dunleavey suggests; but these red stones also speak to powerful Anglo-Saxon associations with the color itself. In a discussion of Anglo-Saxon tastes, Dodwell notes that red was a popular color for Anglo-Saxons, with the "double advantage of being both indigenous and practical" (37).[16] In his praise for the many varieties of shellfish, Bede gives special attention to whelks because of their use in the making of red dye:

> Sunt et cocleae satis superque abundantes, quibus tinctura coccinei coloris conficitur, cuius rubor pulcherrimus nullo umquam solis ardore, nulla ualet pluuiarum iniuria pallescere, sed quo uetustior eo solet esse uenustior.
>
> ———
>
> [There is also a great abundance of whelks, from which a scarlet-colored dye is made, a most beautiful red which neither fades through the heat of the sun nor exposure to the rain; indeed the older it is the more beautiful it becomes] (*Ecclesiastical History* 1.1; Colgrave and Mynors 14–15).

The importance of red pigmentation in *The Ruin* is also stressed in its discussion of the separating tiles: The "teaforgeapa tigelum sceaðeð" ["red-arches separated from tiles"] (30). If the poet was looking upon red stone walls or rust from metal braces, as suggested by Howe ("Landscape" 96), it is significant that the color was a salient feature, and if the detail sprang from the literary imagination, the choice still conveys the value and endurance associated with the shade. In other words, whether the image depicts an actual or imagined structure, the choice of detail is telling all the same.[17]

The structure's roundness is another feature that has been much commented on in the search for archaeological correspondences, one suggestion of course being the circular pool at Roman Bath. Again, the value placed on curves and arches might be more significant to consider than any archaeological source of the image. As with "red," the prominence given to the description of arches is suggestive if the poet is looking upon actual curved ruins, and the choice is no less important if the scene is an imagined one. The wires bound "in hringas" (19), the "hringmere," and the walls that "befeng" the waters within its "beorhtan bosme" all suggest rounded structures,[18] thus investing these ruins with features common in other poetic buildings of great significance (both positive and negative), such as the "beahsele" ["ringed hall"] of Heorot and even the dragon's lair with its "stanbogan" ["stone arches"] (*Beowulf* 1177, 2718).

Though the scene set before the viewer would seem to be a peaceful one, in certain places the phraseology suggests a space with a tumultuous past. For instance, the employment of "harne stan" (43), as we have seen in numerous other texts (see especially chap. 2), denotes imminent danger. Reading behind the literal description to the meaning indexed by the phrase "harne stan," we can deduce that the fallen warriors faced the most formidable, even supernatural forces.[19] The "beorht bosme" of the baths is another seemingly innocuous image that nonetheless denotes possible danger when read against the larger backdrop of the poetic tradition. Elsewhere in Old English poetry, waters described using the metaphor of a "bosm" ["bosom"] are associated with tremendous power, and phraseology applied to *The Ruin*'s baths suggests an inherent power in its walls, reaching beyond purely literal description. Specifically, the "beorht bosme" of *The Ruin* has several parallels in Old English verse, with the phrase usually describing structures of enormous strength that are, like the ruin, associated with water. In *Andreas* we are told that "hwilum upp / astod of brimes bosme on bates fæðm / egesa ofer yðlid" ["terror stood up out of the brine's bosom"] (443–45). The allegorical poem *Panther* also uses the imagery of a "bosom" in its description of water's power: "þisne beorhtan bosm, brim grymetende, / sealtyþa geswing" ["this bright

bosom, the roaring sea, the swell of salty waves"] (7–8). The flood in
Exodus is described as "famigbosma flodwearde" ["foamy bosomed sea
walls"] (494), and in Riddle 3 (KD; Riddle 1, Williamson) deadly rains
descend "of bosme" ["from the bosom"] (47). The imagery is reinforced
as the riddle's speaker withdraws in the metaphoric battle "ofer byrnan
bosm" ["across the bosom of the ocean"] (62). Through an ambient oral
poetics, the presumably still waters that stand before the viewer—and by
extension, the audience—become dynamic, powerful, even fearsome. For
audiences familiar with similar phraseology elsewhere in Old English poetry, *The Ruin*'s "beorhtan bosme" (40) would become far more intimi-
dating than it might initially seem based on a purely literal reading.[20]

To this point, we have seen some features such as height and curves
that connote general worth and value, as well as more specialized phraseology that suggests immense power. Yet while the structure is unquestionably awe-inspiring to the speaker, whether it is seen as inherently
positive or negative is left largely ambiguous. Such phrases as "harne
stan" indicate that *The Ruin* describes a *stone* structure—and a threatening one at that—but other architectural features suggest construction
of a very diVerent type, in terms of both physical composition and associative meanings, sometimes making it diYcult to reconcile conflicting
visual images. Especially problematic is the poem's use at various points
of architectural terminology such as "meodoheall" ["mead-hall"] (23)
and "hrostbeag" [lit., "roof-ring"] (31), which imply typically wooden
structures otherwise referred to as stone, activating the social context of
heroic hall even as it provides dissonant visual cues. Archaeological evidence provides no instances of Anglo-Saxon secular structures, such
as mead-halls, built from stone, and *hrostbeag* has been understood by
most to refer specifically to the *wood*work of a roof (e.g., Hall, *Anglo-
Saxon Dictionary* 194), even though at a purely literal level the compound
breaks apart simply as "roof-ring." Klinck's more recent emendation to
"hrost beam" makes the connection to wood even stronger, a beam of
course being more explicitly connected to a tree. It has been proposed
that the term is used to refer to box tiles discovered at Bath that might
correspond to wooden gables in supporting a roof (Wentersdorf, "Observations" 176). Such an explanation is perhaps possible but not necessary in order for the poem to retain meaning in a way consistent with

the poetic tradition from which it draws its power. More than a mere physical space alone, the ruins on which the speaker gazes serve as a locus for reshaping the past of the structure and its imagined inhabitants in terms of the speaker's own cultural memory. As we have seen elsewhere, Old English poetry seems to regard stone structures and ruins with a degree of ambivalence—admiration but also a certain degree of suspicion. By infusing this stone structure with elements of wood as well, the poet situates the walls clearly in a heroic context that stone alone could not convey.

Also closely connected with the heroic way of life attributed by the speaker to the ruin's original inhabitants are a cluster of images Hume has called the "hall idea-complex" ("Ruin Motif," "Concept of the Hall"). The structure was "full of the joys of men" ["mondreama full"] (23), warriors "proud and flushed with wine" ["gefrætwed, wlonc ond wingal"] (34), who "shone with war-trappings" ["wighyrstum scan"] (34), and "looked on treasure" ["seah on sinc"] (35). In the traditional idiom, such heroism and glory belong in the hall, and it is this former glory that the narrative voice mourns. Thus the distinctly Roman images of the "baths," "hringmere" ["round pool"] (45), "wealstan" ["wall-stone"] (1), and the stone courts are all made traditionally relevant through such specifically Anglo-Saxon images as the mead-hall and accompanying wooden gables. Though architecturally inconsistent, the imagery is nonetheless meaningful, evocative of such locations as Mermedonia that are inhabited across numerous generations and reflect a wide range of traditions and values. Unlike *Andreas, The Ruin* offers no specific narrative but nonetheless takes the reader along the edges of a story, suggesting through traditional idiomatic language a space that was once inhabited by heroic warriors but that later became the site of intense and hostile battle, resulting in the end of the heroic culture, the mixture of incongruous images suggesting ambivalence on the part of the speaker concerning the ruin's current state. As Renée Trilling reminds us, however, the poem's "final image is not one of destruction, decay, or ruin, but rather of the very full lives of the people who once inhabited this spot: it ends not in nostalgia but in redemption" (55). The poet here combines a keen sense of architectural observation with dexterity in the poetic idiom in creating a vivid, highly condensed image that serves as a powerful articulation of transience, loss, and redemption.

THE WANDERER

The Wanderer also poses a number of seeming thematic and architectural inconsistencies as a poem. A number of influential interpretations of *The Wanderer* have sought thematic "unity" in its Christian imagery (Huppé) and in the speaker coming to terms with fate (Greenfield, "The Wanderer"). But Pasternack has since argued quite effectively that all such efforts to find structural and thematic unity arise from our modern expectations based on literary genres and that we would therefore be better off interpreting the poetry on its own terms rather than imposing "unity" based on such preconceived classifications. Accordingly, if one instead acknowledges the oral traditional nature of the poem, a natural "polyphony" emerges. This polyphony is an important concept to keep in mind when considering the architectural significance of the poem's many images, which often evoke multiple spaces simultaneously. Through metaphor (see chap. 4), conflation of man-made and natural structures,[21] and references to various distinct building types and features, the poem employs architectural language to reconstruct the past and then direct audience response to that projected memory.

Metaphorical language, inherently polysemous, frequently employs images of built space to convey emotion, and in *The Wanderer* the speaker's sorrow is expressed in terms of his *ferðlocan* (13), often translated as "heart" but literally the "chamber of the mind or heart."[22] In similar fashion, the sorrow of the earlier, imagined generation of retainers is also held in "ferðloca" (33). The speaker's thoughts are embodied in a *hordcofan* (14), which can be translated as "treasury of thought" (Klinck) or more literally as "hoard-chamber," and these sorrows are also expressed in terms of "hyra breostcofan," their breast-chambers (18). Such metaphors seem especially appropriate here, shaping audience response to an architectural structure by locating thoughts and feelings in meta - phorical chambers, "cofan" and "locan."[23] These roots each have multiple connotations, *cofa* meaning "chamber" or "closet" and *locan* having an even wider semantic range, "that which closes or shuts, a bar, bolt, lock, an enclosed place, locker" (Bosworth).[24] However, taken together and examined in conjunction with other extensive architectural imagery that we will see pervades the poem, the terms point toward the primacy of space and structure in the poem's aesthetic.

But while these terms show the capacity of architectural metaphor to convey emotion, in fact sorrow in the elegies is more explicitly *about* architectural structures, as in the hapax legomenon *seledreorig* (25).[25] Some, such as Wentersdorf, take *sele* as meaning "times" or "season," an interpretation Klinck rejects on the basis of vowel length (110). The high concentration of architectural imagery and vocabulary, however, points toward the reading of *sele* as "hall" and the compound thus as "hall-sorrowful." Later, for instance, the inhabitants are referenced explicitly in relation to the building through such compounds as "selesecgas" ["hall-retainers"] (34) and "burgwara" ["stronghold dwellers"] (86). With these amplified connections between architectural space and human emotions firmly established through employment of such compounds as *seledreorig, hord-cofan, ferðlocan,* and *breostcofan,* the actual structures the speaker contemplates acquire heightened significance. In addition to the speaker seeking the comfort of one who knows him in the "meoduhealle" ["mead-hall"] (27), architecture acts as the focal point for the more generalized and gnomic discussion of earthly transience:

> Ongietan sceal gleaw hæle   hu gæstlic bið,
> þonne ealle þisse worulde wela   weste stondeð,
> swa nu missenlice   geond þisne middangeard
> winde biwaune   weallas stondaþ,
> hrime bihrorene,   hryðge þa ederas. (73–77)

> ———

> [A wise man must see how dreary it will be when all the riches of this world stand in waste, as in different places throughout this earth walls stand, blown upon by winds, hung with frost, the snow-swept buildings.][26]

Ruins of walls throughout the world are invoked here in traditional terms, beaten by winds and covered with frost and snow, in order to metonymically convey the loss of the much larger cultural and social contexts. Unlike the column in *Andreas* that is "storme bedrifene," the walls referenced by *The Wanderer* do not seem to gain power from endurance but lie defeated, serving only as a reminder of previous strength. The decay is then emphasized further as we are told of wine-halls crumbling ["Woriað þa winsalo"] (78).

Like the walls themselves, the men who once inhabited them have also long since fallen, and significantly the men are located spatially in reference to the architectural structure, through a seemingly inconspicuous prepositional phrase: the men fell "by the wall" ["bi wealle"] (80). But this simple phrase actually seems to be one of great import. In *Beowulf* the phrase appears no fewer than three times, with each instance preceding a sudden death or slaughter. Just before cutting off Grendel's head, Beowulf looks "be wealle" (1573), and before entering his final combat with the dragon, the hero is again described as looking "be wealle" (2542). And finally, as poison courses through his veins, Beowulf himself is described as sitting "bi wealle" (2716), a signal of his own impending death.[27] In *Andreas* as well, the phrase appears immediately before devastating retribution. Andreas first sees the column that assists him in bringing terror upon the Mermedonians "be wealle" (1492). Even before the narrative activates a *comitatus* relationship between Andreas and the heroic column (see chap. 3), the phrase "by wealle" tells us that swift retribution is imminent.[28] So in the context of *The Wanderer* the wall serves similarly to guide a reconstructed historical memory: "by the wall" does more here than simply locate the fallen warriors spatially and indicates that the warriors fallen "by the wall" are also imagined to have died violent deaths.

However, of all the architectural images in *The Wanderer,* none has been as closely scrutinized as the "weal wundrum heah, wyrmlicum fah" ["wondrously high wall, decorated with serpent forms"] (98). W. H. French interpreted this wall as being part of a wooden Anglo-Saxon construction, the serpent shapes created by wood-boring insects. Christo - pher Dean sees the wall as part of a barrow built by the Wanderer himself. P. J. Frankis suggests that the theme of dragons inhabiting dwellings abandoned by men may have motivated the serpent imagery (268). Klinck, on the other hand, supports what has become the majority view that "in all probability they refer to some kind of decoration on a Roman structure," the exact nature of which "is impossible to determine" (125). Tony Millns suggests the possibility of Roman herringbone masonry, a method of wall building in which stones are laid diagonally in alternate courses, thus forming a zigzag, snakelike pattern. The Anglo-Saxons did in fact seem to admire herringbone masonry and imitated the technique at a number of sites, including Monkwearmouth, Elsted (Sussex), and Diddlebury (Shropshire) (Millns 435–36). St. James parish church at Selham provides a well-preserved example of Anglo-Saxon herringbone work (fig. 4) and also reflects the cultural fascination with snakes in the intricate snake sculpture on the chancel arch (fig. 11). But a closer look at mentions of serpents in Old English poetry as a whole provides a better idea of exactly what associations may have been evoked through serpentine sculpture and images. Specifically in a discussion of what he has termed the "Cliff of Death" motif, Donald Fry offers a solution based more on such traditional associations than archaeological equivalents. Noting parallel imagery in *Beowulf, Judith,* and *Christ and Satan*,[29] Fry observes a recurring collocation of elements: death, cliffs, serpents, darkness, and deprivation (215), often with repeated phraseology. He argues that we can view the wall both "literally as the wall of the destroyed hall . . . and figuratively as the Cliff of Death" (229). The serpents thus are traditionally appropriate for this contemplation of the former warriors' deaths, regardless of what exact structure we envision. Fry himself seems to imagine a wood construction, asserting that the speaker "looks at the crumbled timbers and sees death in the traditional guise of a cliff covered with serpent shapes standing in the hostile darkness" (229).

Fry's reading of course depends on the poetic interchangeability of walls and cliffs, a conflation of man-made and natural structures that is in fact frequent in *The Wanderer* and in the poetry more widely, with the dualities inherent in the traditional idiom allowing for a range of simultaneous meanings and associations. The *stanhleoþu* of line 101, for instance, have been interpreted variously as "stone walls" (Leslie) or "rocky slopes" (e.g., Dunning and Bliss; Gordon);[30] in the context of the poem, either seems appropriate. The compound also appears in *The Wife's Lament* (48) as the location of the man from whom the speaker is separated: "min freond siteð / under stanhliþe, storme behrimed" ["my friend sits under the stone wall stone slope, frosted by storm" (47–48). In neither instance is it essential for us to know whether the structure is man-made or natural, but what is significant is that the structure is in decay and thus fails to provide required shelter. *The Wanderer*'s use of "gesteal" ["framework"] (110) in reference to the earth also reflects the tendency to view structures natural and man-made in the same terms without passing explicit judgment.[31]

In its final lines the poem shifts back to the voice from the poem's opening, with this original speaker commenting on the Wanderer himself. Here the poem employs one last architectural metaphor to contrast life's transience with the creator's unchanging, never-ceasing comfort, referring to the heavens as the place where one might find "fæstnung," a word that also acts as a gloss for the Latin *munimentum*,[32] "fortification," and, as Klinck observes, "probably suggests 'fortress' as well as 'security'" (126). Though translations must necessarily choose between these dual meanings, most opting for the sense of security or solidity alone,[33] the sense of *fæstnung* as "foundation" here allows for meaningful contrast between the crumbling walls before the Wanderer and the immutable foundations of the "heofonum." While not as explicit in terms of its architecture, *The Seafarer* also provides a parallel for how present and past may be negotiated through images of built space. From his current dwelling of the "hwæles eþel" ["whale's home"] (60), the speaker imagines cities grown more lovely, "byrig fægriað" (48). Like the Wanderer's sorrow, located metaphorically in his "ferðlocan," the Seafarer's grief is made tangible through architectural imagery, as his thoughts turn "over hreþerlocan" ["beyond the breast-chamber"] (58). The hopes for the future are also made spatially palpable, as the speaker asks "hwær we ham agen" ["where we have a home"] (118) and "hu we þider cumen" ["how we come there"] (118). Here, as in many of the Old English elegies, the exile's movement depends on the articulation of multiple spaces, and, in the syncretism of religious and secular imagery so common in Old English verse,[34] this negotiation of spaces contrasts earthly and heavenly spaces through multiple architectural referents.

In addition to ambiguity and polysemy at the level of lexemes and phrases, *The Wanderer* in its entirety perhaps even more notably combines elements from numerous architectural styles in its description of what otherwise seems to be a single structure, a pattern also observed in *The Ruin*. The "winsalo" ["wine halls"] (78) are falling, and one of *The Wanderer*'s fallen warriors is described as now inhabiting an earthen cave, "eorðscræfe" (84), a term that can also mean specifically "grave."[35] Soon after, this same structure is referred to as an "enta geweorc" ["work of giants"] (87) that therefore stands bereft of "burgwara" ["stronghold dwellers"] (86). In a space of only ten lines, there are arguably three distinct building types expressed by the poem: the wine-hall, which would activate the cultural and social contexts of life within the wooden Anglo-Saxon halls; the earth-cave, which evokes an image of a subterranean dwelling and corresponding associations of death; and the work of giants, a phrase that is widely understood as representing Roman ruins.[36]

The narrative polyphony of the poem described by Pasternack is thus paralleled by a different kind of polyphony in the architectural description, one that allows for simultaneous evocations of multiple contexts that work in complementary rather than contradictory ways. The architectural details of the poem—potentially contradictory if taken too literally—work to elicit particular associations, serving less as physical description than as a focal point for the contemplation of memory and history. Standing before a wall in ruins, the Wanderer projects onto the structure a past deeply rooted in contemporary Anglo-Saxon ideals and thus invests the wall with architectural features more closely associated with the heroic social values of the hall. Through the Wanderer's musings, the poem creates a cultural memory through a meaningful hybrid of architectural imagery. While we can have a more complete understanding of the poem with an awareness of the architectural landscape, seeking one-to-one correspondences for the structure in the poem—indeed, assuming that a single structure is being represented at all—potentially misses a crucial dimension of the poem.

THE WIFE'S LAMENT

Where the memory constructed in *The Wanderer* through contemplation of built space is a shared, cultural one, the speaker of *The Wife's Lament* reflects on a private and elusive personal memory by focusing attention on the structure she inhabits. In fact, the space she occupies is described much more specifically than are the cryptic details of her past experience, creating a certain tension between the general and specific that opens up myriad possibilities for interpretations. There is general agreement that the speaker is an exiled female separated from a lover or husband, and references to betrayals suggest some type of feud that has led to the woman's forced isolation underground. But even such basic questions as the identity of the speaker defy simplistic answers. The poem's interpretations have been well rehearsed and summarized elsewhere, but even a few representative examples attest to the poem's fascinating complexities. Though most accept the speaker as a woman,[37] Doane, followed by Luyster, has gone so far as to suggest that the speaker is actually an "old heathen spirit dwelling in the abandoned spot formerly dedicated to the worship of herself" ("Heathen" 89), while Walker-Pelkey has noted significant connections to the Old English riddles and argues compellingly for a metaphorical reading in which the speaker is a personified sword, separated from its bearer and speaking from the grave (227–41). Shari Horner sees a woman but one functioning in contexts of female monasticism (381–91). These and numerous other readings, divergent as they are, demonstrate that the "text can be read convincingly in different ways, functioning coherently on more than one level" (Hough 6). As R. F. Leslie notes, the elegies "present situations without localisation of the settings or identification of the characters" while at the same time including "sufficient concrete detail" to give the impression of "a particular experience" (2).

As with the other elegies here discussed, much of the poem's "concrete detail" lies in the poem's architectonics. But *The Wife's Lament* differs somewhat from the other poems typically designated as elegies in that where exiles such as the Seafarer and the Wanderer travel physically in their movement across space while remembering back to their joys in the hall, the female exile of *The Wife's Lament* occupies a place that "is all too permanent, a space from which she can never escape," a space that "embodies her spiritual inertia and psychological torment" (Klein 116). However, while the woman does not negotiate space physically, she departs from her dwelling beneath the oak tree at least in her mind to contemplate her beloved's distant refuge. The poem is thus not organized temporally but spatially, around these two locations—comprised of earth and stone respectively—which provide the loci for the poem's largely associative meanings. Descriptions of both locations conflate natural and built spaces in their enigmatic descriptions, leading to multiple interpretations of the wife's and her beloved's narrative situations, but the traditional referentiality of the features described provides somewhat more stability with regard to the poem's emotional resonances. The discussion that follows views the descriptive passages of the wife's space, and later her beloved's, within these dual physical and traditional contexts.

The woman's habitation is underground, a foreboding feature in itself, as is the case with Andreas's prison and some of the Old English riddles discussed in chapter 4. While the connections between death and the underground are perhaps somewhat obvious at this point, by viewing the wife's location in relation to actual subterranean spaces present on—or, more precisely, under—the Anglo-Saxon landscape, alongside other Old English poetry employing similar architectonics and against the larger Germanic tradition, we can see more distinctly a simultaneous sense of death and refuge. Whether as a prisoner or for her own protection, the speaker has been forced to dwell in a space beneath a tree:

Heht mec mon wunian   on wuda bearwe,
under actreo   in þam eorðscræfe.
Eald is þes eorðsele,   eal ic eom oflongad,
sindon dena dimme,   duna uphea,
bitre burgtunas,   brerum beweaxne,
wic wynna leas.   Ful oft mec her wraþe begeat
fromsiþ frean.   Frynd sind on eorþan,
leofe lifgende,   leger weardiað,
þonne ic on uhtan   ana gonge
under actreo   geond þas eorðscrafu. (27–36)

[They ordered me to dwell in a grove of woods under an oak tree in the earth-cave. This earth-hall is old; I am all worn out with yearning. The valleys are dim, the hills high up, bitter towns grown over with briars, joyless places. Very often here the departure of my lord has seized cruel upon me. There are loving friends alive on earth; they have their bed while alone at dawn I pass through this earth-cave beneath the oak tree.]³⁸

The wife's dwelling has been interpreted in various ways as a place associated with pagan worship (Wentersdorf, "Situation" 509), a Germanic underground dwelling (Harris, "Note"), a barrow (Leslie),³⁹ a grave, and, more recently, a souterrain (Battles). As these varied solutions indicate, the exact nature of this space is ambiguous. If we accept the narrative ambiguity as a meaningful feature of the verse rather than as an obstacle and accordingly shift our focus away from what space the author might have intended and look instead at the multiple possibilities able to have been imagined by Anglo-Saxon audiences—a subtle but significant difference—these varied possibilities can exist in tandem. There are in fact various kinds of underground structures that would have been observable aspects of the Anglo-Saxon world, most notably graves and barrows, with their obvious connections to death and the dead, and fogous and souterrains, constructed underground passages and chambers that seem to have been employed for purposes of both ritual and refuge (see chap. 4). As G. B. Brown observes, there is always more to a building than its component parts. All Anglo-Saxon built spaces, even underground ones, thus "have a human and historical as well as architectural value, and this is not to be measured by the number of stones that make them up" (*Arts* 2:10).[40] In the poetry it is precisely such "human and historical" dimensions of buildings that are most foregrounded.

The construction of barrows as monuments and places for burials was a fairly widespread practice both before and during the Anglo-Saxon period. Such structures across the landscape would doubtless have reinforced associations of underground spaces with death. As Marsden notes, "Among the wealth of ancient field monuments scattered across the shires of England, the most common and best-known are barrows, long or circular grass-grown heaps of earth or stones, marking the burial places of prehistoric aristocracy" (1). Fulfilling a function parallel to the wife's dwelling in the poem—though at a cultural rather than personal level—the physical barrows themselves were often used by Anglo-Saxons as a means to negotiate the past, often serving to "emulate and evoke the associations of prehistoric and Roman structures" (Bradley 101). The underground space is thus a culturally appropriate one for the wife's contemplation of the past.

Underground constructed fogous (see fig. 12) and souterrains provide additional insights into how an Anglo-Saxon audience may have conceived of the wife's location, in this case more through connotations of refuge than death. Through both archaeological evidence and literary parallels, Paul Battles has previously demonstrated that the wife's dwelling is in fact consistent with both literary and actual souterrains.[41] As but one of numerous examples from medieval Irish, Icelandic, and English literary and historical texts (see also Battles), the Old Norse *Völsunga Saga* includes the description of an earthen underground dwelling being built by Signy as a refuge for her brother Sigurd:

> fór hun nú ok hittir bróður sinn, ok taka þau þat ráð, at hann gerir þar jarðhús í skóginum, ok ferr nú því fram um hríð, at Signý leynir honum þar ok fær honum þat, er hann þurfti at hafa. (Jónsson, ed. 120)

> ───────

> [She went and met with her brother and they decided that he should make an underground dwelling in the woods. This went on for a while with Signy hiding him there and bringing him what he needed.] (Trans. Byock)

Real-world counterparts to Signy's underground shelter for Sigurd, souterrains were frequently built in the woods to provide better camouflage in times of refuge. Evidence of souterrains has been found in Northumbria, Cornwall, Scotland, and Ireland, and the presence of these structures on the physical landscape would have thus provided audiences a potentially powerful mental image of an underground dwelling inhabited by the wife, with oral poetics then further investing the architectonics with powerful traditional associations of not only death but also refuge.

As we saw in chapter 2, the natural associations between death and underground dwellings are heavily utilized in Old English poetry, and the single instance of an *eorðscrafa* paralleling the "earth-cave" of *The Wife's Lament* even more unambiguously juxtaposes the structure with death in *Beowulf,* even if the nature of the "earth-cave" itself remains here also enigmatic: "wæs ða deaðe fæst, / hæfde eorðscrafa ende genyttod" ["He (the dragon) was held fast in death; had used the last of earth-caves"] (3045–46). In this passage a link is created between the earth-cave and death, though the possible use of the *eorðscrafa* as a tomb is specifically disassociated from the dragon who in death no longer needs such a structure. The usage of *eorðscrafa* therefore seems to designate not a grave or dwelling for the dead but rather a dwelling for the living who are facing death. Lot, for instance, in the Old English *Genesis* also flees slaughter by seeking a dwelling in an earth-cave:

Ne dorste þa dædrof hæle
for frean egesan on þam fæstenne
leng eardigean, ac him Loth gewat
of byrig gangan and his bearn somed
wælstowe fyrr wic sceawian,
oðþæt hie be hliðe heare dune
eorðscræf fundon. (2591–97)

———

[Now Lot, the glorious hero, did not dare to dwell longer in that
stronghold for fear of the lord, but he departed from that city, and
his children together with him, to seek a dwelling far from the place
of slaughter, until they found, at last, a cave[42] upon the slope of a
high hill.]

Here, Lot is said to dwell with his "dohtor twa" (2599), translating the Latin
"filiae eius" (19.30), a significant detail, since souterrains often function
as a protection and hiding place in Germanic literature for females more
widely.[43]

Potentially problematic to conceptualizations of such a space as either
a barrow or a souterrain is the phrase *bitre burgtunas* in line 31. The compound *burgtunas*, which literally means something like "fortification-
towns," is unique in Old English poetry, and it is difficult to reconcile the
woman's apparent underground solitude with the presence of such a
grand space,[44] with the designation *bitre* ("bitter") only adding to the
quandary. Leslie offers "protecting hedge" as a gloss and suggests it is "possibly an ancient earthwork" (56). Leslie further argues that *bitre* is used
here in the sense of "sharp," thus describing "briars which have grown
over the protecting walls of the cave or mound, although the abstract
meaning 'bitter' may be intended as well" (56).[45] Even more specifically,
Klinck posits that "the bitter enclosures overgrown with briars" "may be
the remains of an abandoned settlement" (184). But by looking at the
phrase in the context of loss within Old English poetry, especially in the
Exeter Book elegies, we can see that both possibilities might be equally
significant and indeed working together. The speaker of *The Seafarer*, for
instance, experiences "*bitre* breostceare" ["bitter breast-care/sorrow"]
(1) and is "*bitter* in breosthord" ["bitter in breast-hoard/heart"] (55). In

Resignation, we see a figure lamenting his "*bitre* bealodæde" ["bitter wicked deeds"] (20). The sense of *bitter* in these other instances is associative rather than literal, but the space in *The Wife's Lament* works both literally and figuratively. When "bitter" is assigned as an attribute of the entirety of the woman's *burgtunas,* the physical space itself becomes designated as an appropriate locus for grief, regret, and sorrow. By employing language of both natural and man-made constructions, as well as literal and figurative usages of *bitre,* the poem is thus able to idiomatically convey the speaker's sorrow in multiple registers.

As with *The Wanderer,* though, the poem's dominant building type is far from the only type implied by the language, and there are in fact more references in *The Wife's Lament* to built spaces—albeit ones that overlap with the natural world—than direct translation into modern En - glish might suggest.[46] Almost as enigmatic as the woman's location is the situation of her "freond" ["friend"] (33) and "wine" ["friend"/"lord"] (49, 50), described in 47b–50a:

> . . .   min freond siteð
> under stanhliþe   storme behrimed,
> wine werigmod,   wætre beflowen
> on dreorsele.
> _____
>
> [my friend sits under a *stanhliþe,* frosted by storm, my friend,
> mind-weary, surrounded by water in a dismal hall.]

The features of the *stanhliþe* (lit., "stone cliff/rampart") allow simultaneously for interpretation as both a natural space and a built structure. The location has frequently been viewed as a naturally occurring stone cave or cliff,[47] yet the phraseology leaves open the possibility that the space is man-made, since *hliðe* can mean "rampart" as well as "cliff," and *sele* could refer either to an actual hall or a natural structure that the speaker is equating with such a hall. Accepting the poem in all its ambiguity, Klinck observes that "the scene is not presented realistically and need not be regarded as an actual spot," as many of the elements—rocky slope, hoar-frost, storm, water, and anti-hall—"form a composite of traditional elegiac motifs" (187). In this regard, the *stanhliðe* is very much like the wife's *eorðscrafu,* both employing anti-hall imagery to activate an elegiac register despite their marked differences in physical composition. Rather than convey a physically locatable space, the conflation of natural and man-made structures allows the speaker to project onto both the speaker's dwelling and that of her beloved a range of emotionally reso-nant motifs as she considers her situation from various angles and across multiple points in time.

However, despite such shared elegiac imagery, the descriptions of the wife's and her beloved's physical locations also present us with a marked contrast: the wife's dwelling is constructed primarily of earth, her lover's of stone. Unable to be with him, she imagines an experience for him and constructs an image in some ways similar to that of the Wanderer and the speaker of *The Ruin.* Like these other solitary figures, the wife's beloved is located near a stone structure, remembering a happier time and place:

> . . . Dreogeð se min wine
> micle modceare; he gemon to oft
> wynlicran wic. (50b–52a)

> [My friend endures great care in mind; he remembers too often a more joyous place.]

And, as we have seen in numerous other texts,[48] stone as an architectural medium is closely associated with cultures either spatially or temporally distant, not necessarily good or bad, but unfamiliar and thus uncertain. By situating her beloved beneath stone walls, the speaker marks his es-trangement and deepens the psychological ambiguity present through-out the text.

Though the shape of the story is certainly present, *The Wife's Lament* refuses to be limited to its narrative structure. As the medieval architec-tural images that have been discussed by Carruthers were employed to inventory valued knowledge and concepts, the imagined architectural spaces in the Old English elegies have the capacity to key personal mem-ory and response. The speaker thus guides the audience not through time but through space. And the spaces described and encountered in her song, or *gied,* function much like real spaces in that they can accommodate multiple narratives without inconsistency. Within any given elegiac space, countless events can unfold across time as various individuals enter, experience, and depart. If we approach the spaces in elegiac verse in something closer to this dynamic way, then we open ourselves to multiple interesting and productive readings. The details of the poetry's architectonics combined with the relative vagueness of the narratives invite audiences to enter the poems' spaces and fill in the narrative gaps. *The Wife's Lament* can and does evoke riddlic contexts, deeply personal grief, Germanic myth and legend, social exile, and more—and the spaces inside the poem can hold them all.

Figure 1. Roman lighthouse, now on the grounds of Dover Castle. The uppermost section was a later addition.

Figure 2. West tower, All Saints Church, Earls Barton, Northamptonshire, late Anglo-Saxon.

Figure 3. St. Laurence Church, Bradford-on-Avon, Wiltshire, late Anglo-Saxon.

Figure 4. Herringbone stonework, St. James Church, Selham, West Sussex, late Anglo-Saxon.

Figure 5. Church of St. Peter-on-the-Wall, Bradwell-on-Sea, Essex, c. seventh century. Red Roman tiles were reused in the church's construction.

Figure 6. Bathhouse, Chesters Roman Fort, Northumberland.

Figure 7. Hypocaust, Binchester Roman Fort, County Durham.

Figure 8. Hogback stone, Heysham, Lancashire, c. tenth century.

Figure 9. Portal, north door, Durham Cathedral, Durham, Norman.

Figure 10. Two of four columns in the crypt of St. Wystan's Church, Repton, Derbyshire, c. eighth century.

Figure 11. South capital of the chancel arch, St. James Church, Selham, West Sussex, late Anglo-Saxon.

Figure 12. Iron Age fogou, Carn Euny, Cornwall. Photo by Julie Woodhouse. Used with permission.

Figure 13. Ruins of the Mithraic temple *(mithraeum)*, Carrawburgh, near Hadrian's Wall. The altars are replicas of originals now on display in Newcastle upon Tyne at the Museum of Antiquities. Photo by Andrea D. Lively. Used with permission.

Figure 14. Tower, St. Mary's Church, Sompting, West Sussex, late Anglo-Saxon.

Figure 15. Anglo-Saxon stone, possibly cross-shaft, St. Peter's churchyard, Heysham, Lancashire.

Figure 16. Reconstructed Anglo-Saxon hall (completed 2005), West Stow, St. Edmundsbury.

Figure 17. Timber nave, south side, St. Andrew's Church, Greensted, Essex, late Anglo-Saxon.

Figure 18. Wattle and daub, reconstructed Anglo-Saxon hall, Bede's World, Jarrow, County Durham.

Figure 19. Reconstructed Anglo-Saxon hall, Bede's World, Jarrow, County Durham. Based on sixth-century hall excavated at Thirlings, Northumberland.

Figure 20. St. John's Church, Escomb, County Durham, c. seventh century.

Figure 21. Detail, St. John's Church, Escomb, County Durham. Note the Roman tooling on the stones.

Figure 22. West door, All Saints Church, Earls Barton, Northamptonshire, late Anglo-Saxon.

Figure 23. South wall of chancel, exterior, St. Paul's, Jarrow, County Durham, late seventh century.

Figure 24. Chancel, St. Wystan's Church, Repton, Derbyshire, ninth century.

Figure 25. Southwest tower, St. Margaret's Church, King's Lynn, Norfolk, twelfth century.

Figure 26. Roman wall, Pevensey Castle, East Sussex.

Figure 27. Bodiam Castle gatehouse, East Sussex, fourteenth century.

Figure 28. Outer gatehouse, Beeston Castle, Cheshire, thirteenth century.

Figure 29. Cave at Wetton Mill, Staffordshire.

Figure 30. Thor's Cave, Staffordshire.

Figure 31. Ruins of St. Patrick's Chapel, Heysham, Lancashire, c. ninth century.

Figure 32. Annual pilgrimage to St. Peter-on-the-Wall, Bradwell-on-Sea, Essex, July 1, 2006.

PART III

POST-CONQUEST

DEVELOPMENTS

AND

CONTINUATIONS

ARCHITECTURAL AND POETIC TRANSITIONS

Written more than a century after the Norman Conquest, which precipitated the end of the era of Anglo-Saxon timber halls and ushered in an age of medieval English castles, Laȝamon's *Brut* continues to look back with at least some degree of nostalgia at timber halls and the social code with which they were associated. Nowhere is this more apparent than in Arthur's dream (13984–98), which foreshadows Modred's betrayal and the breakdown of Arthur's own *comitatus* through the intense and powerful image of a timber hall literally being torn apart. Arthur dreams that someone places him "uppen are halle" ["upon a hall"] (13984), and as he sits astride this hall alongside the loyal Gawain, Modred, who has marched there with his own army, hacks the posts of the hall with a battle-ax and Guinevere pulls down the hall's roof with her hands. First the hall simply totters, then Arthur falls to the ground, and finally the hall itself collapses: "adun ueol þa halle" ["down fell the hall"] (13996). The obvious similarities between the *Brut*'s portrayal of Arthur's court and the *comitatus* of Old English verse have long been observed. As early as 1916 John Edwin Wells notes that "Arthur is not much the king of chivalry, but is rather the Germanic chieftain with his comitatus" (34). Further, in their commentary on this portion of the *Brut*, Barron and Weinberg observe that "the centrepiece" of Laȝamon's amplification of his sources is Arthur's dream about this destruction of a hall (278), noting in passing that the hall was "a symbol in OE poetry of legitimate royal authority and power" (278). The question remains, however, as to what degree such a symbol would retain its traditional meaning in post-Conquest England, an era for which timber Anglo-Saxon halls would exist only in cultural memory. Any readers of the *Brut* would have been generations removed from the cultural contexts that produced the social and architectural world of Old English poetry. Nevertheless, the imagery continues to find meaningful expression in such passages as this. This chapter seeks to understand the architectural and linguistic processes through which the traditional referentiality of the hall as a poetic image metonymic of *comitatus* ideals was simultaneously fractured and maintained in post-Anglo-Saxon England.

During and following the Norman Conquest, the culture of England was—both figuratively and quite literally—rebuilt, as its language, political structure, literary traditions, and architectural landscape all underwent profound changes so massive in scope as to mark period boundaries for most modern fields of discourse, with "Old English" and "Anglo-Saxon" language and culture giving way to "Middle English" and "Anglo-Norman." As with any such demarcation, the watershed date of 1066 is to some extent arbitrary, suggesting overnight changes that in reality began prior to and continued long after the famous October 14 Battle of Hastings. Yet while "the effects on vernacular verse produced in England were not fully apparent for several generations" (Amodio, *Writing* 131), the architectural break with the past seems to have been both more swiftly and more thoroughly executed than were changes in other cultural arenas. Fernie observes that during the first century of Norman occupation the amount of stone quarried for new construction was at least "as great as that extracted for the building of the pyramids. . . . The sheer volume of construction in the first generation after the Conquest must have turned the country into a vast building site, with almost every city, town and village affected" (*Norman* 19). The new Norman order was powerfully and dramatically asserted through widespread construction of castles, large churches, and other structures that eventually figured as prominently in verse literature as on the landscape itself.

THE ANGLO-NORMAN ARCHITECTURAL LANDSCAPE

One of the most striking differences between Anglo-Saxon and Norman secular architecture involves the displacement of the Anglo-Saxon hall by the Anglo-Norman castle as the dominant aristocratic secular dwelling. The term *castle* itself, however, is not as straightforward as it might appear, as it entered English twice, once directly from Latin and later through French. In its earliest English-language usages, *castel* was introduced during the Old English period to render the Latin *castellum*, with the sense of town or village, or *castra*, meaning "camp."[1] But in French the word developed in a different direction, and for English it was the sense of this later borrowing that eventually became dominant—that of "a large building or set of buildings fortified for defense against an enemy; a fortress, stronghold" (*OED*, s.v. "castle"). However, for some time these Latin- and French-derived senses of *castel* continued alongside one another into the Middle English period, with their primary amalgamated sense being that of a fortified structure or a "moveable tower used in sieges" with secondary senses of fortified camps or walled-villages and towns (*MED*, s.v. *castel*) also existing. Although the sense of towns or camps eventually became obsolete, our reading of early Middle English literature depends on an awareness of these more archaic meanings as well, as they contribute to enduringly strong associations throughout the period between castles and military strength.[2]

Even when limited to its primary and most enduring sense of a fortified structure, *castel* could still refer to a range of architectural types. Nearly eight hundred English castles were built between the Norman Conquest and 1189 alone, the majority of which were motte and bailey structures (Reed 145). This most common type of Norman castle involved the construction of a raised earthen mound (the *motte*) on and around which walls were built, usually of wooden stakes. Within these walled enclosures (*baileys*) could be housed a range of structures, including halls, chapels, and, in some cases, high towers built on top of the mottes. Mottes from the British Isles, which survive today only as grass-covered mounds surrounded by hollows, ranged in height from approximately 3 to 65 feet, in diameter at the base from 160 to 500 feet, and in diameter across the flat tops from 16 to 160 feet (Thompson, *Rise of the Castle* 51). Contemporary with motte and bailey castles were ringwork style fortifications, similar to the motte and bailey structures but without raised mottes (Thompson, *Rise of the Castle* 51). As stone became more dominant, some of these wooden motte and bailey castles were rebuilt in this newly preferred medium, and by the early twelfth century massive stone keeps—that is, the main strongholds of the castles—became commonplace (Reed 145). At least eighty-seven stone keeps from the period before 1216 survive to the present day (Thompson, *Rise of the Castle* 64–65). Norman stone castles were characterized by a tower dwelling encompassing in a single building the central hall, living chambers, and chapel—components that would have constituted entirely separate structures in Anglo-Saxon times. This tower dwelling was a distinguishing feature of the Norman Romanesque style, setting Norman castles apart from the more open Carolingian palace or villa. According to Fernie, the Normans' Romanesque buildings, the "most advanced among standing buildings in Normandy," were reflective of and closely connected to their administrative power, which ultimately contributed to papal support for William the Conqueror's claim to the English throne (*Norman* 14). It was their military function that set them apart, and this aspect of the Anglo-Norman castle continued to become even more pronounced across the late Middle Ages.

During the twelfth and thirteenth centuries, strength was extended beyond the keep of the stone tower, attention being focused also on outer walls equipped with gatehouses and towers erected at regular intervals around the perimeters. It is with these heavily fortified stone castle walls that we see such features as machicolations, which were projecting structures at the top of walls with openings through which boiling liquids or stones could be dropped on would-be attackers; crenellation of walls, which provided regular recesses along the edges through which archers could shoot with cross-bows from positions of relative safety; and port - cullises, grills that slid up and down in grooves in the wall and operated from above, allowing for easier and safer surveillance of approaching enemies than doors or gates alone. The addition of barbicans, structures set just outside the gate to deter direct attacks, provided added protection to the spaces within. Increasingly, such features characterized not only royal castles but private fortifications as well, as at Bodiam Castle (Reed 147; see fig. 27), creating potential threats against area residents, a theme re - flected in the romances of the period, as I explore more fully in chapter 7.

In part because "there were few purely military buildings in Norman England" (Fernie, *Norman* 49), castles as fortified residences acquired an "increasingly military character" due not only "to practical requirements of security" but also "to the need to present a powerful face to those under their rule and to their peers from elsewhere" (Fernie, *Norman* 49). Thus even those buildings that did not require military fortifications nonetheless were provided with "attributes of the architecture of defence and attack" (Fernie, *Norman* 49). Mottes and castle towers (and even castle towers built upon mottes) projected authority and power not only in their imposing height but also through their features of military prowess. Unlike the traditional Anglo-Saxon halls surrounded by but not separated from outlying workshops and residences, both wood and stone castles of Norman England served as an architectural articulation of a new and sharply delineated class system, physically situating the ruling elite above the governed public and embodying in its military features an implied threat against anyone who dared challenge.

The use of architectural space beyond protection against outside invaders, enforcing distance between the new aristocracy and the recently subdued Anglo-Saxons, is especially evident in William of Poitiers' account of the castles built in London for William the Conqueror. William of Poitiers tells us that five hundred Norman knights were sent to force the native troops to "retreat shamefully inside the walls, killing those in the rear. They added fire to the great carnage, burning all the houses they could find on this side of the river, so that the fierce pride of their enemies might be subdued by a twofold disaster" (147).[3] Thus, on William the Conqueror's arrival, the "chief men of the city . . . submitted themselves and the whole city to him" and "produced as many hostages as he required" (147).[4] Not shockingly, the leadership was concerned that there might be some lingering animosity among the London natives following this gruesome turn of events. Although "he hoped above all that once he had begun to reign any rebels would be less ready to challenge him and more easily put down," William the Conqueror "sent men ahead to London to build a fortress in the city and make the many preparations necessary for royal dignity" (149).[5] Shortly thereafter he is said to have retreated from London temporarily to the relative safety of nearby Barking while "fortifications were being completed in the city as a defence against the inconstancy of the numerous and hostile inhabitants" (161–63).[6] In this and other ways the Norman architectural presence asserted its dominance over and distance from Anglo-Saxon culture, divisions that were to become softened over time but that continued to be reflected in poetic architectural description in the *Brut* and across the Middle English period. For instance, following a description of Lud's building of London's great halls ["hallen"] (3534), Laȝamon recites a very brief history of the city's occupation, concluding with the arrival of the Normans, "mid heore nið-craften" ["with their evil-crafts"] (3547): "þeos leodes heo amærden" ["those people they harmed"] (3548). Such explicitly negative commentary is relatively rare but does bring to the surface sympathies for the conquered Anglo-Saxons, sympathies that are made manifest more subtly through both Anglo-Norman architecture and poetic architectural representation.

The architectural style adopted by the Normans and employed to articulate this power over the Anglo-Saxons of course has roots in Europe, and Norman building is perhaps best described as Romanesque. The Normans, who "consolidated their power through their ability . . . to assimilate whatever was useful from the cultures of the peoples they conquered or those of their neighbors" (Fernie, *Norman* 11), adopted and adapted the Romanesque style on settling in northern France, and it is this imposing style that also characterizes Norman architecture of post-Conquest England. The style, as the name suggests, derives from Roman types; however, whereas the Roman world was characterized by communal fortifications (such as city walls) in addition to dedicated military structures (such as army forts), the various military, residential, and communal functions of architecture were largely conflated in Norman construction, leading to castles with more obvious military fortifications. In addition to connections with Romano-Britain, the Romanesque style, both in Europe and later in England, was "exactly contiguous with the extent of the Latin Church" (Fernie, *Norman* 5), and in England this meant the programmatic rebuilding of all cathedrals and larger monastic structures. Though in some cases such reconstruction does seem to have involved a need for greater space, the period also saw the total demolition and rebuilding of Anglo-Saxon cathedrals that recent excavations have shown would have been large by any measure, as evidenced by surviving pre-Conquest foundations at Canterbury and Winchester (Fernie, *Norman* 24).[7]

The surviving architectural record makes the totality of changes in secular and ecclesiastical architecture abundantly clear, with only scattered parish churches from the Anglo-Saxon period having survived the extensive Norman rebuilding program. The writings of William of Malmesbury (ca. 1095–1142), who lived through many of these early changes, provide us with an especially relevant window into the range of attitudes toward these radical changes and also illustrate how Norman perceptions of space were sometimes projected onto Anglo-Saxon architecture. By William's account, "You may see everywhere churches in villages, in towns and cities, monasteries rising in a new style of architecture" (*GR* 461). "At home," William says, "the program is great buildings" (*GR* 461).[8] The histories of William of Malmesbury, long understood as standing "deservedly very high amongst modern English historians," also exhibited an "informed and perceptive interest in architecture" (R. A. Brown, "William of Malmesbury" 9). The careers of ecclesiastical and political leaders are marked and often evaluated in terms of their architectural accomplishments, and it is clear from William's account that demolition of the old and building of the new were part of everyday life. In William's words, the late eleventh century is characterized by the "edifitiis . . . nouis" ["erection of new buildings"] (*GP* 418–19), and the final stages of construction at Durham Cathedral are even marked by an architectural miracle in which unseen divine hands gently lowered the heavy timbers used to support vaulting during construction without damaging the floor or altar as the prior had feared (*GP* 418–19).[9]

For the most part, William's attitude toward innovation is positive. Edward, for instance, is praised for his work on Westminster Cathedral, where he was said to use "for the first time in England the style which almost everyone now tries to rival at great expense" (*GR* 418–19).[10] Fearing that some readers might see the building program as extravagance, William assures readers that Norman leaders maintained a far more temperate existence in their grand buildings than did the Anglo-Saxons in their comparatively humble dwellings: "Unlike the French and the Normans who in proud great buildings live a life of moderate expense," the Saxons "in small, mean houses . . . wasted their entire substance" (*GR* 459).[11] In fact, William of Malmesbury credits William the Conqueror's extravagant spending on a lavish dwelling as a testament to his generosity: "He began and completed one building, and that on the grand scale, his palace in London, sparing no expense to secure an effect of openhanded splendour" (*GR* 567).[12]

Despite the building of castles and the wholesale reconstruction of most cathedrals and monasteries, which served to visually establish a Norman order and effectuate distance from Anglo-Saxon culture, few of the foundations of ecclesiastical centers from the period were built at new sites; most made use of previously built-on spaces (Gittos 93). For Anglo-Norman builders and the bishops who commissioned their work, great value seems to have been placed on historical continuity and the authority of the earlier English church, especially with respect to the age of Bede, whose own stone monasteries anticipated to some extent the dominance of stone in Norman Romanesque construction associated with the Roman church. While the financial advantage of building on preexisting sites rather than developing new ones provides a potentially logical explanation for the practice, "the pattern is so common that it appears to have been largely the result of choice rather than circumstance" (Gittos 93).[13] There were more than ample funds, for instance, for the wholesale reconstruction of Old Minster Cathedral at Winchester on a new site. Yet the builders *chose* to rebuild on the existing foundations, in effect investing the new structures with the authority of history. Wil - liam of Malmesbury reinforces this relationship between continuity and change in his assertion that the convents built through William the Conqueror's generosity had "new buildings" but a "long history of devotion" (*GR* 506–7).[14]

Parallel to the appropriation of spaces was an appropriation of key Anglo-Saxon historical figures connected with such places. In the *Gesta Regum Anglorum* and the *Gesta Pontificum Anglorum*, the values of Norman building are projected onto those Anglo-Saxon kings and bishops still revered in Norman times. Novelty and massive reconstruction projects being the hallmarks of Norman building, Alfred is credited with building a church at Athelney, where he found refuge after having been driven out of his province by the Danes, in a new style ["nouo edificandi," *GP* 312–13] and is praised by William for giving substantial portions of his own revenue to employ builders who worked continuously "on new construction in a remarkable style never seen in England before" (*GR* 194–95).[15] Edward the Confessor is also commended by William for having "aedificationis genere nouo fecit" ["erected a building in a new style"] (*GP* 224–25). And, according to William, the Anglo-Saxon bishop Wilfrid "constructed buildings of remarkable polish" (*GP* 386–87): "It was a popular saying in those days, and one that found its way into writing too, that . . . there was no building like it" (*GP* 388–89).[16] Even Cnut, because of whom monasteries all over England "had been desecrated," is to a degree exonerated by his reconstruction efforts in building new and even better churches "every place where he had fought a battle" (*GR* 323).[17] The associations with this new trend also reflect Norman preferences for the Romanesque style and for construction in stone, as is clear in William's explanation that Wilfrid "learned from stonemasons who had been lured from Rome by hope of a generous reward"[18] and that visitors "coming from Rome nowadays" say that the church constructed at Hexham "gives them a mental picture of the best Roman work" (*GP* 388–89).[19] Benedict, "who educated Bede and was his abbot," is said to be "the first man to invite to England craftsmen able to build stone buildings. . . . Before Benedict buildings in coursed stone were only very rarely to be seen in England" (*GP* 496–97).[20] Of course, Bede's own writings show that associations between stone and the Roman church had a long-standing history (see chap. 2), and the shift in preference for stone construction was not due solely to the Norman Conquest but was brought about by both internal and external forces.

However, beneath the praise lavished on great Saxon and Norman builders, in William of Malmesbury's writings we also see reflected certain misgivings about the construction efforts and a nostalgia for that which is being systematically destroyed. William's accounts convey an anxiety about the drain on public funds for these building projects, most explicitly when he tells of "the grumbles of those who said it would have been better to preserve the old foundations in their former state than to rob them to build new ones while they fell into ruins" (*GR* 506–7).[21] In a somewhat atypical criticism of the new rule, William praises the small church at Lichfield, which "on its cramped site" "gave a good idea of the moderation and restraint of the ancients," virtues that William seems to find lacking in some bishops of his own day who "would not think it a fit place of residence of episcopal dignity" (*GP* 464–65).[22] Embedded in the overall praise for the Norman style, which for William corresponds to a "new devotion" and a higher "standard of religion" (*GR* 460–61),[23] there is in such passages an undeniable esteem for certain values attributed to an Anglo-Saxon mentality. Alfred, for instance, is praised for his extensive building projects but is also said to have accomplished these feats without any cost to the public. William claims that Alfred paid a high price to owners for the land on which to build his projects and that he did so entirely from his own funds: "The king's self-denial was really extraordinary—to be willing to be milked of so much money" (GR 195).[24]

It is in William's poignant account of Wulfstan's (bishop of Worcester) reaction to the rebuilding, however, that we are most clearly shown the perceived value of what was being lost. Despite being loyal to the Norman hierarchy and the only episcopal leader to be retained across the change of monarchs, Wulfstan is nonetheless said to weep at the destruction of a Saxon site:

> When the bigger church, which he had himself started from the foundations, had grown large enough for the monks to move across to it, the word was given for the old church, the work of St. Oswald, to be stripped of its roof and demolished. Wulfstan stood there in the open air to watch and could not keep back his tears. His friends mildly reproved him: he should rather rejoice that in his lifetime so much honour had accrued to the church that the increased number of monks made the larger dwellings necessary. He replied, "My view is quite different. We unfortunates are destroying the works of saints in order to win praise for ourselves. In that happy age men were incapable of building for display. Their way was to sacrifice themselves to God under any sort of roof, and to encourage their subjects to follow their example. But we strive to pile up stones while neglecting souls." (GP 428–31)[25]

It is this gray area between the new Norman order and the sense of an Anglo-Saxon past with which this chapter and the next is most directly concerned. In the midst of the sweeping architectural and literary changes of Norman England, continuations of Anglo-Saxon architectural practice—and poetic representation of this practice—serve as an important frame of reference for interpreting the real-world architecture of the period as well as its fictional counterparts in the settings of Middle English verse.

ANGLO-SAXON ANTECEDENTS IN POST-CONQUEST ARCHITECTURE

While even the most casual glance at Anglo-Saxon architecture and that of later medieval England makes the magnitude of the differences abundantly clear, points of connection are far less transparent. Nonetheless, there is a quite tangible continuity of Anglo-Saxon tradition evident in surviving buildings. In some cases, it is difficult to discern whether building techniques employed in both periods are the result of Anglo-Saxon influence into the Norman period or of a given technique being employed independently by Normans and Saxons; *Saxo-Norman* is the term "used to describe the mixing of Anglo-Saxon and Norman architectural traditions" during the Saxo-Norman Overlap—the period encompassing the earliest Norman Romanesque in the eleventh through the early twelfth century. "By that stage surviving Anglo-Saxon elements had ceased to be used, and those elements which proved adaptable had been entirely absorbed into the English Romanesque style" (Fernie, *Norman* 318). During this period of transition it is often difficult and in some cases impossible to delineate Norman and Saxon influence. Anglo-Norman architects had a wealth of choices in design and technique, with influences arriving from such diverse places as Normandy, Germany, Italy, and Byzantium (cf. Thurlby 119). As we saw with the translations and adaptations of Latin texts into Old English verse (chap. 3), the nature of such choices can be telling, as they can give us at least some small indication of what elements architects and poets saw as most likely to resonate with native values and traditions. And with so many sources of influences, Anglo-Saxon elements became in the post-Conquest period "just one of the factors in a complex equation" (Thurlby 119).

Norman and late medieval structures repeatedly attest to the persistence of certain Anglo-Saxon forms, indicating that such features were not only useful from a utilitarian perspective but also deeply meaningful. At first sight, the massive St. Margaret's Church at King's Lynn bears little resemblance to the relatively small and unassuming churches built during the Anglo-Saxon period. The distinctive plinth on its southwest tower (fig. 25), however, is very similar in structure—high and stepped—to that found in some of these earlier churches, like the plinth of the chancel on St. Wystan's Church in Repton Village (fig. 24) (Thurlby 128). Stepped bases also characterize all three pillared arched structures depicted on the Franks Casket, a rectangular box made of whalebone and dating to eighth-century Northumbria.[26] The panels encompassing these structures depict scenes from three different traditions—Germanic narrative, the Hebrew Bible, and the Christian Gospels—all portrayed in similar architectural settings. As noted in chapter 1, the architectural features selected for inclusion on small spaces provide important insights into what features would have been most salient to contemporary audiences.[27] In this case, the architectural iconography with its stepped plinths helps make important connections for the "informed viewer" (Lang 248), linking seemingly unrelated themes across the time period and placing the varied scenes within the architectural experience of Anglo-Saxon viewers. The stepped plinth was not only a common feature on actual buildings; it was also a defining feature important and salient enough to be included on highly stylized and minimalist sculpture. Its continuation into post-Conquest architecture would thus have served as a visible link to Anglo-Saxon architecture and culture.

A shared aesthetic is also seen in the writings of William of Malmesbury, for instance, who praises the Hexham church built by Wilfrid for its "minaci altitudine murorum erecta" ["menacingly high walls"] and the fact that it was "diuersis anfractibus per cocleas circumducta" ["ringed around by various winding ways"] (*GP* 386–87), indicating a post-Conquest appreciation of high walls, prominent arches, and curved structures, all characteristics likewise prized in Anglo-Saxon architectural aesthetics. Gables ceased to be defining features of ecclesiastical or secular structures, which increasingly were built instead with vaulted ceilings, but other practices of timber construction continued to be implemented long into the post-Conquest period, often at variance with continental practice and in spite of practical difficulties. In addition to temporary functions of timber in scaffolding, machinery, and centering, permanent timber elements in otherwise stone churches included "vertical piles and horizontal beams as reinforcement for walls and foundations" (Fernie, *Norman* 296). Surviving evidence also reveals evidence of wooden vaults in stone churches.[28] And the Farnham Castle keep includes masonry supports in positions "contrary to all common sense," which leads M. W. Thompson to the conclusion "that we are dealing with a 'skeuomorph'" (*Rise of the Castle* 57), that is to say that the supports would be derivative of timber construction but are not needed (and are even counterproductive) in the new medium of stone: "Erected in wood, such structures would not cause surprise, since our knowledge of motte superstructures might lead us reasonably to expect it" (58). Skeuomorphs giving stone structures the appearance of timber counterparts are seen in buttressing techniques as well. In Norman castles and ecclesiastical architecture, the "strength of walls derived from their massive thickness" (68). Although "such thick walls should have made external buttressing unnecessary, . . . pilaster buttresses are practically universal" (69). Again, Thompson suggests that these buttresses, defining features of Norman architecture, are "skeuomorphs, representing the timber posts of earlier wooden structures which could have been carved" (69). That such features are throwbacks to wood is even more likely, given that these pilaster buttresses "are not found on other Continental keeps further east, but are normal on English towers, a fair indication of where the links lay" (38).

The underlying reasons for such skeuomorphs can be explained in terms of both composition and reception, to borrow concepts from studies in oral tradition: Anglo-Norman carpenters familiar with woodworking techniques were now being required to work with stone and very naturally defaulted to certain native building methods; likewise, incorporation of native elements would have helped the new Norman style resonate with audiences accustomed to and appreciative of Anglo-Saxon timber construction.

In other cases, undeniably Norman features of design reveal simultaneous connections with Anglo-Saxon architecture, though the two traditions' radical differences in terms of scale and structure sometimes obscure subtler similarities. Some architectural features that were employed in both England and Normandy prior to the Conquest include herringbone masonry and triangular headed arches (Fernie, *Norman* 210). As an example, triangular openings are seen in Anglo-Saxon construction in the doorway at Jarrow and, independently, in eleventh-century French architecture such as at St. Généroux and Chinon (Fernie, *Norman* 269). Thus it is impossible to say with absolute certainty whether the post-Conquest triangular arch at the Exeter gatehouse is derived from Norman or Saxon practice.[29] Shifting the focus from influence to reception, we can see the potential of such features, regardless of ultimate origin, to resonate with both native and newcomer populations.

THE FRENCH CHEVRON AND ANGLO-SAXON ARCHITECTURAL AESTHETICS

As an extended example of the sharing of Anglo-Saxon and Norman influences, I offer here a discussion of the French chevron, that is, "a moulding forming a zigzag, usually on an arch" (Fernie, *Norman* 314). The design is by definition "Romanesque" (e.g., Fleming et al. 91), but it nonetheless shares visual similarities with the herringbone design of Romano-British and Anglo-Saxon architecture as well as Scandinavian-influenced motifs. Though the chevron was clearly used in architecture and sculpture in Europe, it became much more important in Anglo-Norman culture as "probably the single most characteristic moulding or indeed feature of any kind in Norman architecture in England" (Fernie, *Norman* 276). This chevron ornament is widely visible in many post-Conquest buildings such as Canterbury Castle, the chapel of Anselm's crypt at Canterbury, the choir of the York Minster, St. Mary's Abbey in York, the Lady Chapel at Glastonbury, and, most prominently, at Durham Cathedral (fig. 9). But visually similar designs long familiar to the builders and users of early medieval spaces may also have exerted influence on the preference for the chevron pattern, a design that accommodated both an Anglo-Saxon past and the Norman present.

For instance, an ornamentation similar to the chevron design is featured prominently on Anglo-Saxon sculpture such as Saxon cross fragments at Jarrow, Northallerton, and Ripon (Thurlby 134) and, most notably, the Franks Casket.[30] The lid of the Franks Casket depicts a man—identified by a runic inscription as Ægili and often identified with Egil[31]—defending a house, rendered as an arch supported by two columns. The zigzag pattern forming this arch, similar to the chevron ornament lining the Norman doorways and arches of Durham Cathedral, is repeated on the front panel of the Franks Casket, again in relation to an arched structure supporting two columns, though here at the bottom of the columns.

A number of Anglo-Saxon hogback sculptures found in northern England also show the chevronlike ornament across a curved top, often as a roofline. The hogback sculptures are large monuments, the function of which is largely unknown,[32] with the basic shape of a building. They typically depict decorated "walls" and roofs with stylized shingling. Bailey notes that the shape of these sculptures very likely represents the "boat-shape" of buildings in Scandinavia, a "Viking-period feature of northern Britain" (86). Such Scandinavian links are strong for the hogback sculpture at St. Peter's Church in Heysham, Lancashire, which is believed to depict the story of Sigurd slaying the dragon on one side and Signy's rescue of Sigmund on the other,[33] and on both sides the monument's roofline is indicated with a chevronlike design (fig. 8). The more fully articulated rooflines on hogbacks at the Brompton parish church provide helpful context for understanding their Heysham counterparts. These Brompton hogbacks have beasts at either end, and in several of these sculptures the roofline is indicated by a series of zigzagging lines that seem to represent shingles. The adornments of these various hogback monuments parallel actual construction techniques, as wood-shingled roofs with animal heads at either end do indeed survive in Scandinavian stave churches.

This pattern also has affinities with the herringbone pattern that decorates the exterior of the late Saxon St. James Church at Selham (fig. 4) and can even be found in depictions of artwork in Old English literature.[34] For instance, references to swords in *Beowulf* as "atertanum fah" [lit., "adorned with poison twigs"] (1459), "wyrmfah" ["with serpentine ornamentation"] (1698), and "wægsweord" ["sword with wavy ornamentation"] (1489) are thought to describe a "herringbone-like" pattern, "rippling in its visual effect and thus reminiscent of intertwined serpents" (Fulk, Bjorn, and Niles 205). With such a well-established tradition of similar designs in sculpture, architecture, and even literature, the chevron would have been a natural choice for builders who had inherited an Anglo-Saxon tradition of building but were now working within the parameters of the new Norman style.

In the case of Durham Cathedral, where the chevron design is especially pervasive, the motivation to activate associations with Anglo-Saxon traditions was particularly strong, since at this location tremendous emphasis is placed—even to the present day—on the heritage of

St. Cuthbert and Bede. The cathedral houses a shrine to Cuthbert, with treasures on display,[35] and the remains of the Venerable Bede are also believed to be under the cathedral's Galilee Chapel, exactly in the place where the chevron design is most prominent on the ceiling, walls, and arches. The extensive use of the chevron throughout the cathedral thus allows the building to simultaneously speak to two traditions, harkening back to a Germanic heritage of sculpture and building through the use of a visually similar (if not directly related) tradition of Norman Romanesque building.

THE POST-CONQUEST HALL

The post-Conquest "hall" also develops in keeping with continental practice while consistently demonstrating limited continuations of an Anglo-Saxon architectural aesthetics. Largely subsumed by the castle, the Anglo-Norman hall bears little surface resemblance to Anglo-Saxon halls, yet the subtle ways in which post-Conquest halls differ from their continental counterparts show an undeniable influence of Anglo-Saxon styles and architectural values. Points of connection, however, are largely obscured by the more obvious structural differences as the dominant aristocratic architecture shifted from the hall to the castle. The hall ceased to be a central and unifying entity and gave way to a hall isolated from the outside by increasingly militaristic building designs. Such architectural changes were natural outgrowths of the new priorities of the emerging Norman aristocracy. As seen in William of Poitiers' accounts of William the Conqueror, the native populations were seen as potential threats, and with the growing need for defense and a strong assertion of the new social hierarchy in post-Conquest England the hall became less a central space for congregation and protection and more a space to be isolated and protected.

Even in its new position *within* the castle, however, the English hall was a much more discrete entity than in castles on the continent. Excavations at Goltho in Lincolnshire, for instance, show that when a tower was set on the motte, the hall was kept as a separate structure within the bailey. Later when the motte was spread over the entire bailey, a separate hall was built on top. Throughout this sequence, the hall retained "all the time a separate identity" (Thompson, *Rise of the Castle* 10) within an increasingly militaristic castle. This distinction between the castle as a largely militaristic space and the hall as a separate space to some extent independent of the subsuming castle allows the hall to retain a degree of its pre-Conquest association with Germanic ideals even as the castle that contains the hall represents the rise of the powerful Norman aristocracy.

The points of variance between typical continental and Anglo-Norman castles demonstrate similar continuations of Anglo-Saxon practice, especially with regard to halls. For instance, on the continent upper-story halls were used almost exclusively, whereas in England ground-floor halls were far more common (Thompson, *Rise of the Castle* 90), making for a more accessible hall closer to the central position of the hall in Anglo-Saxon times. Likewise, small "solar" keeps that were round or octagonal in shape were typical in France, while English castles more typically featured large, rectangular "hall keeps" (66), the differences in shape and size aligning the English keeps with Anglo-Saxon architectural style. And within the stone castles, "more often than not the hall was of wood and in some cases the great tower as well" (Fernie, *Norman* 296), the wooden halls continuing to bear a resemblance in material to Anglo-Saxon timber halls.

The open hearth and correspondingly high open roof commonly found and valued in Anglo-Saxon halls also persist in such post-Conquest buildings as the thirteenth-century hall of Stokesay, Shropshire, one of the most intact halls representative of the period. Here the raised cruck roof and open hearth are "virtually unaltered" (125),[36] offering rare incontrovertible proof of the architectural practice.[37] Evidence of open roofs and central hearths, including paved burned areas in the centers of the halls and piers rising from basements to support the weight of the hearth, has been found at many such sites dating through the High Middle Ages, including halls at Oakham (Leicestershire), Winchester, and Ludlow. In contrast, European halls of the same period tended toward fireplaces, flues, and chimneys. The persistence of the central hearth and open roofs of English halls in spite of possible fire damage represents what Thompson calls the "triumph of the native style" (*Medieval Hall* 99). Despite enormous architectural changes in post-Conquest England,

Thompson claims that "a fifteenth-century hall like that of Edward IV at Eltham Palace, Kent, or even a seventeenth-century one at Audley End, Essex, would have been recognizable to King Alfred or even King Edwin" (*Medieval Hall* 74). "Aristocratic culture from 500–1500 was a culture of the hall, where its chief achievements manifested themselves" (Thompson, *Rise of the Castle* 12). The "camaraderie of the Old English hall," that is, the Germanic *comitatus* associated with this social system, "did not survive the introduction of feudalism" (12), but there is in memory a nostalgia for this code, which is reflected in the architecture and in the litera - ture of the Middle English period. Despite its movement toward virtual obsolescence, there was nonetheless "something special about the native style of architecture" (*Medieval Hall* 100) such that "archaisms" in a post-Conquest structure provided "a stamp of approval or even invested it with a special merit" (101). James Earl has persuasively argued that during the migration of Germanic tribes and the eventual conversion to Christianity, the Anglo-Saxon hall "proved adaptive in the drastically changed historical conditions of the Anglo-Saxons' migration and conversion" (*Thinking* 136) and that "the vitality" of the Anglo-Saxons during these transitions "was in part due to the continuity of its development, the survival of traditions that made the difference between growth and just change" (135). In subtler ways this same adaptability can be seen across the cultural changes in the post-Conquest period where the "residues of the past" continue to "provide a repertory of attitudes and responses that can be brought to everyday experience" (135).[38]

ANGLO-SAXON ORAL POETICS AND MIDDLE ENGLISH "HALLS"

The uneasy relationship between the old and the new social orders reflected in Anglo-Norman architecture also finds expression in architectural description in Middle English verse. In its poetic articulation, *castle* more often than not references military strength, whereas images of the *hall* more frequently index codes of behavior associated with heroic conduct, codes that continue the tradition of the Germanic *comitatus*. In fact, usages of *hall* across the body of Middle English texts reflect a retention of its grand sense from Old English times alongside a simultaneous sense reflective of the early freestanding timber halls' subsumption within the stone-dressed castles of the later Middle Ages. The *Middle English Dictionary* gives the dominant sense of *hall* as a freestanding structure, synonymous with *castle:* "a large private residence, a manorial hall; a royal residence, palace, castle" (s.v. *halle*). Its secondary meaning derives from later architectural innovations to castles, with halls being components, albeit important ones, within the larger castle: "the large public room in a mansion, palace, ship, etc., used for assembly, eating, audience, holding court, etc." (s.v. *hall,* sense II). Indeed, definitions of *castle* and *hall* even to the present day reflect an association of halls with social contexts of use and castles with military strength.[39] In poetry there is a heightened sense of such distinctions in verse of the Middle English period, the concepts of hall and castle providing condensed verbal images especially potent in connotative meaning—to use Foley's words, the poetic tradition "works like language, only more so" (*How to Read* 126).[40] In poetry even more than on the landscape, the hall tends to serve as the center of social and heroic activity, where the castle is more likely to serve as a widely visible assertion of dominance and military strength, designed not solely for protection *of* local inhabitants but often as protection *from* the very communities in which they are situated.

Changes in language and literature were less programmatic[41] and more gradual but ultimately no less extreme than those that occurred in the architectural sphere. By the beginning of the twelfth century, linguistic changes that had to some extent begun before the Norman Conquest were now well established, most notably the radical reduction of inflectional endings, the corresponding loss of grammatical gender, and the increasing reliance on word order necessitated by the dramatically reduced case system.[42] And as the Norman style looked radically different from the Anglo-Saxon, the look of the written language changed as well.[43] The greatest impact of the Norman Conquest, which made French the language of the new ruling class, however, lay in the word stock, with many hundreds of words entering English directly from French in the centuries following the conquest, especially vocabulary items involving government or administration, many of which involve the architectural spaces of these newly powerful institutions.[44]

Due to the extreme changes in building practices, architectural language witnesses especially radical changes across this period. New terms such as *prison* and *castle* (in the sense of a building) are established by the end of the eleventh century; *tower* (*tur*), *post* (*postel*), and *chapel* are fixed by the twelfth. During the thirteenth century we see an ever-increasing French influence on both ecclesiastical and secular architectural vocabulary, with words such as *hermitorie* (hermitage), *abbey, cellar, cell, city, kernel* (battlement), *parlour, pilare* (pillar), *sepulchre,* and *palais* (palace) all well attested. Even texts with relatively low percentages of French borrowings, like *King Horn* (Serjeantson 127–30), rely heavily on French borrowings for buildings such as *castel, chapel, palais* (palace), and *ture* (tower). In the late thirteenth and early fourteenth century, terms such as *barbican, chaumbre* (chamber), *schauntillon* (mason's rule), *stage, dungeon, pavilion, pauiment* (pavement), *solere* (sunroom), *balcony,* and *touret* (turret) all come into more common usage, adding to and often displacing Old English architectural vocabulary (Serjeantson 133, 136, 140). And many words of Old English origin become more specialized with distinctly Norman senses, a pattern especially evident in architectural description. The Old English *teldian* ["to spread"], for instance, which, as discussed in chapter 3, originally referred most specifically to the erection of a tent (Bosworth), is applied in *Sir Gawain and the Green Knight* for the erection of towers (795).[45]

More than purely a matter of vocabulary, this influx of French borrowings changed the sounds of English and ultimately shifted its accentual system, which before had primarily involved stress on the initial syllable of words of more than one syllable (with the exception of certain prefixes).[46] With such radical changes to the language, it should be unsurprising that the verse form itself underwent concomitant changes as a result of Norman influence. Alliteration, a defining feature of Old English verse, and initial stress, the norm for Old English multisyllable words, go hand in hand, since initial alliteration is more audible when occurring in stressed syllables. With the shift from stress in initial position of words to variable stress patterns in borrowed items, the alliterative verse of the Old English period gave way to forms of verse that aurally privileged the ends of words through rhyme or primarily iambic metrical patterns. The post-Conquest erosion of the "highly regulated, technically precise, essentially monolithic, continuous tradition" that characterized the Old English verse form "from the composition of *Cæd-mon's Hymn* around 680 until the death of Edward the Confessor and the ensuing Conquest" (Cable 56) led to what has been understood as the "rupture of the poetic tradition" (3), in effect, the "end of the Old English poetic tradition" (55). However, although the period does witness the end of the homogeneity characterizing Old English verse, the poetic system that governed all verse produced in the Anglo-Saxon period did not fall away entirely but instead provided one of many available options to later medieval writers, a pattern similar to that seen in medieval architectural history. Rosamund Allen characterizes the *Brut,* for instance, as "something between the long line of Old English verse, with medial caesura, and the short octosyllabic couplet of much French narrative verse" (*Brut* xxix) and notes that certain features of Old English poetry—such as compounding, alliteration, and formulaic patterning—serve to give the poem " 'archaic dignity,' which Lawman must have considered appropriate to his material" (xxv), even though many of the phraseological patterns are not actually of Anglo-Saxon origin and evoke Old English verse through similarities in structural form rather than lexical content.

Such developments in the poetics can perhaps be better understood in the context of the more obvious patterns in vocabulary discussed earlier. While in some cases French vocabulary items completely displaced native words, in many instances the language simply developed synonyms, such as French *domicile* alongside the native *home, partition* alongside *wall,* or *fortification* alongside *strength,* with some degree of specialization occurring on both sides. The native English vocabulary items retained currency despite the introduction of French-derived terms, giving English speakers a range of connotative meanings in expressing the "same" essential idea. In similar fashion, Anglo-Saxon oral poetics in post-Conquest England provided poets with a highly efficient mode of poetic expression that coexisted with those forms derived from Norman inheritance. As Mark Amodio puts it, the years immediately following the Norman Conquest

> witnessed the decline of the uniform autochthonous oral poet-
> ics that had dominated poetic articulation in England for more
> than four-hundred years and the rise of diverse new systems of

articulating, receiving, and physically encoding poetry, many of which continue to be important constituents of contemporary poetics. Unlike their Anglo-Saxon forebears, Middle English poets do not engage a stable, homeostatic expressive economy, one whose contours remain clearly identifiable across several centuries. Instead, they draw upon the idioms of a number of different expressive economies, some of which descend from and are deeply influenced by Anglo-Saxon oral poetics, some of which derive from continental traditions and hence owe no direct debt to medieval English oral poetics, and some of which can best be described as deriving from a mix of oral and literate poetics (both insular and continental). (*Writing* 79)

This diversity in poetic expression closely parallels not only the period's expanding vocabulary but also the multiplicity of architectural styles employed in post-Conquest England. And, as the architecture of the period manifests continuations of Anglo-Saxon aesthetics and practice even in the midst of radical and widespread reform, the poetic language employed to describe fictionalized architecture likewise draws from multiple modes of expression, a process that can be brought into sharper focus by exploring selected terms in a representative early Middle English text, specifically the usages of *hall* and *castle* in Laȝamon's *Brut*.

ARCHITECTURAL POETICS IN THE *BRUT*

Tensions between the Anglo-Saxon and Anglo-Norman social orders found physical expression in the transitional architecture of this period involving tumultuous change, with older structures rapidly being replaced by newer, grander buildings, which nonetheless betrayed an indebtedness to and inherent respect for prior modes of architectural expression. In presenting his version of British history, with all its successive changes in rule, it is only natural that Laȝamon would have used architectural imagery in marking shifts in power and authority, and leaders' prowess in the *Brut* is frequently signified by the destruction of old and/or the erection of new structures. Yet at several points, especially in the poem's employment of hall imagery, seemingly generic architectural language indexes a social code that had already to some extent been displaced in post-Conquest England, though it was no less revered. Through its employment of oral traditional poetics, the *Brut* conveys great respect for the hall and its concomitant social culture even amid a poetic world that—like the real one inhabited by Laȝamon and his earliest audiences—is dominated by military castles.

Laȝamon's *Brut,* variously dated from the late twelfth to the early thirteenth century, occupies something of a transitional position along the medieval English "oral-literate nexus."[47] In the autobiographical prologue, Laȝamon situates his text unequivocally in the realm of literacy and scholarly learning, claiming Wace's French *Roman de Brut* as the primary source among three texts and self-referentially describing his actual writing process in some detail (lines 26–28). As a verse chronicle, the *Brut* has no generic precedent in English-language texts, and its linear manner of historicizing Britain's leaders from Brutus through Cadwalader further demonstrates the poem's production within a culture of literacy and linear thinking. Its daunting 16,000 lines and its "highly inconsistent" rhythms and metrics (Amodio, *Writing* 94) would argue against the likelihood of its having been intended for oral performance,[48] and, unlike much Middle English verse, the *Brut* makes no reference to a listening audience and provides no indication that the author envisions any such performative context. Nevertheless, despite its entrenchment in literate culture, "evidence of demonstrably written composition *does not preclude* the presence of nonperformative oral poetics" (Amodio, *Writing* 93). In fact, as Amodio has established, the *Brut*'s "lexicon, thematics, syntax, metrics, narrative patterning, and verbal collocations all witness the centrality of oral poetics to Laȝamon's compositional process" (95), even as the text negotiates "among the disparate, unique, and often conflicting constellations of elements that constitute early Middle English culture" (101). In terms of its architectural representation, the connotative meanings of the hall and its evocation of *comitatus* ideals are sustained throughout the poem, but hall imagery is more subtle and far less frequent than in Old English verse. The architectural landscape of the *Brut*—very much like Laȝamon's own—was one characterized by multiple stylistic influences but dominated by strong, well-fortified castles.

The *Brut*'s Castles

While the leaders of the *Brut* inhabit and interact with numerous buildings that appear in the poem, the *Brut* of course does not attempt complete architectural accuracy across the centuries it spans. The word *castle*
itself is fairly generic in the poem and cannot be understood as representing any particular building type. It occurs over two hundred times
in reference to buildings from numerous geographic regions spanning
millennia. In the absence of more specific details, what might the term
castle have conjured in terms of physical images and associative meanings for Laȝamon's earliest audiences? What metonymic meaning under-
lies this fairly ubiquitous and architecturally vague term? To approach
these questions, let us turn now to the narrative and phraseological contexts in which buildings denoted as *castles* most frequently appear.

Though the architectural referents for *castle* vary considerably
throughout the narrative, its distinctly military function is quite consistent in the *Brut*. The poem's opening being representative of patterns
that continue consistently throughout the poem, an analysis of the first
1,000 lines can clearly illustrate the employment pattern of the word in
distinctly military and proprietary senses. In the first 1,000 lines of the
Caligula version,[49] four leaders are identified as having castles, with a
total of 25 occurrences of the words *castle* or *castel* involved, and here
every structure referenced explicitly as a *castle* is marked in terms of its
strength and military fortifications.

Aeneas, the first leader of such a structure, built a castle named Lavi-
nium after his beloved Lavinia, a building described as a "*stronge* castel
mid starke ston walle" ["strong castle with sturdy stone walls"] (96; emphasis mine)[50] and referred to as a "castle" also at 97 and 114. Assaracus
similarly possesses three castles given to him by his father, all of them
explicitly described as "*stronge* castles" (202).[51] The militaristic function
of these buildings is also underscored by the "seoue þusend kempen"
["seven thousand warriors"] assigned to their protection, a number twice
repeated (217, 233).

Like those of Aeneas and Assaracus, Pandrasus's castle Sparatin
(Sonatin in the Otho MS.) is also marked as "strong"—"Nes castel nan
swa strong" ["There was not a castle as strong"] (302), and its designa-

tion as a *castle* is repeated eight other times (301, 305, 308, 310, 318, 322, 330, 418). Finally, the last leader of these 1,000 lines is Britain's legendary founder, Brutus himself, whose "strong" (827) dwelling is actually referenced as a castle no fewer than nine times (826, 827, 831, 839, 841, 843, 848, 854, 865).[52] All of these usages from the Caligula manuscript are also included in the first 1,000 lines of the Otho manuscript, and, in addition, the Otho manuscript includes a reference to a *castel* found by Brutus and his men (corresponding to Caligula *burh*) that follows the same pattern in marking the structure's strength: "Hii funde in þan ilond: anne castel swiþe strong" ["They found on that island a castle very strong"] (569).

These opening 1,000 lines of the more than 16,000-line poem thus effectively establish the world of the *Brut* as one of *castles*, structures that are consistently designated as *strong* throughout the length of the text[53] and that frequently serve as displays of military prowess and appropriate sites for battle. Though the narrative of the *Brut* is of course not treating Norman history directly, the usage of *castel* is still consistent with the military appearance and function of castles on the Anglo-Norman architectural landscape contemporary with the poem's production. Like the post-Conquest England of the poem's first readers, the world of the *Brut* as rendered by Laȝamon is characterized by rapid and large-scale construction, especially with regard to castles that symbolically validate and physically maintain military strength and political authority.

The *Brut*'s Halls

Whereas castles are fairly ubiquitous in the *Brut*, structures lexically designated as *halls* are far less common—a pattern very much in keeping with the growing importance of the castle and a corresponding diminishing role for the hall not only on the Anglo-Norman landscape but also in the period's literature. While forms of *castle* occur 25 times in the first 1,000 lines alone, forms of *hall* appear only 39 times in the entire length of the 16,000-line poem, six of which are localized within the short space of Arthur's dream. As with *castel*, the usages of *hall* in some respects reveal much more about Anglo-Norman architectural attitudes than about those of the cultures being described in the *Brut*'s narrative. Halls in actual medieval construction took a number of forms, gradually shifting from self-contained structures to spaces within the larger castle, and the term *hall* itself in the *Brut* similarly denotes a range of architectural possibilities. At points *hall* designates a structure separate from but parallel to the *castle,* as when Arthur acquires castles and halls during the fall of Paris: "bitahten him halles: bitahten him castles" ["delivered to him halls, delivered to him castles"] (11995). At other points, the *hall* is more discernibly a space *within* the larger structure, as when Brutus discovers a stronghold within which lie wasted halls: "Heo funden i þon eit-londe: ane burh swiðe stronge: / To-hælde weoren þe walles: weste weren hallen" ["They found on the island a very strong fortress: broken were the walls; wasted were the halls"] (569–70). At this point in the Otho manuscript, the hall's presence inside a castle specifically is made still more clear, the *burh* of the Caligula becoming a "castel swiþe strong" in the Otho.[54] And in a description of great devastation, halls again are presented as components of the larger stronghold but also distinct within that space when enemies are said to "berne[ð] heore halles / seælle[ð] heore tures. 7 swaleð heore bures" ["burn their halls, assail their towers, and set fire to their bowers"] (3063–64). Finally, Belin repairs his "castles" by attending to their component parts, including the halls: "rihten alle þæ hallen: 7 stronginen þæ walles" ["righting all the halls, and strengthening the walls"] (2983). These senses of *hall* as sometimes parallel to but distinct from castles and at other times constituents of encompassing structures are certainly consistent with the reality of what constituted a hall at various points and in various structures in early post-Conquest England. Thus the term *hall* in itself does little to convey a specific type of built space, and the physical appearance of the *Brut*'s halls must be left largely to audience visualization.[55]

But while the physical structures of the *Brut*'s halls vary widely in their architectural features, the phraseological and syntactical structures in which the term *hall* is employed are surprisingly quite consistent in connotative meaning. In subject and direct object position, buildings marked lexically as *halls* almost always occur as items of property— generally alongside one or more possessions—being destroyed, built, or distributed during a transition from one leader to another. On the other hand, as the object of a preposition, *hall* exhibits throughout the poem a much more specialized and traditionally freighted meaning. It is in this particular placement that buildings designated as *halls* occur in conjunction with distinctly *comitatus* ideals.

Temporarily leaving aside Arthur's dream, which includes especially complex usages of hall imagery that are discussed below, 11 of the 33 remaining references to a hall are in subject or direct object position. (See complete list of lines at the end of this chapter.) In each of these cases the halls figure into the narrative primarily as physical property, usually as one of multiple items being built, repaired, destroyed, or distributed. For instance, in lines whose halves are linked by rhyme, *walls* are most frequently paired with *halls* in being built or destroyed. Not only do Brutus and his men discover halls and walls laid waste (570), as noted above, but Gurguint commands his warriors to "brekeð heore walles. 7 berne[ð] heore halles" ["break their walls and burn their halls"] (3063), and Octa likewise destroys walls and halls (8272): "greiðeden walles: to-halden þa halles" ["prepared the walls and broke the halls"] (8272). In contrast, the conquest of Rome by Belin and Brennes is followed by commands to have halls built and walls mended ["timbrien þa hallen: bæten þa walles"] (2963), and Belin later commissions further repair and fortification of halls and walls: "rihten alle þæ hallen: 7 stronginen þæ walles" (2983). And though the halls do not appear in the same line with walls, King Lud does erect halls immediately after constructing the walls of London (3532, 3534), and yet another collocation of the two structural elements appears when Bedivere is warned of a foe who destroyed numerous structures within Howel's castle, including gates (12919), doors (12921), and hall walls (12920).

King Aurelius is twice said to have erected halls, the halls again being items in a list of constructions, first alongside walls ("He letten stronge walles: he lette bulden halles" ["He had strong walls built; he had halls built"] (8459) and later with churches "þer he lette wurcchen: [halles 7 chirchen]" ["there he had halls and churches made"] (8464).[56] The pairing of halls with churches in destruction or building efforts is seen also in the Otho manuscript's treatment of Childric's demolition projects: "þe chirchen for-barnd: þe halles to-fallen" ["the churches burned, the halls fallen"] (11025).[57] In the description of Arthur's leadership, the usage of the term follows the same pattern of being syntactically in subject or direct object position in occurrence alongside other items, but for Arthur the halls are parallel not with walls or other component parts of castles but rather with the castles themselves: "bitahten him halles: bitahten him castles" ["delivered to him halls, delivered to him castles"] (11995). As I discuss more fully below, the hall as a symbol of heroic ideals is closely associated with Arthur's court in the *Brut*, and it is thus very appropriate that we find here halls elevated syntactically to the same status as castles. Living and writing in an era of widespread demolition and construction, Laȝamon quite naturally depicts shifts in power structure throughout his history in terms of radical architectural change. And, given the importance of halls even within the construct of larger castles, it is also unsurprising that halls figure especially prominently among the items destroyed, built, and restored by great leaders.

What is perhaps surprising is how the associative value of the hall shifts according to its syntactical positioning. As objects of a preposition, the halls of the *Brut* are typically not items in lists of property destroyed, built, or distributed, as we have seen was the case for those instances occurring in subject or direct object position, but rather these preposition-governed halls serve as indexed loci for heroic behavior. In these instances, rather than being linked with militaristic strength such as that stemming from the Anglo-Norman *castle*, the term *hall* consistently appears in conjunction with ideals most similar to those of the Germanic *comitatus*. Men are led together "to hallen" (7137), hear stories "in . . . hallen" (12072), receive and respond to challenges "in-to halle" (12346), drink and harp "in halle" (7461), and throng together "to halle" (9242). As can be seen in the appendix to this chapter, halls as the objects of prepositions almost always appear in conjunction with communal ideals and social conventions typical of the Germanic *comitatus*, and these consistent and repeated patterns of use doubtless created meaningful channels of communication for Laȝamon and his medieval audiences.[58]

There are three arguable exceptions to this pattern at lines 11919 ("heo clumben uppen hallen: heo clumben uppen wallen"; "they climbed upon halls; they climbed upon walls"), 1014 ("mid bouren 7 mid hallen"; "with bowers and with halls"), and 9855 ("þe wes on-væst þere halle"; "which was near the hall"). The prepositions in these three instances—*vppen*, *mid*, and *on-væst*—are unattested with "hall" as object elsewhere in the poem, forms of "to" and "in" being far more frequent and thus more likely to develop into patterns of associative meaning through repetition. These three instances are further removed from the usual usage of hall in object of preposition position in that they are only being referenced in conjunction with other physical spaces within larger castles or grounds. In the cases of 11919 and 1014, the halls are items in lists (referenced alongside walls and bowers respectively), more like the halls in subject/object position discussed earlier. (In the case of line 11919, the corresponding point in the Otho manuscript does not include a preposition with "hall" at all, suggesting even less of a formulaic or traditionally fixed quality for this particular usage.) While the "hall" referenced in 9855 is not an item in a list of multiple objects or spaces, it is also only referenced in relation to another physical space and would seem to serve primarily to provide the physical location of a well outside the hall. This is not to say that these three instances would not evoke the concept of *comitatus* ideals or relationships for reading or listening audiences, but in terms of narrative context and syntactical placement these three usages do not seem as closely linked to *comitatus* ideals as other usages. Nevertheless, all of the other instances of *halle* in object of preposition placement clearly do occur in conjunction with (or in direct subversion of) *comitatus* ideals.

The three possible exceptions above aside, it is in object of preposition placement where clear associative patterns emerge that transcend the lexical meaning of a hall as a purely physical space. That the pattern is more than mere coincidence whereby the knights happen to be in a hall is suggested by its usage at points when the knights are arguably *not* in halls. Three phraseological patterns, accounting for twelve of the employments of *hall* in object of preposition placement, receive special attention here due to their remarkable consistency in syntactical form and narrative context. Each of these compositional devices involving the word *hall* also shares repeated rhyming words that link the first and second halves of the line.[59] The first involves the word pair *alle/halle,* and the second two have *halle* linked via rhyme[60] and other structural features—or what we might call near-rhyme[61]—to the adjective *stille.*[62]

alle/halle Word Pair.   In collocation with *alle,* the word *halle* when placed as the object of a preposition is consistently the locus of knightly solidarity. The motives behind that solidarity may be good or ill, but the ideal of unity for knights within the hall at these points is unambiguous. When traitors of King Belin make a boast—albeit a boast not to fight bravely but rather to wear a unified front in treachery—their loyalty to one another in their evil endeavors is expressed in reference to the hall: "Þa seiden heo *in halle* þisne read halde we *alle*" ["Then said those in the hall: 'This council hold we all'"] (2673). At another convening of men by a leader, this time in Arthur's court, the Otho manuscript also employs the *halle/alle* word pair with the effect of emphasizing the solidarity of Arthur and his *comitatus:* "answerede alle: in boure and in halle" ["answered all, in bower and in hall"] (Otho, 11116).

Another usage in the Otho that is unattested in the corresponding portion of the Caligula manuscript further illustrates this pattern, again linking through identical phrasing a convening of *alle* with the men's physical placement "in hall." King Coel on his deathbed calls his men together. "And hii him radde alle; in boure and in halle" ["and they all counseled him, in bower and in hall"] (Otho, 5498). The Otho manuscript situates the men "in halle" despite the fact that Coel at this point in the narrative is said explicitly to be in an encampment, "in comelan" (5491). The Caligula manuscript, which has the men convene without the explicit reference to the hall, would seem to be more logical, but from the perspective of the surrounding traditional poetics, the men's placement around their leader "in halle" is perfectly appropriate. As in numerous other cases of seeming inconsistency, the traditional import of such phraseology supersedes purely lexical meaning, the invocation of the hall underscoring the men's solidarity with one another and with Coel at the time of his death.

This pattern linking the hall with knightly solidarity becomes especially evident in the cycles of loyalty and treachery in the episodes involving Vortigern, his son Vortimer, and his father-in-law Hengest, in their continuing struggles for power. The solidarity of Vortigern's men and their unwavering loyalty to Vortigern and one another are marked by the *alle/halle* word pair when the men conspire to kill Constance and thus bring Vortigern to power: "eoden heo *alle:* þurh-ut þære *halle*" ["They all went throughout the hall"] (6767).[63] Vortigern himself assumes the role of *comitatus* leader and is said to go into the hall now surrounded by his retainers: "He wende in-to *halle:* 7 his heleðes mid him *alle*" ["He went into the *hall,* and all his retainers with him"] (7126), the placement of the men together in the hall thus underscoring the solidarity between and among Vortigern and his men. Hengest's power as a leader and the soli-

darity of his loyal retainers are likewise marked by the *halle/alle* collocation: "Heo comen *in-to halle:* hændeliche *alle* / ["They came *into the hall,*
noble all"] (6977).

This solidarity conveyed through the *halle/alle* lines is reinforced
by surrounding associations between the *comitatus* social system and
the physical structure of the hall, consistently designated as a space for joy
and feasting among retainers: "bemen heo bleowen: gomen men gunnen
cleopien. / bord heo hetten breden: cnihtes setten þer-to: / heo æten heo
drunken: dræm wes i burhȝen" ["they blew trumpets; men began to shout
joy; the boards they ordered to be spread; knights sat down at them; they
ate and they drank; joy was in the stronghold"] (7127–29). In conjunction
with this space of *comitatus* feasting complete with not only camaraderie but also music, food, drink, and joy, the treacherous Rowena is then
led into the *hall:* "Hæȝe iborenne men: heo lædden *to hallen*" ["High-
born men led her into the hall"] (7137). By explicitly noting Rowena's entrance as "into the hall," the language suggests that Rowena is not only a
threat to Vortimer himself but also to the entire social system that the hall
embodies and metonymically represents. Rowena's entrance into the hall
thus anticipates the disruption to the social system of the hall that is indeed realized when she seduces Vortigern. The subsequent marriage between Vortigern and Rowena greatly empowers the calculating Hengest
and his followers, much to the dismay of the British people, who in response turn against Vortigern and raise his son, Vortimer, to the throne.

As with the hall of Vortigern his father, explicit designations of the
space of Vortimer's "hall" are invariably linked with the image of a king
surrounded by retainers feasting, drinking, and playing music on the
harp, all aspects of the hall-idea complex in Old English verse: "Þa þe
king hafde iæten: þa eoden þeines-men to mete. / in *halle* heo drunken:
harpen þer dremde" ["When the king had eaten, then the lord's thanes
took food. In the hall they drank, harps there resounded"] (7460–61).[64]
And, once again, it is the treacherous Rowena ["swicfulle Rouuenne"]
(7462) who shatters the social structure of the *comitatus* by poisoning
Vortimer at the feast.[65] As these examples attest, the term *hall* in collocation with *alle* is consistently associated, either by contrast or by fulfillment, with ideals of loyalty to king and companions, with ideals that
occur in conjunction with other *comitatus* values, including generosity to

and among retainers, promises and fulfillment of valor, and celebratory/
anticipatory joy, feasting, and music.

stille/halle Word Pair: *hit wes/sæt stille in halle.* The second formulaic
pattern to be addressed here occurs exclusively within the Arthurian
portions of the text. Indeed, the highest concentration of explicit references to the hall—especially in the more marked object of preposition
placement—do lie in these episodes where the *comitatus* ideals of loyalty, bravery, and reciprocity are most pronounced. This is not to say that
castles do not figure prominently in the Arthurian portions of the poem
as well, but Arthur's world is characterized more than any other portion
of the poem by the social culture, and attendant architecture, of the hall.
In a great celebration with Uther Pendragon, Arthur's father, men are
said to throng to the hall: "þa þe mæsse wes isungen: *to halle* heo þrungen" ["when the mass was sung, to the hall they thronged"] (9242). And
while virtually all of *Brut*'s halls in this object-of-preposition placement
demonstrate a strong relationship—though sometimes subverted—to
comitatus ideals, Arthur's halls in particular are associated with distribu-
tion of treasure and land to loyal and worthy retainers, harping, singing,
and joy:

> þus Arður þe king delde; his driht-liche londes.
> after heore iwurhte; for he heom þuhte wurðe.
> þa weoren bliðe spelles; *in Arðures hallen.*
> þer wes harepinge and song: þer weoren blissen imong. (12070–73)
>
> ———
>
> [Thus Arthur the king dealt out his royal lands,
> According to their works, for he thought them worthy.
> Then there were happy tales in Arthur's halls:
> There was harping and song; there were joys as well.]

Thus it is in the hall that Arthur is challenged by messengers from Rome:
"Þer comen *in-to halle:* spelles seol-cuðe" ["There came into the hall
strange tales"] (12346) and here that his knights must subsequently pledge
themselves to victory. The messenger warriors who issue the "spelles" are
described very much in keeping with *comitatus* values—armed, noble,

loyal to one another, and bearing treasure[66]—as they challenge and boast, claiming that unless Arthur submits entirely to Rome's jurisdiction the kaiser will seize him and lead him bound before the people of Rome (12389–91). However, in a demonstration of their own adherence to the values of the *comitatus* relationship, Arthur's knights respond with an even more threatening boast, swearing "uppen mære ure Drihten / þat alle heo dede weoren: þa þeos arunde beden: / mid horsen al to-draȝene. dæð heo sculden þolie" ["upon our glorious Lord that they all will be dead, those who brought this message, with horses all dragged. Death they must endure"] (12394–96).

But there is of course more to the *comitatus* relationship and the social culture of the hall than fierceness and feasting, as the repeated pairing of *stille* with *halle* conveys. The successful *comitatus* embodies an implicit respect for leadership and control within an assembled body of knights, an order characterized formulaically through silence or stillness in the hall. While the purely lexical meaning of the assertion that "all was still in the hall" would make it appropriate in numerous narrative contexts, such as at nighttime when knights sleep or in times of peace, the line invariably occurs following an uprising of Arthur's knights in response to a grave threat. When Arthur and his men convene following the threat from Rome discussed above, they retire to an "ald stanene worc" ["old stone work"] (12419), seat themselves at benches ["to benche"], thus evoking the configuration of mead benches in the traditional Germanic hall even within the physical space of ancient ruins, and remain silent until Arthur speaks: "þa wes hit al *stille:* þat wuneden inne *halle*" ["Then it was all still, that dwelled in the hall"] (12423). The two lines that immediately follow then explicate the silence—though not its explicit referencing of the hall itself—linking this stillness with both respect and fear for their king: "þer wes vnimete æie: mid mære þan kinge./ ne durste þer na man speken: leste þe king hit wolde awreken" ["There was immense awe for the glorious king. No man there dared speak, lest the king punish them for it"] (12424–25). Following the silence, Cador speaks first as the highest-ranking knight, followed by Gawain. When a subsequent disagreement between Cador and Gawain threatens to disrupt the unity of the "hall," Arthur again calls them to order, this time on pain of death (12462). Once again there is stillness in the hall: "Al hit wes still: þat wunede inne halle"

["It all was still, that dwelled in the hall"] (12463), but this second time the silence is effectively sustained until "spak þe king balde" ["the king spoke boldly"] (12464).

In the lengthy and long-awaited speech that follows, Arthur justifies the plans to conquer Rome on the grounds that Rome rightfully belongs to the Britons by means of rightful inheritance from King Belin and his brother Brennen (12500–12501), and "þus we mid rihte ahten Rome us biriden" ["thus, by right, we ought to besiege Rome"] (12506). Arthur's claim to the physical space of Rome thus helps explain the earlier and potentially confusing references to the stone fort as a "hall" since here it is the connotative rather than denotative sense of "hall" that propels the sequence forward. The *comitatus* relationship implicitly invoked by the stillness of the hall simultaneously validates Arthur's authority as leader, reestablishes the ordered solidarity of the knights, and sets the stage for the leader's boast, all as Arthur and his men symbolically appropriate Rome by assembling in the physical space of stone walls reminiscent of Roman ruins. Indeed, even Merlin's initial prophesy of Arthur's conquests is conveyed through a distinctly architectural image whereby stone walls fall before him: "scullen stan walles: biuoren him to-fallen" ["stone walls must fall before him"] (9415), a prophesy that comes to fulfillment only through the loyalty of the *comitatus*. Thus even as they occupy these stone walls and make plans to take over the city of Rome itself, the body of retainers continues to embrace and embody the social codes of the timber halls that the references to knights in the hall (12600) and stillness in the hall (12462) idiomatically convey. The traditional import of the phrase as appropriate for assembled knights thus supersedes the immediate narrative context and physical space.

The final two usages of this formulaic pattern would seem to occur in actual halls but are no less laden with connotative force. As in the previous cases, these employments of the *still/halle* word pair signal the respectful and appropriate deference of retainers to their lord. Ironically, the first of these two usages applies to the court that Modred has treacherously appropriated. During Arthur's journey to conquer Rome, he trustingly leaves his nephew Modred in charge of all his lands and men. Modred's retainers at this point do not know that he is treacherous, and, indeed, they cannot even imagine the possibility (12718), so deeply en-

grained is the *comitatus* code of conduct. Thus it is that "al hit wes *stille·*
in hirede and in *halle*" ["it was all still in court and in hall"][67] (12717). The
line here has the effect of exonerating (at least initially) the duped retainers who, in trusting Modred and retaining the proper hierarchy of the
court, actually maintain rather than violate the *comitatus* system. Without this qualification, it might appear that Arthur himself had not earned
the loyalty of his men. But the statement of the knights' lack of knowledge combined with the traditionally encoded assertion that all was "still
in the hall" suggests instead that the men fail to challenge Modred precisely because they *do* respect the traditional hierarchy and Arthur's leadership within it. Arthur has left Modred, his own nephew and Gawain's
brother, in command, and they thus maintain the traditionally appropriate order in his hall.

In the final usage of this *stille/halle* pairing, Arthur's court in Rome
has just been told the tragic details of Modred's betrayal. The men "mid
sele þan kinge" ["with the noble king"] (14053) are stricken with grief at
the news of such an unfathomable occurrence. This grief is marked by a
deferential silence, one designated as appropriate through the line "þa
sæt hit a *stille·* in Arðures *halle*" ["then it all sat still in Arthur's hall"]
(14052). It is only after this initial deferential silence that the men "stefne
þer sturede" ["stirred their voices"] to make numerous boasts vowing to
bring Modred to righteous death. What all four of these usages show is
that while a ready willingness to fight is certainly central to the ideal of
the *comitatus*, equally important in this delicate balance of hall ideals is
a leader able to control potential chaos and channel the fury of loyal retainers into fierce but controlled vengeance and victory. Arthur is such a
leader, as our final formulaic line involving "hall" demonstrates even
more forcefully.

stille/halle Word Pair, with Imperative Form of *be* or *sit.*   This final formulaic line type invoking the architectural space of the hall as the object
in a prepositional phrase serves an overlapping function with the "all was
still in the hall" line, the primary difference being the use of the imperative to actually bring about order as opposed to the indicative statement
that order has already been attained. In each of its four occurrences, the
line includes a command to "sit" or "be" still followed by the tag, "cnihtes

in halle." Each usage is preceded by a potential or actual threat to the court and a chaotic, unordered furor on the part of assembled knights. The formulaic command invariably results in an ordered silence and is followed by an orderly but forceful boast and attendant call to arms. Despite the difference created by the imperative rather than indicative verbs, both of these formulaic lines involving the *stille/halle* word pair are also more specialized than their lexical meanings alone would convey and are employed exclusively at times of threat to the *comitatus,* just as was the case for their indicative counterparts.

One such instance involves the threat to Arthur's court from Rome and precedes the debate between Cador and Gawain regarding whether a course of war or peace is best. Similar to the previously discussed *still/halle* examples, the command to be still in the hall once again formulaically restores order to a disruptive court and reasserts Arthur's role as ultimate leader. The knights' collective infuriated response to the messengers from Rome threatens to lead to a battle on the spot, but Arthur responds with the command to "sitteð adun stille; cnihtes inne halle" ["Sit down still, knights in hall"] (12409), and the men sit in silence "on hire benches" ["on their benches"] (12412), as they respectfully submit to the hierarchical order and share their thoughts with Arthur in this tradition-encoded space. The speech of Angel, "Scotlondes deorling" ["Scotland's darling"] (12568), elicits an especially strong response from the knights, requiring Arthur to once more reassert his command to "Sitteð adun still; cnihtes inne hall" ["Sit down still, knights in hall"] (12600). And, as in the other usages, the knights immediately fall silent and defer to the higher authority of Arthur, who then follows with the boast for which the sequence has laid the groundwork, vowing to bind the emperor of Rome, hang him, lay waste all his land, and put all opposing knights to death (12605–7).

The first instance of this full-line formulaic command in the *Brut,* however, is more complicated. It is actually employed not by Arthur but by his father, Uther. At the point in the narrative when the command is issued, Uther and his men have recently captured Gorlois, earl of Corn - wall. Uther, through Merlin's magic, has disguised himself as Gorlois in order to enter Tentagel castle and make love to Ygerne, Gorlois's wife with whom Arthur has fallen in love. When Gorlois's men learn of their leader's capture, they quickly and urgently assemble in Tentagel, where-upon Uther (still disguised as Gorlois) leaps from Ygerne's bed at once, "swulc hit an liun weore" ["as if he were a lion"] (9565), to assure them that their leader is indeed alive (which at this point is still true enough, though Gorlois's death at the hands of Uther's knights is imminent). He then effectively quells their furor with the following command: "Beoð stille beoð stille: cnihtes inne halle" (9567). Gorlois's men, convinced that they are truly looking upon Gorlois himself, respond immediately and ap-propriately to Uther's command. As in every other instance of this formu-laic call to order, Uther's directive is met by silence, after which he makes the expected boast. Uther's pledge here, though, is cleverly worded in such a way that Uther does not compromise the integrity of the boast itself. He vows not to slay Uther and his knights (which in this unusual circum-stance would of course amount to suicide) but to "me wurðiche awrake" ["avenge myself worthily"] (9575), effectively satisfying the expectations of Gorlois's own men—and the expectations put in motion for the audience by the formulaic command—while still making a boast appropriate to his own true identity. The command to "sit/be still, knights in hall" is thus far more complex than it might at first appear. The line effectively estab-lishes the knights' heroism, drawing attention to their intense and collec-tive fury while at the same time granting ultimate authority to the leader, who alone is able to convert the justified anger into respectful silence and eventually channel that heroic fury through a call to arms.

The pattern of fury, restoration through formulaic command, si-lence, boast, and fulfillment is firmly established by the poem's final use of this powerful command, which occurs just prior to Arthur's final boast. After his decisive victory over Rome, Arthur anticipates a return to England, where he expects to rule both Rome and his native homeland. Arthur, however, is told that Modred, not only his retainer but also his nephew, has treacherously taken his lands and even his wife, Guinevere, as his own. Arthur's loyal men are justifiably outraged, fiercely and loudly plotting revenge, when Arthur, "hendest alre Brutte" ["the most noble of all Britons"] (14060), makes his demand for order: "Sitte[ð] a-dun stille: cnihtes inne halle" ["Sit down still, knights in hall'"] (14061). After thus restoring order to the hall, Arthur makes his boast. In a *beot* as powerful as any in Old English verse, Arthur vows that "Moddred ich wulle s[l]an:

7 þa quen for-berne. / and alle ich wulle for-don: þa biluueden þen swike-
dom . . . and iuorþ(e) m(i) beot seo[ð]ðe: bi mine bare life" ["I shall kill
Modred and burn the queen to death / And I shall destroy all of them
who gave assent to the treason. . . . And then I shall fulfill my vow, upon
my very life"] (14065–73). However, just as Beowulf could not survive the
dragon after the flight of his own men, so too does Arthur fulfill his own
beot by killing Modred and all those who were against him, though following the collapse of the *comitatus,* he falls in the process, with his reign
passing on to Constantine.

By this late point in the *Brut,* audiences have seen numerous leaders betrayed and countless changes in power. But the consistent development of *comitatus* themes throughout the Arthurian episodes amplifies
the tremendous magnitude of this particular breach. The ideals of Arthur's
court belong to the social culture of the hall, and Arthur's end is foreshadowed in the image of a collapsing hall. *Comitatus* ideals having been consistently situated within the physical space of the hall (even when potentially illogical in some narrative contexts), Arthur's dream, with which
this chapter began, does much more than anticipate Modred's betrayal:
it marks the breakdown of an entire social culture.

Down Fell the Hall.   Thus it is that the communal ideals held by Arthur's
court and his rightful leadership of that court are marked by repeated
idiomatic references to halls. Arthur's successes are attained largely by
rallying his men, following through on all boasts, and earning loyalty of
his retainers as their "aðelest kingen" ["noblest king"]—an epithet given
to Arthur (and to no other ruler) some thirteen times over the course of
the poem. The subsequent downfall of Arthur and the collapse of the
comitatus that long sustained his successful reign is signified to Arthur
(and to the *Brut's* audience) through a dream centering on the powerfully resonant architectural image of a collapsing timber hall:

> Me imette þat mon me hof: uppen are *halle.*
> þa *halle* ich gon bi-striden: swulc ich wolde riden.
> alle þa lond þa ich ah: alle ich þer ouer sah.
> and Walwain sat biuoren me: mi sweord he bar an honde.
> þa com Moddred faren þere: mid unimete uolke.

he bar an his honde: ane wiax stronge.
he bigon to hewene hardliche swiðe.
and þa postes for-heou alle: þa heolden up þa *halle.*
er ich iseh Wenheuer eke: wimmonnen leofuest me.
al þere muche *halle* rof: mid hire honden heo to-droh.
Þa *halle* gon to hælden: and ich hæld to grunden.
þat mi riht ærm to-brac: þa seide Modred Haue þat.
Adun ueol þa *halle.* . . . (13984–96)

————

["It came to me that someone lifted me upon a hall.
I was astride the hall, as if I were riding.
All the land that I possess, all I oversaw there.
And Gawain sat before me. My sword he held in his hand.
Then Modred came marching there with an enormous host.
He bore in his hand a strong ax.
He began to hew with great force
and then slashed all the posts which held up the hall.
I saw Guinevere there also, the woman I love best.
The whole hall roof, with her hands she pulled down.
Then the hall began to break, and I fell to the ground,
which broke my right arm. Then Modred said 'Take that!'
Down fell the hall. . . ."]

That the passage has no precedent in either Wace's *Roman de Brut* or
Geoffrey of Monmouth's *Historia Regum Britanniae* would seem to support the argument that meaning is to be found in the native tradition instead (Donahue, "Lawman's Formulaic Themes" 93–94). As we have seen,
Old English tradition imbues Arthur and his hall not only with legitimacy of rule, as Barron and Weinberg assert, but also with a distinctive
and highly revered code of social conduct. By the point of Arthur's dream,
the links between Arthur's halls and *comitatus* ideals are in fact well established, and this dream represents the disintegration of his loyal *comitatus* explicitly through the fall of a timber, freestanding hall, a hall that
more than any other in the poem physically resembles the halls of the
Anglo-Saxon landscape and Old English verse. Modred's betrayal, the ultimate breach of the *comitatus* relationship, is here symbolized by the

destruction of the hall, Modred's cutting through the timber posts visually conveying the fall of the social system on which Arthur's rule was
dependent. The roof, the most significant aspect of halls in Old English
poetry, is ripped off by the bare hands of his wife, Guinevere, whom
Modred—the son of Arthur's sister and his own knight—had taken as
his own after usurping Arthur's power in Britain.

In this dream the building on which Arthur sits is referenced specifically as a *hall* no fewer than six times in the space of only thirteen lines.
It clearly is more than a space within a castle and is described as a freestanding structure; moreover, it is one constructed with vertical wooden
posts rather than the stone methods of building contemporary with the
Brut's production. Syntactically, the language at this point marks the hall
as both a physical possession and as the appropriate locus for heroic activity. In the first reference, the hall is in object of preposition placement, suggesting its social significance, but the centrality of the hall imagery here and the density of hall terminology conflates the distinctions
between subject/direct object and object of preposition seen elsewhere in
the poem, the hall calling to mind at once the many halls raised and destroyed throughout the poem as well as the many halls that embodied
their ever-important *comitatus* behavior.

In the *Brut,* an example of a relatively early post-Conquest and somewhat transitional text, then, we see the traditional referentiality of architectural imagery and language sustained from the Old English period
at the same time that it is "created anew"[68] with myriad changes that re -
flect architectural and literary developments of post-Conquest England.
Thus it is that in the spheres of architecture as well as verse, the "hall" of
Old English was eventually to become a component of the dominant
categorical construct of the "castle," but in this new context it retained a
more discrete status than halls within castles on the continent. In summary, *castle* denoted a range of styles and functions in the Middle Ages,
but its associations in early Middle English verse involve first and fore-
most the structure's militaristic function as a locus of strength and dominance. The traditional referentiality of the "hall" in connoting ideals of
loyalty to king and family, generosity to and among retainers, and boast-

ing and fulfillment of heroic deeds, however, was still largely retained and sustained during this period of upheaval, even as the structure itself became subsumed by an architectural form closely connected with hierarchical feudalism rather than the Germanic *comitatus*.

The persistence of native architectural associations in the work of poets with a wealth of poetic models at their disposal attests to the enduring expressive capabilities of oral poetics for many poets and their implied audiences across the Middle English period. As we move further and further from Old English verse, the specific features of the mead-hall—an abundance of gables, prominent arches, elevated location, building height, and wooden construction—are evoked with increasingly less consistency.[69] In the next chapter I explore later developments in architectural imagery across an even wider range of Middle English verse narratives, examining survivals from as well as the continuing fragmentation of the earlier architectural oral poetics.

APPENDIX: HALLS AND CASTLES IN LAȜAMON'S *BRUT*

Except where otherwise noted, all lines below are from the Caligula manuscript. In most cases, the usages here parallel those of the Otho. In the few instances where the Otho differs significantly in its treatment of these terms, the lines of both manuscripts are provided.

castel or *castle* in first 1,000 lines

Aeneas's castle:
96: he makede enne stronge castel: mid starke ston walle.
97: Lauine hehte his leuemon: þene castel he clepede Lauinion.
114: 7 Lauinion þene castel: 7 muchel lond þar-to.

Assaracus's castles given to sons:
197: He ȝef Assaracum his sune: sele þreo castles.
202: for he heold þe stronge castles: þurh staðele his fader ȝefe.
217: bote seoue þusend kempen: þa he in-to þane castlen dude.
233: Ich abbe i min castlen: seoue þusend kempen.

Pandrasus's castle:
301: þat heo comen mid him: to þane castle of Sparatin. (Sontatin in Otho)
302: Nes castel nan swa strong: i þon londe of Griclond.
305: idon into þan castle: 7 þear heom quic heolde.
308: In þon castle he dude hende: six hundred of his cnihten.
310: Þe king to þan castle forð mid his ferde:
318: Þa cnihtes of þan castle: quic-liche heom wið-stoden.
322: He tæh hine aȝein ane þrowe: 7 þreateð þene castel.
330: I þon castle weoren monie men: 7 muchel mete þer bihofede.
418: Sparatin he aredde: heh an his castel.

Brutus's castle:
826: He nom ræd æt his monnen: þat he wolde þar castel makian.
827: Þa þe castel vp stod: he wes strong 7 swiðe god.
831: Þa Goffar þe king: þene castel kennede:

839: Brutun & his kempan: heo driuen into þan castle.

841: 7 æl dai heo ræmden: 7 resden to þan castle.

843: I þon castle wes muchel dred: a þa mid-niht heo nomen read.

848: Brutus wes i þon castle: 7 hine wel wuste.

854: Vp heo duden heora castles ȝæten: 7 cofliche vt wenden.

865: Brutus hine funde dead: 7 into þane castle dude.

In Otho MS. but not Caligula:

Otho 569: Hii funde in þan ilond: anne castel swiþe strong.

Instances of the word "hall" in the *Brut*

in subject or direct object position

hall(s) destroyed or decayed

570: To-hælde weoren þe walles: weste weren hallen.

3063: and brekeð heore walles. 7 berne[ð] heore halles

8272: 7 greiðeden walles: to-halden þa halles. [not at corresponding point of Otho]

11025: þat Childric al for-barnden: 7 þa hallen alle clæne. [Otho: *þe chirchen for-barnd: þe halles to-fallen.*]

12920: He nom þare halle wah: and helden hine to grunde [Otho: *He nam þe hilewoh*]

hall(s) built or repaired

2963: timbrien þa hallen: bæten þa walles. [corresponding point in Otho damaged]

2983: rihten alle þæ hallen: 7 stronginen þæ walles. [corresponding point in Otho damaged]

3534: He letten bulden þe hallen. swiðe muchele mid alle.

8459: He letten stronge walles: he lette bulden halles.

8464: þer he lette wurcchen: [halles 7 chirchen] [reconstructed text based on corresponding point in Otho]

halls distributed

11995: bitahten him halles: bitahten him castles. [not at corresponding point in Otho]

in object of preposition position
communal activities in hall (men led to hall, feasting, singing, storytelling)
7137: Hæȝe iborenne men: heo lædden to hallen.
7461: in halle heo drunken: harpen þer dremden.
9242: Þa þe mæsse wes isungen: to halle heo þrungen.
12072: Þa weoren bliðe spelles: in Arðures hallen.
12346: Þer comen in-to halle: spelles seol-cuðe.

solidarity in hall conveyed through all/halle *word pair*
2673: Þa seiden heo in halle þisne read halde we alle.
6767: eoden heo alle: þurh-ut þære halle.
6977: Heo comen in-to halle: hændeliche alle. [Otho: *Forþ hii wende alle: to Vortiger his halle.*]
7126: He wende in-to halle: 7 his heleðes mid him alle.

hit was still in halle
12717: Ah al hit wes stille: in hirede and in halle. [not in corresponding point in Otho]
12423: þa wes hit al stille: þat wuneden inne halle. [not at corresponding point in Otho]
12463: Al hit wes stille: þat wunede inne halle
14052: Þa sæt hit al stille: in Arðures halle.

Sit/Be still, knights in hall
9567: Beoð stille beoð stille: cnihtes inne halle. [Otho: *Cnihtes in halle: beoþ swiþe stille.*]
14061: Sitte[ð] a-dun stille: cnihtes inne halle.
12409: Ah sitteð adun stille: cnihtes inne halle.
12600: Sitteð adun stille: cnihtes inne halle.

less common usages
1014: mid bouren 7 mid hallen: mid hæȝe stan walle. [Otho has *mid boures and halles*]
9855: irne to þere welle: þe wes on-væst þere halle.
11919: heo clumben uppen hallen: heo clumben uppen wallen.

compounded with *dure*

10478: and leggen i þare halle-dure: þer æch mon sculde uorð faren.

15049: wið-uten his halle dure: and sæide þu art wilcume. [Otho: *boures dore*]

Arthur's Dream

13984: Me imette þat mon me hof: uppen are halle.

13985: þa halle ich gon bi-stride: swulc ich wolde riden.

13991: and þa postes for-heou alle: þa heolden up þa halle.

13993: al þere muche halle rof: mid hire honden heo to-droh.

13994: Þa halle gon to hælden: and ich hæld to grunden.

13996: Adun ueol þa halle: 7 Walwain gon to ualle.

Otho halls not in Caligula

alle/halle word pair, with phrasing *in boure and in halle*

11116: þo answerede *alle: in boure and in halle*. [no corresponding space in C]

5498: And hii him radde *alle: in boure and in halle:* [no corresponding space in C]

stille/halle word pair, with form of "steal out"

1177: and hehte him swiþe stille: stelen vt of halle. [corresponds to *vt of hirede* in C]

8871: and þe leche stille: bi-stal vt of þan halle. [corresponds to *bistal of þan tune* in C]

CHAPTER SEVEN

THE POETICS OF BUILT SPACE IN MIDDLE ENGLISH NARRATIVE VERSE

The tendency to invoke the hall as a space emblematic of the communal ideals inherited from Anglo-Saxon tradition reflects a larger pattern in which poetry across the Middle English period continued to employ traditional themes and, to a lesser extent, phraseology inherited from the Anglo-Saxon poetic tradition but with decreasing stability and in increasingly less traditional contexts. As Amodio has compellingly demonstrated, "the history of the specialized register of oral poetics after the close of the Anglo-Saxon period was largely one of steady loss and continued fragmentation" (*Writing* 133). Because the groundbreaking connections Amodio makes across Old and Middle English verse are so central to the arguments about architectural poetics that follow, I cite his discussion on the complex nature of such continuity at some length here.

> Those post-Conquest poets who deploy oral poetics do not do so because they wish to preserve an antiquated and archaic mode of composing verse—one, moreover, that is very likely to be at least partially if not wholly inaccessible to their target audience. Rather, these poets employ oral poetics because its dedicated register

continues to offer them an affectively powerful and economical way to express meaning, just as it provides those who receive their poems—whether visually as private, perhaps silent, readers or aurally as members of textual communities—with long-established and, more importantly, still functional channels of reception. Because oral poetics remains so freighted with traditional meaning(s) and because it continues to be compositionally useful (on both the lexical and narrative levels), post-Conquest poets are able to use it to express traditional, inherent meaning. . . . All the poets who engage oral poetics are also able to and frequently do use the traditional idiom to confer idiosyncratic, post-traditional meaning(s) upon their narratives, something that witnesses not just the flexibility of oral poetics but the degree to which it is able to combine seamlessly with literate poetics to create a powerful expressive economy. (130)

As discussed in chapter 6, the period's architecture and architectural description evince these complex developments in especially tangible ways, the hall becoming subsumed by the Norman castle and Anglo-Saxon ecclesiastical centers being systematically replaced by stone cathedrals and monasteries. These new structures, however, were often built, quite literally, on Anglo-Saxon foundations. Amid the rapidly changing poetic landscape, we frequently find parallel "foundations" in Old English themes and phraseology. In the steady fracturing of Anglo-Saxon oral poetics that characterizes the later Middle English period, there is a vast range in both the degree and the nature of the employment of oral traditional elements as native themes are put to innovative uses alongside Anglo-Norman and continental modes of expression in newly emerging and ever-evolving literary contexts. To illustrate continuities with aspects of architectural poetics treated most extensively in previous chapters, the discussion here is centered largely on a detailed and extended analysis of the complex of communal ideals associated with halls in four thirteenth- and fourteenth-century verse romances whose landscapes are increasingly dominated by castles. As a way to revisit phraseological issues treated throughout the volume, I then close by returning to the phrase "by the wall," discussed at length in chapter 5, as an example of traditional referentiality sustained from the Old English period but put to new purposes in various Middle English contexts.

ARCHITECTURAL THEMATICS IN MIDDLE ENGLISH NARRATIVE VERSE

At a thematic level, the more distinctly Germanic architectural and social ideals embedded in the concept of the hall still have resonance well into the Middle English period but undergo a certain weakening of associative meaning. In Old English verse we saw a distinct correlation between features associated with the hall—timber construction, arched structures, preponderance of gables, site on an elevated location, building height—and the set of social ideals associated with the Germanic *comitatus*—dedication to one's lord, courage in battle, public boasts (and their subsequent fulfillment), giving and receiving of treasure as reward, and, above all, loyalty to one's companions in battle. In the early Middle English *Brut,* however, this connection continues between halls and *comitatus* ideals but on a more general thematic level rather than through emphasis on specific architectural features.

The architectural poetics of the hall, whether freestanding or within a castle, as emblematic of a distinctly Germanic heroism continues for some time amid numerous other architectural and poetic conventions.[1] By continuing the previous chapter's exploration of the contexts of use surrounding the concepts of the hall and the castle we can better understand the survival and fragmentation of architectural traditions in Middle English narrative verse. The poems treated here include *King Horn, Havelok the Dane, Sir Orfeo,* and *Sir Gawain and the Green Knight.* These texts have been chosen because they share enough structural and topical features to enable valid and viable comparison while still reflecting the great diversity that exists across Middle English verse. Though differing significantly in subject matter, metrical form, and style, the four texts share several generic features and have all been tied in various ways to both oral and literary conventions within medieval romance. Each has also been shown to rely on the Return Song story pattern,[2] the elements of which include a hero's Absence, Devastation, Return, Retribution, and

Wedding. This is not to say that these texts employ the pattern in equally traditional ways but rather that the persistence of such patterns into texts produced in cultures of literacy attests to continuing importance of traditional modes of narrative expression. Not only does the story pattern help establish a common basis for more productive and valid comparative analysis,[3] but this pattern is especially well suited for analysis of architectural description, as it requires a hero to journey between his home—with its corresponding architectural space—and the place of withdrawal—which usually necessitates a different physical space—allowing for comparative study of built spaces presented within a single poem. Taken together, the four narratives exhibit a transformation of Anglo-Saxon architectural ideals as they were sustained and adapted well into the Anglo-Norman period.

Although all four of these poems display continuations of Anglo-Saxon oral poetics through architectural description, they do so to varying degrees and in markedly different ways. In *Horn* we see a highly traditional employment of architectural imagery, *halls* consistently connected with the loyalty and courage of the poem's protagonists, and heavily fortified stone *castles* with their power-hungry villains. In *Havelok,* we see a similarly traditional employment of hall imagery, the hall consistently linked with the *comitatus* ideals of the hero and his band of retainers, yet these ideals become embedded in an intensely hierarchical class structure reflected in and reflective of the poem's numerous castles, castles built and inhabited by heroes and villains alike. *Sir Orfeo* traces the hero's voluntary exile from the hall as he journeys to and from the threatening and well-fortified castle of the Fairy King. More operative here is the separation from the hall and its attendant *comitatus* culture experienced by the poem's solitary hero, a sense of isolation evocative of Old English elegiac verse. Finally, *Sir Gawain and the Green Knight* presents the most architecturally complex landscape of the four poems, with the narrative framed around not just two but three divergent settings: Arthur's hall, the castle Hautdesert, and the Green Chapel. The traditional associations of the hall with heroic conduct and the castle with military strength seen in such poems as the *Brut* and *King Horn* are all employed but ultimately subverted as the narrative brings into sharp focus the contrast between traditional communal ideals of hall culture and the emergent values of innovation architecturally conveyed through the admired novelty of the castle and the interiority of the private chapel.

KING HORN

King Horn, which traces the hero's rise in power as he journeys to avenge his father's death and marry a king's daughter, dates to the late thirteenth century and represents a later phase in verse narrative than the *Brut*.[4] While all three surviving manuscripts of *King Horn* were clearly produced in literate, and literary, cultural contexts, the poem nonetheless demonstrates a significant indebtedness to oral poetics. Its formulicity, its treatment of character, and its employment of the Return Song story pattern all share characteristics with traditional oral narrative and attest the "importance to our written texts of concurrent oral tradition" (Bradbury, *Writing Aloud* 67).[5] In terms of its architectural imagery, the representation of halls in *Horn* provides an especially powerful example of traditional referentiality sustained from corresponding halls in Old English verse as well as the early post-Conquest *Brut*.

The Hall and the *Comitatus*

In *King Horn* (Cambridge MS.), the term *hall(e)* appears fourteen times, always in object of preposition placement, consistently evoking the hall as the realm of knights loyal to one another and to their lord.[6] The phrase "into [or "in the"] hall among the knightes alle" occurs four times, reinforced by the rhyme but also serving to strongly link the hall with solidarity among knights in a manner reminiscent of the *alle/halle* word pairing of the *Brut*. When King Aylmar returns to his castle having taken the foundling Horn into his protection, he "com into halle / Among his knightes alle" (227–28). The phrase appears a second time in conjunction with *comitatus* behavior when Rymenhild is unable to speak with Horn apart from the other knights, so strong is the solidarity of this unified band "in the halle / Among the knightes alle" ["in the hall, among all the knights"] (259–60). The third usage marks Horn's return from a decisive victory against the Saracens: "He verde hom into halle, / Among the knightes alle" ["He went home into the hall among all the knights"] (629–30). And the phrasing occurs a fourth and final time when King Thurston has lost his two sons and leaves his kingdom to Horn. The poem legitimizes the succession by prefacing the transfer of power with the now well-established phraseology: "The king com into halle / Among his knightes alle" (901–2).[7] Each of these displays of solidarity is situated specifically within the traditionally appropriate space of the hall, thus aligning the poem's heroes with an inherited tradition of heroic ideals.

Two additional instances of *halle* appear in conjunction with Horn's pledges to prove his loyalty and courage. Twice Horn leaves his beloved Rymenhild to establish his worth, and twice his valiant boasts are linked explicitly with feasting and halls. In the first instance, Horn, who has been accused by the treacherous Fikenhild of plotting against King Aylmar, tells Rymenheld, "Mid spere I schal furst ride, / And mi knighthod prove" ["With spear I shall first ride and my knighthood prove"] (548–49) and, after Rymenheld's weepy response, he "in to halle cam" ["came into the hall"] where the knights were appropriately feasting: "The knightes yeden to table" ["the knights went to the table"] (590–91). Much later, Rymenhild has been captured by Fikenhild and is being kept in the castle against her will. Immediately after boasting, "Today I schal hem teche / And sore hem areche" ["Today I shall teach them and strike them sorely"], "Horn sprong ut of halle" ["Horn sprang out of the hall"] (1231–33). The hall thus provides not just a physical space for the poem's narrative events, but a traditionally appropriate locus for the boasting, feasting, and public displays of valor associated with the hall since Anglo-Saxon times.

Four other occurrences of *hall(e)* more directly involve a retainer or servant demonstrating loyalty to a king. When Athelbrus seeks Horn to deliver a message from Rymenhild, the king's daughter, he finds him in the hall: "Horn in halle fond he tho / Bifore the kyng on benche" (372–73). Since later the evil Fikenhild, "that was the wurste moder child" ["who was the worst child of a mother"] (652), tells King Aylmar that Horn desires Rymenhild only as a means to the throne, the phraseology in this scene helps establish Horn's loyalty to Aylmar, "the gode Kyng" (345), whom he at this moment is serving as a dedicated retainer in the hall. Later when Rymenhild asks Athelbrus to speak to the king on Horn's behalf, she suggests that he humble himself "Bifore the king in halle" (460), and, when Athelbrus does ask the king "to knight Childe Horn," he "Wente to halle blive" ["went to the hall immediately"] (476). By setting these exchanges in the hall and prefacing them with acts of fealty to the king, the poet authorizes both Horn's relationship with Rymenhild and Horn's own right to knighthood. Horn's relationship to Thurston is also marked by his public display of deference in the hall. On arriving in Ireland, Horn, now disguised as "Cutberd," is led by Berild "in to halle" where he "grette wel the gode king" ["greeted well the good king"] (785). Contextualized within the hall, these isolated acts of subservience thus reach beyond their immediate local contexts and mark Horn's participation in a much larger network of *comitatus* ideals.

Not only is *Horn*'s hall imagery employed in keeping with the poetics of Old English heroic verse, but some usages also parallel that of elegiac poetry. Two instances of *hall* in particular are especially evocative of the hall/anti-hall parallels seen in Old English lyric, where the hall is referenced more in terms of the speaker's separation from its joys. On Murry's death, his devoted wife, Godhild, "wente ut of halle / Fram hire maidenes alle / Under a roche of stone / Ther heo livede alone" ["went out of the hall from all her maidens under a rock of stone"] (75–78). Her departure from hall life and subsequent refuge beneath a rock thus evokes something of the pathos seen in *The Wife's Lament*. And the sense of this rock as Godhild's anti-hall, similar to the Wife's *eorðsele*, is reinforced near the poem's conclusion when Horn retrieves her: "He com to his moder halle / In a roche walle" ["He came to his mother's hall in a rock wall"] (1397–98).[8] As in Old English verse, evocation of the "hall" complex in reference to Godhild's voluntary exile and subsequent return has the effect of magnifying the loss, and in this case eventual recovery, of the heroic community that the hall physically embodies and metonymically references.

The remaining two usages of *hall* more distinctly reflect Anglo-Norman manifestations of "hall" as a space *within* a castle rather than a freestanding structure, but even in these instances "hall" retains its associations with heroic *comitatus* ideals. Rymenhild is kept prisoner in two castles during the course of the narrative. She is held as a bride by Modi "in strong *halle*, / Bithinne castel walle" ["in a strong hall within the castle wall"] (1051–52) and later by Fikenhild until Horn rescues her by entering "right at *halle* gate" ["right at the hall gate"] (1488)[9] in his disguise as a harpist. Although these two usages occur in reference to halls within the castles of villains, they nonetheless retain something of their positive valence in their associations with the poem's protagonists: even within the castles of these villains, it is not Modi or Fikenhild but the heroic Horn and the noble Rymenhild who are described specifically in relation to the hall.[10]

The Castles of *King Horn*

In arguing for the possibility of "continuous Anglo-Saxon influence" on the composition of *Horn,* Sonya Veck notes especially "the importance of reciprocal self-giving, loyalty, and communal bonds among characters" (3), all ideals upheld by Horn in his rise to power and all ideals traditionally associated with the hall. Although Horn clearly has military and political power, avenging his father and conquering as many as three kingdoms, neither Horn nor his esteemed father, Murry, is ever said to build or even dwell in a "castle." The word *castle* itself appears only four times in the poem (1052, 1409, 1455, 1480) and always in conjunction with motives of treachery and greed. As in the *Brut, King Horn*'s castles are explicitly designated as "strong" (1409), aligning them with military strength rather than heroic ideals.[11] Only the poem's villains dwell in buildings designated as castles, and the explicit and primary purpose of the poem's two castles is to force others to the villains' wills. The first castle is Modi's, where Rymenhild is trapped as an unwilling bride "bithinne castel walle" ["within the castle wall"] (1052). The second castle belongs to Fikenheld, Horn's childhood friend turned traitor. Fikenhild, "prut on herte" ["proud in heart"] (1403), betrays the *comitatus* ideals and, in an act of all-consuming jealousy, tells Rymenhild that Horn is dead. He then attempts to forcibly marry her himself. Rather than earn the respect and loyalty of his men as would be appropriate for a leader in a *comitatus* band, Fikenhild is said instead to bribe them (1405–6). Toward fulfillment of his wicked plan, he builds a fortified castle to keep out Horn: "Ston he dude lede, / Ther he hopede spede, / Strong castel he let sette" ["Stone he had transported; there he hoped to succeed; a strong castle he had built"] (1407–9). This castle is equipped with numerous defensive devices, including a moat (1410–12),

a tower (1467), and a gate (1488). Horn and his men do not know the castle because it is so new (1455), a circumstance that perhaps reflects a very
real anxiety about the rapid erection of castles on the real-world landscape at this time. Of course, none of this analysis polarizes halls as "good"
and castles as "bad." Rather, the poetic and architectural traditions invested halls with *comitatus* ideals and castles with military strength. While
in this particular poem this strength of castles is associated exclusively
with the dominance of power-usurping villains, the distinctions are not
always so straightforward, as the following discussion of *Havelok the Dane*
illustrates.

HAVELOK THE DANE

Havelok the Dane's connection to oral tradition has long been established
through its employment of traditional formulas, development of characters, use of traditional themes and story patterns, and use of proverbs.[12]
As with the poems discussed in this and preceding chapters, connections
to oral tradition do not at all signify purely oral provenance; rather they
point toward the persistence of a powerfully resonant oral poetics in
meaningful interplay with conventions of Anglo-Norman literate culture. The buildings that appear in the poem carry fairly traditional connotations; however, such associations with *castles* and *halls*, in particular,
are put to innovative uses in this post-Conquest text.

Heroic Halls and "Castles Stronge"

Like the world of Old English verse, *Havelok*'s setting is largely "uncarpentered," to use Earl Anderson's term, with the poet relying instead on
the audience's ability to visualize the narrative's space without detailed
description. What few specific details we are given serve more to evoke
established associations than to create specific architectural images. All
six explicit references to the hall occur in object of preposition placement,
and all are consistently linked with codes of conduct very similar to those
of Old English verse. Shortly before the great Aþelwold's death, the unity
of his men and their loyalty to their king is asserted through their en-

trance as a body "Thanne he weren comen alle / bifor þe king into þe halle / At Winchestre þer he lay" ["when they all came before the king into the hall where he lay at Winchester"] (156–58).[13] When Aþelwold dies, the heroic associations of the hall are again activated as the "leuedyes in boure, knictes in halle" ["ladies in bower, knights in hall"] (239) lament his passing by reinforcing the role of the knights specifically within the hall.[14] Like these two, the third specific reference to a hall again has unambiguously positive connotations, aligning the hall with *comitatus* values of loyalty. The narration of Havelok's loyal band being presented to Ubbe involves a reference to their coming "to the halle" as a body (1694). The unity of the men at Ubbe's court at the moment when they recognize Havelok's identity is also marked by Havelok's proximity to the hall: "Als the knithes were comen alle, / Ther Havelok lay ut of the halle" (2121), and oaths of Havelok's new retainers are taken "in the halle" (2267) as well, implicitly linking medieval vows of fealty with the loyalty of the Germanic *comitatus*. After Havelok has proven his strength in the famous stone-putting episode, news of his deed reaches the hall but specifically the hall within a castle: "In þe castel, up in þe halle, þe knithes speken þer-of alle" ["in the castle, up in the hall, the knights all spoke of it"] (1068–69). As this usage suggests, the hall is a discrete entity within the castle with its own set of associative meanings; however, castles are not portrayed as antithetical to heroism as was the case in *Horn*.

Instead, *castel* is here simply linked with the notion of military strength, as Havelok dreams of and eventually acquires "castles stronge" (1294) and "strong castles" (1302). Unlike *Horn*, which predictably linked villains with castles and heroes with halls (which sometimes are situated architecturally within castles), *Havelok* employs a much broader, more neutral semantic range for *castle*, evoking strength but not necessarily in a negative sense. In *Havelok*, it is the *castle* and not the *hall* that emerges as the dominant architectural form, forms of *castle/castel* appearing some thirteen times. In *Havelok*, the lexeme usually occurs in the plural and can refer to residences of both positive and negative figures. The knights whom the evil Godrich most trusts, for instance, are put into "castels" (252). The noble Berkabeyn also leaves "casteles and tunes" (397) to the care of Godard, who in turn imprisons Havelok and his sisters in the tower of "þe castel" (412). Like Rymenhild in *Horn*, Havelok and his sisters,

Swanborow and Helfled, are placed "in the castel" (412). Goldborough is also kept in a "castel," "pourelike in feble wede" ["poorly in wretched clothes"] so that "non micte comen hire to" ["so that none might come to her"] (323–25). In more positive usages, the noble Ubbe summons help "After alle that castel yemede" ["from all that had charge of castles"] (2277), and Havelok himself promises "castles ten" (1443) to Grim's sons should they assist him after his prophetic dreams of holding "alle þe castles" in Denmark (1322). In the context of the poem, *castle* denotes power — power that can be used positively or negatively — while *hall* evokes purely positive heroism. Over the course of the poem, Havelok lays claim not only to the two kingdoms of Denmark and England but also to two modes of architectural expression, possessing heroic halls *and* strong castles.

The poem infuses the castle with the ethos of the hall in more tangible ways as well. For instance, details concerning Ubbe's residence in Denmark that emerge through the narrative show the dwelling to be a castle with a high tower (2073) but one made of wood. After Havelok has fended off intruders, Ubbe offers Havelok and Goldeboru "a bowr / þat is up in þe heye tour" ["a bower that is up in the high tower"] (2073–74). Then, to assure Havelok of his safety and to denote Havelok's status as equal to himself, Ubbe tells Havelok, "it ne shal noþing ben bitwene / þi bour and min . . . But a fayr firrene wowe" ["There shall be nothing between your bower and mine . . . except a fair fir wall"] (2076–79) and reinforces the safety of the structure by referencing the same "rof" ["roof"] that will "hile us boþe" ["cover us both"] (2083). When Havelok's telltale light once more betrays his identity, Ubbe and his men see it through a hole in the wooden wall, "at a bord" ["in a board"] (2107). To be sure, wooden castles did exist in England (see chap. 6), especially when circumstances made more expensive stone difficult to obtain, but in poetry the choice of material involves more than practical considerations, since *writing* about stone is no more costly than writing about wood. Unlike Vortigern's castle in *Brut* or Fikenhild's castle in *Horn,* which are explicitly identified as stone, Ubbe's castle is made from wood, linking it through architectural description with the timber Germanic halls and corresponding *comitatus* ideals, appropriate for Ubbe in practical terms, since he is a ruler in Denmark, and in traditional contexts, since he is clearly aligned with the poem's hero.

And like the gables in Heorot and the column in Andreas's prison, certain elements of Ubbe's home figure prominently in the climactic battle. When over sixty intruders attack Ubbe's residence, it is the wooden bar from the door that Havelok chooses as his weapon: "Hauelok lifte up þe dore-tre / And at a dint he slow him þre" ["Havelok lifted up the door-tree and slew three with one dint"] (1807–8). The bar is referenced numerous times, clearly aligned with Havelok in a fight well won. "Wit þe barre" ["with the bar"], he "clapte him on þe crune" ["banged him on the head"] (1812, 1814). Later he "le[t þe] barre fleye and smot him sone ageyn þe brest" ["let the bar fly and struck him at once against the breast"] (1828–29). "With þe barre . . . he cowþe sore smite" ["with the bar he could strike mightily"] (1854–55). Rather than being used to keep enemies out, the bar is taken off the door and used to attack intruders in public displays of valor. Havelok commands Robert and William to fight likewise with weapons of wood: "Gripeth eþer unker a god tre, / And late we nouth þise doges flee" ["Both of you grip a good wooden beam / And we will not let these dogs flee"] (1883–84). They follow his command: Robert grabs a "staf strong and gret" ["staff strong and great"] (1891) and William "grop a tre" ["gripped a tree"] (1893). Bernard fights with a weapon used to cut wood, holding "his ax ful faste" ["his ax very firmly"] (1895). In contrast the intruders fight with weapons of stone: "He gripen sone a bulder-ston, / and let it fleye, ful god won, / Agen þe dore, þat it to-rof" ["They at once gripped a builder-stone and let it fly, with very high expectations, against the door so that it shattered"] (1791–93). Later they assail Havelok "with flintes" (1864). The wooden weapons are rustic to be sure, marking Havelok and his men as somewhat unsophisticated and unrefined but unquestionably heroic all the same. In fact, it is this very ability of Havelok to bridge aristocratic and popular cultures that distinguishes him as a hero.

Architecture and Class in *Havelok*

In addition to setting its action in castles and halls, the poem displays a keen awareness of more humble architectural forms, fitting for Havelok prior to his restoration to power. After a change of heart that leads him to rescue rather than kill Havelok,[15] Grim builds a new home. Unlike his earlier stone house, however, this new house is made "of erþe" ["from earth"] (740–43). However, even though he is a significant figure in the narrative development, Grim, at least in the version that we have,[16] is not heroic in the same way that Havelok and even Grim's sons show themselves to be. In fact, when Havelok returns ready to enter battle with enemies, Grim has already died. More modest than wood or stone, the earthen construction speaks to the family's weakened financial condition, but it also carries potential connotations from Anglo-Saxon poetics. As we saw in previous chapters, earth dwellings are often associated with protection: for Lot in the Old English *Genesis* (see chap. 3) and the fox of the Exeter Book riddles (see chap. 4), as well as for figures in comparative Germanic traditions, such as Sigmund in the earth dwelling of *Völsunga Saga* built for him by his sister Signy. The protection afforded by earth lodging links Grim firmly with the refuge he affords Havelok. And, despite his humble home, Grim goes down in history as the founder of Grimsby.

The poem also uses images of building to mark Havelok's identification with craftsmen. Though Havelok is shown here to be working on the construction of the boat, the trade encompasses both shipbuilding and domestic architecture, since in medieval Grimsby carpenters' work involved housing construction as well as shipbuilding (Rigby 72). Refitting, repairing, and building were all done at the port.

> Hise ship he greyþede wel inow:
> He dede it tere an ful wel pike
> þat it ne doutede sond ne krike,
> þer-inne did a ful god mast,
> Stronge kables and ful fast,
> Ores gode an ful god seyl—
> þer-inne wantede nouth a nayl. . . . (707–14)

> ———

> [His ship he trimmed well enough: He did tar and caulk it very well so that it feared neither sand nor creek. Therein (he) made a very good mast, strong and very fast cables, good oars, and a very good sail. There was lacking not a nail. . . .][17]

Having dwelled at various points in his trajectory to power in wooden halls, stone castles, modest houses, and even an earthen hut, Havelok is thus portrayed through his architectural affiliations as a hero with connections across the hierarchy of social spheres.

Although Havelok's rise from orphan through various working-class positions to king of two realms might seem a "peasant fantasy," Susan Crane convincingly argues that the poem actually reinforces and idealizes the existing social order. The poem "creates a world remarkable for its social complexity and breadth, yet unites that world in harmony with the hero's purpose" (47). Bradbury concurs that though *Havelok* "draws on a flourishing English legend," this legend "is not one that opposes and ridicules authority" but one retold in ways "compatible with what are clearly [the poet's] own values of justice and legitimacy" (*Writing Aloud* 76).[18] As in *Horn,* castles in *Havelok* denote strength and halls are associated with the loyalty and courage of the *comitatus.* However, unlike the *Horn*-poet, the poet of *Havelok* does not present the categories in opposition to one another. Whether freestanding or contained in stone castles, the halls of *Havelok* serve as appropriate spaces for feasting, boasting, and fighting by the poem's hero and his loyal following. Likewise, narrative developments suggest that leaders and warriors in the rigid feudal system can and do possess the heroic qualities of idealized Anglo-Saxon lords and retainers. The poem ultimately reinforces rather than challenges the existing hierarchy but does so in part by investing the newly dominant power structure with traditional Germanic values and furthermore by providing the hero with experience in architecture of the working and lower classes. Architecturally, this means linking Havelok with both the traditional ethos of the hall and the military dominance of castles.[19]

In subtle but significant ways, the poet of *Havelok* thus guides audiences through the narrative by nuanced usage of architectural imagery and phraseology, consistently aligning heroic ideals with hall imagery. Although the images and associations of Germanic halls and Norman castles are brought together in innovative ways, expectations established by traditional usage are consistently met by the narrative's developments. Hall references, for instance, consistently activate the register of heroic idealism and never appear in the absence of such associations, not even in parody or satire. Rather, each usage carries with it the full authority and force of a dynamic tradition. But, as I discuss below, traditional architectural language and imagery does not have to follow traditionally established patterns of use in Middle English verse. Unlike *King Horn* and

Havelok the Dane, Sir Orfeo and *Sir Gawain and the Green Knight* take advantage of the traditional language of architectural imagery but often do so in decidedly nontraditional ways, frequently stripping traditional-freighted images of their narrative predictability for rhetorical effect.

SIR ORFEO

As an adaptation of a classical myth, *Sir Orfeo* is clearly a work produced in a culture of literacy and cannot be understood as "oral" or even "oral-derived" in the same sense as Anglo-Saxon verse. Nonetheless, its poetic articulation bears a debt to oral traditional structure and thematics. Like *King Horn* and *Havelok the Dane, Sir Orfeo* follows the Return Song story pattern, which takes the hero through multiple architectural spaces in his journey of exile and return. *Sir Orfeo* also shares with the other texts treated here the loose generic classification of "romance," *Orfeo* being more specifically a Breton lay. In keeping with the conventions of this genre, which is closely linked with song, the text evokes a context of oral performance.[20] Though the primary source of the story lies in the classical Orpheus and Eurydice myth that was "well known in the Middle Ages from the versions of Virgil, Ovid, and Boethius" (Bliss xxxiii), "with these were fused elements from a Celtic story of a very popular type" (xxxiii). Drawing from multiple traditions, yet allowing none to exact its full authority in the narrative's context, the poem thereby cleverly manipulates audience expectations by drawing from intertwining and sometimes competing poetic conventions. The casting of the tragedy of Orpheus and Eurydice into the genre of the Breton lay—with its implied likelihood of a happy outcome[21]—is among the most obvious ways the poem provides the audience with seemingly discordant contexts for reception. Instead of being killed as classical legend would lead us to expect, Heurodis is simply abducted and is in time recovered by Orfeo. In his incarnation within a Breton lay, the Hades figure—the Fairy King—does not forbid Orfeo to look back, and the reunited couple eventually return home to live happily ever after. These multiple influences are evident in the poem's manipulation of architectural description as well, in particular, in the contrast between Orfeo's dwelling and that of the Fairy King. From Orfeo's hall to his tree-hollow refuge to the Fairy King's castle to a beggar's house and back again, *Orfeo* reveals its indebtedness to an Anglo-Saxon oral poetics, even as it deviates from the very expectations its traditional usages would seem to establish.

Tradition and Manuscript Variation

Sir Orfeo is extant in three separate manuscripts: the Auchinleck MS., dated by Bliss to about 1330; the MS. Harley 3810, most likely written in the early fifteenth century; and MS. Ashmole 61, written sometime after 1488.[22] Differences among these manuscripts indicate that the texts are unlikely to have been stemmatically related to each other through a direct written transmission process.[23] Instead, there seems to be a high probability that transmission was directly affected by oral/aural reception, with resulting textual variation that is in line with what would be "both expected and encouraged among medieval *romanciers* in the telling of their stories" (Bliss 2).[24] As opposed to the case of *King Horn,* where the three extant manuscripts exhibit consistency in their employment of architectural terminology and description with the few differences that exist indicating a weakening of affective dynamics in the later manuscripts, such is not the case in the three surviving manuscripts of *Sir Orfeo.* Striking differences emerge among these different versions in their treatment of the "hall," and, somewhat surprisingly, it is the latest manuscript, the Ashmole, that demonstrates the strongest oral poetics in its articulation of built space.[25]

Hall appears in the Auchinleck three times (219, 410, 524), in the Harley four times (213, 379, 470, 474), and in the Ashmole seven times (159, 221, 243, 270, 509, 514, 540), almost exclusively in object of preposition placement;[26] *castle* occurs six times in the Auchinleck (159, 245, 355, 377, 386, 519) and only five times in the Ashmole (158, 251, 358, 396, 430). These statistics alone would indicate that the Ashmole, although it is the manuscript with the latest date, is more concerned with the culture of the traditional hall than of the more modern castle. The contexts in which these terms appear also point toward a more consistent usage of oral poetics in the Ashmole. Two instances of *hall* in the Ashmole are formulaic usages that do not appear in the Harley or Auchinleck, both times in conjunction with the phrase "castles and towers." When Heurodis recounts her abduction to Orfeo, she explains that the Fairy King showed her his "castles and towers" in all three versions (Auchinleck 159, Harley 158, Ashmole 158). The Ashmole alone then follows the phrase with "and hys hey haules & boures" ["and his high halls and bowers"] (159). The Ashmole-poet includes a similar reference, also in conjunction with castles and towers, when outlining the contrast between Orfeo's wilderness home and the kingly life he has recently left. Where the Auchinleck refers to Orfeo as one who "hadde castels & tours" (244) and the Harley makes no reference to specific buildings, the Ashmole heightens Orfeo's loss as one who "wyst not wher he was" ["knew not where he was"] (242) by adding that he once "sate in boure & halle" (243). Only as a separate item does he possess "castellus & tourys" (251). Though the phraseology is similar at both points in the Ashmole, slight but significant differences are apparent between the architecture of the Fairy King's dwelling and that of Orfeo. When applied to the Fairy King's land, the "hey haules" seem to be part of the "castles and towers," and the Fairy King himself is not located in any particular space. In contrast, Orfeo is said to reside specifically within a hall (243, Ashmole), with his castles being itemized as altogether separate possessions. The detached hall of Orfeo in this way displays greater affinity with native architectural practice (see chap. 6) than the Fairy King's hall within the castle. Further, the hall of Orfeo is more closely linked not only with traditional architectural practice but also with ideals traditionally connected with such a hall. All three texts situate the weeping for Havelok's departure, and the unity his men display in their collective loss, in the hall: "þer was wepeing in þe halle / & grete cri among hem alle" (Auchinleck 219–20; cf. Harley 213–14 and Ashmole 221–22). As this shared reference to a hall suggests, what we are dealing with here is not the hall filled with boasting and rejoicing retainers but the hall *deprived* of such joys, which is more evocative of Old English elegiac verse.

Though all three manuscripts mark Orfeo as leaving a hall, only the Ashmole locates him in an anti-hall during his self-imposed exile. In passages describing Orfeo's wanderings in his search for Heurodis through wilderness and woods, all three manuscripts make reference to a particular tree, but each gives different details.[27] The Auchinleck version says that Orfeo used the tree for storage: he "hidde in an holwe tree" ["hid in a hollow tree"] (268) his lyre, the only material possession he took with him on his journey; and the Harley says that he himself lay *beneath* the tree. Both of these versions contrast the rustic woodland habitat with the castles and towers he formerly occupied: "He þat had castel & toure" ["He who had castle and tower"] (248) now "haþ he no-þing þat him lykeþ" ["he had nothing that he liked"] (251).[28] The Ashmole manuscript, however, goes further, indicating that Orfeo lived *in* the tree and referring to the tree as his "hall": "Ther was hys haule euyn & morow" ["there was his hall evening and morning"] (269–71). The tree of the Ashmole manuscript thus replaces the "halle" that Orfeo previously occupied and becomes an "anti-hall," reminiscent of similar structures inhabited by exiles in Old English verse, such as *The Wife's Lament's* "eorðsele" ["earth hall"].[29] As Orfeo travels alone in great despair separated from all the joys and comforts of his castle and home, the Ashmole's evocation of the tree as an anti-hall simply furthers the exilic theme by making more liberal use of oral traditional associations. Like the Old English Seafarer who, deprived of the joys of the hall, finds solace in the songs of birds, Orfeo also re-creates the ethos of the hall in nature, playing his harp for the animals who congregate to listen.

The Ashmole's greatest concentration of *hall* usages occurs near its end, when the *comitatus* ideals of loyalty to king and themes of joy in the hall are most pronounced. And where the Auchinleck has the steward admit Orfeo into a "castel" (519), the steward of the Harley and Ashmole manuscripts leads the disguised Orfeo into a "halle" (Harley 470; Ashmole 509). Where the Auchinleck refers to Orfeo sitting "stille in þe halle" (524), the Harley and the Ashmole directly link joy with the hall: "þer was grete myrthe in þe halle" (Ashmole 514; cf. Harley 474). But in the steward's final test, the Ashmole alone invokes the hall. Orfeo, still in disguise, tells the steward that the owner of the harp he carries was killed by lions. The steward falls "to grounde" in the Auchinleck and made "grete mone" (489) in the Harley, but in the Ashmole "on swon he fell in þe halle" ["in a swoon he fell in the hall"] (540). The Ashmole also departs from the Auchinleck and the Harley in drawing attention to the public display of the steward's loyalty "be-for hym alle" (541). By specifi-cally referencing the context of a hall at this point, the testing of the stew-ard's loyalty, the most central characteristic of retainers in a *comitatus* relationship, is underscored, and the scene's conclusion conveys a restora-tion of the music and feasting in the traditional Anglo-Saxon hall and brings the narrative full circle from the "wepyng" in the hall that occurred at Orfeo's initial departure.

The one point where the Ashmole does *not* reference a hall mentioned in the Auchinleck and Harley further demonstrates the Ashmole's linkage of "hall" with the hero Orfeo. When Orfeo is admitted into the Fairy King's presence he is said in the Auchinleck and the Harley to go into the "halle" (Auchinleck 410; Harley 379), but in the Ashmole he simply sees the king "Jn þat castell" (396), not in the hall specifically. As we have seen in previous instances where there are differences in the versions, the Ashmole once again retains a closer relationship to Anglo-Saxon oral poetics through its choice in terminology. By the fourteenth century the term *hall* had a broad semantic range, and two meanings were current during a time frame spanning all three manuscripts.

The older of the two meanings, attested from 1175–1606, refers to "a large place covered by a roof; in early times applied to any spacious roofed place, without or with subordinate chambers attached; a temple, palace, court, royal residence" *(OED)*. The later, attested from 1225 onward, denotes a smaller, more specialized space: "The large public room in a mansion, palace, etc., used for receptions, banquets, etc." The "hall" in the Fairy King's castle as described in the Auchinleck and Harley manuscripts must refer to a more specific location within a larger structure in keeping with the later definition; already inside the castle, Orfeo moves into the "halle." The Ashmole, on the other hand, more consistently restricts the term *hall* to its earlier and more traditional sense of a freestanding structure and employs *castell* at this point instead. Although the Auchinleck text is generally considered the "standard," assumed by virtue of its age to be closer to an "original," such traditional associations are not present in this text.[30] It is the latest of the three texts, the Ashmole, that most retains traditional usages of poetic space.[31] Literacy and orality were far from mutually exclusive categories, and the relative ages of extant manuscripts do not directly correlate to the degree to which they were influenced by traditional oral poetics.

Oral and Literate Modes of Architectural Description

Having established these subtle but significant differences across the three manuscripts, let us turn now to more general patterns of architectural space shared in all surviving manuscripts and the relationship of the poem's built spaces to one another. The dominant settings of the poem are Orfeo's hall and the Fairy King's castle. While the foregoing analysis revealed differences between the two spaces—most notably the relationship of the hall to the overarching structure—what is much more striking is the difference in the *manner* of description used for these spaces. Whereas in *King Horn* and *Havelok* the mode of description and level of specificity are more or less the same with regard to the spaces encountered by these poems' respective heroes, in *Orfeo* we find different levels of description at various points in the poem, the language employed for Orfeo's own residence being reminiscent of the "uncarpentered" landscape of Old English poetry, which left specific details largely to audience imagination, and the language applied to the Fairy King's dwelling, contrastingly displaying a level of detail very uncommon in traditional verse.

As with much of the earlier Old English verse, description in *Sir Orfeo* serves more to convey a social ethos than a portrait, our first description being of a "city of noble [or, in the Ashmole manuscript, "great"] defense."[32] Just as with the king's dwellings in *Havelok* and *Horn,* the specific features of this regal home are left to the imagination of the audience, with adjectives such as *noble* or *great* provided in place of more concrete physical details. We know little about his residence aside from its general magnitude and praiseworthiness. Instead, the specifics of Orfeo's dwelling are left to be filled in by the audience's own imagination and architectural awareness, in a dynamic mode of description closer to that of an oral tradition. But whether or not the poet and audience had the *same* type of dwelling in mind is to a certain extent irrelevant; without being provided with specific details, an audience must default to *familiar* architectural features, whatever those features might be, thereby creating a more all-encompassing and immediately applicable sense of a "home" from which Orfeo—like all Return Song protagonists—must soon depart. This expected (to an audience familiar with the Return Song pattern if not to Orfeo himself) departure is then effected shortly afterward following Heurodis's sudden abduction, as Orfeo is said to go in search of her "out of town," a phrase shared by all three extant manuscripts.[33]

The space to which Orfeo journeys, on the other hand, receives an abundance of physical details, as all three manuscripts provide lengthy descriptions of the Fairy King's castle during Orfeo's approach, with most architectural features remaining constant among them. As noted above, the dwelling's status as a "castel"/"castell" is made explicit in all three manuscripts, and all versions also include a specific reference to its height: "Riche & real & wonder heiȝe" ["rich and royal and wondrously high"] (Auchinleck 356); "Noble & ryche, ryȝt wonder hie" ["noble and rich, right wondrously high"] (Harley 341); "A feyr castell, ryall & hyȝe" ["a fair castle, royal and high"] (Ashmole 355). In each text, the outermost wall is likened to crystal (Auchinleck 358; Harley 344; Ashmole 361), and an abundance of towers (Auchinleck and Harley) or turrets (Ashmole) is also a consistent feature. These towers number a hundred in two texts (Auchinleck 358 and Ashmole 362) and are "stout" in all three (Auchinleck 360; Harley 346; Ashmole 362), and the presence of battlements is specifically mentioned in the Auchinleck (360) and the Ashmole (363).[34] Precious stones also appear in all three texts (Auchinleck 366; Harley 352, 354; Ashmole 369). In two texts, animal carvings are mentioned, on the vaultings of the Auchinleck version's castle (364) and on the building's front in the Ashmole text (366–67). Gold also figures prominently in all three descriptions: "burnist gold" in the Auchinleck (367), towers and dwellings "of golde" in the Harley (347, 349–50), and "pylers" "of gold full ryche" in the Ashmole (364–65).[35]

This high level of objective detail sets this descriptive passage apart from architectural description in Old English verse as well as in the *Brut*, *Horn*, and *Havelok*, where architectural details are more scarce and serve largely to evoke certain associations or to further the plot. Heorot, for instance, embodies the heroic ideals of the *comitatus*, and those few physical characteristics we are provided either serve to convey that sense of hall life and culture (such as the prominent gables and high walls) or are mentioned in reference to specific events directly relevant to the plot (such as the door through which Grendel enters). In the *Brut* we also see little in the way of objective description, and architectural references follow more traditional patterns, with stone castles being connected to military strength and halls most frequently referenced in terms of the leaders and retainers within their walls. In *King Horn* we continue to see largely traditional modes of architectural description, with the few details provided directly relevant to plot. We know, for instance, that Fikenhild's castle has a bridge not because the building is described at length but because someone is thrown from it. We know of the castle's gate not because the poet describes its construction but because Horn has to carefully negotiate its entrance. The portrayal of Orfeo's home in this regard parallels the mode of description employed in the more traditional *Havelok,* which avoids itemizing architectural features in any sort of detached description and instead limits architectural detail to those aspects of the buildings with which the poem's characters directly interact; we know, for example, that Ubbe's castle is made of wood because his men peer through a hole in the fir-wall, and we know that his door is locked with a timber bar because Havelok and his men use the bar to smash hostile intruders. The tendency to ground such details firmly in the narrative action rather than to provide itemized descriptions is typical of works relying on oral traditional modes of expression, where lists of features "devoid of a human action context" would be more characteristic of works produced in more literate contexts.[36] What makes *Sir Orfeo* especially interesting in this regard is that the poet employs *both* styles of description in telling the story, at certain points employing architectural imagery in traditional ways and at other points objectively itemizing architectural features in great detail. The difference is especially notable in the contrast between Orfeo's hall and the Fairy King's castle.

The description (or, more precisely, the lack thereof) of Orfeo's hall displays features more typical of oral and oral-derived narrative, suffusing the residence with human ideals of honor rather than offering objective details, where the description of the Fairy King's castle allows the reader, at least initially, to analyze objectively the visual details of the structure outside the context of human interaction in a manner more typical of narratives produced in cultures of literacy. Thus not only is the poet drawing from multiple traditions in classical, Celtic, and Anglo-Saxon components of plot, but the poet also demonstrates an adeptness at both oral and literate modes of description in storytelling, taking advantage of a vast range of expressive styles with the effect of creating a highly nuanced narrative.[37] A powerful effect of the traditional style to describe Orfeo's hall is to create a sense of familiarity and identification with the space and, in turn, the character.[38] In contrast to the sparse detail that allowed room for audience identification with Orfeo's dwelling, the accumulation of details of the Fairy King's castle serves to distance the structure from familiar experience, emphasizing those ways in which the castle visually asserts its singularity.

In keeping with patterns established in previously discussed Middle English texts, numerous details establish the castle as one of great military strength, such as the battlements and high outer walls, where others serve to underscore the opulence of the space, such as the precious gems, animal carvings, and burnished gold. Just as important as the specific visual features conveyed by the details, however, is their very inclusion. Unlike references to Orfeo's own castle and his subsequent tree dwelling, in which recognizable spaces were left to be filled out by the audience, in the Fairy King's castle the high level of detail serves to heighten a sense of contrast and otherness, creating a productive tension that is exploited throughout this portion of the narrative.

For instance, the deceptively pastoral landscape that Orfeo first encounters in the Fairy King's lands evokes what turns out to be a false sense of ease: "he com in-to a fair cuntry / As bry3t so sonne on somers day" ["he came into a fair country as bright as the sun on a summer's day"] (Auchinleck 351–52; cf. Harley 337, Ashmole 353). As Orfeo arrives, the castle provides the promise of the journey's end, but of course one fraught with the possibility of danger. Initially, though, the scene is described as serene and nonthreatening. The "fair cuntray" surrounding the castle is in general "a gentler and more hospitable place than the wilderness wherein [Orfeo] has wandered ruing the ten years of his self-imposed exile" (Longsworth 7). But the "architectural grandeur" of the Fairy King's castle itself is duplicitous, concealing "a scene of grim desolation, of mutilation and arrested motion" (7), and the poem carefully introduces us to this ambiguous space by elaborating on every detail and leaving little to the imagination. The Fairy King's castle is marked by its stone construction, simultaneously awe-inspiring but most decidedly "other," the associations closely paralleling those of Old English verse. The otherness of the castle leads to the possibility—in this case realized—of duplicity: Men only "þink" ["think"] that it is the "proude court of Paradis" ["proud court of Paradise"] (Auchinleck 375–76), when in fact it is the very space that corresponds to the underworld in the classical Orpheus myth.[39]

After the lengthy descriptions of the castle and its surroundings, the tensions between the space within the castle and the impressions created from the outside are finally negotiated through the character of the porter, who eventually unlocks a gate and admits the visitor Orfeo. Though there are variations among the three manuscripts, the presence of the gate and the wall inside are made explicit in each, helping to mark this entrance as a liminal space beyond which lies grave uncertainty. In the Auchinleck, we are told that "þe porter vndede þe ȝate anon/ & lete him in-to þe castel gon" ["the porter undid the gate at once and let him go into the castle"] (385–86). In the Harley the "porter" is replaced by the pronoun *he*, who "vnded þe gate anone & lete hym in-to þe castel gone" (369–70), where Orfeo "sawe folk sit vnder þe wal" ["saw people sit under the wall"] (372). In the more traditional Ashmole, Orfeo, like King Horn entering Modi's castle, is admitted in the role of a minstrel: "The porter vndyd þe ȝate anon / And as a mynstrell lete hym gon" ["The porter undid the gate at once and as a minstrel let him go"] (376–77). As it turns out, the potential danger anticipated by the detailed descriptions of the spaces is very quickly mitigated, as Orfeo fairly easily negotiates the return of his bride. Just as the plot itself at first follows the basic structure of a classical tale with a grim ending only to replace the expected outcome with a happy one, the architectural description suggests a dangerous space that turns out to be relatively safe.

Once Orfeo leaves the Fairy King's home with Heurodis, the earlier lack of specificity in architectural detail once again reappears (in all three manuscript versions), indicating a return to the familiar and traditional world of the poem's hero. The beggar's house where Orfeo temporarily resides with his wife after her rescue is visualized only vaguely: "Bot with a begger, y-bilt full narwe / Ther he took his herbarwe" ["But with a beggar, housed very poorly, there he took his lodging"] (459–60). And at the poem's climax, just before revealing his true identity, Orfeo is said to return merely to the "hall" (Harley 470, 474; Ashmole 509, 514) or, in the case of the Auchinleck, "castel" (519), signifying a return to the traditional and familiar.

The pattern here is consistent with Orfeo's relationship to an oral poetics more generally and with its specialized employment of the Return Song story pattern more specifically. Whereas *Havelok* and *Horn* frame their narratives around a fairly predictable—and more wholly traditional—sequence involving the hero's absence, devastation during his absence, his eventual return and retribution, and, finally, a wedding, the pattern in *Orfeo* operates very differently and might, in fact, at first appear to be completely irrelevant as the poem includes neither a wedding nor retribution. As Amodio demonstrates, however, the poem actually offers "a rather paradigmatic instantiation" of the story pattern (*Writing* 196). In place of the retribution typically enacted by the returning hero, the *Orfeo*-poet instead offers a testing of the loyal steward, following which no retribution is required. And in place of the wedding that usually concludes the Return Song, in *Orfeo* we see "the reassertion and public resumption of Orfeo and Heurodis's marriage" (197).[40] The simultaneous evocation and departure from the conventional Return Song pattern thus markedly illustrates "the vital, ever-shifting nature of oral poetics" (197) as it appears in the post-Conquest period. Manipulation of conventions in architectural description contributes to these patterns, as the poem's characters negotiate tensions between the familiar and the new in spaces and story patterns alike. The employment of an increasingly fractured but still powerfully expressive oral poetics becomes even more fraught in the architectural description of *Sir Gawain and the Green Knight*.

SIR GAWAIN AND THE GREEN KNIGHT

As with *Sir Orfeo, Sir Gawain and the Green Knight*'s placement within a European-influenced literary tradition is in many ways far more readily apparent to modern readers than its employment of native English oral poetics. However, "although almost certainly produced by a highly sophisticated and undoubtedly literate poet," the poem's versification, diction, and structure nonetheless "owe a large debt to the oral tradition" (Amodio, "Tradition, Modernity" 49). In its versification, the poem participates in what has become known as the "Alliterative Revival," even as it forges new and arguably less traditional poetic ground. Amodio aptly describes the poem as "gesturing back toward the traditional past and forward towards modernity," resisting rather than reinscribing the "evolutionist view of cultural change" (49), and the poem's transitional nature has been observed in its complex employment of ring structure,[41] the psychological interiorizing of both heroes and villains,[42] and its ambiguous relationship to traditional heroic ideals in the face of modernity.[43] "But far from securing the poem firmly within the bounds of the oral tradition, its verse form, formulaic language, and oral traditional themes and type-scenes serve rather to point its distance from the very tradition the *Gawain*-poet so consciously strives to invoke" (Amodio, "Tradition, Modernity" 50). As with these larger narrative patterns, so too with the poem's architectonics.

In terms of its architectural language and imagery, the poem demonstrates the continuing connection between hall imagery and *comitatus* ideals, yet employs these associations to challenge some of the very ideals on which the culture of the hall is based. The varied styles of architectural description employed for Camelot and the castle Hautdesert bring into sharp relief the contrasts between the traditional ideals of Arthur's court and the value placed on individuality and innovation in Bertilak's realm. It is in the "chapel," though, a socially and architecturally ambiguous space that conflates man-made and natural structures, that the poet most directly pits communal ideals against intensely private and individualized notions of ethics and morality. Far from being mere settings and backdrops for the narrative action, these three distinct spaces help articulate and negotiate some of the poem's most probing questions.

Halls and Comitatus Ideals

Although the fourteenth century was decidedly an era of castles, the language of *Sir Gawain and the Green Knight* is in many respects far more concerned with the *culture* of the *hall*. Despite the dominance of the castle as a narrative setting, the word *castle* itself appears only four times, always in reference to Hautdesert (767, 801, 1365, 2067) and never in reference to Camelot. Unlike the modifier *strong* employed with the castles of *Brut, Horn,* and *Havelok,* adjectives such as *comly* (1365) and even *comlokest* (767) employed with "castle" in *Sir Gawain and the Green Knight* suggest a preoccupation with the structure's more superficial beauty and grandeur rather than its military strength (although the defensive features are enumerated at some length, as will be seen below). *Hall,* on the other hand, appears eighteen times in the text, eleven times in reference to Camelot and seven times in relation to the castle Hautdesert. To the extent that the traditional referentiality of the terms *hall* and *castle* remains operative in the fourteenth century, these numbers would suggest that Arthur's court, housed more explicitly in a "hall," is more closely connected with the complex of ideals associated with the hall in earlier British medieval literature. As discussed below, the poem does indeed rely on such associations but at the same time challenges these very ideals that the poem's hall imagery evokes.

In addition to the sheer number of references to Camelot as a "hall," differences in the architectural features attributed to the "hall" of Camelot and the "hall" of Hautdesert show more distinctly Anglo-Saxon architectural patterns in the poem's treatment of Camelot. For instance, the Green Knight rides straight up to Arthur's court and "þe halle entres" ["enters the hall"] on horseback, indicating that the hall is on the ground floor, in the more common fashion of English halls, and that the hall is an open and freestanding structure. In contrast, the hall of Hautdesert, whose name is French in origin,[44] is "ful hyȝe" (794), seemingly on an upper floor or lodged within a high tower more in line with continental architectural practice (see chap. 6). Further, unlike Camelot, the castle Hautdesert can be entered only by passing over a bridge and through a guarded gate (820–21), also more in keeping with Norman and French practice.

Although the architectural referents of "hall" differ with respect to Camelot and Hautdesert, the term itself retains associations with communal ideals of honor in both spaces. In Camelot, "þe kyng watz cummen with knyȝtes into þe halle" (62), communal feasting occurs "in halle" (92), and there is "wynne" in the "halle" (2456). Further, Gawain boasts that he will meet the Green Knight's challenge "in þis halle, herande þise knyȝtes" ["in this hall, in the hearing of these knights"] (450). The hall within the castle Hautdesert also serves as the locus for communal activities and the celebration of heroic ideals, though less explicitly and to a lesser extent than in Camelot. In Hautdesert, as in Camelot, men play "gomnez in halle" ["games in hall"] (989; cf. 459). Further, the contracts of gift exchange are said to be fulfilled when Bertilak sees Gawain "in halle" (1620), and when he first arrives at the castle, Gawain is led cere-moniously by a host of men into the "halle" (825, 831). Thus even the halls within the mighty castle of Hautdesert become suffused with heroic associations. Whether as a freestanding hall at Camelot or as a hall within an impressive castle at Hautdesert, spaces marked lexically as "halls" are conveyed as appropriate loci for communal *comitatus* ideals and activities.

Similar patterns emerge with *hall*'s synonym *sale*, which, like *hall*, denotes a rather vaguely described but seemingly freestanding structure in reference to Camelot and a more specialized space within a larger heavily fortified structure in the castle Hautdesert.[45] Such connections between "sale" and the social activities inside are consistent with the sec-ondary sense of "sale" as "the persons present in the hall" (*MED*, s.v. *sale*) attested at this time, the hall itself and the people therein able to be ref-erenced by the same term.[46] Like the term "hall," "sale" is applied more fre-quently to Camelot (four times; 197, 243, 349, 558) than to the castle Haut-desert (twice; 1372, 1651), again pointing toward a heightened narrative presence of the hall and its corresponding communal ideals in Arthur's court.[47] Also like *hall*, *sale* in both spaces is employed in association with communal acts and values. When Bertilak summons the people of his household together as a body, he is identified in relation to the hall, the "lorde in þat sale" (1372), and the feasting of the group, characterized by "myrþe" and "ioye" (1007), takes place "al þe sale" (1005). Back at Came - lot, when Gawain magnanimously offers to accept the Green Knight's challenge in place of Arthur, he appeals to Arthur's position "so hyȝe in your sale" ["so high in your hall"] (349), and the collective lamenting of Gawain's comrades on his departure is also described in terms of the hall: "þere watz much derue doel driuen in þe sale" ["there was much griev-ous lamenting made in the hall"] (558).

Though the terms for "hall," *hall* and *sale*, are fairly consistently em-ployed in this poem specifically in relation to heroic conduct and rela-tionships in patterns similar to those seen in *Horn* and *Havelok*, these traditional associations are then put to very untraditional purposes in *Sir Gawain and the Green Knight*, as the narrative raises the question of whether Arthur's hall is truly the home of heroic men. As soon as the Green Knight enters the hall ["the halle entres"] (221), he issues a chal-lenge to "alle the heredmen in halle" ["all the courtiers in the hall"]

(302) that ultimately calls into question the very values on which their *comitatus* is based. When the Green Knight suggests that perhaps no men are actually brave enough to pit themselves against him, he lessens Camelot's status architecturally by referring to it only as a "hous": "if any so hardy in this *hous* holdes hyselven" ["if any in this house hold themselves so hardy"] (285–86). Still not receiving a response, he again refers to the court in rather common and domestic terms: "'What, is this Arthures *hous*,' quoth the hathel thenne, 'That al the rous rennes of thurgh ryalmes so mony?'" ["'What, is this Arthur's house,' said the knight then, 'Of which fame runs through so many realms?'"] (309–10). Since "hous" and "halle" fill the same metrical needs for the alliterative verse and since, as Camargo notes, the poem's structure is in many ways "overdetermined," the choices between the two architectural terms should not be dismissed as purely accidental.[48]

It is only after Gawain has risen to the occasion, sworn to find the Green Chapel, and performed his valiant though unsuccessful beheading of his challenger, that the Green Knight lexically restores Camelot's status as a "hall" and validates the hall's correspondent ideals: "As þou hatz hette in þis *halle*, herande þise knyʒtes. / To þe grene chapel þou chose" ["As you have promised in this *hall*, in the hearing of these knights, to the green chapel you go"] (450–51). Then finally, in typical ring-structure fashion, the hall door is mentioned explicitly on the Green Knight's departure, just as it was at his entrance, though the subtle detail of the door is likely overshadowed for many readers by the fact that the knight is now carrying his head in his own hands: "he . . . halled out at þe hal dor, his hed in his hande" ["he . . .went out the hall door, his head in his hand"] (458). Almost a year later, of course, Gawain himself follows, and, in leaving the hall and its concomitant social structures encounters new and unfamiliar architectural spaces. My interpretation of Gawain's subsequent journey is guided in part by architectural representation, as the poem moves not only through multiple spaces but also through various modes of architectural description that inevitably shape audience response.

Castles and Emerging Modernity

As discussed at length in chapter 6, the centuries immediately following the Norman Conquest turned England into a vast building site for new castles, a phenomenon that made its mark in contemporary literature as well as on the landscape. Though from Gawain's perspective the castle was only a lengthy side stop on his mission to the Green Chapel, the castle at Hautdesert and the events therein occupy the center and the greatest portion of the poem's narrative content. Adventures of errant knights during side stops in castles are of course a commonplace in medieval French as well as English romance, but the *Gawain*-poet innovatively pits the architectural commonplaces of the French-influenced romance in direct juxtaposition with those of pre-Conquest England. My focus here is thus on the contrasts that emerge between the portrayal of the hall at Camelot and the castle at Hautdesert. In the spaces themselves and in the language used to describe them, Hautdesert calls to mind architectural and social aspects of the new Norman social order, whereas Camelot aligns itself more directly with native Germanic architectural traditions and codes of conduct. This effect is accomplished in part through the vocabulary choices discussed above, with *castle,* a word and structure closely associated with military strength and political prowess, being reserved for Hautdesert, and *halle* and *sale,* terms more typically evoked in relation to heroes and their noble deeds, employed more frequently with regard to Camelot. However, not only is Camelot referenced with vocabulary that indexes communal ideals more frequently than Hautdesert, but the very modes of description employed in the treatment of these two spaces also mark Hautdesert's distance from the traditional and communal ideals of Camelot. Like the buildings on the actual landscape, these descriptions of built spaces verbally and visually articulate the complex social and cultural dynamics that Gawain must negotiate as he journeys from Camelot to Hautdesert and back again.

Camelot is described with vocabulary connotatively potent but descriptively vague, much like the uncarpentered world of traditional Old English verse. The castle Hautdesert, however, is described in language much more vivid and precise, more in keeping with patterns of literate culture. As with *Sir Orfeo,* the hero of *Sir Gawain and the Green Knight* initially resides in a visually indistinct space that the audience must envisage based on experiences from outside the poem and then journeys to spaces rendered with increasing specificity and detail. The manner of description, like the vocabulary itself, aligns the Hautdesert portions of the text with non-native French influence and Camelot with traditional

Germanic. According to Andrea Clough, the "descriptive passages of a more highly ornamented nature" are characterized by a preponderance of "French loan words, exploited for their elevated or specialised status" to the extent that the borrowings "overshadow the native element almost entirely" (190). In the case of the castle Hautdesert, the "architecture of the castle is mirrored in the elaborate ornamentation of the diction itself" (195).[49] In contrast to Hautdesert, Camelot in this poem is treated without minute physical description and analysis, belonging instead to a world of communal and largely unexamined (except by Gawain himself) ideals and values.

In keeping with these patterns, most of those details of the hall at Camelot come not through objective description but through characters' physical interaction with the respective spaces. Unlike the bolted gates itemized objectively alongside myriad other details of the castle Hautdesert at its first appearance, the doors of Camelot are referenced only to the extent that they are directly engaged by characters, as when someone passes through them (e.g., 136, 458). During the scenes in Camelot, characters are frequently identified in terms of their relation to the buildings but without physical description of such spaces. For instance, although Arthur himself is introduced first as a builder, the best of "alle þat here bult" (25), no specific details are given for the buildings he erected.[50] Buildings and their component parts at Camelot are never referenced simply for the sake of description.

Instead, it is Arthur's relationship to the space that is highlighted rather than its physical details, Arthur welcoming the Green Knight "to þis place" ["to this place"] (252) and introducing himself as "the hede of þis ostel" ["head of this hostel"] (253). When he first arrives at Camelot, the Green Knight himself is also introduced specifically in reference to Arthur's hall: "þer hales in *at þe halle dor* an aghlich mayster" ["there rushes in *at the hall door* a terrifying man"] (136), and the happiness of Arthur's court is conveyed in terms of space as "al wats hap vpon heȝe in hallez and chambres" ["all was happiness up high in halls and chambers"] (48). Verbal images of Arthur arriving "with knyȝtes into þe halle" ["with knights into the hall"] (62) and the splendid feast shared "among his fre meny in halle" ["among his noble men in the hall"] (101) are highly evocative of the *comitatus* ideals and culture so prized in *Beowulf*'s Heorot and Old English poetry in general. Much like the kings' halls in *Havelok* and Orfeo's hall in *Sir Orfeo*, Camelot is thus presented in idealized though largely unspecific terms.

Gawain himself is at the poem's opening very much a part of Camelot's communal ideals, as is reflected in his position in the hall; he is "glad to begynne þose gomnez in halle" ["glad to begin those games in the hall"] (495), as he is surrounded by "þe best of þe burȝ" ["the best of the stronghold"] (550). But as Gawain proceeds from his recognizable world into the uncertain realm beyond, the poem's conception of space shifts toward the specific with its first given historical place-name: "Til þat he neȝed ful neghe into þe Norþe Walez. / Alle þe iles of Anglesay on lyft he haldez" ["Until he had approached very near to North Wales. All the Isles of Anglesey he holds on the left, and goes over the fords by the forelands"] (697–98).[51] At this point in the narrative, we see an attendant change in architecture, as the structures themselves begin to mark Gawain's distance from familiar terrain. Through these portions of the text, we see a proportional change in the narrative's use of language, as the architectural description, like the architecture itself, becomes less and less like that found in oral traditional narrative. In Gawain's journey from Camelot to Hautdesert, the mode of architectural description shifts from one that emphasizes buildings' relationships to the human life world to a more neutral and detached cataloguing of features.

Thus, in contrast to King Arthur's idealized hall, which is portrayed almost exclusively in relation to the poem's characters, Bertilak's castle receives detailed and relatively objective physical description long before Gawain or any other character is said to directly interact with it. On approaching, Gawain is first struck by the height and isolation of the structure:

> er he watz war in þe wod of a won in a mote,
> Abof a launde, on a lawe, loken vnder boȝez
> Of mony borelych bole aboute bi þe diches. (764–66)

> [Then he was aware in the wood of a dwelling within a moat,
> above a land, on a mound, secured under boughs of many great
> tree trunks near the ditches.]

Shortly afterward, we are given sixteen more lines of detailed description of the castle Hautdesert:

> Þe walle wod in þe water wonderly depe,
> Ande eft a ful huge he3t hit haled vpon lofte
> Of harde hewen ston vp to þe tablez,
> Enbaned vnder þe abataylment in þe best lawe;
> And syþen garytez ful gaye gered bitwene,
> Wyth mony luflych loupe þat louked ful clene:
> A better barbican þat burne blusched vpon neuer.
> And innermore he behelde þat halle ful hy3e,
> Towres telded bytwene, trochet ful þik,
> Fayre fylyolez þat fy3ed, and ferlyly long,
> With coruon coprounes craftyly sle3e.
> Chalkwhyt chymnees þer ches he inno3e
> Vpon bastel rouez, þat blenked ful quyte;
> So mony pynakle payntet watz poudred ayquere,
> Among þe castel carnelez clambred so þik,
> Þat pared out of papure purely hit semed. (787–802)

———

[The wall went wondrously deep into the water, and then went up a great height, made of hard hewn stone up to the cornice molding, built[52] under the battlement in the best fashion. And then very bright turrets were fashioned in between, with many lovely windows (loop-holes) that locked very cleanly. That warrior had never looked upon a better barbican. And inside he beheld that hall very high, towers erected between, provided with very thick troches (tines of a deer's horn),[53] fair fitted pinnacles exceedingly long, with carven ornamental tops craftily made. Chalk-white chimneys in abundance he perceived there upon the tower roofs, that gleamed very white; So many painted pinnacles scattered everywhere, throughout the castle embrasures in the battlement, clustered so thickly, that it seemed purely carved out of paper.]

As Clough has noted, "One cannot help being struck by the large number of words used in unusual, technical, or specifically poetic senses to suggest elaborate ornamentation and architectural splendour" (195).[54] The contrast with the simple, traditional language employed during the Camelot portions has the effect of distancing the space architecturally and poetically from native traditions and aligning Hautdesert with the higher social classes more reminiscent of an Anglo-Norman elite.[55] The highly specialized vocabulary demonstrates the poet's "exploitation, and possibly even creation, of rare words" to portray features especially valued "by virtue of their associations with the tasteful and highly decorative architecture of the fourteenth-century aristocracy" (Clough 193). The contrast stylistically marks Gawain's passage from a familiar space governed by traditional and communal ideals to one characterized by innovation, individuality, and a new social order. In short, the detailed description of Hautdesert invites individual analysis, where the portrayal of Camelot assumes through its absence of detail a shared and collective worldview.

That Camelot's depiction is more "conventional" and that Hautdesert "seems to have a real background" (Thompson, "Green Knight's Castle" 324) has led to numerous theories attempting to place the "real" Hautdesert in a phenomenon that Robert Barrett refers to as "assertive localism" (Barrett 136). Awareness of real-world counterparts can of course provide useful context and increase our understanding of how contemporary audiences might have visualized the poem's architecture, but this context need not assume direct correspondence with any single structure.[56] In surveying and exploring the proposed candidates for real-world corollaries to Hautdesert castle and, later, the Green Chapel, I neither affirm nor deny any single claim regarding the poet's original inspiration. Instead, as in previous chapters, I argue only that real-world landscapes can and do shape audience response to texts and that the relationship of the imagined landscape of *Sir Gawain and the Green Knight* to the real landscape inhabited by the text's earliest readers can complement and enhance our reading of the narrative's architectural poetics. Two proposed candidates for Hautdesert's inspiration are Beeston Castle, Cheshire (e.g., Thompson, "Green Knight's Castle" 319), and Swythamley Park in Staffordshire (e.g., Elliott, *Gawain Country* 3). The argument for Swythamley is based largely on the terrain and its proximity to Lud's Church, a proposed location for the Green Chapel, though Elliott explains

that "there was never a castle at Swythamley such as Sir Gawain so op-
portunely discovered" (3). Beeston Castle (fig. 28) shares with the Hautdesert castle its construction in finely dressed stone (789), its battlements, and the walls behind the parapet with periodic projecting towers
corresponding to the poem's "garytez" (791). Its height, visibility, isolation, and rocky terrain also have precedent in Beeston.

Moving beyond the question of whether Hautdesert is modeled on a
single, specific castle or is, rather, a composite of vague architectural features observable on the fourteenth-century landscape, we can find models for productive middle ground in oral theory. The question is not unlike the nineteenth-century Unitarian/Analysts controversy "over one or
many Homers" (Foley, *Theory* 5), a debate that became more or less moot
with the growing awareness of the epic's traditional nature. The concept
of Homer posited by Milman Parry was neither a "sequence of poets and
redactors posted by the Analysts" nor an "original master bard imagined
by many Unitarians" (Foley, *Theory* 20) but one "able to harness the artistic idiom fashioned by his many predecessors" and thus "bring to his
poems something more" (*Theory* 20). Cockcroft makes a parallel argument for *Sir Gawain and the Green Knight,* contending that the imagery and phraseology surrounding Hautdesert is likewise best understood as neither an exact portrayal of a single castle nor a "patchwork" of
fourteenth-century architecture. Rather, by utilizing expectations based
on tradition *and* architectural features observable to contemporary audiences, the Gawain-poet also "brings to his poems something more" in
his unconventional combinations. Thus while the evidence is convincing that something *like* Beeston Castle or Swythamley was being evoked
and while it certainly enhances our interpretation to have the visual context these and other such buildings provide, the poem also employs "lapses
in strict physical and spatial realism" that serve to "enhance the moral realism of the poem, even as they frustrate the enthusiast of military architecture" (Cockcroft 460).

While seeking a single "source" for the castle can be unnecessarily
limiting, being aware of the features in view to fourteenth-century audiences can nonetheless productively shape our readings of the text. For instance, while looking at a structure such as Bodiam Castle, a private castle
constructed in the fourteenth century and roughly contemporary with
Sir Gawain and the Green Knight, one might find it easy to understand

how Gawain, unschooled in reading the details of Anglo-Norman construction, naively looked on the beauty of the castle without full awareness that much of its attraction derived from protective and dangerous
defense fortifications. Bodiam's well-preserved examples of crenellated
battlements, narrow windows, moat, and barbican (fig. 27) all convey
beauty at the same time that they provide protection. Yet, as was previously noted for *Brut, Havelok, King Horn,* and even historical writings of
the period, the rise of the castle corresponded to the emergence of feudalism and the displacement of native rulers and social systems. The concept "castle" was closely tied with military prowess, and the abundance
of castles, especially private ones, was eyed by many with suspicion and
some degree of fear, as we saw in the historical accounts of William of
Poitiers and William of Malmesbury. At this point in the narrative of *Sir
Gawain and the Green Knight,* the court of King Arthur and the authority
of his leadership has, if only within the construct of a game, been challenged by an unknown and outside presence whose residence—though
Gawain does not yet know to whom the castle belongs—bespeaks a new
and powerful social structure that traditional ideals prove insufficient to
negotiate, an architectural and social presence whose potential threat an
audience might recognize even when Gawain himself does not.

That multiple widely visible castles come fairly close to the description of the castle Hautdesert suggests that the poem's audience would
have had multiple images from actual experience to contribute to the visualization of this fictional place. The effect would be to put the audience
a step ahead of Gawain, who seems to be encountering such architecture
for the very first time, marveling at every tiny detail. By dwelling on features of the castle (and later the Green Chapel) with which an audience
was already likely familiar, the poem's architectural language serves to
create a distance between Gawain's perspective and the reader's. While to
Gawain the castle might appear to be "pared out of papure purely" ["cut
purely out of paper"] (802), a West Midlands audience familiar with such
imposing architecture would likely have seen Gawain's response to potentially dangerous defense mechanisms as uninformed and perhaps
quite naive.

The analytical description of the castle "verges on what we would
now call psychological realism" (Elliott, *Gawain Country* 40), thus interiorizing Gawain's character and moving him not only physically but also

psychologically further and further from the communal codes of conduct that characterize Arthur's court. Instead of describing the scene in
its totality, the poet gives us selected, though still plentiful, details as they
might enter the consciousness of an actual viewer. As Alain Renoir observes, such minute detail does not necessarily correspond to greater
narrative importance, especially in oral-derived texts; using an "analogy
of the cinematograph" ("Descriptive Techniques" 132), Renoir argues that
though "the importance assumed by a given detail depends largely upon
the portion of that space it occupies," the relationship in *Sir Gawain
and the Green Knight* is an inverse one: "the greater the magnitude of the
picture before us, the less the importance of the individual detail" (127).[57]
Rather, the intensity of detailed description shifts the reader's/viewer's
attention away from external action and instead moves toward internal, psychological perceptions, in this particular case underscoring "the
mounting anxiety of Gawain as he inexorably approaches the time and
place of his supposedly impending death" (Renoir, "Progressive Magnification" 245).

Yet, ironically, while Gawain is intensely anxious about his upcom-
ing meeting with the Green Knight, he expresses no such anxiety when
he first sees the castle Hautdesert, an arguably naive response given not
only the eventual revelation of the host's identity but also the potentially
threatening nature of the castle's architecture. For an audience contemporary with the poem's production, such a castle would have been a possible
source of very real anxiety during a period of rapid architectural change.
The nature of the description at this point in the narrative thus sets up
an uneasy tension between Gawain's perceptions of this new space and
the essence of the features being described. Although Gawain looks on the
sight with innocent awe and admiration, a number of the castle's features
are potentially quite threatening. Gawain sees a well-constructed barbican, tightly locking windows, and an unimaginable number of embrasures and crenellations in the battlements, through which enemy warriors
might send projectiles from a well-protected location, as merely "luflych"
and "fayre."[58] The distinction between guest and captive is somewhat obscured when we are reminded at Gawain's departure that the bridge was
raised and the gates locked during the entirety of his stay: "The brygge
watz brayde doun, and te brode ʒates / Vnbarred and born open vpon

boþe halue" ["The bridge was brought down and the broad gates unbarred and opened on both sides"] (2069–70).

The potential divide between a knowledgeable reader and a seemingly oblivious character creates a literal and figurative space for the poem to challenge and question the traditional ideals that seem to have governed Gawain's world up until this journey. Inside the castle, of course, Gawain's sense of duty toward women is thrown off balance by the advances of his host's wife. His ideal of keeping his word at all costs is pitted against a very real fear of death. After making a formal agreement such as Gawain has made with his host, a more traditional hero such as Beowulf or even Havelok would have no moment of self-doubt. Gawain, however, experiences true fear and, despite the oath he made to share with his host all that he obtained during the day, keeps the green girdle that the wife promises can save his life. The trials that Gawain faces in the castle are deeply personal, and the communal ideals of Camelot are simply insufficient to fully address the choices he must make. While, as noted above, Hautdesert does have a hall that serves as an appropriate space for traditional and communal social activities, the ideals associated with the hall-idea complex now struggle against the surrounding culture of the castle. It is not until Gawain finally reaches the Green Chapel, however, that these tensions reach their climax.

The Green Chapel and Negotiations of Space

Thus far we have been viewing the relationship between Camelot and Hautdesert within a dual structure, one that highlights the differences between traditional and literary culture in ways similar to the dual patterning of *Sir Orfeo*. But, as in other regards, the Gawain-poet thwarts simple binary relationships, triangulating and complicating the poem's architectural landscape through the presentation of the enigmatic Green Chapel. In the space of Camelot, communal *comitatus* values are largely unexamined and govern all decisions, and in Hautdesert these values are put to the test as Gawain is confronted with new and unfamiliar challenges. At the Green Chapel, Gawain is judged for his failure to live up to his own ideals of honesty, receiving a nick from the ax for his breach of the agreement made with his host. However, by *only* giving this nick, the

Green Knight also implicitly judges the ideals themselves, prioritizing these lofty values somewhat below the needs required by individual circumstance and natural human fear. It is thus here at the Green Chapel that the tensions built across the poem between the individual psyche and communal ideals are negotiated.

In terms of its architectural features, the Green Chapel is the most ambiguous of all the poem's built spaces, a "chapel," yet seemingly a work not of man but of nature. However, despite such ambiguity, the appropriated term for referencing the space is much more consistent than for either Hautdesert or Camelot. Where *castle* appears only four times in the text and the spaces of Camelot and Hautdesert[59] are identified by name only once each (37, 2445), the Green Chapel is referenced specifically as such thirteen times and is identified as a "chapel" without the designation "green" nine additional times. The three remaining instances of "chapel" occur in reference to private spaces within courts, at Camelot (63) as well as at the castle Hautdesert (930, 1857). The choice of *chapel* as the term to designate these disparate spaces brings the tensions between communal ideals seen in the hall of Camelot and the individualism and modernity embodied in the castle Hautdesert into the foreground. Audiences contemporary with the poem would no doubt have seen a "chapel" primarily as a private space very distinct from the public parish churches. At this point in English-language history "chapel" most often designated a place of worship "*other than* a parish church or cathedral" (*MED*, sense 1; emphasis mine), a "sanctuary for *private* worship" (sense 2), or a space "not subject to the jurisdiction of the ordinary (such as a bishop)" (sense 1c). Gawain, however, obscures potential differences between public and private spaces in comparing the Green "Chapel" with "churches" he has known. By referring to the Green Chapel as the "corsedest kyrk þat euer I com inne" ["most cursed church that ever I came in"] (2196), he conflates these public and private functions, setting the stage for the tensions between public and private honor that he later negotiates within this very space. The Green Knight absolves him for breaking his oath, but Gawain remains unable to reconcile the breach with the communally held ideals of Arthur's court.

Given the unwavering designation of the space as a "chapel" (or in the single instance in Gawain's words above, a "kirk") elsewhere, the language used by the Green Knight to describe his own space at this point is conspicuous; the knight welcomes Gawain not to his "chapel" or even his "house" but simply to his "place" (2240). It is only when the Green Knight envisions a retelling of the event that the space is once again described in man-made terms, as he directs Gawain to remember the "chaunce of þe grene chapel" ["adventure of the green chapel"] (2399). And Gawain does in fact later tell King Arthur's court of "þe chaunce of þe chapel" (2496). The chapel is only identified specifically as such in stories before and after the fact. In the immediate moment of its description, the exact nature of its reality is unclear, a seemingly natural space invested with architectural significance and temporarily appropriated for the Green Knight's mysterious contest.

The ambiguous nature of the space contrasts with the consistency of its attribution in similar ways throughout the poem. For instance, the Green Chapel on the surface shares little with other buildings designated as "chapels" earlier in the poem. The three usages of "chapel" that do not refer to the Green Chapel establish such structures as spaces for "chauntré" ["singing of the mass"] (63), "euensong" of chaplains (930), and private confession (1857). With these concepts of chapel in place, it is understandable that the Green Chapel differs so markedly from Gawain's expectations that it is some time before he even notices it as such: "And ofte chaunged his cher þe chapel to seche: / He seȝ non suche in no syde, and selly hym þoȝt" ["And he often changed his position to seek the chapel: He saw no such thing on any side and it seemed a marvel to him"] (2169–70). Like the castle at Hautdesert and the castle of the Fairy King in *Sir Orfeo,* the Green Chapel is marked by a high level of detail in its description:

> Saue, a lyttel on a launde, a lawe as hit were;
> A balȝ berȝ bi a bonke þe brymme bysyde,
> Bi a forȝ of a flode þat ferked þare;
> Þe borne blubred þerinne as hit boyled hade. (2171–74)

> ————
>
> [He saw a little way off on a lawn, a mound as it were; a rounded mound by a bank beside the water's edge, by a ford of water that flowed there; the stream bubbled therein as if it had boiled.]

So confused is Gawain that he dismounts his horse and walks about the structure for closer inspection (2180–84), at which point further description is provided from this new angle:

> Hit hade a hole on þe ende and on ayþer syde,
> And ouergrowen with gresse in glodes aywhere,
> And al watz holȝ inwith, nobot an olde caue,
> Or a creuisse of an olde cragge, he couþe hit noȝt deme
> with spelle.

> ———

> [It had a hole on the end and on either side, and was overgrown with grass in glades everywhere, and all hollow within, only an old cave, or a crevice of an old crag, he could not tell for certain.]

The contrast between Gawain's expectations and the structure he encounters is then expressed by the words of the hero himself: "'We! Lorde,' quoth the gentyle knyght, / 'Wheþer þis be þe grene chappelle? / Here myȝt aboute mydnyȝt / þe dele his matynnes telle!'" ["Oh! Lord," said the gentle knight, "I wonder whether this be the Green Chapel? Here about midnight the devil might say matins!"] (2185–88).[60] Gawain continues by describing the structure as "wysty" ["bleak"] (2189), "ugly" (2190), and "with erbes overgrowen" ["overgrown with grass"] (2190). The subterranean nature of the dwelling is also underscored as Gawain walks up even to the structure's roof: "He romes up to the roffe of tho rogh wones" ["He wandered up to the roof of that rough dwelling"] (2198). Both Gawain's reactions and the descriptive patterns themselves establish the individuality of the space and its distance from anything familiar or traditional.

As with the castle, this high level of specificity seen for the Green Chapel has led to searches for exact real-world locations. As R. E. Kaske has asserted, "Though no one would argue that a poetic description of this kind must necessarily mirror an actual piece of terrain, the present passage does seem to push the imagination inevitably in that direction" (112). Kaske notes the "unparalleled" setting of the chapel, a setting that is "singular to a really remarkable degree—an effect greatly heightened by the unusual fullness and specificness with which they are described" (112), and Ralph W. V. Elliott has therefore proposed the natural rock formation of Lud's Church as a possible location ("Sir Gawain" 12), noting that the formation lies clearly within the dialect boundaries of the poem's likely composition. Local sentiments also side with the Lud's Church theory, widespread and tantalizing enough that a Cheshire travel Web site even makes an unqualified claim that the formation "acted as the model for the 'Green Chapel' in the classic mediaeval poem 'Sir Gawain and the Green Knight', and the aura of mediaeval romance still seems to stick to it."[61] Indeed, the travel sections of the *Independent* (London), *Sunday Telegraph* (London), and *Sentinel* (Stoke) have all linked the site with the Gawain legend.[62]

Two additional locations in the Manifold Valley have also been posited: the Wetton Mill cave (fig. 29) and Thor's Cave (fig. 30).[63] Thor's Cave is surrounded by a lush, green landscape, and, sitting high above the valley, it is visible from a great distance. With its "walls" rising high into an arched peak and its mouth a perfectly rounded "doorway," the structure leaves open many suggestive possibilities. Elliott notes that prehistoric artifacts have been found here ("Landscape" 116), making it even more imaginable as an ancient dwelling. Because of its multiple openings and houselike structure, the rock shelter at Wetton Mill has also had its case forcefully presented, first by Mabel Day in 1940 and more fully by Kaske in his 1970 analysis.[64] Such real-world assignments of a poetic locale are made possible only by the specificity with which the poet describes the chapel in the first place.

The obvious connection shared by all of these possibilities is the link to a natural rather than man-made environment. Continuing the narrative style employed with the description of the castle, the specificity itself marks a stylistic difference from Camelot, taking Gawain even further from the familiar and traditional realm of Arthur's court at the same time that it renders the space more familiar to an audience who knows the Staffordshire landscape, with not one but several similar structures visible in the area. As with the castle, that there are strong correspondences between the Green Chapel and geographic features of the Staffordshire landscape would likely serve to underscore the distance between a Staffordshire audience familiar with such a landscape and Gawain, who is clearly out of his element. Someone familiar with such geographic structures as Thor's Cave or Wetton Mill likely would have recognized the architectural paradox long before Gawain does.

As ambiguous as the space is at a literal level, it is perhaps even more so in terms of its associative meaning, seeming to simultaneously evoke and reject the architectural poetics of earthen built spaces of Anglo-Saxon times. Just as the halls of *Sir Gawain and the Green Knight* share connections with heroic ideals seen in Old English verse, so too does the underground Green Chapel share associations with death seen in Old English underground dwellings such as the dragon's barrow in *Beowulf,* the subterranean dwelling in *The Wife's Lament,* and the watery habitation of Riddle 1's speaker. All of these underground structures evoke ominous traditional associations of danger and death. (See chaps. 2 and 5.) When Gawain arrives at the site of the much-anticipated chapel, he sees not a church but a "balȝ berȝ bi bonke" ["round mound by the bank"] (2172), "berȝ" deriving from Old English *beorg* ["barrow"]. The natural imagery continues (2180–83) as the structure is described as "ouergrowen with gresse" (2181) and likened to an "olde caue" (2182) or "creuisse of an olde cragge" (2183). Viewed from the perspective of an inherited traditional poetics, this underground space evokes strong connotations of death. The eerie combination of natural and man-made imagery and the sharp contrast between Gawain's expectations and what he finds serve to heighten the sense of foreboding.[65] Throughout the poem, the mode of description thus evokes traditional Anglo-Saxon poetics. At the same time, however, the poem manipulates, subverts, and ultimately refutes such tradition-encoded meanings. The description of the Green Chapel activates a register of architectural description that calls to mind funerary and ominous associations. The narrative, however, does not follow through. The threat of death haunts Gawain almost to the poem's very conclusion. In the end, however, not only does no one die, but the poem's hero and his opponent actually part as friends.

The "architecture" of the Green Chapel has meaning on several levels. It can be read in light of Anglo-Saxon architectural spaces as a funerary "anti-hall," in the common usage of *chapel* as a religious space outside the jurisdiction of the official church, or according to its physical characteristics as a natural space completely outside the realm of human interaction. The chapel becomes the locus for the testing of traditional ideals and retribution based on modern and individualized criteria. Gawain is judged for his failure to be completely honest, yet such communal ideals are in part rejected, the retribution for his failure to live up to these ideals being mitigated through the Green Knight's more nuanced and introspective evaluation of Gawain's motives. With the Green Chapel, the "structural duplicity" contrasting the hall with the castle works in tandem with a triadic structuring of the narrative,[66] accomplished in part through a duality in architectural description and a narrated triangulation of three distinct building types: King Arthur's hall at Camelot, Bertilak's castle at Hautdesert, and the Green Knight's chapel.

After taking us from the hero's home to the distant castle and chapel, the ring composition of the Return Song story pattern is completed as we are brought back to the hall at Camelot and the hero finally makes his way home to King Arthur's court. As before, the contrast between the language used to describe and reference built space is extreme. Having left the heavily described spaces of Hautdesert and the Green Chapel, we return once again to a space provided with only the most limited physical description. This familiar location of Camelot is referenced solely in terms of traditional social function: without gazing on the features of the hall, in fact without any buildup at all, Gawain simply "commes to the court" ["comes to the court"] (2489). Like the ideals of Arthur's court, the architecture of Gawain's surroundings receives no further unpacking and relies exclusively on audience awareness to fill in gaps. By allowing the audience to visualize this space for themselves, the sparse language virtually guarantees that the architectural image created will not be at odds with the familiar and traditional associations being invoked. The unexamined architecture at this point parallels the court's inability to accept or even understand Gawain's close self-examination. So sharp is the divide between the psychological interiorization seen at Hautdesert and the externally conveyed ideals of Arthur's court that Gawain's shame at personal failure seems to have little or no meaning in Arthur's court. When Gawain confesses his own "vntrawþe" (2509) and bares his scar to Arthur's court, the perplexing laughter indicates the vast chasm between Gawain's recently explored individual psychology and the communal and largely unexamined ideals that dominate Camelot. Arthur's hall is not a space for individual exploration or interior contemplation. As Amodio argues, Gawain's actions and assertions are "from the perspective of the court, incomprehensible because they are untraditional and unexpected"

("Tradition, Modernity" 60). The court reacts to all things as a unified body. Confronted with Gawain's shame "alle þe court" (2514) laugh and immediately reinstate Gawain into the *comitatus* through a gesture of solidarity in which "vche burne of þe broterhede, a bauderyk schulde haue" ["each knight of the brotherhood, a baldric should have"] (2516).

Depictions of built space in *Sir Gawain and the Green Knight* thus reflect the precarious position that the work occupies on the orality-literacy continuum, as the poem's treatment of architectonics repeatedly probes the relationship between tradition and modernity, between the communal and the individual, much as Gawain himself has to do. As fanciful as it is as an imagined space, the castle Hautdesert nonetheless reflects patterns in architectural reality and offers a fictional space in which to explore the rapidly changing social world of post-Conquest England.[67] The poem's nuanced employment of oral poetics speaks powerfully to the tangled relationships between oral and literate modes of poetic expression in the late Middle Ages so that as Gawain moves physically from the traditionally resonant world of Camelot to the morally ambiguous realms of the mysterious Green Knight and back again, previously shared traditions and ideals can no longer be assumed to hold their ultimate authority. But, challenged though they are, these ideals—conveyed through the employment of both oral and architectural poetics—continue to exert a discernible and potent influence on the poem's narrative and psychological developments. When Bertilak invites Gawain to stay and spend the new year at the castle Hautdesert, he declines, choosing instead to return to the hall at Camelot. He does so, however, with much ambivalence. Through a parallel ambivalence in its architectural imagery, the poem draws attention to its own transitional position between tradition and innovation and leaves the reader, much like Gawain, not quite at home in either space.

CODA: BY THE WALL

In closing, let us turn from these larger narrative patterns to one final and more tightly focused example of traditional referentiality, one whose development can be traced across all the periods treated in this volume and extending even into modern times. Where the continuity of oral poetics across the Old and Middle English periods is often sustained most strongly at the level of thematics, usages of "by the wall" demonstrate that there is also at least limited continuity in phraseology sustained in Middle English verse, variations of the phrase operative in Old English verse (as discussed in chap. 5), in the *Brut*, and in each of the previously discussed verse romances.

Just as "by the wall" preceded, and in some instances predicted, slaughter in such Old English poems as *The Wanderer*, *Beowulf*, and *Andreas*,[68] so too it is consistently followed by slaughter in the post-Conquest *Brut*. The connection between walls and slaughter is quite logical from a number of perspectives. In terms of its etymology, *wall* derives from Latin *vallum* (palisade), entering English with the military sense of fortifications. Its earliest sense in English is of a "rampart of earth, stone, or other material constructed for defensive purposes" (*OED*, 1.a). Thus to be by such a wall would involve being quite literally on the very dangerous edges of potentially hostile territory. Sound correspondences further account for the connection, since, as noted in chapter 5, *weal* (wall) is phonetically quite similar to *wæl* (slaughter, or the slain). During the Old English period, these lexical and phonological characteristics likely helped establish associative patterns, frequent usage eventually developing into traditional idiom. It is perhaps the combination of etymological and phonological associations that helped sustain this particular phraseological pattern across the Middle English period in a transition that most traditional idioms did not manage to bridge.

As in Old English verse, occurrences of the preposition *by* (*be* or *bi*) followed by the object *wall* (*wealle/walle/wal*)—even if additional words intervene—are in Laȝamon's *Brut* consistently followed by or concurrent with narrated slaughter. Brutus finds Turnus killed in battle and buries him "*bi* ane stan *walle*" (866; emphasis mine). At a later point in the poem Dunwale and his men take swords that were lying "*bi* þisse *walle*" (2088), and Dunwale then gives orders to "slæð heom mid sweorde" ["slay them with swords"] (2107), a slaughter that soon becomes reality (2115). Later, Constance, Uther's brother the monk, is deceived and ultimately killed by Vortigern. When monks faithful to Constance enter his quarters, they see his clothes lying by the wall, "liggen *bi* þan *waȝes*"

(6560) and expect the worst, grieving the loss of Constance. At this point in the narrative Constance manages to temporarily escape, but his inevitable slaughter, anticipated in the phrase "by the wall," follows soon after (6780).

In the fourteenth-century verse narrative *Havelok the Dane*, "by the wall" also retains something like the full force it had in Old English narrative and thus serves to guide audience response and forecast narrative events. After Godard's brutal murders, Havelok sees his sisters sprawled in blood "bi þ[e] wawe." And when Havelok and his men hear of the sixty intruders, they too are described as being "bi þe wowe" ["by the wall"] (1964) just before they brutally defeat these foes. We see the phrase yet again when the men Ubbe has called together in judgment of Godard assemble "bi þe wawe" (2471), where they later determine that Godard will be flayed alive. The consistency with which "by the wall" is associated with such acts of violence would suggest that these walls act as much more than mere architectural details and are employed by the poet to shape and condition audience response—even to the extent that in the last example an audience familiar with such patterns would automatically intuit from this phrase that Godard will not be shown mercy, even though the actual judgment of his case has not yet occurred.

Usages in *King Horn* and *Sir Orfeo* demonstrate continuing expressive force of the phrase, even as the phraseology itself begins to break down. In *King Horn* and *Sir Orfeo* any prepositional phrase in which "wall" is the object fills a similar function. The system here thus can be modified as "(x[preposition]-) the wall." In the only prepositional phrase where "wall" is an object to be found in *King Horn*, Rymenhild finds her servant dead "under hire chambre wowe" ["under her chamber wall"] (982). The phrasing is likewise altered in *Sir Orfeo*, though the wall as the object of a preposition is still seen specifically in conjunction with slaughter. When Orfeo first encounters the many slain individuals in the Fairy King's court, the victims are described in relation to the wall in all three surviving manuscripts: "a-boute þe walle" in the Ashmole (378), "wiþ-in þe wal" in the Auchinleck (388), and "vnder þe wal" in the Harley (3810). Though not employing the exact phrasing "by the wall" seen in Old English verse and in *Havelok*, the juxtaposition of death and stone walls evokes associations similar to those we observed in chapter 5 for the heroes fallen beside stone walls in Old English poetry, where such phraseology is used to create expectations of death and loss. And, of course, such loss is exactly in line with the narrative of the well-known classical versions of the tale, where Orfeo (as Orpheus) retrieves his wife only to have her quickly snatched away from him back into the underworld. Here, however, Orfeo and his wife are able to counter such a disaster by making good on their escape from the castle of the Fairy King. The impact of the poem's happy ending is thus heightened not only by literary expectations generated from classical source texts but also through traditional associations of the architectural details the poet(s) chose to include, "(x[preposition]-) the wall" anticipating a slaughter that is threatened but never actualized.

The "(x[preposition]-) the wall" system is also present in *Sir Gawain and the Green Knight,* with continuing associations of death and slaughter but in far less traditional contexts. As Gawain seeks entrance to the hall at Hautdesert, he is greeted by a "porter pure plesaunt" (808). Their exchange as the porter learns Gawain's errand is described as taking place "on þe wal" (809), a phrase that should lead a contemporary audience to question the porter's superficial pleasantries. Based on this phrase (as well as the extensive description of the castle's military features discussed above), a reader might quite reasonably fear that Gawain will meet his death inside, but the poet invokes this idiomatic language only to subvert expectations in the narrative development. The anticipation of death signified by the phrase suggests to the audience a very real danger in the temptations and games that follow, but of course in the end Gawain and his host part as friends and Gawain returns from his journey with only the smallest nick. "On þe wal" seems to accomplish more than mere physical description, playing to audience expectations even as it undercuts the very traditional referentiality on which its meaning rests.

Such retention across the Old and Middle English periods of traditional referentiality at the phraseological level is rare, this particular system's stability likely enhanced by the homophonic relationship between *wall/weall* (wall) and *wal/wæl(e)* (slaughter), both of which date back to Old English times, though the latter became obsolete fairly early in the Middle English period.[69] Nevertheless, it demonstrates the process that traditional idioms and themes underwent in their developments from

Old into Middle English poetry. In fact, the pattern does not end even with Middle English.[70] From the seventeenth century to the present day "to go to the wall" has had the sense "to give way, succumb in a conflict or struggle" (*OED*, s.v. *wall*, sense III.13); "to lie by the wall" could be "spoken of a person dead but not buried" (*OED*, s.v. *wall*, sense III.17), and since the seventeenth century, "to turn one's face to the wall" has been "said of a person on his deathbed conscious of the approach of the end" (*OED*, s.v. *wall*, sense III.19). This deceptively simple but powerfully evocative phraseological pattern in "by the wall" and its later developments illustrates both the pervasiveness of traditional oral poetics far into the Middle English period and the increasingly varied ways that such traditional language could be employed during—and even since—the Middle English period. Though the phrase itself denotes death, it has survived through numerous periods of linguistic change and attests to the persistent rhetorical force of living tradition across and within literate culture.

AFTERWORD

MODERN

ENCOUNTERS

WITH

ANGLO-SAXON

SPACES

On the first Saturday of July each year, anywhere from one thousand to five thousand people congregate in the small village of Bradwell-on-Sea for a pilgrimage to the seventh-century St. Peter's Chapel (fig. 5). Though the chapel is used regularly throughout the year by the neighboring Othona community (itself named after the Roman fort believed to have occupied the site at a still earlier point in history), it is this annual pilgrimage that brings the highest concentration of visitors. The interdenominational pilgrimage begins at the parish church of St. Thomas, and participants walk two miles to the Anglo-Saxon chapel, which sits prominently on the headland overlooking the River Blackwater estuary (fig. 32). The 2006 pilgrimage that I attended, held on July 1, opened with a Celtic hymn, and the procession was led by a banner of St. Cedd, a figure closely tied to the Celtic church and believed by many to have founded St. Peter's Chapel. The vicar of Lindisfarne, who led the day's ceremonies, made numerous references to the chapel's Anglo-Saxon origins, and local residents were quick to point out to visitors the Roman tiles scattered throughout the chapel's fabric. Very much a dynamic and living space, St. Peter's Chapel is highly valued for connections to its varied Celtic, Roman, and Anglo-Saxon traditions. Far from a static space to be merely observed, this building, like many other Anglo-Saxon churches, continues to speak to the multiple traditions from which it derives.

Anglo-Saxon spaces continue to be utilized in radically different ways. At Jarrow, for instance, an interpretive center and museum have been built as a part of Bede's World, which also features a re-created Anglo-Saxon village and a tourist information center. The nearby Saxon church of St. Paul is likewise geared toward dissemination of information, with visiting schoolchildren dressed as monks having lessons in the chancel, which has a staffed museum shop at the rear. Many Anglo-Saxon churches, such as St. Wystan's at Repton and St. Laurence at Bradford-on-Avon, have stalls in the back where one can leave money for postcards or guides. But St. Paul's at Jarrow, closely connected with Bede's World, is much more explicitly a tourist site with an extensive selection of merchandise. Far more common, however, are those churches that continue to have weekly, sometimes daily, services that at times have posed impediments to archaeological study.[1]

The dynamic nature and continued use of the buildings and their surroundings have also been a source of frustration for some visitors seeking a sense of the early medieval world. Of St. Peter's and St. Patrick's at Heysham, one guidebook cautions that "much imagination is required to conjure its original solitude out of the present throng of sweet shops and cafes around the lower edge of the churchyard" (Kerr and Kerr, *Anglo-Saxon Sites* 56). Of St. John's Saxon church at Escomb, the same guide laments that "its majestic antiquity is unmarred by the tasteless modern houses which surround it" (35). It can be risky, however, to presuppose that there was ever a homogeneous cultural identity even during the Anglo-Saxon period itself. Many of these sites from the time of their very construction bear signs of multiple time periods and cultural associations. The "unmarred" and "majestic" Escomb Church actually bears marks of Roman tooling on the stones with which it was constructed (figs. 20 and 21). On the building's interior one can still see a Roman inscription on a stone, turned on its side however, indicating that the inscription itself was not relevant to the mason who placed it there. The pair of Anglo-Saxon churches at Heysham bear witness to Scandinavian influences in the hogback monument (fig. 8) and to Celtic influence in the doorway of St. Patrick's ruin (fig. 31). Indeed, the very fact that the two churches are in such close proximity to one another has suggested to some local residents that tensions necessitated separate places of worship among even the earliest residents.[2]

The spaces today continue the synthesis of traditions. A woman I spoke with at St. Andrew's Church at Greensted was just as proud of the handmade shingles added to the Victorian tower in 1987 as of the Anglo-Saxon timbers I had come to see (fig. 17). A man I met at St. Mary's in Sompting pointed out a "millennium tree" planted on the church grounds just a few years ago before proceeding to show me the famed Anglo-Saxon tower (fig. 14). These spaces continue to be used, not simply as museum artifacts and tourist sites, but as dynamic and vibrant spaces. The Greensted *Church Guidebook* opens by welcoming visitors to "the oldest wooden church in the world" (3) and closes by asking, "Why is it that visitors always seem surprised when they learn that Greensted is a living church?" (10). Today's Greensted church community is certainly proud of its rich historic heritage but values even more the fact that "people have worshipped here continuously for 1300 years" (3). Likewise, the Sompting church guide concludes its architectural history with an adamant testimony to its vibrancy: "After all these years, this is still very much a Church in action" (6). And the Selham church guide, after carefully summarizing the academic debates regarding the Saxon and Norman components of the architectural structure, reminds visitors of the continuity of function amid numerous external changes, noting that "upwards of 30 generations of Selham folk have offered their worship, said their prayers, confessed their sins, celebrated the baptisms and marriages of their sons and daughters, and come reverently to lay their loved ones to rest" (n.p.).

In compiling the church guide to All Saints Church at Earls Barton, Andrew Hart more directly confronts potential tensions between conceptions of the space as the static object of archaeological appreciation and the dynamic locus of activity for the social community: "Some commentators, whilst enthusing about the tower, have summarily dismissed later features as being of little interest. However, there is much else worthy of note, and every century from the tenth onwards is represented in the fabric and fittings of the building which bears witness to the continuity of Christian life and is still a very active place of worship" (1). When faced with a choice between retaining historic function or historic form, Sompt-ing parish church opted to keep the space dynamic: "Within the ruins of the mediaeval chapel, which for centuries had proved a romantic but disturbing feature north of the tower, a new building was at last erected in 1971, to serve as a chapel and as a parish room and thus to continue the historic functions of the original" (6). Like the oral poetics underlying much Old English poetry, these Anglo-Saxon churches have been flexible through centuries of great cultural change and continued use.

While these and numerous other parish churches survive from Anglo-Saxon times, none of the secular timber buildings that figure so prominently in poetry and historical records remain on the landscape, a situation that has led to creative and insightful reconstruction projects that give the public at least some sense of long-vanished early medieval spaces. For instance, at West Stow Country Park and Anglo-Saxon Village, visitors are invited to consider, "What was it like in early Anglo-Saxon times?"[3] This reconstructed village at West Stow is a vast and ongoing project led by Stanley West, archaeological consultant for the Anglo-Saxon Village Trust. Since the initial period of excavation (1965–72), archaeologists and curators at West Stow have attempted to reconstruct spatial relationships and buildings as they might have existed on the site during its Anglo-Saxon period of occupation, roughly 420–650 C.E. West explains that six or seven houses would have surrounded a typical Anglo-Saxon hall, and West Stow shows evidence of three or four such settlements. Remains of such tools as axes, augers, and chisels found during excavation give some indication of how they were built. Speaking of the buildings that have been reconstructed from such limited surviving evidence as "interpretations" rather than reconstructions, West affirms the experimental and creative nature of the process (*West Stow*).

From remains of charred wood, for example, it is difficult if not impossible to discern many specific details of timber construction for any given building, leading carpenters to experiment within a range of viable possibilities. One such experiment involved literally putting square pegs in round holes for increased stability. Even the most accurately reconstructed building will never be utilized in Anglo-Saxon ways, necessitating very different strategies for upkeep. West describes "never-ending procedures of repair and maintenance" because far more people visit today than would have inhabited the spaces in Anglo-Saxon times. The reconstructions have also been supplemented with interpretive information for schoolchildren and others with little knowledge of Anglo-Saxon culture. One sign, for instance, invites children to "imagine sitting around the hall fire at night asking riddles. One person describes something in an unusual way and the others guess what it is."[4] A more chilling feature of the park visually and powerfully demonstrates the threat of fire for buildings constructed entirely from timber; a reconstructed farmhouse burned to the ground in February 2005, and the ashes—all that was left—are fenced with a sign explaining that "a fire fighting crew came but . . . were unable to save the house."[5] West notes the importance of this archaeological experiment as an educational resource and hopes that future additions to the site include more attention to historical context, especially from Iron Age, Roman, and Saxon developments. For those of us visiting the sites today, the difference between stone and wood construction, a difference that can seem trivial when reading surviving literature at over a thousand years remove, becomes palpable. The interior of a wooden building not only looks but also smells and even sounds different from a stone structure. The poet of *Beowulf* takes full advantage of his audience's familiarity with wooden structures, evoking Heorot not only as a place grand in its appearance but also one that can be experienced through multiple senses, as the wooden floors could be heard and felt reverberating during Grendel's attack.

Bede's World, another experimental archaeology project at Jarrow that attempts to reconstruct buildings of the period (fig. 19), is an English Heritage site offering visitors slightly different interpretive frameworks for understanding Anglo-Saxon life and culture. Unlike West Stow, which aims for representation of a particular village focusing primarily on evidence from on-site excavation, the Gyrwe Anglo-Saxon Demonstration Farm at Bede's World aspires "to re-create the landscape familiar to Bede" and includes reconstructions based on archaeological evidence not just in Jarrow but throughout Northumbria.[6] For many of the same reasons outlined by Stanley West, Susan Mills, director of the project and former curator of Bede's World, finds "reconstruction" inaccurate and prefers the term *creation*. As discussed in chapter 2, the painstaking efforts taken throughout the buildings constructed at Jarrow to maintain authenticity have led to numerous insightful conclusions about Anglo-Saxon architectural practices, yet as Fowler and Mills explain, the dynamic process of re-creating such spaces must also take into account new audiences and purposes:

Yet, for all our aspirations, we also know now for certain that it is quite impossible to re-create a 'true' past, for none such existed or exists; that is particularly so of a past as specific as our core idea. Furthermore, quite apart from philosophical and theoretical objections, the demands of our own time, populist and statutory, make it very difficult even to remain close to our principles. How, for example, do you accommodate in an early medieval landscape, with any pretensions to former realism, rain shelters for the visitors, seats for the tired and breathless, railings beside the pond, and other safety precautions as defined by law and insurance companies? . . . At the physical level alone, our creation can never be more than a severely compromised approximation to what a seventh-century landscape with buildings may have looked like, in its form and very being almost certainly saying more about us and the late twentieth century than about Bede and his time. (122)

In fact, revision and adaptation have *always* characterized such spaces, since it "was already an old landscape for those who saw it thirteen hundred years ago" (115).

Nicholas Howe expresses a similar view in reflections on his visit to Bede's World. Howe writes that at first glance its placement in an industrial center makes it a less than ideal location, that it "would seem better sited anywhere in the Northumbrian countryside" (39). "Sometimes, though," he goes on to say, "the scholar's purism misses the point" (39), since the space is able to "hold in suspension two radically different moments in British history separated by twelve hundred years— agricultural village and industrial landscape" (39). The sense one has now is perhaps not unlike the dissonance Bede himself recorded in the "transition in Britain from pagan to Christian" (39). Howe's comments remind us that there is no "pure" state of Anglo-Saxon culture, and there truly never was.

While we can of course no longer hear medieval voices that spoke within these walls or witness the performance of early medieval poetry, we can, even today, share many spaces contemporary with poems now fossilized in surviving manuscripts. To return to Tolkien's apt metaphor, we can benefit from the "towers" of scholarship in literary and archaeological studies alike. We can interact with these buildings not as static relics of the past but as the dynamic spaces that they were and, in many cases, still are. As fictional narrative, as translation, as metaphor, and as locus of memory, the many and varied buildings in early medieval English poetry speak to the complex network of traditional associations in which they were produced. And if we attempt to engage the poetry in the same dynamic way that we might enter these surviving buildings, not as mere spectators or tourists, but as active participants, we are likely to develop a much more nuanced understanding of medieval verse produced in the dual contexts of oral tradition and literate culture. By increasing our awareness and appreciation of the architecture created by medieval builders and the corresponding spaces described by contemporary poets and scribes, we can come at least a little closer to understanding their respective crafts, the buildings they inhabited, and the traditions they shared.

NOTES

Preface and Acknowledgments

1. For instance, "Siblings and Suitors in the Narrative Architecture of The Tenant of Wildfell Hall" (O'Toole), "The Narrative Architecture of Rasselas" (Braverman), *The Semantic Architecture of the Old English Verbal Lexicon* (Diaz Vera), *Negational Architecture in Old English Poetry* (Andres), *Constructing the Architext* (P. Mitchell), "Architexture in Short Stories by Flannery O'Connor and Eudora Welty" (Gretlund), "Dickensian Architextures" (Wolfreys).

2. For a survey of such scholarship, see Catherine Hills, "*Beowulf* and Archaeology."

3. The nineteenth-century Burnham High Lighthouse at Burnham-on-Sea, for instance, is praised for its status as a "real ivory tower," in color if not material. www.holidaylettings.co.uk/rentals/burnham-on-sea/9330.

4. Reuters News, April 10, 2008.

5. See Foley, *Theory of Oral Composition* and *Oral-Formulaic Theory and Research,* with updates in *Oral Tradition.*

6. Any views, findings, conclusions, or recommendations expressed in this book do not necessarily reflect those of the National Endowment for the Humanities.

CHAPTER 1. Oral Tradition and Vernacular Architecture

1. Text from Krapp and Dobbie, *Anglo-Saxon Poetic Records,* vol. 3. Except where otherwise noted, all translations are my own.

2. The approximation of thirty follows Nicholas Howe. As Howe notes, "Since this poet does repeat some of these images and does not always state clearly the particular nature of each one, a completely accurate count of the conventional images in his poem is not possible" (*Old English Catalogue Poems* 106).

3. Russom argues that all these skills are also especially valued in the Anglo-Saxon heroic code: "The class of distinguished attributes is in some ways very broad; yet it also has distinct boundaries. Rigorously excluded from all lists of talents are all skills involving mercantile or agrarian life: that is, talents which enable one to earn a living outside the *comitatus*" (Russom, "Germanic Concept of Nobility" 13).

4. Lines 35–36, 49–50, 52, and 91–94a address performance in speech and/or song; lines 44–48 and 75–76 address skills in planning and constructing buildings. Significantly, acts of writing are treated separately from acts of oral performance in lines 94b–96.

5. See Howe, *Old English Catalogue Poetry,* on repetition. Howe suggests that the poet repeated those elements "that he valued especially," noting that "if repetition is an aesthetic weakness, it is rarely, as most teachers know, a didactic one" (111).

6. While later in the poem we do see a builder, *bilda,* constructing a home without specific reference to the planning process (lines 75–76), we never see a designer working in isolation.

7. Cf. the description of musicians in *Fortunes of Men* (80–84) and *Christ* (668–70), both of which catalogue gifts in a form similar to that in *Gifts of Men.* Neither of these works, however, juxtaposes the performer with the builder and neither conflates physical skill and mental knowledge. Both emphasize instead the relationship with the audience: e.g., in *Christ,* "Sum mæg fingrum wel hlude fore hæleþum hearpan stirgan, gleobeam gretan [A certain one is able with fingers to play the harp loudly for men, to greet the joy-wood]," the verb *mæg* emphasizing physical ability rather than mental knowledge. The variation possible across the repetitions of this image within a genre most often noted for its lack of any originality attests to the subtle meanings that can be conveyed through even minor variation on a conventional theme. The same phrases that distinguish the harpist in *Gifts* from the harpists in *Christ* and *Fortunes* are those that make it most parallel with the builder.

8. As Mary Carruthers has amply demonstrated, architectural metaphors to describe the composition process were pervasive in texts and images throughout medieval Europe, with verbal composition and building especially closely connected in the minds of readers and orators alike. For monastic monks, memory was not merely a rote exercise, Carruthers explains, but a craft, like carpentry or masonry. Spontaneous and creative oral composition was a primary goal of the reader (*Craft of Thought* 9), and this reader was seen as an architect building his interpretation on the foundation laid by the printed text (20). Such connections explicitly evidenced in the use of this trope throughout Europe are demonstrated paratactically in the Old English *Gifts of Men.*

9. The images at the end of this volume are of course intended as specific illustrations of points throughout the book but also serve as a general visual over - view of Anglo-Saxon architecture, as well as Roman and even Iron Age structures with which Anglo-Saxons may have been familiar and which likely informed their interpretations of poetic architectural description. For representative Romano-British architecture, see figures 1, 6, 7, 13, and 26. For surviving Anglo-Saxon structures, see figures 2, 3, 4, 5, 10, 11, 14, 15, 17, 20, 21, 22, 23, and 24. For modern reconstructions of Anglo-Saxon dwellings, see figures 16, 18, and 19. For an example of an Iron Age dwelling, see figure 12.

10. Cf., e.g., Jennifer Neville's sensitive exploration of the concept of nature in the Anglo-Saxon world (1–19). Neville convincingly demonstrates that even the process of classification itself would have been relatively foreign in Anglo-Saxon England. Neville's point about "nature" could be made for "architecture" as well: "The problem cannot be solved merely by seeking a different label or more inclusive definition . . . for the Anglo-Saxons did not have a word to designate 'the Other,' either" (3).

11. *Oxford English Dictionary*. The meaning "master-builder" is attested as early as 1563; the more general sense—"loosely, a builder"—does not appear until 1665. The ultimate source of *architect*—Greek "chief" and "builder"—likewise emphasizes the individual.

12. On "the terminological quagmire surrounding the term *burh*," see Fernie, *Architecture of the Anglo-Saxons* 28–31.

13. *DOE*, s.v. *burh*. Where enough information is available to make such a determination, the *Dictionary of Old English* organizes senses based on history and frequency of use. Its ordering of meanings within the entry for *burh* thus indicates that the sense of individual fortification was earlier and/or more frequent than the broader sense of "city." On the ordering of senses, see preface to *Dictionary of Old English*: "Historically early or etymological senses (where they can be established) may be given first; frequent senses are often given early in an entry where no other logical pattern obtains" (6). Bosworth and Toller make the primacy of *burh* as an individual structure more explicit (s.v. *burh*): "the original signification was *arx, castellum, mons, a castle* for defence. It might consist of a castle alone; but as people lived together for defence and support, hence *a fortified place, fortress, castle, palace, walled town, dwelling surrounded by a wall* or *rampart of earth.*" On ways "the figure of the hall merges in Old English poetry with that of the city," see Magennis, *Images* 40–42.

14. The mere quantity of entries and subentries in the *Dictionary of Old English* devoted to *burh* and its compounds gives some sense of the lexeme's semantic range. *Burh* alone receives almost ten pages of text (2429–38), and compounds beginning with *burh* receive over thirty (2439–71).

15. *DOE* s.v. *burh-bot, burh-weg*. See also *burh-loca*, which denotes either an enclosure of a specific structure (most often a prison) or an entire city enclosure (*DOE* s.v. *burh-loca*) and *burh-wylla*, which can refer to a city well or to a "well within an individual stronghold" (*DOE* s.v. *burh-wylla*).

16. Even the modern English equivalents provided for *burh* have to be somewhat ambiguous, the more open-ended "fortification" or "stronghold" being employed in the *DOE* rather than "structure," "building," or "architecture."

17. See further chapter 4 below.

18. Bosworth and Toller, s.v. *burh, burh-hleoþ*.

19. The mind and heart are often described in spatial terms, as *ferðlocan,* "soul's enclosure" (Bosworth and Toller), and *hordcofan,* "place where thoughts are stored" (Bosworth and Toller). On metaphorical uses of architectural imagery, see chapter 4.

20. The chapters that follow offer much more in-depth analysis of these and many other terms and phrases, but even a few brief examples can illustrate the protean and sometimes vague nature of Old English architectural descriptive language. The adjective *geap*, for instance, is among the few details we are given in reference to Heorot's specific physical characteristics and is used also to describe the subject of *The Ruin*, but lexically the term provides us only the most general sense of "open, spread out, extended, roomy, spacious, wide." Bosworth and Toller, s.v. *geáp*. Klinck adds to its specificity, glossing it as "curved; arched" (*Old English Elegies* 405). Likewise, *horn*, another term that frequently appears in descriptions of buildings, has been defined variously in its architectural sense as a "horn-shaped structure on the gable end of a building," the gable itself, or an arched structure more generally. Bosworth and Toller, s.v. *horn*; *Klaeber's* Beowulf (Fulk, Bjork, and Niles 398), gives *hornas* in the plural as "gables"; Klinck, *Old English Elegies* (420), gives *horngestreon* as "abundance of arched structures."

21. Bosworth and Toller, s.v., *horn, sele, ræced*.

22. On the interdisciplinarity of vernacular architecture as a field, see Wells, "Introduction" 5; Adams and McMurry xvii; and Groth, "Making New Connections in Vernacular Architecture." On its influence in preservation and policy planning in the United States, see Carter and Herman, "Introduction" 2.

23. Vicky Richardson defines *vernacular* in this sense as "the unconscious work of craftsmen based on knowledge accumulated over generations" (6). As such, "vernacular architecture" is "surely a contradiction in terms" (6), since "architecture" most typically implies a "premeditated design process with a conscious appeal to the intellect" (6). Like most in the field, Richardson seeks to break down these and other binaries resulting from a vocabulary insufficient to accommodate the range of building practices across time periods and cultural traditions. This amorphous and expanding concept of architecture might appear to render all related attempts at analysis meaningless. Can anything potentially be defined as "vernacular architecture"? Where do we draw the line? Fortunately, these are not the questions being asked here. My inquiry instead focuses on questions of reception: How is built space conceived of by those who create and use it? Precisely how do various building types and architectural features convey cultural meaning? For these and related questions, rigid definitions would be very limiting. Thomas Carter and Bernard L. Herman express succinctly what seems to be simultaneously the field's greatest potential weakness and its greatest asset: "In the end it may be that all definitions of vernacular architecture fail when compared to the material and contextual complexity of the objects we study. This may not be such a bad thing" ("Toward a New" 5).

24. This influential series began in 1982 as the proceedings of Vernacular Architecture Forum. Though it has since expanded its purpose and scope, this aspect of the field remains unchanged more than twenty years later, vernacular architecture continuing to be "defined less by what is being examined than by the method through which the built world is investigated" (Hoagland and Breisch xiii). As an approach, it is interested in "the subtle, often cloaked, meanings that buildings and

places convey through form" (xiii). It involves analyzing "the built environment as a cultural product," confronting "how built landscapes are shaped by the social political, economic, and cultural structures of the people who produced them" (Adams and McMurry xxix). Vernacular architecture involves "questions of cultural and cognitive process" (Carter and Herman, "Introduction" 3), questions that closely, and not coincidentally, parallel those we frequently ask in our analysis of literary traditions.

25. Camille Wells notes that the study of vernacular architecture "has expanded dramatically beyond the lists and antiquarian and nostalgic interest in quaint, usually rural buildings" ("Introduction" 3). Ten years later Hoagland and Breisch continue to maintain that "although the field of vernacular studies has expanded beyond its core fascination with 'common' buildings and places and how they were put together, its attention remains fixed on the social function of building" (xiii). This insistence on an all-inclusive approach continues to be echoed: "Of course monumental buildings have never been totally neglected by the Vernacular Architecture Forum, but in recent years the organization and the discipline have been moving beyond a simple definition of the vernacular as common or typical building to embrace both the ordinary and the extraordinary and to consider them in relationship to one another, which is, after all, how they existed in past time" (Adams and McMurry xviii). It is true that Henry Glassie and others use the term in reference to buildings seen as "neglected," those that "embody values alien to those in the academy" (20); however, even Glassie sees the term as highlighting "the cultural and contingent nature of all building" and one that "will be obsolete" once architectural studies more widely embrace "the whole of the built world" (21).

26. The pattern for the surviving Anglo-Saxon architectural record is consistent with what Wells has observed for the study of vernacular architecture more widely. "In many cases," she explains, "surviving buildings offer little or no better picture of life among common folk than do other sources" ("Old Claims" 8).

27. Martin Perdue, for instance, unapologetically treats temporary habitations constructed by Civil War soldiers from caves, sticks, logs, mud, stone, and leafy branches as "architecture." "Whether it was a patch of ground with a small tent and a fire or a picketed regimented camp, shaping the nearby landscape gave the men a chance to govern one aspect of their lives during a time of tremendous upheaval and imminent peril. They made the unknown familiar by contriving small shelters with homelike qualities of scale and a degree of comfort" ("Hiding Behind Trees and Building Shelter without Walls" 101). See also Leech, "Impermanent Architecture in the English Colonies of the Eastern Caribbean."

28. See also Zumthor's discussion of medieval poetry and poetics. For Zumthor, "poetics" "deals with the overall signifying structure constituted by a realized discourse" (xxi). Thus the signifying structure of a given "poetics" can operate even in works that might not be categorized as "poetry." This distinction between poetry and poetics is crucial to my arguments here, which explore overlapping poetics in verbal and nonverbal media.

29. As Brian Stock has powerfully argued, "a new hermeneutics of society and culture" emerged across Western medieval Europe, one whose "salient feature is that it is simultaneously oral *and* written" and one in which performative acts "were increasingly contextualized by writing in a manner that implied shared values, assumptions, and modes of explanation" (*Listening* 20; original emphasis).

30. Until quite recently discussions of orality and literacy "tended to be rather polarized, with oralists and nonoralists alike accepting that orality and literacy were opposing, perhaps even competing cultural forces whose interaction could best be understood in decidedly Darwinian terms" (Amodio, *Writing the Oral Tradition* 1). In response to subsequent division (and perceptions of division) within the field, Mark Amodio offers a much more nuanced model—and one that is fundamental for the present study—for understanding the many relationships of oral tradition to literate culture in medieval England. Amodio's model openly acknowledges the many facets of textuality in early medieval English poetry—"the nonperformative nature of the oral poetics discoverable in them, the *author*ity of the poets who composed (and in some cases inscribed) them, and the literate character of the culture within which vernacular poetry was composed and received throughout the period" (xvii). Looking at European medieval culture more broadly, Brian Stock has also worked very hard to complicate the often oversimplified and dichotomized concepts "orality" and "literacy." "If we take as our point of departure the admittedly arbitrary date of A.D. 1000," Stock writes, "we see both oral and written traditions operating simultaneously in European culture, sometimes working together, but more often in separate zones, such as oral custom and written law" (*Listening for the Text* 19). Recent work in parallel fields has also effectively argued against reductive dichotomizing views. In his second edition of *The Oral and the Written Gospel,* for instance, Werner Kelber aggressively challenges the polarizing frame and asks readers to "avoid any implications of what has come to be referred to as the Great Divide" (xxi): "I do not myself use the term *the Great Divide,* nor was it part of our vocabulary in the late seventies and early eighties. . . . Indeed, the attentive reader will observe that my understanding of tradition and gospel is more nuanced than the label of the Great Divide gives it credit for" (xxi). Like most responsible studies of oral-derived texts, Kelber's work does not argue that the Gospel of Mark is a direct product of oral composition or in any way purely oral. His premises are far more logical, that "in ancient and medieval media history, manuscripts functioned in an oral contextuality" and that "by way of compositional dictation, recitation, and auditory reception, they were closely allied with the oral-aural medium" (xxii). In similar fashion, Susan Niditch argues against a "diachronic approach to orality and literacy" (*Oral World* 3), noting that "there is an interplay between the oral and the written in traditional cultures, modern or ancient, and a continuum or sliding scale of oral styles" (4). Rather than literacy superseding orality, she says, "literacy in ancient Israel must be understood in terms of its continuity and interaction with the oral world" (1). Close analysis of these and other studies on orality and literacy would generally suggest that the "divide" has been much more in the

perception of the field from the outside than an accepted distinction taken at face value by those working most closely with oral and literate modes of communication. If in its earliest formulations the distinctions were presented in simplified terms, these binaries have long since been complicated and nuanced in many productive and insightful ways.

31. This concept of performance arena is related to Richard Bauman's notion of a "performance frame," in which "each speech community will make use of a structure's set of distinctive communicative means from among its resources in culturally conventionalized and culture-specific ways to key the performance frame, such that all communication that takes place within that frame is to be understood as performance within that community" (*Verbal Art as Performance* 16). Foley "favor[s] this spatial metaphor, together with its geographical and ritualistic overtones, because it implies a recurrent forum dedicated to a specific kind of activity, a defined and defining site in which enactment can occur again and again without devolution into a repetitive, solely chronological series" (*Singer of Tales in Performance* 47). Since the present study examines space in a very literal sense, this spatial model for understanding oral tradition is especially relevant.

32. Approaching this relationship between oral and written composition as parallel speech acts, Leslie Arnovick observes that "natural narrative and literary narrative share structural forms because, on some basic level, they are utterances of the same type" (10). Extending this notion beyond verbal discourse, I argue here that architecture and poetic depictions of architecture are also, in many cases, "utterances" of the same type, drawing from a shared set of associative values and ideals.

33. Walter Ong has persuasively demonstrated that "a writer's audience is always a fiction," that writers distanced in time and/or space from their readers nonetheless construct an imagined audience. Carol Braun Pasternack argues that "instead of implying an author, Old English verse implies tradition. Formulaic echoes and patterns that are frequently used to express an idea function as a code that readers can interpret as 'tradition.' In doing so, they recognize the present text's place in a network of expressions and thought" (*Textuality* 19). It is in this sense that the following chapters employ the notions of "audience" and "tradition." As Thomas Bredehoft has demonstrated, the "author function" is not absent from Old English texts. Rather, "the mode of their implication is historically situated in ways that may not be familiar to us" (10). On the "act of reading" "as opposed to the potentially separate act of vocalizing a text," see Bredehoft (10). My own analysis does not seek to isolate "tradition" from "author" but follows Amodio in exploring "how what was once a living oral tradition . . . comes to find expression through the pens of authors engaged in very different, private moments of composition" (*Writing* xv).

34. Medieval culture across Western Europe "was an eclectic heritage: it arose from Greek and Roman education, from Jewish scripturalism as transformed by early Christians, and from Germanic languages and institutions, which originally lacked writing" (Stock, *Listening* 19). In this regard, Anglo-Saxon syncretism is characteristic of Western medieval culture more widely.

35. The Old English "Nine Herbs Charm," for instance, includes references to Christ as well as Woden. (See, further, Garner, "Anglo-Saxon Charms in Performance.") The elegiac *Seafarer* likewise recasts traditional Germanic exile imagery in distinctly Christian terms. (See Foley, "Genre(s) in the Making.")

36. Paralleling cultural syncresis is linguistic syncretism, a feature that is especially apparent in oral-traditional language and texts. As Foley observes, "It is characteristic of these specialized idioms . . . that they consist of a somewhat unusual version of the contemporary language, perhaps maintaining archaisms and different dialect forms alongside more current, streamlined speech, as in the case of the Homeric register" (*Homer's Traditional Art* 23). On the multiple traditional registers employed in Homeric and South Slavic epic, see further Foley, *Homer's Traditional Art* 74–88.

37. For further discussion of this church, see Pocock and Wheeler; Fernie, *Architecture of the Anglo-Saxons* 55.

38. Cf. Tolkien's famous metaphor comparing scholarship to the architectural process of building upon "old stones" ("Monsters" 11), discussed in the preface.

39. In similar fashion, Simon Bronner argues that just as verbally adept speakers use time-tested proverbs, "builders can use forms and techniques that they recognize from tradition as socially accepted and time tested, and residents alter and apply their experiences in the house" (7). Like an oft-repeated proverb, "the house can be a constant, longstanding reminder of tradition, and often its standing in a culture" (Bronner 7).

40. It is worth noting that from both directions such metaphors and similes are generally employed to counter oversimplifications—that of viewing poetry as purely artistic and lacking any practical function, or "folk" architecture as purely utilitarian and lacking any recognizable aesthetic. In truth, aesthetic principles can very seldom if ever be wholly separated from issues of functionality and form.

41. E.g., Cramp, "The Hall"; Hills, "*Beowulf* and Archaeology"; Kleinschmidt.

42. E.g., Keenan; Wentersdorf; Dunleavy. See also Orchard, "Reconstructing *The Ruin*" 45–46, for a brief overview of theories.

43. *Wen* is generally translated as "tumor" or "cyst," from Germanic **wanja*, "swelling."

CHAPTER 2. From Structure to Meaning in Old English Verse

1. The following definitions are provided in Bosworth and Toller: *scippan*, "to shape, form" (sense I), "to create" (sense II); *scop*, "a poet"; *scippend*, "the creator." The notion of God as architect has been more fully explored by Wehlau; see esp. 15–28.

2. Unless otherwise noted, all citations to *Beowulf* are from Fulk, Bjork, and Niles, eds., *Klaeber's* Beowulf, 4th ed.

3. The concept "gaps of indeterminacy" ultimately draws from Iser's reception-oriented model of interpretation (see, e.g., "Indeterminacy" 11 ff. and

42 ff.; and *Implied Reader* 48, 283). On applications of Iser's "affective criticism" as related specifically to oral poetics in *Beowulf,* see Amodio, "Affective Criticism."

4. On log houses in Europe, see Weslager 68–98. On Swedish and Finnish log houses in the Delaware region, see Weslager 148–205; and Shurtleff 164–73. On the Pennsylvania Germans and Scotch Irish, see Weslager 206–60; and Shurtleff 175–80. On the origins and development of the log cabin more generally, see Van Dine 132–43.

5. For a more thorough discussion of the many tourist sites associated with Lincoln and featuring log cabins, see Weslager 288–99.

6. For thorough documentation of Harrison's log cabin campaign, see Weslager 261–75; Shurtleff 188–90; and Van Dine 138–39.

7. Van Dine observes, "As for the log cabin as an architectural genre, it is roughly as American as apple pie, which was invented by the Romans" (133).

8. While horizontal log dwellings did exist in Europe and elsewhere, the phrase "log cabin," with all its associative power, is first attested not in England but in the United States (*OED* s.v. "log cabin"), the first attributed usage in 1770.

9. See chap. 1 above.

10. On how traditions are created in memory—and sometimes lead to falsehoods—through repetition, see Drout, who argues that repetition "not only leads to stability, but generates the impression—whether true or untrue—that a repeated practice has *always* been repeated. This idea in turn creates continuity, because if we believe that individuals in the past were performing the same actions we are today, we are more likely to see ourselves as being fundamentally like them. Thus not only repetition but also identity is projected back into the past" (168). It is such a projection "back into the past" that we see here with log cabin imagery and language.

11. See, e.g., the discussion of Bede and Alfred below.

12. This strategy is especially important since the majestic descriptions of Heorot stand in stark contrast to assumptions often made regarding Anglo-Saxon timber construction, the medium used almost exclusively for Anglo-Saxon secular buildings and also employed in the legendary Heorot, described as a "sæl timbred" ["timbered hall"] (307). This value placed on wood construction may seem counter to modern views of medieval construction methods. Even some of the most significant and authoritative sources on early British architecture sometimes seem to view this period as lesser in comparison with the earlier Roman and later Norman periods. One important study of Anglo-Saxon buildings even restricts the term *architecture* to "the *art* of building in *stone*" as opposed to the more native "construction" of *timber* halls. Another has argued that the art of architecture was "lost" following the departure of the Romans, who constructed largely from stone. Kerr and Kerr, *Anglo-Saxon Architecture* 5 (emphasis mine); Yarwood 2. Such dismissive comments, though, perhaps betray an incomplete understanding of how wood was perceived in the Anglo-Saxon world. Even those Anglo-Saxon structures

that rely heavily on Roman techniques and materials are sometimes disparaged. One study, for example, praises the seventh-century Anglo-Saxon builders who began to "revive stone and brick architecture in Britain" but at the same time accuses them of "robbing" and "ransack[ing]" former Roman sites in the process (de la Bédoyère, *Architecture in Roman Britain* 66).

13. Archer calls this building "the most remarkable survival of all" (22). For a detailed analysis of construction methods in this wall, see further Christie, Olsen, and Taylor.

14. Labeled A2 in Addyman.

15. For a recent overview of hall construction, see Pollington, chap. 2, esp. 65–77.

16. This discussion applies to Anglo-Saxon vernacular architecture a phenomenon frequently noted in traditional verbal arts, that of "variation within limits." This principle allows "for compositional flexibility at the same time that it delivers a resonant context that frames each of its occurrences" (Foley, *Homer's Traditional Art* 170). Oral tradition, Foley explains, "thrives on its ability to vary within limits. Every instance of a 'classic' situation or incident is somehow different from all others; every context is unprecedented as well as generic; each poet and poem and performance is in some fashion unique. If we fail to take realistic account of these aspects of uniqueness, we falsify the hybrid nature of oral poetry as both traditional and particular" (*How to Read an Oral Poem* 140). Like these oral traditions that vary within certain communally accepted parameters, each building exhibits innovations of particular builders while still retaining those elements necessary for the larger community to recognize and appreciate the structure as a "hall."

17. The question of influence in Anglo-Saxon architecture is a complex one. Radford has argued for parallels with Saxon villages in Germany, such as Warendorf, comparing the archaeological evidence of sunken huts in England with the German *grübenhaus* and the Anglo-Saxon halls with the German long-house. Fernie *(Architecture of the Anglo-Saxons)* also posits significant connections between continental and Anglo-Saxon building types, focusing especially on excavations at Elisenhof. My interest here lies not in establishing a definitive chronology of influence or locating a real-world Heorot but rather in understanding how the Anglo-Saxons themselves perceived various building materials and types and how we, in turn, can most productively interpret descriptions of such features in the surviving poetry.

18. See Niles et al. 190 (47m by 7.5m).

19. Modern examples might include a wood-grain look in tile floors, vinyl automobile dashboards made to imitate leather, or marble designs in Formica countertops. We continue to carry positive associations with such valued materials even after changes in technology or economy render their use impractical or inaccessible.

20. A building technique consisting of long stones on end between flat ones. This method provides especially good bonding for corners and is common in Anglo-Saxon architecture.

21. Fernie claims that this view is highly unlikely both because of its late date and because the one surviving wooden structure at Greensted provides no useful parallels. He argues instead that the likelier source of the Anglo-Saxon strips lies in Roman construction; here "long and short work" was used to increase the strength of rubble walls, rubble masonry involving rough, unhewn building stones. In either case, the strips on this and other buildings appear to serve little practical function, and, as Fernie notes, "what began as a practical aid was swiftly prized by the Anglo-Saxons for its ornamental possibilities" (*Architecture of the Anglo-Saxons* 145).

22. A faceplate is a disk attached to the supporting spindle of a lathe. This disc holds in place the work to be turned.

23. For details on the Sompting tower, see Taylor and Taylor 558–62.

24. One such collapse occurred in Barton-upon-Humber in 1979 (Rodwell 172).

25. Lap joints are formed by placing one piece of wood partially over another as a form of bracing or, in some cases, temporary framing.

26. On Bradwell-on-Sea, see Taylor and Taylor 91–93.

27. On the Earls Barton Saxon tower, see Taylor and Taylor 222–26.

28. On the church at Jarrow, see Taylor and Taylor 338–49.

29. In a general sense, "gable" refers to the "generally triangular section of wall at the end of a pitched roof, occupying the space between the two slopes of the roof" or, in some cases, the "whole end wall of a building or wing having a pitched roof" (*American Heritage Dictionary,* s.v. "gable"). In architectural contexts Old English *horn* (which elsewhere can refer to drinking horns or musical horns) can have either of these senses and can also refer more generally to any projections from the roof. It typically occurs in the plural or in adjectival usages. The word *gable* does not appear until Middle English, having developed from Norman French *gable* and Old Norse *gafl.* "Gable" in English can also refer to triangular (and often ornamental) sections above arched doors or windows, though this more specialized meaning does not seem applicable to Old English "horn."

30. See Kerr and Kerr, *Anglo-Saxon Sites* 56–57.

31. See drawing in Kerr and Kerr, *Anglo-Saxon Architecture* 33.

32. This discussion of Lindisfarne appears in III.25:
"Interea, Aidano episcopo de hac uita sublato, Finan pro illo gradum episcopatus a Scottis ordinatus ac missus acceperat. Qui in insula Lindisfarnensi fecit ecclesiam episcopali sedi congruam, quam tamen more Scottorum non de lapide sed de robore secto totam conposuit atque harundine texit. quam tempore sequente reuerentissimus archiepiscopus Theodorus in honore beati apostoli Petri dedicauit." [Meanwhile, after Bishop Aidan's death, Finan succeeded him as bishop, having been consecrated and sent over by the Irish. He constructed a church on the island of Lindisfarne suitable for an episcopal see, building it after the Irish method, not of stone but of hewn oak, thatching it with reeds; later on the most reverent Archbishop Theodore consecrated it in honor of the blessed apostle Peter.] The undesirable wood is later covered with sheets of lead: "Sed et episcopus loci ipsius Eadberct

ablata harundine plumbi lamminis eam totam, hoc est et tectum et ipsos quoque parietes eius, cooperire curauit." [But it was Eadberht, who was bishop of this place (Lindisfarne), who removed the reed thatch and had the whole of it, both roof and walls, covered with sheets of lead.] On Bede and the "mixture of admiration and antagonism" that "characterized the English attitude towards Irish learning," see Wright 42.

Regarding the church at York, Bede explains that Edwin "baptizatus est autem Eburaci die sancto paschae pridie iduum Aprilium, in ecclesia sancti Petri apostoli, quam ibidem ipse de ligno, cum cathecizaretur atque ad percipiendum baptisma inbueretur, citato opere construxit" [He was baptized at York on Easter Day, 12 April, in the church of St. Peter the Apostle, which he had hastily built of wood while he was a catechumen and under instruction before he received baptism] (II.14). Soon after, he "curauit docente eodem Paulino maiorem ipso in loco et augustiorem de lapide fabricare basilicam" [he set about building a greater and more magnificent church of stone, under the instructions of Paulinus] (HE II.14, Colgrave and Mynors 186–87).

33. On the Utrecht Psalter, see further chap. 3. Pointing toward the complexities of architecture and depictions of architecture, Carver explains that "it remains possible that later Saxon architecture drew its ornamented ideas from manuscripts, rather than vice versa" ("Contemporary" 144).

34. Quotations from Alfred's preface from Carnicelli's edition.

35. Cf. Harbus 725; Bately 21. See also Wehlau 23–24 for a discussion of the ways Alfred makes the metaphor more "concrete" than its analogue.

36. More positive treatment of wood is also reflected in the translation of Gregory's *Patrologia Latina* attributed to Alfred. In this forest metaphor, wicked people are represented by timbers that must be cut down and "dried" prior to productive construction. In Gregory's Latin original, the forest timbers in their native state are characterized by a "greenness" that is "harmful" and "excessive": "nimitum prius vetiosa ejus viriditas" (Migne, ed., *Patrologia Latina* 77.118). In his adaptation of the metaphor, however, Alfred eliminates much of the negativity associated with the forest wood, which must dry simply because of its "grennesse" ["greenness"], not because it is inherently "harmful" or "excessive." On classical analogues of Alfredian forest metaphors and instances of the trope in later medieval texts, see further Bhattacharya 162.

37. Anderson, for instance, applies an evolutionary model for understanding the lack of description, arguing that more precise terms were a later development ("Uncarpentered" 67). Pickles also finds little value in the scribal renderings that sometimes bear only vague physical resemblance to the buildings they purport to describe. Such "copying at a distance," Pickles argues, "occurs far more frequently in verse" (9), and it was not until the twelfth century that writers began to "venture into truly detailed descriptions" (11). The perception of distance, however, assumes we are expecting a detailed, verbal "copy" of a fixed "text," and what poses a

problem for Pickles's archaeological analysis can actually enhance our interpretation of surviving poetry. The power and pervasiveness of traditional associations are not advantages a poet or scribe will quickly give up in favor of a more "accurate" description stripped of such meanings.

38. As John Hines has demonstrated, for "the richest possible reading of *Beowulf*," "archaeology is neither an illustrative curiosity nor a pedantic factual burden. The archaeology is truly a vital part of the poetic composition" (105).

39. Cf. Earl's argument that "the stubborn preservation of this ancient form of building is related to the hall's symbolism. . . . In its traditional form and usages the hall defined and structured a traditional way of life. It preserved a constellation of values and distinctions essential to the culture and therefore was not to be exchanged lightly for some more 'advanced' form" (*Thinking* 114–15). As Earl notes, "The symbolism of traditional dwellings is an anthropological commonplace. . . . To understand the meanings and functions of the hall, then, is to understand one of the most basic, pervasive, and persistent structures in the world of the Anglo-Saxons. Perhaps the survival of the traditional hall in architecture, social life, and literature was vital to England's rapid and successful development after the conversion" (115). See also Pollington, chap. 3 (99–118), who offers additional discussion of the hall as "ritual space" and "ideal dwelling," giving special attention to Heorot (101–4).

40. On the predominance of arches and absence of angles, see Anderson, "Uncarpentered," who argues that Anglo-Saxon verse existed at an early stage in "the evolution of geometric terms" (67). In Anderson's view, Old English was "limited in technical architectural terminology" and thus had "terms for circularity only" (80). For further discussion of what Anderson perceives as the "comparatively impoverished vocabulary of geometric shapes compared to modern English and ancient Greek, even though Anglo-Saxon and medieval England was not an architecturally impoverished culture" (267), see chap. 7, "Geometric Shapes," in his *Folk Taxonomies*; the tendency toward "curvilinearity" in particular is treated on pp. 269–71. Wehlau argues convincingly that "'uncarpentered' may be misleading here. . . . The real distinction is not so much in the absence of straight lines, as in the poetry's reluctance to categorize or organize" (130).

41. *The Ruin*, with its "hringmere" ["round pool"] (45) and binding "hringas" ["rings"] (19), further indicates the tendency toward curves in poetic architectural description. See further chap. 5 on *The Ruin*.

42. Pickles observes that even in descriptions of actual buildings we are seldom given enough information to fully visualize a construction. In Latin and Old English prose, as well as in the verse of the period, architectural descriptions are highly selective and not sources of accurate physical details. He cautions against viewing written descriptions prior to this period as we might a modern description: "There was no such thing as a paradigm" (9) for churches or other architectural descriptions, and "politico/religious" agendas often underlie any physical details provided. What Pickles refers to as an "agenda" (9) can perhaps be more accurately understood as an

aspect of the period's newly emerging literacy. In an oral tradition, associative meanings are often more important than literal, descriptive detail.

43. The compound *horngeap* is a unique occurrence, and "horn" in reference to gables is usually in the plural, *hornas*. Klaeber, followed by numerous translations and editions, glosses it as "wide-gabled" (398). Klaeber's original edition included a question mark beside the definition, removed in the fourth edition, reflecting the growing scholarly consensus on the meaning. The sense is consistent with architectural description elsewhere in heroic verse. On the phrase "heah ond horngeap," see further chap. 3. On the burning of Heorot, see further below.

44. On the positive value of gold in the poem, see Greenfield, "Gifstol" 113. For an alternate view, see Wentersdorf, who argues that the presence of gold in the structure "serves to underscore the poet's repeated theme that the obsession with the acquisition of gold . . . was both morally and politically hazardous" ("*Beowulf*-poet's Vision of Heorot" 425–26).

45. On the fluid boundaries between the natural and human worlds, see further Neville 1–3; and chap. 5 below. On potential overlap between built and natural environments, see discussion of vernacular architecture, chap. 1.

46. As with the hall of Heorot, the mere landscape has been thought by some to be analogous with that of Lejre. For a discussion of the relevance of Lejre and a succinct summary of other real-world counterparts that have been posited, see Niles et al. 217–22. My own argument involves associative meanings embedded in description rather than historical origins and does not negate the possibility that stories of Lejre and/or a related locale passed through multiple generations across the migration to England. In fact, historical correspondences embedded in the memories transmitted from one generation to the next could only strengthen the associations of these architectural types. The particular features isolated for inclusion in architectural description are equally telling whether fictional or actual. Returning to the log cabin parallel, evocation of what can be understood as "log cabin ideals" is brought about by specific features of the log cabin. Its modest size, rustic wood construction, and rural location could all contribute to a sense of its log cabinness, but other details that might be equally important from a practical perspective, such as the dimensions of windows, types of door locks, or ceiling height, would not. Verbal depictions of fictional and actual log cabins share a particular combination of features selected for inclusion. Even if Heorot and the mere do have their origins in Lejre or a similar location, the details chosen for inclusion, at the exclusion of others, are no less telling from an interpretive angle.

47. On the mere as hell, see Neville 75 n. 83. On hell as an architectural space in Anglo-Saxon poetry, see chap. 3. See also Wright's chapter, "The *Visio S. Pauli* and the Insular Vision of Hell" (106–74); Grendel's mere is treated specifically on pp. 117–21 and 132–36.

48. For cautious parallels between the mere and the landscape surrounding Lejre as well as a summary of previous speculations regarding real-world counterparts, see Niles et al. 218–22.

49. For further discussion of this wood above the mere in relation to Heorot as "two arboreal extremes—wild and domestic, hewn and unhewn" (96), see Bynum. Bynum tracks the motif of the "two trees" across the Indo-European tradition. Most relevant to the present discussion is Bynum's notion of "complementarity" of two kinds of wood: wood in the wild associated with ogres in the wider Indo-European tradition and wood "cut and fashioned for human use" often in the form of a "redemptive tree" (96–97).

50. *Har* in isolation, which can refer to the lichen that grows on rocks or the shade of such lichen, also has strong associations with age, as Anderson has discussed (*Folk Taxonomies* 129).

51. On this passage in *Andreas*, see chap. 3 below.

52. On shared traditions linking this passage in Blickling XVI and Grendel's mere, see Wright 118–19. Similarities have also been noted by Clemoes (181); Morris (I, vii); and Klaeber (1st ed., 183); Healey (*Old English Vision* 52); and Magennis (134).

53. For extensive treatment of Roman ruins in relation to Anglo-Saxon poetry, see chap. 5. On the phrase "enta geweorc" specifically, see also chap. 3.

54. *The Wanderer* 87; *The Ruin* 2; *Beowulf* 1679, 2717, 2774.

55. On flooring in *Beowulf* and Anglo-Saxon archaeology, see Pollington 86–87.

56. The *DOE* gives "floor" as the primary sense of *flett*, "ground" being an overlapping sense based primarily on these applications to the mere in *Beowulf* (s.v. *flett*). With twenty-eight instances, "disproportionately frequent in poetry, esp. in *Beowulf*," *flett* can also refer to a dwelling or hall more generally. Bessinger notes that *flett* typically refers specifically to the floor of a hall. Compounds in *Beowulf* beginning with *flett* also bear out the associations with the hall, *flett-werod* referring to a "troop gathered in the hall," *flett-rest* meaning a "hall-couch, resting-place in a hall" *(DOE)*.

57. Bessinger cites 16 uses of the "wall" sense in the poetry and 84 instances of the "wave" usage (80). See Anderson, "Uncarpentered," on the "homologizing" of natural and man-made structures.

58. On *gæst* ["gist"] as applied to various characters in *Beowulf*, see Carolyn Anderson.

59. On *sele* compounds, see Marjorie A. Brown, who argues that there is a "demonization of the hall" in such poems as *Judith* and *Juliana* (10) and that Christian concepts of sin seem to have altered depictions of banqueting scenes.

60. For further analysis of architectural imagery in *Andreas*, see chap. 3 below.

61. See chap. 3.

62. *Stear(c)ne* is a more recent emendation (Fulk, Bjork, and Niles), previous editions providing "steapne," also potentially positive with its connotations of height.

63. Fulk, Bjork, and Niles. Previous editions of Klaeber take the text as "eorð -(hu)se," instead of "eorðse(le)."

64. Most *eorð* compounds included in the *DOE* do have secondary, and sometimes primary, senses associated with graves and death. The primary sense given for *eorðhus* is "earth house," "underground chamber," or possibly "cave"; a secondary sense "refer[s] to a tumulus or grave." After "cave" and "fissure in the earth," the third sense of *eorþ-scræf* is "grave." Sense b of *eorþ-ærn* is likewise "grave." As with many other architectural terms, the multivalence of these and related *eorð* compounds allow for multiple simultaneous associations, evoking a "cave" in the immediate narrative context while activating connotations of death at a larger level.

65. Marjorie Brown has also noted similarities in the depictions of Heorot and Beowulf's memorial barrow (8).

66. Fulk, Bjork, and Niles. Previous editions of Klaeber provide *hliðe*. Both renderings convey the location's valued height.

CHAPTER 3. **The Role of Architecture in Verse Translations**

1. De la Bédoyère's study of Romano-British architecture asserts that "the church at Bishop Escomb (Durham) was built of blocks from the nearby fort at Binchester" (*Architecture in Roman Britain* 66), and Kerr and Kerr's guide to Anglo-Saxon sites likewise claims that many of the stones "were doubtless taken from the nearby fort at Binchester" (*Anglo-Saxon Sites* 36). More cautiously worded discussions state that the Roman materials are "*thought* to have been brought from nearby Binchester" or that the church "was built *partly* with stones from the Roman fort of Vinovia at Binchester" (Archer 24; Ousby 715; emphasis mine).

2. On mason marks on reused Roman stone, see Alexander 77.

3. I am grateful to David Mason, archaeology officer of Durham County, for sharing these findings and suggestions. E-mail correspondence, July 20, 2006.

4. David Mason, conversation, June 27, 2006. For more on the site of Escomb Church and the Roman objects found there, see Pocock and Wheeler.

5. This is not to say that architecture on the British landscape would have been the only model for all Anglo-Saxon poets and scribes. In "Rome: Capital of England," Nicholas Howe discusses the "institution for English pilgrims in Rome that was founded in the late eighth century" (147) and argues that the Anglo-Saxons found an intellectual and spiritual *patria* that had Rome as its capital, though "this new relation did not lead the Anglo-Saxons to abandon the Germanic tradition" (148). With this tradition of pilgrimage, a number of Anglo-Saxons likely did have other building traditions from which to draw in both the composition and the reception of architectural description. Buildings in translated and adapted works were nonetheless likely less familiar than those on the British landscape and warrant separate treatment in this analysis.

6. For a compelling discussion of "straightforward text-to-text comparison" as "a dangerous approach to source study," see Foley, *Singer* 183−85.

7. For an alternate view, see Robert Stanton, who argues that Old English poetry is not translation as such but should be regarded instead as "adaptation" (5). Although he omits poetry from his discussion of the "culture of translation," his observation that "all translation is transformation" (4) is quite relevant to verse as well as prose. And, as he acknowledges, "when we see the changes wrought by even the closest translation . . . we begin to see the power inherent in interpretation itself" (5). Stanton's decision to omit poetry may also be due in part to his views of English as a language that "lacked the age" of Latin (7). The characterization of "written Old English" as a "young," "precocious" language (7) might be nuanced with a consideration of the inherited oral poetics that influenced products of early literacy.

8. For brief descriptions of known analogues, see Boenig, trans., *Acts of Andrew* ii–iv. As Foley has noted, *Andreas* occupies a "curious slot" in the canon of Old English poetry (*Singer* 183). While it is generally regarded as a translation, the exact source is much less clear than generically related texts such as *Judith,* which is generally accepted without qualification as an adaptation of the Latin Vulgate Bible. See, e.g., Marie Nelson, who cites the Vulgate as a "probable source" for *Judith* (5). Though there is general agreement that the Greek *Praxeis Andreou kai Mat - theia* is "by far the closest in structure and language of any surviving version of the Andreas legend" (Boenig, *Saint* 23), some favor the idea of a lost Latin intermediary to explain discrepancies between the Greek *Praxeis Andreou kai Mattheia* and the Old English *Andreas*. Foley argues, however, that we need not posit a "lost" source to account for variants because the oral tradition surrounding the text provides ample reason for points of departure as the story was adapted for an Anglo-Saxon audience.

9. Following Liebermann, Harding et al. give the dates as 892–93 (291).

10. Text and translation of laws, Attenborough 62–65.

11. The semantic range for *tun* is quite broad, possibilities including "enclosure," "garden," "field," "yard," "farm," "manor," "homestead," "dwelling," "house," "mansion," "group of houses," "village," "town." Attenborough takes *cyninges tune* to mean the king's own quarters rather than the broader notion of a "town" in the more modern sense.

12. It is worth noting that typically neither Roman nor Greek law used public imprisonment as a form of punishment in itself. The *Oxford Classical Dictionary* states that public prison *(carcer, publica vincula)* did serve for a "short incarceration, whether used as a coercive measure by magistrates against disobedience to their orders or for convicted criminals awaiting execution" (1248).

13. Attenborough 64–65.

14. Attenborough 66–67.

15. Attenborough 66–67.

16. A law against the confinement of innocent persons includes debatable phraseology: "Gif he hine on hengenne alecgge, mid xxx scil. gebete" ["If he places him in the stocks, he shall pay 30 shillings compensation"] (35.2; Attenborough

78–79). Though Attenborough translates *hengenne* very narrowly as "stocks," Hall gives a broader semantic range that includes torture and more general imprisonment (177). Bosworth and Toller define the term in this sense as anything "on which any one is hung." Pugh's discussion of imprisonment assumes the sense as "stocks," citing the passage as evidence that prison "may have been as simple as the stocks" and that " 'the stocks' is probably our earliest 'prison' " (1; 1 n. 4). Whether translated as "stocks" or "confinement" more generally, *hengenne* here does not suggest a need for any architectural space dedicated to confinement or detainment. Images of hanging in conjunction with sin and punishment are also consistent with the "Hanging Sinner Motif" discussed by Wright 113–45.

17. Attenborough 130–31.

18. Attenborough 168–69.

19. Attenborough 168–69.

20. Riddle 50 in Williamson. Also spelled *ræplingas*. Multiple solutions have been proposed for this riddle, such as two pails, oxen led by a slave, and a flail, the solution accepted by Krapp and Dobbie (348). Unambiguous, however, is the *ræpingas'* role as prisoners entering the hall.

21. On architectural imagery in the Old English riddles, see chap. 4 below. Riddle 50 has no known Latin analogue (Allen and Calder 162–74).

22. Lines 57, 90, 130, 991, 1075, 1082, 1250, 1460, 1560, 1578. Line numbers follow Brooks.

23. The *DOE*, noting that the appearance in *Andreas* is its only occurrence, translates it as "prison cell." The primary sense of *cleofa* alone is translated "chamber" or "cell," specifically a "sleeping closet" or "bed chamber." Def. 1a.ii has underground associations, "den," "lair."

24. The *DOE* notes that there is only one occurrence of the word, that in *Andreas*. It provides "dungeon" as a definition, suggesting a relationship with Old High German *tunc*, which has been used to gloss "hypogeum," "subterranean chamber."

25. See chapter 2 on heroic ideals associated with the Anglo-Saxon hall and the specific implications of the term *sele*.

26. *DOE* s.v. *clustorcleofa*. *Clustor* alone means "lock, bolt, bar" or can refer metonymically to the entire "cell" or "prison" (*DOE* s.v. *clustor*).

27. *Clustor* derives from Latin *clustrum*. Based on five occurrences, all occurring in poetry, the primary definition in the *DOE* is that of "lock, bolt, bar" with a secondary sense of "cell, prison." The most explicit connection to prison occurs in the *Meters of Boethius* (1.72): "He hine inne heht on carcernes cluster belucan." For the usage in *Genesis* in particular, Doane gives "bar, gate, lock" *(Saxon Genesis)*, and Gordon translates it as "prison." For discussion of the metaphorical use of *clustor* in *Christ I*, see chap. 4 below. "Clustor"/ "cluster" also appears in *Descent into Hell* (37).

28. This description of doors in *Juliana* seems to have been an innovation of the Anglo-Saxon poet, since in the *Passio S. Iulianae* Belial simply appears,

"apparuit" (6, ed. Strunk) or is viewed as "ueniens" (Lapidge, "Cynewulf" 159), without an indication of the doors themselves in either proposed source text.

29. It is the substitution of the "hammers" where we would expect "giants" that conveys a negative sense here, not the use of hammers in and of itself. Most, if not all, constructions from wood would technically be the "work of hammers," but only these isolated instances are marked explicitly as such.

30. The "praetorium" is not referred to specifically in the *Passio S. Iulianae* edited by Lapidge, "Cynewulf" 162.

31. Because two manuscripts have been posited as possible source texts (see n. 37), I offer comparison of the Old English against both throughout this discussion. I argue for neither of these texts as an ultimate source but focus instead on ways the Old English poet departs from *both* in adapting the narrative in a distinctly Anglo-Saxon poetic idiom and architectural construct.

32. E.g., verses 4, 5, 12.

33. *Enge* has more negative connotations, however, than simply "narrow" and can also mean "vexed," "troubled," "anxious," "oppressive," "severe," "painful," or "cruel."

34. *Nydcleofa* occurs only in verse, appearing also in *Elene* (711).

35. Lapidge has argued for the influence of *Andreas* on the composition of *Juliana* (54).

36. While both terms are generally translated as "prison," the elements of the compound are less clear-cut. *Hlin* has the sense of "latticed" or "grated" and is used to refer to gratings on prisons or prison doors but metonymically can refer to the prison itself. Thus *hlinræced* literally means "grated building" (Brooks 150) or "a place with grated doors" (Bosworth) but can be taken as simply "a prison" (Bosworth). Rendered literally, *hlinscuwa* would translate something like "dark grated structure" but is more accurately understood as "dark prison," with *hlin* meaning prison (Bosworth). The related compound *hlinduru* (treated at more length below) refers to "a door formed of lattice-work, a grated door" (Bosworth) but also denotes prison doors specifically.

37. *Bibliotheca Hagiographica Latina no.* 4522. See Lapidge, "Cynewulf" 166 n. *Juliana,* long held as a translation from the Latin *Acta Sanctorum,* has been more recently discussed by Lapidge in relation to the *Passio S. Iulianae* in Bibliothèque Nationale de France, lat. 10861, hereafter BNF.

38. For a chart showing correspondences between the *Acta Sanctorum* (BHL) and the Old English *Juliana,* see Strunk 50. Lapidge's edition of the *Passio S. Iulianae* (BNF) also marks correspondences in and divergences from the Old English poem. On Strunk's discussion of the poet's elaboration of an architectural metaphor in lines 648–55 specifically, see chap. 4 below.

39. *Genesis* 91 ("under hearmlocan"), 2539 ("under burhlocan"); *Andreas* 95 ("under hearmlocan"), 144 ("under heolstorlocan"), 940 and 1065 ("under burhlocan"), 1005 ("under heolstorlocan"), 1065 ("under burhlocan"); *Elene* 485 ("under

þeosterlocan"), 695 ("under hearmlocan"); *Christ* 769 ("under banlocan"); *Juliana* 43 ("under hordlocan"); Riddle 73, Riddle 71 in Williamson ("under hrægnlocan"); *Beowulf* 1928 ("under burhlocan").

40. Translations such as "jail" (e.g., Boenig, *Acts* 74) lose the force of this referentiality.

41. Citations of *Genesis* are from Doane's edition. Significantly, the phraseology employed to describe prisons is shared to a great extent in describing the architecture of hell. (See further below.)

42. Nelson 57; Gordon 166. Bradley translates the passage "had in store treasures" (303).

43. The phrase is also unprecedented in the *Passio S. Iulianae* (BNF). See Lapidge, "Cynewulf" 157.

44. On the extended architectural metaphors in *Christ I*, see chap. 4 below.

45. See further Doane's note on *Genesis* 2535–2546a (312) on these lines as a "greatly elaborated paraphrase of 19.23–24." On the related *banhus*, see discussion of architectural metaphor, chap. 4 below.

46. J. R. C. Hall; Bosworth. "Grated door" providing a confusing image, *hlinduru* is often translated simply as "door" (e.g., Gordon 255).

47. Significantly, no doors are mentioned in the Latin *Physiologus*, making it more likely that the phrase is an Anglo-Saxon innovation operative in an Old English poetic idiom. On possible sources and influences on the Old English *Physiologus* more generally, see Allen and Calder 1:156–57.

48. Other references to doors in hell appear in *Christ and Satan* (379, 465, 720), *Genesis* (447), and *Descent into Hell* (53).

49. As Fulk, Bjork, and Niles observe, the presence of *irenbendum* shows that "in regard to its construction as well as its adornment Heorot is distinguished from ordinary buildings" (162), which are not described as having iron bands. On the landscape as in the poetry, iron bands are present but not common: "iron hardware (chiefly in the form of clench bolts) have been detected in connection with some timbered buildings of AS England and Scandinavia, though the evidence is not always conclusive" (162).

50. Wright focuses especially on the Iron House motif in "The Devil's Account of the Next World" (189–206).

51. This portion of the poem does not have a parallel in the fragments of the Old Saxon *Genesis*; however, Doane suggests that the bondage theme was in the Saxon original, noting that *Genesis B*'s use of *irenbenda* (where a corrector added an *s* to make it masculine) would be consistent with the Old Saxon feminine *bendi*.

52. In the case of Heorot the door's opening is emphasized through the use of two, arguably redundant verbs: The door is said to *onarn* ["open"] (721) when Grendel first touches it, and we are told two lines later that Grendel *onbræd* ["pulled open"] (723) the door. For a reading of the text that eliminates potential redundancy, see Bommesberger 119–20.

53. See further chap. 2 above.

54. Cf. the "ellenrofum / fletsittendum" in *Beowulf* (1787–88).

55. Representing the most common renderings of "tent" and "pavilion," Treharne translates both *træfe* (43) and *geteld* (57) as "tent"; and Bradley translates both as "pavilion."

56. Bosworth gives also "tilt" or "covering of a tent" as a definition and provides an etymology of *bur* ["a bower"] and *geteld*. For *geteld* alone, Bosworth gives a broader semantic range: "tent, tabernacle, pavilion, tilt, cover." The term is related to the verb *teldian*.

57. See, e.g., the patterns provided at www.42nd-dimension.com/NFPS/nfps_geteld.html, the supply list and detailed instructions given at www.regia.ca/getelds/article.html, the reconstruction information at www.regia.org/houses.htm, and connections to manuscript evidence at www.mathomhouse.com/regia/notes/tents.

58. Basing his theories on manuscript images, such as the eleventh-century British Library, MS. Cotton Claudius B IV, Harrison argues that "the tents appear to be made up of coloured panels, of canvas or heavy linen which are perhaps painted rather than dyed" (23). He speculates that "on campaign, senior thegns sheltered under structures of this kind" (23).

59. Measurements are those posited by the reenactment society Regia Anglorum for constructing an Anglo-Saxon tent. These reconstructions are based on a combination of surviving archaeological evidence, manuscript illustrations, and experiments with various configurations within known parameters.

60. Noel cautions us not to understand the Harley Psalter exclusively as a "copy of the Utrecht Psalter," noting that such connections often result from "an accident of survival" (7). Like the Roman stones of Escomb Church and Old English translations of Latin texts, the exact "source" of the illustrations is more complicated than the term *copy* alone would suggest. On "the intended reader of the Harley Psalter," see Noel 196–202.

61. Bosworth; Hall. The usage of *træf/traf* to mean "temple" is discussed further below.

62. Treharne translates each occurrence of *træf* in *Judith* as "tent." Gordon translates it as "pavilion" twice (43, 268) and "tent" once (255).

63. Boenig translates *helltrafum* as "hellish temples" (*Acts* 121) in keeping with Brooks, who gives "hellish" with the note "i.e., heathen" (148). Gordon also translates as "temples" (210). For *træf* in isolation, Brooks provides the more general meaning "building."

64. *Hærgtrafum* is reconstructed because the *æ* in "hærg" is unclear. The *trafum* portion of the compound, however, is not in question. (See Fulk, Bjork, and Niles 12 n.).

65. For more on the *hearg* portion of the compound, see Thomas L. Markey's discussion of Germanic *harg* (367–70). Though *hærgtrafum* is often translated as "pagan" or "heathen temples," Markey's etymological study of words for *temple* and *cult* indicate that the Old English *hearg* "originally denoted an (ele-

vated) area in the open where pagan rites were conducted, but there is no clear indication of a temple or enclosure as a referent" (369). Klaeber's edition glosses as "heathen temple," the commentary to the most recent edition (4th) noting that *træf* can denote "either a tent or pavilion or a more substantial building," while place-name evidence indicates that a *hearh* would have been "a relatively important, perhaps public, shrine in a high, commanding place" (128). While evidence of cult houses has been located at Yeavering as well as at Germanic sites in Europe, such as Lejre, the poet of *Beowulf* "need not have had any definite knowledge of Scandinavian religious practices of an earlier age, and he mentions them here only to condemn them" (128).

66. E.g., Treharne; Raffel. Such observations point not toward inadequacies in these and other highly effective translations but rather toward the incredibly powerful yet subtle nuances of meaning invested in the architectural language of Old English verse.

67. *DOEC.* In both cases *fleohnet* is given as equivalent to *conopeum.*

68. The *DOE* gives "floor of a building" as the dominant meaning for *flor/flore* with "surface of the earth, the ground" and "the lowest part, the bottom of anything" (such as the "depths of hell" or "the bottom of a body of water") offered as secondary senses (*DOE* s.v. *flor,* senses 1, 2, 3). Hall gives "ground" as a secondary meaning for *flor;* Bosworth does not. Cf. the *fagne flor* of Heorot (725) or the *flor* that Beowulf crosses after Æscere has been killed (1316).

69. On this slaying as a battle, see further Garner, "The Art of Translation in the Old English *Judith.*"

70. Irving writes, "This camp is not named in the poem, but it is clearly the camp 'contra Phihahiroth, quae respicit Beelsephon' on the shore of the Red Sea. Cf. Exod. 14:1–2" (*Old English* Exodus 77).

71. Irving offers "struck their tents" as an alternate reading (*Old English* Exodus 82).

72. Of this usage, Irving writes that "perhaps the association of the previous camp, Succoth, with tents was in the poet's mind" (*Old English* Exodus 74).

73. Etymology from Bosworth, s.v. *bælc.* Based on its only instance, this in *Exodus,* the *DOE* suggests "covering, perhaps specifically canopy" and also offers the possibility of "beam, plank of wood" as "a metaphor for the pillar of cloud" (s.v. *bælc, bælcu*). Lucas offers an extended discussion of the etymology of *bælc* ("The Cloud" 302 ff.).

74. The *DOE* defines *ealh/alh* as "temple," with a secondary definition "referring to a pagan temple."

75. *Ealdstede* is defined in the *DOE* as a temple, "referring to a heathen temple" in such texts as *Andreas* 1638. It can also have the broader sense of "city," as in *Daniel* 671, 686.

76. *Wih,* however, by the Old English period "denotes 'idol, image,' and appears to have lost its original meaning of 'hallowed ground or sacred grove'" (Markey 374).

77. The claims put forth here are specific to Old English verse. Usages of "temple" in surviving prose are not limited to positive contexts. As in many other cases, poetic usages tend to be more specialized, with narrower ranges of connotation.

78. For "Anglo-Latin" and "Frankish Latin" synonyms for *church*, see Pickles, Appendix II, pp. 155–57.

79. The pattern put forth here is limited to verse. In prose works, *tempel* is employed in reference to Christian and pre-Christian structures and in positive as well as negative contexts.

80. See also 707: "he in temple gestod" ["he stood in the temple"].

81. Old English prose, on the other hand, includes non-Christian temples such as Ælfric's references to a "hæðen temple" ["heathen temple"] and "feondlican temples" ["fiendish temples"] in "Depositio Sancti Martini," Godden, ed. *Ælfric's Catholic Homilies,* 2nd ser. 293). The sense of "temple" in Old English poetry, however, is unequivocally positive.

82. Tolkien links the building of the temple to I Chron. xxi.18, I Chron. xxii.6–19, and 2 Chron. iii. I (66). Irving writes that "the identification of the hill on which Isaac was to be sacrificed with the mountain on which Solomon built the temple is nowhere made directly in the Vulgate" (*Old English* Exodus 90). Following Moore, he claims a probable source in Josephus (Jewish Antiquities I, 26).

83. According to Bede's account a letter from Pope Gregory to Mellitus declared that "the idol temples of that race should by no means be destroyed, but only the idols in them" (*HE* I.30): "uidelicet quia fana idolorum destrui in eadem gente minime debeant, sed ipsa quae in eis sunt idola destruantur" (Colgrave and Mynors, ed. and trans., 106–7). However, assimilation was not always the mandated practice. Pope Gregory's letter to King Ethelbert as quoted in Bede does call for the overthrowing of the structures themselves: "idolorum cultus insequere; fanorum aedificia euerte" ["suppress the worship of idols; overthrow their buildings and shrines"] (Colgrave and Mynors, ed. and trans., 112–13; *HE* I.32). Bede also recounts a story in which Coifi destroys the pagan temples which he himself had consecrated (*HE* II.13). The space, though, is appropriated in its commemoration as "Goodmanham, the place where the high priest, through the inspiration of the true God, profaned and destroyed the altars which he himself had consecrated" ["Godmunddingaham, ubi pontifex ipse inspirante Deo uero polluit ac destruxit eas, quas ipse sacrauerat aras"] (*HE* ii.14.197). On this and related appropriations of "heathen" spaces, see Richard North (12), who shows that not only did the Christian Anglo-Saxons build on heathen sites, but Christian kings claimed genealogies tracing back to pre-Christian gods.

84. On the many superlatives in this passage, including those pertaining to the architecture itself, see Hall, "The Building of the Temple in *Exodus.*" On connections with the parting of the sea and its metaphorical building, see chap. 4 below.

85. For a fairly thorough discussion of Mermedonia as it appears in all known versions of the story, see Brooks xxvii–xxx.

86. Brooks 62.

87. Magennis has argued that the description of Mermedonia "recalls that of the coast of Denmark in *Beowulf*, seen from the perspective of Beowulf and his men as they first approach it," but with a "forbidding aspect" (174).

88. See chap. 2 above on this phrase; and Swisher 133. In *Beowulf* this phrase is used to describe the entrances of both Grendel's mere and the dragon's lair (1415, 2744), and it appears also in the embedded story of Sigemund, as the hero ventures alone (887) under the gray stone to slay his dragon. Its usage in Blickling Homily XVI discussed in chapter 2, indicates that the phrase, with its traditional implications of supernatural danger, was thought to resonate with both the clerical audiences giving the homily and the lay audiences who might hear it.

89. Cf. Gordon's translation of "buildings" (195). Boenig's translation gives "towers" (95).

90. In *Beowulf* the term also appears with highly negative connotations as the Danes, desperate to rid themselves of Grendel, are said to worship at "hærgtra-fum," and in *Judith* the tent of the evil Holofernes is three times referred to as a "træfe." *Beowulf* 175; *Judith* 43, 255 ("wlitegan træfe"), 268 ("þeodnes træf").

91. On the Colchester temple in particular, see R. North 103–4. Leaders in Romano-British as well as Anglo-Saxon times were concerned with royal apotheosis, and genealogies of Christian leaders reflect the same syncretism as the Christian churches built on sites of Romano-British and Germanic pre-Christian sites.

92. See also Foley, *Singer* 198.

93. See Kerr and Kerr, *Anglo-Saxon Architecture* 43–44.

CHAPTER 4. Architectural Metaphor and Metonymy

1. Dobbie emends from "scesne" (128).

2. On the distinction between metaphor and metonymy, Gillian Overing states that "the metaphor always mediates between the reader and a meaning that lies beyond the immediate reference; meaning is *transferred* to another descriptive term and is always connected to a larger central meaning or point of reference. The metaphor is not self-referential. The metonym, in contrast, is a *substitution* of meaning, an expression used *instead* of the name of a thing" ("Some Aspects of Metonymy" 89). Old English poetry relies heavily on both metaphor and metonymy.

3. Much has been written on Old English narratives as metaphor (e.g., Lionarons; Lee). The present emphasis, however, is on those passages in which such metaphors are made explicit in the poems being studied, descriptive passages whose primary purposes lie in analogy. Wehlau's study of metaphor in Old English poetry offers a useful overview of the subject. Architectural metaphor is treated specifically in chapter 1 (15–54), with special attention to metaphors of creation in religious texts and metaphors of the body.

4. Walter Ong has argued that where writing is able to "structure knowledge at a distance from lived experience," primary oral cultures are more likely to "conceptualize and verbalize all their knowledge with more or less close reference to the human lifeworld, assimilating the alien, objective world to the more immediate, familiar interaction of human beings" (42). While Old English verse, of course, is not the product of a "primary oral culture," as poetry produced in a period of early literacy and deriving in part from an oral poetics, this literature nonetheless manifests certain features of oral and oral-derived works.

5. These and related metaphors "give a sense of God building not just any construction but a house; the architectural metaphors are a means of portraying God as a protector" (Wehlau 21). In contrast, Wehlau argues, the same imagery in biblical analogues "serves to emphasize human insignificance" (21).

6. To these Martin adds a third, "rhythmic," approach in which we notice the ways that similes "punctuate the narrative, giving it an almost musical rhythm and providing episodic definition" (144). For the *Iliad* he shows "a key performance factor in the uses of similes—namely, the way in which they demarcate segments" (144).

7. In a discussion of interdisciplinarity, James Clifford uses assumptions about the nature of metaphor as an example of the problematic separation between literary and other academic disciplines. He has noted that "literary texts were deemed to be metaphoric and allegorical, composed of inventions rather than observed facts" (5). Toelken's model allows for more productive connections across anthropological and literary fields of discourse.

8. Leslie Webster, for instance, has noted the "fondness for the visual" that "goes back into pagan Germanic culture" ("Iconographic" 227). Powerful Germanic visual imagery was not replaced with the advent of literacy and classicism but actually "reinforced and extended after the conversion by the introduction of the learned traditions and expositive techniques of classical and Christian visual narrative" (227). Significant parallels can certainly be seen between the metonymic language of Anglo-Saxon wisdom poetry and the "abbreviated representations" of the stories carved on the Franks casket (227), a small Anglo-Saxon whalebone chest with runic inscriptions and various scenes from Germanic and biblical narrative engraved on all four sides and the lid. A brief gnomic statement calls forth a much larger context of proverbial wisdom just as even the barest image can recall an entire narrative for an audience familiar with the larger story. For the Anglo-Saxons, oral and literate, Germanic and classical, visual and verbal were not mutually exclusive categories.

9. Muir notes that "the architectural imagery introduced here reappears sporadically in other texts in the [Exeter] manuscript, and may be considered one of the unifying strands in the anthology (consider especially in this respect *The Wanderer, The Seafarer,* and *The Ruin*)" (2:384).

10. Bradley, for instance, translates "heafod" as "headstone" (205).

11. Burlin follows Cook in this line of thinking. See Cook 74. Gordon is another who renders *healle* as "temple" (133). In contrast, see Wehlau, who takes the term *healle* at face value, describing the metaphor in terms of a "house" and "hall" (25–26).

12. On this passage in Ælfric, see chap. 3, which discusses descriptions of temples in Old English verse.

13. Although her primary analysis involves Christological imagery frameworks, Kramer briefly discusses such secular associations in her analysis of the Book of Kells illustration, noting that "this building, presumably the temple in Jerusalem, has the shape of a medieval insular hall, with heavy beams framing the house" (101).

14. On similarities between *Maxims II* and *The Ruin* (though not *Advent Lyric I*), see also Orchard, "Reconstructing" 58.

15. Psalm 117.22. The phrase "caput anguli" appears elsewhere in the Vulgate at Matthew 21.42, Mark 12.10, Luke 20.17, 1 Peter 2.7.

16. Bosworth, s.v. *hyrne.*

17. With *eorðbold,* I follow Muir, who explains that the new digital image of this folio shows clearly part of a rounded letter following *b*" (2:385). Cf. earlier *eorðb . . .* in Burlin, *Old English Advent* 57; and *ASPR*'s emendation of *eorðburh.*

18. Burlin notes that "the striking figure by which the antiphonal source of this division is identified is surprisingly underplayed. It is, in fact uncertain that the 'key' actually occurs in the Old English text" (*Old English Advent* 71). Campbell sees such omissions as negative, asserting that "some of the finest things in the Latin text . . . apparently did not interest the poet at all" (*Advent Lyrics,* 13). On the confusion surrounding the line, see also Greenfield, "Of Locks and Keys." Muir follows Greenfield's reading of Christ *as* key (2:387).

19. Riddles 42 and 87 in Williamson. A less prominent key also appears in Riddle 42 (40 in Williamson), which employs the key imagery in a bawdy meta - phor, one far removed from the kingly nobility of *Advent Lyric I.*

20. See further Williamson, *Old English Riddles* 389; Whitelock 152; Thorpe, *Ancient Laws,* 1:418.

21. For further discussion of keys and women's economic status, see Fell, who explains that "women's graves contain both keys and key-shaped objects" (59–60).

22. Based on a survey of a Kentish cemetery (Fell 60).

23. On Latin sources of *Juliana,* see chap. 3. See also Lapidge, "Cynewulf"; Strunk.

24. Employing slightly different phrasing, the Juliana of *Passio S. Iulianae* (BNF lat. 10861) likewise urges her listeners: "aedificate domus uestras super petram uiuam, ne uenientibus uentis ualidis disrumpamini" (Lapidge, "Cynewulf" 164–65). For a chart showing correspondences between the Latin and Old English texts, see Strunk 50.

25. Biggam gives *grund* as the more common term for "foundation" (though it can also mean "ground" more generally). See also Stanley, who convincingly argues that the sense of "foundation" is metaphorical, with the underlying literal sense "the place to which we are all rooted" (326).

26. The poet then takes even greater advantage of this metaphor by adding contrasting architectural imagery in the description of Heliseus's afterlife, providing details once again absent from posited source texts. Unlike those who build in their hearts homes of firm foundations and walls, Heliseus and his thegns must dwell "in þam þystran ham" ["in that dark home"] (683), the "winsele" devoid of all joys associated with the Anglo-Saxon hall (686).

27. On paratactic structures in Homeric epic, see Notopoulos, "Continuity" and "Parataxis in Homer."

28. Also, like the stone in *The Ruin* and *Maxims II*, this stone is described as "wrætlic" ["wondrous"], heightening its connection to grand and positively charged buildings. The temple Elene ordered built to house the cross, for instance, is also described as "stan" and "wrætlic" (*Elene* 1019–20).

29. Like the verse *Exodus*, an Old English prose rendering of *Exodus* (*Old English Version of the Heptateuch*) also supplies architectural details in adding a reference to a street at this point: "and læg an drige stræt ðurh ða sæ" (Ker, ed.). In both instances, the wall is made more tangible by providing the metaphor with more specific, visually focused elements.

30. Irving emends to "wæter *on* wealfæsten," translating the passage as "The wave builds the water into a fortress-wall" (*Old English Exodus* 85).

31. Tolkien takes with the sense "from now back into eternity" (*Exodus* 60 n.).

32. Charles Kennedy translates *wolcna* as "heavens," but "clouds" seems more consistent with the established pattern of imagery in which a natural element corresponds to an architectural one. Cf. Tolkien, *Exodus* 26.

33. Bradley, for instance, translates as "piled" (58), and others have provided "steep."

34. Richard Buxton makes a compelling case for distinguishing between simile and metaphor, noting that some see metaphor as "abridged simile," with the implied analogy compressed (139–40), where others see metaphor instead as primary, creating (rather than compressing) resemblances. Setting aside the question of primacy, Buxton argues that the distinction is useful "when we are trying to distinguish between different kinds of poetic language, and different kinds of poets" (140).

35. See discussion of this passage in chap. 5 below.

36. Further heightening the passage's immediacy, the Old English poet embeds this more detailed description of the scene in a speech by Moses, unlike the Latin exemplar. Irving claims that "it is strange that the poet chooses to have Moses describe such a striking event, particularly since he departs from the biblical source by so doing" (*Old English Exodus* 85). It is possible, however, that this portion of the narrative was recast in Moses' speech precisely because it is such a "striking event."

The first-person, rather than omniscient, viewpoint gives a tangible speaker and an immediately present audience, placing the powerful description in a vivid and distinct performance context. The significance of the shift to first-person becomes even more apparent in the line, "þa ic ær ne gefrægn ofer middangeard" ["which I have never heard over middle-earth"] (287). Cf. "Ne gefrægn ic" ["I have not heard"] (*Beowulf* 1027), which heightens the significance of the treasures received at the feast celebrating Beowulf's defeat of Grendel, and "Ne gefrægn ic næfre" ["I have not ever heard"] (*Finnsburh* 37), which verifies through this traditional phraseology the loyalty and dignity of Hnæf's warriors.

37. See, e.g., O'Donnell 159.

38. As Joanne Spencer Kantrowitz argues, the poet speaks within "traditional allegory" and thus provides a general interpretation for the allegory. "Our part," she says, "is to understand the details" of precisely how the allegory works (13). See also C. A. M. Clarke for further analysis of *The Phoenix* as "a self-conscious and assured integration of Latin and Anglo-Saxon features" (43), specifically with regard to the poem's use of space and landscape.

39. Text, Thorpe 210 ff.; trans., Allen and Calder 116.

40. While some translations leave the connection open-ended, "either a nest or a tomb" (Roberts and Donaldson), Allen and Calder insert "rather" in brackets to shift the emphasis to that of "tomb," a connection common in Latin texts.

41. Meanings include dwelling place, country, region, and native land (*DOE*, s.v. *eard*). While there are approximately 600 instances of *eard* in Old English literature *(DOEC)*, the *eardstede* compound appears only in *The Phoenix* and is defined by the *DOE* as "dwelling-place," or "habitation," "referring to the nest of the phoenix" in this instance.

42. For further connections between *The Phoenix* and Riddle 5, see Williamson, *Old English Riddles* 151–52.

43. Like other riddling traditions, Old English riddles are essentially what Toelken calls "ambiguous metaphors" (*Morning Dew* 17).

44. Except where otherwise noted, numbers in this chapter refer to Williamson's numbering system. The disparity across editions results from Williamson's consolidation of Krapp and Dobbie 1–3, 75–76, and 79–80. The result is a total of 91 riddles in Williamson's edition, as opposed to 95 in Krapp and Dobbie. For the benefit of those more familiar with Krapp and Dobbie's earlier numbering system, a chart with correspondences is provided in an appendix to this chapter. Other riddles with "ship" as solution include 30, 34, and possibly 62. (Other proposed solutions for 62 include "falconry" and "writing.") Only 17, however, refers to the ship directly as a built structure.

45. Williamson notes that *be wege* can be read either "by the way" *(wēg)* or "by the water" *(wēg, wæg)*. Pope says that the meter supports the "water" reading, but also gives credence to Pearson's suggestion that "by the way" is preferable, with the understanding that lighthouses marked waterways (Williamson, *Old English Riddles* 340).

46. Hall gives "beautiful" as the definition for the compound *hleortorht* (*Anglo-Saxon Dictionary* 186).

47. Old English kennings, he says, "often utilized one term for *sea* and one for *horse*" (189). Examples include "brimhengest" (*The Ruin* 47; *Andreas* 513), "mere-hengest" (Riddle 12, line 6), "sæmearh" (*Andreas* 267; *Elene* 228, 245; *The Whale* 15), and "lagumearg" (*Guthlac* 1332).

48. Cf. the nailed board "nægledbord" (5) of Riddle 56.

49. Williamson's translation of *eðelstol* as "home-stones" (*Feast* 59, line 33) may be misleading, given the predominance of wood for domestic structures and the relatively few references to stone in such poetic contexts. Poetic and archaeological evidence indicates that *eðelstol* would refer to wooden structures rather than stone.

50. Williamson translates this section as "prison," but it is worth making a distinction between confinement or imprisonment and a dedicated prison. See further chap. 3 on prisons and imprisonment in Anglo-Saxon society.

51. Williamson explains the metaphor of light between the horns thus: "When the moon is only a thin crescent, old or new, we can often make out the rest of the disc faintly illuminated by sunlight reflected from earth to moon" (*Old English Riddles* 227–28).

52. Williamson notes that this riddle is informed by an Anglo-Saxon belief that the moon received its light directly from the sun.

53. Cf. discussion of parting waters as the walls of a building in *Exodus*, chap. 3 above.

54. On *timbran* as a generic term referring to any type of construction, see chap. 2.

55. The Grendel mere provides another example of an underwater "hall" working in tandem with its inhabitants. As the fish and its *sele* are created (*scop*) to work together (*ætsomne*), the mere, as anti-hall, to use Hume's term, is invested with subversive features that parallel the antiheroic nature of its own ghastly residents.

56. Other suggested solutions include "badger," "porcupine," and "hedge-hog" (Williamson, *Old English Riddles* 173–75).

57. Williamson's translation gives "hall," but the nature of the structure does not carry the associations more typical of a hall.

58. See further Clark.

59. For discussion of fogous and souterrains as represented in Germanic litera-ture more broadly and for possible connections with *The Wife's Lament,* see Battles. See also chap. 5 below.

60. Still, other suggestions have been made. Wyatt, for instance, has sug-gested that eggshells are hung on a wall as a charm (Williamson, *Old English Riddles* 169).

61. See further Anderson on the frequency of "homologized" descriptions, simultaneously man-made and natural (*Folk* 276).

62. Notably, "there is no archaeological evidence for the existence of an Anglo-Saxon battering ram" (Williamson, *Old English Riddles* 297). Rather, the ram would

have been familiar primarily through knowledge of Roman war tools. That the referent is a foreign rather than a native implement may help explain why the metaphor is cast in terms of enslavement. Instead of being utilized by an unambiguously positive hero, the noble wood is enslaved by a "grim" and presumably non-Germanic warrior, but nonetheless the wood that constitutes the ram and its captor are portrayed as fighting "atgædre" ("together") in a mutual endeavor.

63. See Williamson, *Old English Riddles* 315.

64. Williamson translates this loosely as "native land" *(Feast of Creatures).*

65. Bosworth suggests "among the hills" as the meaning of *geond weallas.* Williamson says that the "reference may be to domestic gardening" (*Old English Riddles* 243) but argues that "about walls" is far more likely since *weall* usually means "wall" or "cliff." Given the pervasiveness of building imagery throughout the riddles, I would argue that "wall" provides the best meaning.

66. Williamson, *Old English Riddles*; Krapp and Dobbie.

67. Williamson notes that this theme is shared with Aldhelm's Latin Riddle 80, "Calix Vitreus" (*Old English Riddles* 323).

68. For the full text of Aldelm's riddle, with Old English parallels noted, see Williamson, *Old English Riddles* 266.

CHAPTER 5. (Re)Constructions of Memory

1. The model Wesley Trimpi describes for ancient Greece in *Muses of One Mind* offers a way of thinking more analogous to medieval thought than that provided in the more sharply delineated modern modes of discourse. For the ancient Greeks, Trimpi argues, literature was not a discrete art form; rather all art was thought to draw from the same ultimate source. Hesiod, Trimpi explains, describes the nine Muses as being "of one mind" (ix) at their birth. "The 'discourse' of the Muses, then, might be considered the project of a single purpose insofar as they collectively express and realize these potentialities of the human intelligence as a whole rather than as fragmented into the more exclusively didactic or formal intentions of particular artistic doctrines" (x).

2. Eric Fernie, for instance, includes parallels with archaeology in Germany *(Architecture of the Anglo-Saxons),* and Nigel Kerr and Mary Kerr devote much discussion to Scandinavian parallels (e.g., *Anglo-Saxon Architecture* 58).

3. See Cramp, "Changing Image," for further implications of the initial separation of "the study of the Anglo-Saxon language and its texts," which "had begun seriously in the eighteenth century," from "consideration of the physical remains of the post-Roman/pre-Norman period" (3).

4. The corresponding titles assigned in this early catalogue—such as the "History of Beowulf," the "Ode on the Battle of Brunanburh," "The Exile's Complaint" ("Wife's Lament"), and the "Song of the Traveler" *(Widsið)*—all evoke spe - cific genres and establish contexts in which the poems are to be understood, contexts

that have not always been revised as new information on Anglo-Saxon poetry and culture is acquired.

5. For Eaton, the move was one of hostile appropriation, as the church at Ripon was "built from massive blocks of Roman stone robbed from the town of Aldborough."

6. See Klinck 12 ff. for an extended discussion of the condition, dialects, and possible dates of the Exeter Book poems.

7. Most treatments of elegy include *The Wanderer, The Seafarer, Deor, Wulf and Eadwacer, The Wife's Lament, The Husband's Message,* and *The Ruin* in the discussion. Klinck's edition includes also *The Riming Poem,* Riddle 60, and *Resignation.*

8. Significantly, Klinck's definition follows her examination of the poems, consistent with her belief that the generic categories should be determined by the patterns that emerge within the poetry itself rather than be imposed by outside systems of classification. María José Mora goes a step further, making a convincing case that modern readers have created the category of elegy, a "mode" of expression rather than a "genre" in its own right.

9. For instance, John Pope's well-known claim in 1965 that the poem contained two distinct narrative voices, later retracted in 1974. See also Greenfield, "*Min, Sylf,* and Dramatic Voices."

10. We need not decide on one genre in favor of the other, however. Both Greenfield and Renoir ("Reading Context") view the poem as being simultaneously elegy and a representative of the traditional Germanic women's songs.

11. "Movement in or into exile," one of four conventions that Greenfield has associated with the exile theme that is so prominent throughout the Old English elegies, typically conveys a sense of motion toward the path of exile and, as might be expected, involves description of physical space. Additional elements include deprivation and state of mind as sorrowful. On the exile theme in this passage and the multigeneric nature of Old English narrative, see Garner, *Oral Tradition and Genre* 103–6. On this "nested" lament in relation to the narrative's larger themes of sonless fathers, see Harris, "*Beowulf* as Epic."

12. See also Orchard, "Reconstructing" 45–46.

13. *Wig* has two senses, the more common one having to do with war or conflict and the second with idols or images. Klinck, like many others, has taken the compound with the first sense, translating as "bastion."

14. Dunleavy also specifies the massacre described in the poem as "the massacre at Chester of members of the nearby Welsh monastery at Bangor Iscoed" in 613 (113). (See fig. 7 for a photograph of the more well preserved Binchester hypocausts.)

15. Dunleavy, for instance, justifies the search for archaeological correspondences, saying that the details "encourage speculation on the identity of a city which the poet may have seen personally or had described to him by travelers in Britain" (115).

16. The privileging of red among other colors is not specific to Anglo-Saxons. See Anderson, *Folk Taxonomies*, for comparative linguistic treatment of the term, where he demonstrates that "red is the color par excellence in languages around the world" (129).

17. In fact, the specific shade is likely far less important to our reading than the associative meanings of the word, if we accept Anderson's argument that "red" denotes a range of colors "obtainable through the artistic preparation of ocher and hematite: red, reddish brown, orange, and reddish yellow" (*Folk Taxonomies* 137). Red, Anderson argues, is "mainly earthen, mineral, or metallic in its focus" (138), certainly appropriate for the description of a stone wall.

18. Anderson attributes the prevalence of curved forms to "five-stage development" of "the evolution of geometric terms across languages" ("Uncarpentered World" 67). According to this theory, "the language of Old English poetry belongs at stage two, while the prose texts show evidence of a transition to stage three" (68). This evolutionary model, however, risks underestimating the power of traditional motifs. Even though the language could more than accommodate angular forms, the choices in the poetry reflect the resonance of traditional aesthetics.

19. The description at this point in *The Ruin* closely parallels the skyline of Mermedonia in *Andreas*. The fearsome Mermedonians' dwellings include several of the features seen in *The Ruin:* gray stone ("harne stan"), towers ("torras"), and tiles ("tigelfagan") (841–42).

20. It is worth noting that these instances account for several of the only twenty or so instances of *bosm* in Old English verse, but most others still have a strong association with water, such as the bosom of a ship, *scipes bosme* (*Genesis* 1306), *lides bosme* (*Genesis* 1332, 1410; *Brunanburh* 27). In Riddle 12 (Williamson; 14 KD), typically solved as drinking horn, the speaker's *bosm* is filled with liquid (9, 15; line numbers follow Williamson).

21. See further Anderson, "Uncarpentered World," on the frequency of "homologized" descriptions, simultaneously man-made and natural.

22. E.g., Raffel and Olsen. Klinck provides "container of spirit."

23. None of these three compounds is especially common in Old English writings; each occurs six times *(DOEC)*. In the case of *ferðloca(n)*, all six are in verse *(DOEC)*. (Other appearances include *Andreas* 1671; *Juliana* 79, 234.) Likewise, *breost-cofa* is more common in verse (specifically in *The Creed, Genesis, Precepts,* and *Meters of Boethius*), with only one of the six occurring in a prose text. *Hordcofa* occurs only twice in verse, the other instance being in the Paris Psalter 118.2. Making specific reference to *feorh-hus* ["life-house"], Overing asserts that such compounds "mix, indeed fuse the visual with the more abstract; they collocate the functional, literal, emotional and spatial attributes of the 'image.' The compound is an event; a split second of illumination, of imaginative 'seeing'" (89). Such "fusions" of the emotional and spatial are especially pronounced in the elegies, and understanding the breadth of their associative meanings goes far to help us unpack the emotional core of the poems.

24. As noted in chapter 4, *cofa* has a secondary sense of "cave" or "den" *(DOE)*.

25. Klinck takes this as one word, whereas Krapp and Dobbie divide it into two. Klinck's compound here follows Fischer (299–301).

26. Of the multiple possibilities for *eder,* including "hedge" and "house," Bosworth translates *ederas* more specifically as "houses" for this line. An analogous relationship with the formulaic *in under edoras* in *Genesis* 2447 and 2489 and *Beowulf* 1037 supports a meaning close to "buildings" (122) rather than "precincts," the meaning offered by Leslie.

27. The phrase is often considered insignificant enough for modern readers to be omitted in translation. See, e.g., Heaney 183.

28. As I discuss in chapter 7, the phrase continues to carry traditional force into the Middle English period in such texts as *Sir Orfeo* and *Havelok the Dane.*

29. Holoferne's death in *Judith* 111–21; hell in *Christ and Satan* 24–32, 89–105; Grendel's pool in *Beowulf* 819–23, 1357–75, 1408–40. It is worth noting that although Fry is the first to name the motif and cast it specifically in oral traditional terms, Millns had previously observed the connection between serpents and death in Old English verse and had noted shared phraseology and imagery in *Judith, The Wanderer,* and *Christ and Satan* (437–38).

30. Klinck provides "rocky slope," rocky cliff," and "stone rampart" as equally viable possibilities (447).

31. On the use of *gesteal,* Klinck notes that this "is a rare word which seems to mean some kind of supporting structure" (126). Dunning and Bliss take the term as "foundation" on analogy with *wealsteal* in line 88. (See Dunning and Bliss, "Introduction" 66–67.)

32. E.g., the Lindisfarne Gospels, Mark (Skeat 5.5).

33. E.g., Treharne's translation of "security" (47) and Bradley's translation as "immutable" (325).

34. Liuzza is one of many to observe that in "the rich matrix of Anglo-Saxon culture," "Latin-Christian and native vernacular lines of thought were hardly kept distinct" ("Tower of Babel" 8).

35. This sense of *grave* is especially clear in "Soul and Body" (112). *Scræf* alone indicates a "cave," "cavern," or "hollow place in the earth" (Bosworth).

36. On *enta geweorc,* see chap. 2 above.

37. See Klinck for an overview of the poem's scholarly history.

38. Some have interpreted an earlier reference to her abode at line 16, MS "her heard." Leslie and others emend to *her eard* (53) making the reference applicable to a general "dwelling." Krapp and Dobbie suggest a reading of *he(a)rg hearh,* interpreting the compound as "heathen temple." For a full description of readings, see Klinck 180. Klinck herself leaves the manuscript intact, taking the line as "My lord commanded, cruel, to seize me here" (181).

39. Leslie asserts that the poem's speaker is ordered to live in "a cave or tumulus in the woods in wild and solitary surroundings" (7). The location itself is

less important than her state of mind, and "her surroundings are not only desolate in themselves; she has invested them with something of her own desolation of spirit, summed up in "wic wynna leas" (line 32) (11). The repetition of description in lines 28 ("under actreo in þam eorðscræfe") and 36 ("under actreo geond þas eorþscrafu") "indicates how deeply the nature of her dwelling has branded itself on her mind" (12).

40. It should be noted that G. B. Brown's foundational study of Anglo-Saxon architecture admits that "Saxon earthworks exist" but dismisses them on the grounds that they "have no distinctive character and are in no way architectural" (*Arts* 2:7). The early tendency of scholarship to dismiss the value of earth construction (perhaps because so little of Anglo-Saxon earthwork survives today) neglects the strong traditional associations such structures might have had for medieval audiences.

41. That these underground dwellings captured the later medieval imagination as well is evidenced in Thomas Herron's studies of Spenser and archaeology, which posits the existence of souterrains in Books V and VI of *The Fairie Queene*.

42. The widely acknowledged source of the Latin Vulgate provides *spelunca* at this point in the narrative (19.30).

43. See chapter 3 for further discussion of this earth-cave as a prison. See also Battles on souterrains in Germanic literature as places of refuge.

44. As noted in chapter 3, the varied senses of *tun* include both smaller spaces such as "enclosure," "homestead," or "dwelling" and larger spaces such as a "group of houses," "village," "town." Thus we need not assume that *tunas* refers to towns in a more urban or modern sense. The open-endedness of *tunas* allows for the literal sense of the woman's seemingly small, enclosed space while also evoking a larger emotional space in which to focus the magnitude of her sorrow. Rather than the bitterness contained "in breosthord" or the "heart" of *The Seafarer*, with which *The Wife's Lament* has often been compared, this speaker's sorrow potentially requires entire towns to encompass the bitterness.

45. Arguing that the wife's dwelling is the more solitary souterrain rather than an actual city, Battles offers an alternative view that "*burgtunas* is probably a variation of the preceding *duna uphea* (1. 30), since the hills near the dwelling resemble walls around a city" (267).

46. Kennedy's translation, for instance, interprets the woman's dwelling as natural, "earth-cave under the oak," a "cave-dwelling," as does Raffel's translation of "earthen cavern under an oak, ancient hall." Bradley's indicates intervention by man in creation of the space, with "earthen dug-out" and "earthen abode." Treharne's translation conveys both; the space is an "earth-cave" but also a "hall in the earth." The connotative force of the phraseology in the Old English poem renders both natural and man-made spaces simultaneously.

47. See, e.g., Leslie (58 nn., 80) and Wentersdorf ("Situation" 610).

48. See esp. chap. 2.

CHAPTER 6. **Architectural and Poetic Transitions**

1. The *DOEC* includes 140 occurrences, primarily in chronicles. The primary sense throughout Old English usage was "village, town, frequently rendering *castellum*." (*DOE,* s.v. *castel,* sense 1). In late (i.e., eleventh-century) manuscripts, it had a secondary sense of "castle, fort," more comparable to Anglo-Norman *castel* (*DOE,* sense 2).

2. On the potential for confusion regarding these multiple usages (and the dominant sense of fortified building later in the period) the *OED* offers as an example a seeming misinterpretation in the *Cursor Mundi* in which a reference to Bethany as the "castel" of Mary and Martha is understood not as the town, as it would have been intended in the Vulgate, but instead as the castle of an English feudal lord (s.v. *castle*).

3. Text and translation of William of Poitiers from Davis and Chibnall. "egressam contra se aciem refugere intra moenia impigre compellunt, terga caedentes. Multae stragi addunt incendium, cremantes quicquid aedificiorum citra flumen inuenere, ut malo duplici superba ferocia contundatur" (146).

4. "principes ciuitatis . . . sese cunctamque ciuitatem in obsequium illius"; "obsides quos et quot imperat adducunt" (146).

5. ". . . praesertim sperans ubi regnare coeperit rebellem quemque minus ausurum in se, facilius conterendum esse. Praemisit ergo Lundoniam qui munitionem in ipsa construerent urbe, et pleraque competentia regiae magnificentiae praepararent, moraturus interim per uicina" (148).

6. "dum firmamenta quaedam in urbe contra mobilitatem ingentis ac feri populi perficerentur" (160–62).

7. This wholesale rebuilding program sets the Norman era of building apart from both previous and subsequent architectural periods. For instance, "after the arrival of the Gothic style in the third quarter of the 12th century, new work consisted largely of the rebuilding of parts of structures, with only a handful of examples being completely rebuilt" (Fernie, *Norman* 24).

8. "Domi ingentia, ut dixi, edifita . . . " All citations and translations from William of Malmesbury *Gesta Regum Anglorum* are from Mynors, Thomson, and Winterbottom.

9. All citations and translations from *Gesta Pontificum Anglorum* from Winterbottom. See Thomson, *Gesta Pontificum* ii, 191, fig. 9, for a photograph of the late-eleventh-century Romanesque vaults at Durham Cathedral.

10. ". . . quam ipse illo compositionis genere primus in Anglia edificauerat quod nunc pene cuncti sumptuosis emulantur expensis."

11. "Paruis et abiectis domibus totos absumebant sumptus, Francis et Normannis absimiles, qui amplis et superbis edifitiis modicas expensas agunt."

12. "Vnum edifitium et ipsum permaximum, domum in Lundonia, incepit et perfecit, non parcens expensis dum modo liberalitatis suae magnificentiam exhiberet."

13. Architecturally, this also meant that the basic form of newly constructed buildings often depended to a certain extent on the nature of the original design, a process which could potentially provide misleading evidence as to how spaces were used, since we might expect that the newly designed spaces would fit the precise needs of the church at the time of construction. Gittos observes that "early medieval liturgical manuscripts can inform interpretation of architectural function, but they rarely coincide in a precise manner" (92).

14. ". . . monasteria surgebant religione uetera, edifitiis recentia."

15. "nouarum edium extructionibus mirabili."

16. "Ferebaturque tunc in populo celebre, scriptisque etiam est inditum, nusquam citra Alpes tale esse edifitium."

17. ". . . excursionibus partim fedata partim eruta reparauit. . . . "; "loca omnia in quibus pugnauerat . . . aecclesiis insigniuit . . . "

18. "sed et cementariorum quos ex Roma spes munificentiae attraxerat magisterio . . . "

19. ". . . ambitionem Romanam se imaginari iurent. . . . " Thomson, *Gesta Pontificum* (177), notes that the source for William's claim is not known. Because Richard, prior of Hexham, in or soon after 1141 also claimed that Wilfrid brought in foreign workmen, Thompson says that "William's statement may therefore reflect local tradition" (177). What is verifiable is that the crypt was built of reused Roman stone (recognizable from Roman tooling on the stones' surface). Most significant for present purposes is the clear admiration for Roman stone work seen in William and later writers.

20. "quod artifices edium lapidearum et uitrearum fenestrarum primus omnium Angliam asciuerit. . . . "; "Nec enim lapidei tabulatus in Anglia ante Benedictium nisi perraro uidebantur. . . . "

21. "Sed hic animaduerto mussitationem dicentium melius fuisse ut antiqua in suo statu conseruarentur quam illis semimutilatis de rapina noua construerentur."

22. "Aecclesia angusto situ erat, antiquorum uirorum mediocritatem et abstinentiam preferens: locus pudendus nostri aeui episcopis, in quo episcopalis dignitas diuersari deberet."

23. "recenti ritu patriam florere"; "religionis normam."

24. "Stupenda profecto regis abstinentia, ut tanta se pateretur emungi pecunia. . . . " William does include a somewhat comical account of what could be seen as Alfred's overexuberance in building two churches too close together: "The two churches were so close, the walls actually touching, that the voices of those chanting in either interfered with the other" (195).

25. "Cum aecclesiae maioris opus, quod ipse a fundamentis inceperat, ad hoc incrementi processisset ut iam monachi migrarent in illam, iussum est ueterem aecclesiam, quam beatus Oswaldus fecerat, detegi et subrui. Ad hoc spectaculum stans sub diuo Wlstanus lacrimas tenere nequiuit. Super quot modeste a familiaribus re - dargutus, qui gaudere potius deberet quod se superstite tantus aecclesiae honor accessisset ut ampliatus monachorum numerus ampliora exigeret habitacula,

respondit: 'Ego longe aliter intelligo, quod nos miseri sanctorum opera destruimus ut nobis laudem comparemus. Non nouerat illa felitium uirorum aetas pompati- cas edes construere, sed sub qualicumque tecto se ipsos Deo immolare, subiec- tosque ad exemplum attrahere. Nos e contra nitimur ut animarum negligentes ac- cumulemus lapides.'" The story is also told in *Vita S. Wulfstani* iii. 10.3., in William of Malmesbury, *Saints' Lives* 8–155. A reconstruction drawing of Bishop Wulfstan's cathedral church at Worcester is provided in Thompson, vol. 2, p. 197, fig. 10. For further discussion of this church, see R. Gem, "Bishop Wulfstan II."

26. On further connections between these three panels of the Franks Casket, see Lang 248. Lang notes that the "pillared and arched structure" represents "the canopy over the virgin and Child, the frame around the lady in Egil's house on the lid and the Temple with its empty Ark of the Covenant on the back plate.... All three arches share triple-stepped bases and capitals" (248). Through these images, Lang argues, "a route is established from front to back over the lid of the casket implying that the front and back work together, even though they are not adja- cent" (248).

27. As Carol Neuman de Vegvar has observed, "The same interpretive skills must be brought to bear to make sense of the assemblage of scenes on the Franks Casket" as for the "partially oral context" of Old English wisdom literature (150–51).

28. See Hearn and Thurlby on wooden ribbed vaults in early medieval Brit- ish architecture. Fernie argues, "Despite the large numbers of masonry buildings which can be attributed to the Norman period in England, it is possible that those built in wood, even among structures of some prestige, were more numerous" (*Rise of the Castle* 296).

29. In the case of the Exeter gatehouse, Fernie leans toward Anglo-Saxon models.

30. Images of the Franks Casket where this design can be seen and additional information about its history are readily available at the British Museum's Web site: www.thebritishmuseum.ac.uk.

31. See Webster, who explains that "the lid may depict an otherwise un- known scene from a lost Egil legend, since it contains an archer labeled Ægili, an Old English name possibly related to the Old Norse Egill" ("Stylistic Aspects" 21). On Latin and other Anglo-Saxon instances of the "plain two strand interlace" on the lid's arch column, see Webster, "Stylistic Aspects" 27.

32. While the hogbacks are often thought to be tombstone covers or funer- ary sculpture, evidence is limited. Bailey observes "no grave has been found in clear association with one of these stones" (99).

33. The sculpture has since been moved inside the church for better protection.

34. On the herringbone pattern in Romano-British and Anglo-Saxon archi- tecture, see chap. 5.

35. The Durham Cathedral Web site shows the continuing pride in the heritage of the Anglo-Saxon saint: www.durhamcathedral.co.uk/story_st_cuthbert.htm.

36. Cruck-style roofs were made from curved timbers.

37. For an illustration, see Thompson, *Medieval Hall* 126, fig. 63.

38. From this perspective, architecture functions in similar ways to Victor Turner's concept of ritual as "a cultural means of generating variability, as well as of ensuring the continuity of proved values and norms," "a repertoire of variant deep cultural models" (69, 70).

39. To some degree the senses of "hall" and "castle" put forth here have survived even to the present day. *Castle* continues to be defined predominantly in terms of its strength and military function, a "large fortified building or group of buildings with thick walls" (*AHD*4, s.v. *castle*), and the semantic changes of *hall* reflect its dual senses in the Middle Ages of a self-contained structure and of a dominant room within a larger building. The reversal of orders from medieval times to the present is indicative of the subsumption of the hall within larger structures and a dissolution of the ideals represented by the hall across the period. The subordinate sense gradually acquiring primacy, the dominant sense today of "hall" develops from its earlier sense of a room within a large structure but has grown much more modest: "1. A corridor or passageway in a building" (*AHD*, s.v. *hall*). Its other senses are retained, however, *hall* referring also to grander structures, as in a "concert hall," with the sense of "a building for public gatherings or entertainments" or "the large room in which such events are held" (*AHD*, s.v. *hall*, sense 3). As in medieval times, "hall" in its grandest sense can still refer to a "castle" itself or to a "principal room" within a castle. "a. The castle or house of a medieval monarch or noble. b. the principal room in such a castle or house, used for dining, entertaining, and sleeping" (*AHD*, s.v. *hall*, sense 7). To this day, hall in the freestanding sense of Anglo-Saxon halls and the more hierarchical sense of a room within a grand structure recurs in almost every sense of the word: "A building for public gatherings or entertainments" *or* "The large room in which such events are held" (sense 3); "A building belonging to a school, college, or university that provides classroom, dormitory, or dining facilities" *or* "A large room in such a building" (sense 5); "The castle or house of a medieval monarch or noble" *or* "The principal room in such a castle or house, used for dining, entertaining, and sleeping" (sense 7). Also as in medieval times, the term *hall*, whether freestanding or not, differs from *castle* in being defined more clearly in terms of what goes on inside its walls, a building "for public gatherings" or a room "in which such events are held," a building "used for the meetings, entertainments, or living quarters" of particular groups. To this extent, the distinctions put forth here about usages in Middle English texts are somewhat consistent, taking into account a shift in the ordering of senses, with those of modern times.

40. The sense here is that oral poetry "uses a special language to support highly focused and economical communication, taking advantage of implications unique to that language" (126). For Foley, "oral poetry *is* a language" (126), and "because registers are more highly coded than everyday language, because their 'words' resonate with traditional implications beyond the scope of multipurpose street language,

they convey enormously more than grammars and dictionaries . . . can record" (*How to Read* 116). These tendencies can be witnessed in written works deriving from oral traditions because such oral registers "can and do persist beyond live performance and into texts" (*HROP* 116).

41. As Amodio observes, "Although it may be tempting to read a large political motive into this situation, we need not do so, for the Normans who invaded England and then settled there may simply and understandably have preferred (and hence supported and fostered through their patronage) verse founded upon their inherited, familiar tradition, verse that celebrated their own cultural heritage and that was, moreover, composed in the foreign tongue and alien metrics of a conquered people but in the language that they themselves spoke and in metrical forms with which they were long acquainted" (*Writing* 132).

42. For a basic overview of the linguistic changes from Old to Middle English, see Algeo and Pyles 123–52.

43. For instance, French scribal practices were responsible for such Middle English spellings as *qu*, which replaced Old English *cw* in such words as *queen; ch,* which replaced Old English <c> in representing the affricate [č]; and the introduction of <v>, an angular form of <u> that could be used to represent consonant or vowel but that in Old English times would have been spelled with <f>.

44. A standard study of vocabulary is Serjeantson. On French influence, see 104–69. On vocabulary involving buildings, see 106, 108, 110, 113, 115, 117, 119, 122, 128, 129, 131, 133, 136, 137, and 140.

45. See further Clough 195.

46. For many French loanwords, the position of the accent eventually shifted to the stem-syllable in words that in French had been placed on the final syllable, such as *vírtu* and *hónour* from French *virtú* and *honóur*. However, the change was gradual, with bilingual speakers retaining the French pronunciations and many poets as late as the fifteenth century varying between English and French modes of accentuation (Serjeantson 295).

47. See Amodio, *Writing* 1–32.

48. See also R. Allen, who shares the belief that *Brut* "mediates a world where the oral and written modes of communication are interdependent" but concludes that it is "designed for an audience whose response is primarily aural" ("Counting Time" 91).

49. The *Brut* survives in two manuscripts, the MS. Cotton Caligula A ix and the later, slightly shorter Cotton Otho C xiii.

50. Unless otherwise noted, citations from the *Brut* are from the Caligula version edited by Brook and Leslie. Translations are my own.

51. These same castles are also referenced at 197, 217, 233.

52. Other buildings associated with great leaders but not marked as "strong" do figure into the narrative in these 500 lines. For instance, Ascanius builds a *hehe burh* (111) and Brutus's mother died in a *burhe* (149), but these structures are never

referenced specifically as *castles*. The reference to the structure is absent in the Otho version, where it is simply asserted that she died. As in Old English (see chap. 1), the Middle English *burgh* has a wide semantic range. It could refer to entire cities or towns (*MED*, s.v. *burgh*, sense 1) or to individual structures as castles, strongholds, or fortified dwellings (sense 3).

53. E.g., "þa þe castel vp stod; he wes strong 7 swiðe god" (827); "stronge castles" (201); "castles stronge" (2225); "ane stronge castle" (2340); "castel swiðe strongne" (3187); "twenti castles stronge" (4225); "stronge enne castle" (4342); "þe castles heolden stronge" (5331); "ane stronge castle" (5671); "stronge castle" (6100); "castles swiðe stronge" (6250); "caste[l] wurche. mid stronge stan walle" (7707).

54. For another *hall* within a *borhe*, see 1013–14.

55. The obvious exception to this lack of physical specificity is the hall of Arthur's dream, which is discussed at more length below.

56. This reconstructed text by Brook and Leslie is based on the corresponding point in the Otho manuscript.

57. The corresponding point in the Caligula omits the reference to churches ("Childric al for-barnden; 7 þa hallen alle clæne"), but the halls are here also one of multiple items in a list as the preceding line describes the destruction of the city walls.

58. Omitted from discussion are instances where "hall" functions more adjectivally, compounded with *dure* [*halle dure*, 10478, 15049]. Evidence from the Otho manuscript further suggests that this compounded form of *hall* lacks the same connotative meaning as typically seen in object of preposition placement. The point in the Otho manuscript corresponding to 15049 references not a hall door but a *boures dore*. Similarly the *halle wah* at 12920 (which occurs in the direct object position) is rendered as a *hilewoh* in the Otho.

59. These patterns can all be classified as full-line formulas, as defined by Dennis Donahue for the *Brut* in particular: "word groups (consisting of the key words or words and specific context words) that verbalize a given concept" and that "can be repeated in different syntactic shapes" (*Lawman's* Brut 136). In Donahue's configuration, word pairs linked by rhyme or alliteration "can be classified as formulas when they consistently verbalize a specific concept" (136). Whether or not we label these repeated compositional devices as "formulas," the "concept" being verbalized through their iteration is crucial to our understanding of the narrative contexts in which they are employed.

60. If rhyme were a defining feature of the verse throughout Laȝamon's *Brut*, it might be tempting to reduce the patterns to metrical necessity (though, as we have seen elsewhere, metrical necessity is not mutually exclusive of traditional and idiomatic meaning). However, the verse form is very highly inconsistent, some lines marked by alliteration, some by rhyme, and some lacking any discernible poetic features at all.

61. As Rosamund Allen notes, the concept of rhyme is not always in line with patterns that would be considered rhyme today, as in the case of *stille/halle*, which

follows a fairly common pattern in the *Brut* involving words that "have identical or nearly identical consonants with distinction of vowels" ("Counting Time" xxix). Sound patterns involving rhyme and alliteration frequently suggest units of half-lines within the longer line. The pattern does not characterize the entire poem, but enough lines do demonstrate this pattern that Barron and Weinberg provide half-line caesuras in their edition of the *Brut*.

62. A third pattern, albeit attested only by two examples, emerges in the Otho manuscript. At two points in the Otho manuscript there is a usage of *hall* as an object of preposition in rhyming position with *stille* and in lines with forms of the verb *steal*. In the first instance, Locrin takes one of his men whom he trusts well ("þat wel he treste con," 1176) in typical *comitatus* fashion "and hehte him swiþe stille: stelen vt of halle" (1177). In the second instance Appas is described as stealing out of the hall through similar syntax and phraseology: "and þe leche stille: bi-stal vt of þan halle" (8871). At the corresponding point in the Caligula MS. Appas does speak with his men, "spec wið his monnen" (8871), but is said simply to steal away from "þan tune" (8872) rather than the hall. This pattern is less established in that it only occurs twice and only in the Otho manuscript, but it does reinforce the overarching pattern of halls in object of preposition placement linked with *comitatus* actions and ideals.

63. The corresponding line in the Otho differs slightly, with "knights" being in the same line as "hall."

64. An effect in this particular scene of evoking elements of the hall is to juxtapose "the treachery of Rowenne to the joy of Vortimer" (Donahue, *Lawman's Brut* 286) and thus heighten the effect of Rowena's poisoning of Vortimer, "þe gode king" (7485). On the "Feast Theme," which is closely connected with hall life and ideals, see Donahue, *Lawman's Brut* 74–80.

65. The argument put forth here does not presuppose that the evocation of hall ideals is an automatic endorsement of the leaders and retainers involved. Much has been written on the "ambivalence" of Laȝamon toward Saxon leaders. See, e.g., Donahue, who argues that the inconsistent treatment of Saxon leaders reflects a more general "ambivalence toward the past" and is part of a "wider cultural ambivalence in 12th- and 13th-century England ("Laȝamon's Ambivalence," 537); and Noble, who argues instead that there are in Laȝamon's historical representation not one but two groups of Saxons portrayed. In this reading, the poem is "both pro-English and anti-Saxon" (181). The question of nationalistic identities represented in the poem is very complex indeed and beyond the scope of this study. Even if the treatment of the leaders themselves remains ambiguous, the *comitatus* ideals represented through the hall clearly have Laȝamon's endorsement.

66. They are depicted as "hehȝe" (high) men, armed with weapons ["on wepne"], wearing great rings of gold ["grætne ring of golde"] and approaching in pairs clasping hands (12351–52).

67. Translating the phrase in terms of physical space as some have done risks losing the force of the idiom. For instance translating *halle* here as "court" (e.g.,

Allen) locates the assembly of men appropriately but risks losing the traditional and idiomatic import of the *halle/stille* word pair.

68. Speaking to the simultaneous consistency and flexibility of traditional art forms, Cable writes, "a tradition, though perceived as a single entity by those who join or define it, is upon closer examination a set of discontinuous parts, sequenced only by time. The tradition must be created anew, recapitulated, and sustained within each individual poet—perhaps with changes (intentional or otherwise)" (Cable 133).

69. The features attributed to the hall are more limited to height and timber construction, with fewer, if any, explicit references to gables or arches in structures referenced as "halls." This pattern is consistent with Amodio's contention that "the specialized lexemes of oral poetics" are likely to "become obsolete and disappear once their specialized register fractures" but that "its thematics remains relatively intact throughout the Middle Ages" (Amodio, *Writing* 188), the specific features being the architectural equivalent to "specialized lexemes."

CHAPTER 7. **The Poetics of Built Space in Middle English Narrative Verse**

1. I refer here to the process by which "what had been for hundreds of years a univocal and metrically uniform system for articulating verse became a polyphonous (if not cacophonous) one marked by a hitherto unknown metrical diversity" (Amodio, *Writing* 132).

2. Story pattern, a component of oral theory developed by Lord and Parry, refers to "narrative patterns that, no matter how much the stories built around them may seem to vary, have great vitality and function as organizing elements in the composition and transmission of oral story texts" (Lord, "Theme of the Withdrawn Hero" 18). The schema presented here is Albert Lord's. Lord posits an Indo-European origin to the story pattern ("Theme of the Withdrawn Hero" 19) with manifestations in South Slavic, ancient Greek, and Germanic traditions. On the Return Song pattern, see further Foley, *Traditional Oral Epic* 13. On *Sir Orfeo* as Return Song, see Ward Parks, "Return Song and a Middle English Romance" 222 ff. The view of *Orfeo* as Return Song has subsequently been accepted by Longsworth, Falk (147 n.), and Amodio (*Writing* 196–97), among others. On *Havelok* as Return Song, see Henderson 93. On the Return Song as an "underdeveloped but nevertheless present and functioning compositional element" of *Sir Gawain and the Green Knight,* see Amodio, *Writing* 197–98.

3. See Foley's discussion of "genre dependence," in *Traditional Oral Epic* 3–4, 8–9. While Foley's model is designed for comparative work across cultural traditions, it provides a responsible point of departure for comparison across the vast range of medieval English texts, which in some ways can be understood as "cross-traditional" themselves, drawing from multiple and widely divergent cultural influences.

4. *King Horn* appears in three manuscripts: British Library MS. Harley 2253 in London (hereafter, London MS.) dating to the mid-fourteenth century, Bodleian Library MS. Laud Misc. 108 in Oxford (hereafter, Oxford MS.) dating to the late thirteenth or early fourteenth century, and the University Library MS. Gg.4.27.2 in Cambridge (hereafter, Cambridge MS.) dating to the end of the thirteenth century. Hall, whose edition includes all three texts, follows scholarly consensus in placing the Cambridge MS. as the earliest but viewing it as a likely copy of a still earlier text. Most critical editions thus work primarily from the Cambridge MS. Sands, for instance, cites the Cambridge MS. as the "oldest" and "best" (15), and Allen also uses the Cambridge MS. as the basis of her edition. On the relationship of surviving texts to one another, see Hall, *King Horn* vii–xv. Unless otherwise noted, all citations are to the Cambridge MS., Herzman, Drake, and Salisbury's 1999 edition. The occasional references to the London and Oxford MSS. are from Hall. While there are significant differences at some points in the manuscripts, the Oxford being 23 lines longer than the London and 45 lines longer than the Cambridge, the differences in architectural description are too slight to affect the arguments put forth here. Those minor differences that do exist are described in the notes.

5. See, e.g., Hurt, who argues that *Horn* shows signs of oral-formulaic composition and that the poem was likely copied by scribes familiar with the oral-formulaic method (47–59). Wittig also makes reference to the "oral-composition origins" of the text (170). Henderson discusses *Horn* as a "more traditional romance" (91) and explores the implications for character development and the poem's "strongly didactic nature" (91). See Amodio, *Writing* 194–96, on the role of the traditional Return Song story pattern in this narrative and Veck for discussion of parallels with Old English narrative that can be attributed to "continuity via oral tradition," especially in the Midlands region (24), which "was more inclined to resist assimilation" and thus to preserve Anglo-Saxon traditions. The persistence of oral techniques does not, however, negate the view that *King Horn* "was composed by a literate author" (Allen, *King Horn* 110). The premise I follow here is simply that an oral poetics continues to have resonance and to convey meaning within literate cultures and thus provide some among many expressive options for Middle English authors.

6. Thirteen times in the London MS., the latest of the three.

7. This is the only instance in which the word *hall* does not appear in all three extant manuscripts. The London MS. reads "þe kyng lette forþ calle / hise knyhtes alle" (Hall, ed., 907–8), evoking the unity of the knights without the context of the hall. This difference in the latest manuscript may speak to the weakening of the oral poetics across the period.

8. Allen observes the difference in employment here, noting that "hall" is "used ironically" (*King Horn* 385).

9. In the London and Oxford MSS. Horn enters through a hall "door" rather than a "gate" (Hall, ed., L 195, O 1523).

10. Rymenhild's position in the hall is further established by the description of her pouring drinks in the "sale" (1117). Not from the same root as the Old English *sele, sale* derives from Old English *sæl* and Old French *sale,* with the sense of a room within a castle rather than a freestanding structure.

11. In the later London and Oxford MSS. the castle is referenced but not designated explicitly as "strong" (Hall, ed., L 1411, O 1444), reflecting a lessening of the associations between castles and military strength, a phenomenon discussed at more length in relation to *Sir Orfeo* and *Sir Gawain and the Green Knight* below.

12. See, e.g., Henderson's discussion of character development in "more traditional" romances (esp. 91), Quinn and Hall's discussion of formulaic density in conjunction with rhyme as oral compositional devices (49–76), and Park's response to Quinn's approach ("Oral Formulaic Theory" 670); for a comparison of proverb usage in *Havelok the Dane* and the more rhetorical usage of proverbs in Chaucer's *Troilus and Criseyde,* see Garner, "Role of Proverbs." Arguing that protagonists in narratives "closer to a hypothetical oral provenance" reflect traditional codes of ideals rather than tending toward the psychological complexity and narrative ambiguity of less traditional works, Henderson places *Havelok,* with its idealized heroes and unwaveringly evil villains, far closer to an oral outlook than more ambiguous narratives such as *Sir Gawain and the Green Knight.* Traditional proverbs in *Havelok* also carry their full associative force throughout the narrative, guiding audience response with an unquestioned traditional wisdom that is never contradicted by the narrative's plot.

13. *Havelok the Dane* is extant in its entirety in one manuscript, Bodleian Library, Oxford, MS. Laud Misc. 108, with fragments surviving in Cambridge University Library Add. 4407. Unless otherwise noted, all citations from *Havelok* are from Smithers's edition.

14. Cf. Uther's and Arthur's commands to "knights in hall" discussed in chap. 6. Ronald B. Herzman, Graham Drake, and Eve Salisbury explain the usage thus: "The 'bower' and 'hall' were two fundamental units of a castle or noble dwelling that persisted in some form throughout the Middle Ages. The hall was an open, public space used for dining, entertaining, or convening of nobles; the bower was a relatively more secluded area used for sleeping. The bower, it should be noted, was not necessarily a more private place. Yet the association of bower with ladies and hall with knights is appropriate; while one could find either sex in either place, the bower is associated more with the more intimate love of women, the hall with the masculine world of celebrating achievements and swearing loyalties to comrades. Compare with *Beowulf,* where the king and queen retire to the *burgh* while Beowulf and the retainers sleep on and around the same benches where they have feasted."

15. On the proverbial wisdom accompanying Grim's shift from villain to helper, see Garner, "Role of Proverbs" 262–63.

16. The prominent position of Grim and his portrayal in armor on the seal of Grimsby (named of course for Grim himself) would suggest that in local legend

perhaps Grim had a more explicitly heroic role. On this seal and its relationship to local legend, see Bradbury, *Writing Aloud* 71–72. On the seal more specifically, see Smithers 160–67.

17. Smithers takes *doutede* (709) as "unequal to." Sands translates *doutede* as "feared" and *sand* as "sound," making the line read, "So that it [should] fear neither sound nor inlet" (76 n.). Given the tendency in early medieval English poetry to personify objects, especially built works, the emendation to "sound," though "orthographically possible" (Sands 76 n.), seems far from necessary.

18. Opie and Opie observe that stories commonly understood as "rags to riches" fantasies seldom are: "In the most-loved fairy tales, it will be noticed, noble personages may be brought low by fairy enchantment or by human beastliness, but the lowly are seldom made noble. The established order is not stood on its head. Snow White and Sleeping Beauty are girls of royal birth. Cinderella was tested, and found worthy of her prince. The magic of the tales (if magic is what it is) lies in people and creatures being shown to be what they really are" (14). While *Havelok* of course is not a "fairy tale" in the same sense, it does share a use of magic that reifies rather than subverts the traditional hierarchy. Like Cinderella and other fairy tale protagonists, Havelok is brought low and moves through the lower classes of society in order to reclaim (with the aid of supernatural elements) his entitled position.

19. Havelok has been seen as a "hybrid figure" in other regards as well, most notably in his fusion of a Danish and English identity (Rouse 77). Rouse argues that the narrative, situated "in the Anglo-Saxon past," "makes use of the popular post-Conquest view of the Anglo-Saxon period as a Golden Age of law and order" (77). The portrayal of "hybrid" architectural elements further reinforces the positive valence of Anglo-Saxon ideals within an emerging Norman social order.

20. See further Bliss xxvii–xxxi, who notes that "the manner in which Breton minstrels performed their *lais*" is "far from unambiguous" (xxix).

21. On Latin variants with happy endings, see Dronke 198–215. On fragments of a Scottish version of the story, see Stewart.

22. See further Bliss xix–xx. For more on the three manuscripts, see Bliss ix–xv. Unless otherwise noted, quotations from all three versions are from Bliss's thorough edition. Determination of date and dialect are also problematic, as features from Anglian dialects (southern and western) are admixed with other linguistic features that point clearly to the Southeast, and the vocabulary itself seems to conflate not only regional tendencies but also lexical usages from various periods. Such multiple influences from various dialects and time periods are of course typical of orally transmitted narratives, with examples ranging from Homeric epic to modern South Slavic poetry and beyond (e.g., Foley, *Homer's Traditional Art* 23–34). Taken together the three surviving manuscripts allow us to analyze what Foley has called "variation within limits" in oral traditional and oral-derived works. Variation within certain traditionally accepted parameters allows for "composi-

tional flexibility at the same time that it delivers a resonant context that frames each of its occurrences" (Foley, *Homer's Traditional Art* 170).

23. Though he posits the possibility of lost originals and missing intermediary texts, Bliss notes, "It is impossible to establish the affiliation of the three manuscripts with any certainty" (xiii).

24. Bliss explains that "the establishment of a definitive text for any specific 'adventure' was not often thought important" (2). Specifically, variations in spelling and rhyme throughout the manuscripts seem to suggest "the work of an idiosyncratic scribe freely adapting a sound copy" (Bliss xvii). Another feature indicative of oral transmission that we can witness through comparison involves the frequent transposition of the two lines in a rhymed couplet (Bradbury, *Writing Aloud* 19). Before welcoming the disguised Orfeo into his hall, the steward of the Auchinleck MS. says, "Euerich gode harpour is welcom me to / For mi lordes loue, Sir Orfeo" ["Every good harpist is welcome to me, for the love of my lord, Sir Orfeo"] (517–18). However, in the Harley text, the order of the lines is reversed: "For my lordys love, Syr Orpheo, / Al mynstrellys ben welcom me to" in the Harley ["For the love of my lord, Sir Orfeo, all minstrels are welcome to me"] (467–68). (The Ashmole MS. follows the order of the Harley: "For my lordys loue, Syr Orfeo, / All herpers be wecum me to" (506–7). Using as a comparison a passage of equiva-lent length from Chaucer's "Knight's Tale," a text known to have been transmitted via writing through various manuscripts, Bradbury notes that *Sir Orfeo* has a significantly higher number of these transpositions: "Even allowing the greater cultural prestige that would help to preserve Chaucer's texts and for the increased syntactic and intellectual complexity that makes his couplets less subject to transposition without disruption of meaning, the difference, then, is sufficiently striking to suggest a difference in the means of transmission," the difference suggested being that between "the copyist's short-term recall" and "the performer's long-term memory" (*Writing Aloud* 19): Bradbury draws her statistics from McGillivray, who observes seven such transpositions in the Ashmole MS., where among the manuscripts of the "Knight's Tale" "only three out of fifty include more than one such transposition and no manuscript exceeds three" (19). On fluidity in the medieval romance, see also Baugh, who argues that variation results from improvisation.

25. Notably, it is also the Ashmole that evinces transposition of couplets indicative of oral/aural transmission (Bradbury, *Writing Aloud* 19; McGillivray 90–91).

26. The two exceptions are Ashmole 159, where "halls" occur alongside multiple possessions in the same pattern seen in the *Brut,* and Ashmole 270, where the tree is said to be Orfeo's hall, a metaphor discussed at more length below.

27. Robert M. Longsworth observes the dual influences on *Sir Orfeo,* arguing that medieval romances more generally "have as it were a foot in both worlds," oral and literate (1). "The duality of this formal heritage should be reckoned with in the interpretation of all medieval romances, for differences between textual and

non-textual expectations and conventions can produce unacknowledged but manifest differences in thematic and stylistic conventions" (2). In a comparison of the three extant versions of *Sir Orfeo,* Longsworth points specifically to the tree dwelling, whose hollowness is mentioned in only one version. Longsworth also points out the parallelism with the queen's position under a tree in the fairy kingdom (5).

28. Harley 249, 251; cf. Auchinleck 245; Ashmole 251.

29. In fact, all characteristics of the Old English exile theme as characterized by Greenfield (status as a solitary exile, sorrowful state of mind, separation from desired objects and situations, and movement into or within exile) are present here.

30. Sands's edition of *Middle English Verse Romances,* for instance, uses the Auchinleck (omitting the prologue). This version, he says, "antedates the two by over a hundred years." Lending it further authority, he says that this particular manuscript "may have been seen by—may indeed, have belonged to—Geoffrey Chaucer" (185). The Auchinleck is also the version used in the TEAMS text, following *The Middle English Breton Lays* (ed. Laskaya and Salisbury).

31. For instance, when the steward falls into a swoon on thinking that Orfeo is dead, the Auchinleck describes him as falling "to grounde" (549), and the Harley omits the swoon altogether. The Ashmole, however, reinforces the steward's associations with heroic ideals by having him fall "in þe halle" (540).

32. The treatment of the city itself varies. Thrace is spelled *Traciens, Tracyens,* and *Crassens* in the various manuscripts and in the Auchinleck is linked with Winchester. The various spellings here are yet another indication of the possibility of aural rather than purely written transmission. Auchinleck: "þis king soiournd in Traciens, / þat was a cité of noble defens" ["For Winchester was cleped þo Traciens"] (47–50). Harley: "Orpheo sugerneþ in Crassens, / þat is cyté of noble defens" (47–78). Ashmole: "The kyng jorneyd in Tracyens, / That is a cyté off grete defense" (41–42).

33. Auchinleck MS. 236. Cf. Harley "out of towne" (230), Ashmole 61 "out off þe tounne" (238).

34. For an image of battlements somewhat contemporary with the manuscripts, see fig. 27.

35. Where the texts do vary in their description, the Ashmole consistently defaults to traditional architectural imagery. In all three texts, for instance, there is reference to the surrounding moat [*diche/dyche*], but the structure emerging from the moat varies—buttresses in Auchinleck (361) and the outermost (presumably towers) in Harley (347), but pillars in the Ashmole, more in keeping with the vertical timbers of Anglo-Saxon architecture and this manuscript's tendency toward Old English poetic imagery (364). The Auchinleck and Harley texts heighten the strangeness and uniqueness of the structure and depart from traditional phraseology by explaining that no man could tell of or even imagine the richness of the work (Auchinleck 373–74; Harley 359–60). In the Ashmole, however, the contrast is implied rather than explicitly stated, and these lines are absent entirely.

36. Ong has argued that writing allows for a structuring of knowledge "at a distance from lived experience" (42), where primary oral cultures tend to conceptualize and verbalize knowledge "with more or less close reference to the human life-world, assimilating the alien objective world to the more immediate, familiar action" of the participants (42). With literacy comes an increased tendency to "distance," "itemize," and make "neutral," to allow for description and lists "devoid of a human action context" (42). Writing "makes possible increasingly articulate introspectivity" and objectifies "the external objective world quite distinct from itself" (104), where "primary orality fosters personality in structures that in certain ways are more communal and externalized" (68). None of this is to suggest that any of the medieval narratives discussed here are products of "primary orality." Without reducing these patterns to binaries, we can nonetheless appreciate the oral modes of expression that are employed alongside and interact with more clearly literate features.

37. The employment of multiple influences from oral tradition as well as literate culture is typical of medieval verbal art. As Stock explains, the medieval period saw a "transformation" of oral modes of expression alongside the growing influence of literacy; thus the literature produced during the medieval period reflects a shift "not so much from oral *to* written as from an earlier state, predominantly oral, to various combinations of oral *and* written" (Stock, *Implications* 9 [original emphasis]; see also 12). As Howe has astutely observed, "There is in fact no clear point of transition from a nonliterate to a literate society" (*Migration* 9), and it is to our benefit to recognize and understand the implications of oral as well as literate tendencies in narrative description.

38. Again, while more characteristic of oral traditional verbal art, this mode of expression, in appealing to the direct experience of an audience, can be, and is, employed for rhetorical effect in print culture even today, primarily to convey a sense of immediacy or to situate an event outside an audience's experience within the realm of the everyday. For instance, Margaret McDonald opens a collection of ghost stories, "A House Like Yours—Only Haunted," employing second person as if addressing an immediately present audience and inviting readers to supply the settings of the stories that will follow with details from their own experience. By limiting description to "like yours" (26), McDonald relies on the architectural awareness of the book's audience in somewhat the same way that the medieval narratives discussed above leave specific visual details to the reader's imagination and experience.

39. The shared wall joining the peaceful landscape and the prison of the Fairy King's victims also displays connections to conventions of allegorical verse found in medieval verse. Kolve, for instance, discusses the "striking juxtaposition" in the prison and garden in Chaucer's "Knight's Tale" as emblematic of "the 'wele' and 'wo' of human life" (87). That *Orfeo* sustains readings at all of these various levels is a testament to the poet's adeptness in multiple registers.

40. See also Ward Parks's convincing argument that *Orfeo* is in fact a Return Song and that awareness of this pattern explains a number of plot developments

that are otherwise inconsistent, such as the testing of the steward when we have no reason to suspect his loyalty ("Return Song" 224). As Parks notes, "*Sir Orfeo* belongs to a state in the development of literary culture in which distinctly 'literary' forms were still emerging out of oral-traditional proto-types" (340). In *Orfeo* traditional forms retain much of their "power and integrity" even as the "specific poetic instance is beginning to individuate itself from the generic pattern, to stand in a greater degree of 'otherness' to the structures from which it is ultimately derived" (240). The testing sequence is typical of Return Song patterns.

41. Camargo observes a highly complex ring-structure in the poem, noting that "none of the extant romances is a transcription of a genuine oral composition" (126). It is far more productive to understand Middle English romance as "transitional or oral-derived" and to keep in mind that "the habit of formulaic composition could and in fact did form part of the 'education' of the literate poets who wrote those romances" (126). In fact, he argues that the structure of the poem is actually "*over*determined" (123; original emphasis). Camargo encourages us to "recall the widespread use of ring composition in living oral forms such as the ballad and the folktale, which were familiar to the fourteenth-century audience," and thus recognize the "competence" this audience likely had in "oral grammar" (127). A fourteenth-century audience would likely have been more attuned to "annular and trinary structuring devices in oral narrative" (127).

42. The poem's inherent ambiguities have also been observed at the level of character development. Henderson notes that ambiguity of character in heroes and villains alike distances *Sir Gawain and the Green Knight* from more "traditional heroes like Beowulf," characters who "behave in conformity to codes of conduct or patterns of behavior that are inscribed in the memories of traditional audiences" (99). Gawain's interiority and complex psychological development lead him to move from an illusory perfection in Camelot to a "fragmented vision" of self (97). Likewise, the Green Knight is "a correspondingly less traditional 'heavy' villain, and we cannot even call him 'villain' at all times. In the resolution scene at the Green Chapel, his wry humor may even endear him to audiences, creating a rather diffuse resonance between this scene and the challenge episode" (99).

43. Amodio observes that in its final scene the poem "reveals both the irresolvable tension that binds tradition and modernity and the poem's uneasy situation between them" ("Tradition, Modernity" 49). "Marked by its interiority and introspection, this newly emerged self is based on unique, recently formed, and internal precepts rather than the collective, traditional, external ones still operating for Arthur and the rest of the court" (61). "Gawain's dislocation from the court may be seen as the ineluctable result of the tension that exists between tradition and modernity" (62).

44. Noting that the place-name Hautdesert "has been variously explained," Twomey suggests a compound from the French components *haut* and *dese* read as "high wasteland" or possibly "high hermitage" (105).

45. For instance, Gawain, while feasting in the "sale" (1372) gives to his host the gifts that he earned "þis wonez wythinne" ["within these walls"] (1386), indicating that the private bedroom quarters where he dallied with the host's wife were lodged within the same walls as the feasting hall. Although the French *salle* and the Old English *sæl* both mean "hall" and ultimately derive from the same source, the two have very different connotations by their development in the later Middle Ages. In France "the principal room in a medieval aristocratic dwelling was called the 'sal,'" "merely a room," while the English hall, in contrast, "was a separate entity open to the roof" (Thompson, *Medieval Hall* 9).

46. The first example provided for this second usage is from *Cleanness*: "So watz served fele syþe þe *sale* alle aboute" (1417).

47. The pattern is slightly different for *flet*. In Old and Middle English alike *flet* has the sense of "hall," but this sense derives metonymically from its primary meaning as "floor." The *OED* gives "the floor or ground under one's feet" as occurring as late as 1450 and cites the usage in *Gawain* specifically (line 568). The second meaning, which derives from the first, of "dwelling, a house, hall," also had currency in Old as well as Middle English. Unlike "hall" or "sale," "flet(te)" appears in reference to Hautdesert (859, 1376, 832, 1653, 1925) more than to Camelot (568, 294). Since *flet* sometimes does have the sense of "floor" (and in some cases, either sense could apply in context), the increased usage is in keeping with the heightened specificity in architectural description that we see of the castle Hautdesert, for instance, the description of the decorations on the walls and "on þe flet" (859).

48. In a discussion of synonyms in Gawain's alliterative verse, Benson shows that the *Gawain*-poet frequently conveys meaning "not by explicit statement but by the synonyms he uses" (143). "This kind of variation," Benson asserts, "is a device of oral poetry" that for the *Gawain*-poet serves as "a delicate and expressive part of the poetic technique" (143).

49. Sarah Stanbury has written one of the most extensive and insightful studies available on description and perception in the works of the *Gawain*-poet. For *Sir Gawain and the Green Knight,* in particular, Stanbury demonstrates substantial stylistic differences between "Gawain's single gaze" and "collective gazes," such as of the court of Camelot. In Stanbury's reading, the extensive details provided, often with little or no interpretation, throughout the Hautdesert scenes make *Gawain* "in many ways a fourteenth-century detective fiction" (109). Stanbury's observations here are in keeping with predictable stylistic differences between oral and literate modes of expression.

50. This identification in terms of built structures is consistent with the poet's treatment of other leaders mentioned in the opening stanzas. Romulus is said to have built "þat burȝe" ["that stronghold"] "with gret bobbaunce" ["with great pomp"] (9), Tirius "teldes bigynnes" ["founded dwellings"] (11), and Langaberde in Lumbardie "lyftes vp homes" ["built up homes"] (12). This identification of leaders

with the buildings and cities they erect is reminiscent of the *Brut* and of historical writings, such as those of William of Malmesbury. See further chap. 6.

51. That Malory later places Camelot specifically in Winchester speaks even further to the intentional vagueness of Camelot's description in this earlier work.

52. The *Middle English Dictionary* defines "embaned" as follows: "Provided with horn-work, i.e. projecting masonry, to impede assault." Tolkien provides the following more simplified translation for the rather technical term: "provided with projecting horizontal coursings" (*Gawain* 178).

53. The term derives from hunting, as appropriate given the prominence of hunting at the castle: "A cluster of three or more tines at the summit of a deer's antlers" (*MED*, s.v. *troche*). Tolkien translates "provided with ornamental pinnacles." The image is reminiscent in some ways of the gabled Anglo-Saxon halls, also described in terms of horns.

54. Wehlau has also commented on the distinctive style of this passage, specifically in comparison with Old English architectural description: "The sense of place that is so important in *Beowulf* develops out of the symbolic value of Heorot as the centre and metaphorical body of a community rather than from any clear visual image of the hall. One need only contrast the short description of Heorot in *Beowulf* with the lengthy description of Bertilak's castle in *Sir Gawain and the Green Knight* to see what a more detailed enumeration of architectural attributes looks like" (131).

55. See also Wehlau, who asserts that "the description of barbican, towers, and chimneys paints a picture of the whole by analyzing it into parts but, ironically, this careful analysis distances us" (132).

56. It is worth noting that the level of descriptive detail, if not the features themselves, is paralleled also by the description of the otherworldly Fairy King's castle in *Sir Orfeo*, though of course the tendency in scholarship on that poem has not been to seek equivalences on the British landscape despite such specificity. Longsworth, in fact, argues that the scene "is redolent of the Holy City described in the Revelation of St. John" (9).

57. See also Benson, who argues that at such moments "the viewpoints of the narrator and the hero coalesce, and scenes and characters are presented as they appear to Gawain, with his eye and emotions providing the process by which the details are organized" (183).

58. For audiences familiar with the features of such heavily fortified castles, the effect might have been something like when Little Red Riding Hood innocently admires her "grandmother's" big teeth, completely unaware of the danger those teeth pose.

59. On Hautdesert and whether it refers to the castle, the chapel, or the larger geographic region, see Twomey 105–7.

60. The significance of this speech is underscored by its employment within the bob and wheel structure, which, as Benson observes, is "always aurally significant in its abrupt shift in meter" (116).

61. www.cressbrook.co.uk/cheshire/cheshatxt.htm.

62. "Reliving a Knight's Tale," *Sentinel* (Stoke), August 7, 2004; "Who Was Sir Gawain?" *Sunday Telegraph* (London), December 10, 2000; "Into the Chasm of Death," *Sunday Telegraph* (London), December 10, 2000; "Great Escapes," *Independent* (London), May 11, 2003.

63. Day's analysis seems to conflate the two locations (xx), a pattern followed by Randall (488). On the confusion of the two locations, see further Kaske 113–14. Thor's Cave is actually much larger and higher than the more easily accessible Wetton Mill cave, now adjacent to a tea and ice cream shop.

64. In a less formal presentation, Twomey has further argued that Wetton Mill "fits the poet's description of the place somewhat better" than Lud's Church, noting that "like the Green Chapel, it lies above a stream, projecting above the surrounding terrain (2171–74), it is open at both ends and overgrown on top, and it has openings on two sides (2180–84)" ("Travels with Sir Gawain," www.ithaca.edu/faculty/twomey/travels/SGGK_tour_GreenChapel.htm).

65. Elliott recognizes the "supernatural, if not funerary," associations of the chapel but is careful to distance these impressions from the language by which the chapel is described: "it is important to remember that both the word 'ber3' (2172) and the word 'lawe' (2175) are normally used in Middle English toponymy to denote simply a hill" ("Landscape and Geography" 113). "Both words," he argues, "must be regarded as largely bereft of whatever funerary associations they may have carried in Old English" (113). The *OED* shows *lawe* attested during the thirteenth through fifteenth centuries with the meaning "hill, esp. one more or less round or conical." *Lawe* derives from the Old English *hlaw*, which could mean "arch" or "burial mound" (*OED*, "low"). During the Old English period as well as Middle English, *beorg*, later *ber3* had the sense of "hill." The associations with death and burial, however, were not entirely lost. The *OED* entry for *barrow*, which derives from *beorg*, gives the meaning, "a mound of earth or stones erected in early times over a grave; a grave-mound, a tumulus," as active through the Middle English period and as late as the twentieth century. Tolkien's "barrow-wihts," for instance, suggest this darker sense.

66. Both of these features are noted by Camargo.

67. As Elliott observes, "The turreted, pinnacled, and chimneyed elegance of Bertilak's castle is a brilliant anticipation of what was to happen when the solid medieval stronghold of the past gave way to the castellated mansions of the fifteenth century" (*Gawain Country* 53).

68. See chap. 5, p. 165.

69. *Wal/wæl(e)*, meaning "death" or "slaughter," is attested as late as the early thirteenth century (*OED*, s.v. *wal*), well past the Norman Conquest, but is long obsolete by the writing of *Sir Gawain and the Green Knight*.

70. Thanks to Michael Leslie for pointing out the existence of modern-day counterparts.

Afterword

1. Warwick Rodwell's comments testify, "Rivenhall, Deerhurst, Repton, and Hadstock all have living churches, and the extent to which their sites and fabrics can be disturbed in pursuit of academic knowledge must, perforce, be limited" (156).

2. Many thanks to Mary Wright, a lifelong member of St. Peter's Church, for sharing with me her valuable perspectives regarding its history.

3. Information on the park can be found on-line at www.stedmundsbury .gov.uk/sebc/play/weststow-asv.cfm.

4. These details are based on exhibits during my visit to West Stow in June 2006.

5. All reconstructed houses now have fire extinguishers placed inconspicuously inside, another way that modern needs have led to departure from "authenticity."

6. Information on Bede's World is available on-line at www.bedesworld.co .uk/bedesworld-farm.php. Detailed information on the building projects in particular are available at www.bedesworld.co.uk/academic-buildings.php. Personal observations here are based on a visit in June 2006.

BIBLIOGRAPHY

Adams, Annmarie, and Sally McMurry. "Exploring Everyday Landscapes: Introduction." *Perspectives in Vernacular Architecture* 7 (1997): xvii–xxx.

Addyman, P. V. "The Anglo-Saxon House: A New Review." *Anglo-Saxon England* 1 (1972): 273–307.

Ahrens, Claus. "An English Origin for Norwegian Stave Churches?" *Medieval Life* 4 (1996): 3–7.

Alexander, Jennifer S. "The Introduction and Use of Masons' Marks in Romanesque Buildings in England." *Medieval Archaeology* 51 (2007): 63–81.

Algeo, John, and Thomas Pyles. *Origins and Development of the English Language.* 5th ed. Boston: Wadsworth, 2004.

Allen, Michael J. B., and Daniel G. Calder, trans. *Sources and Analogues of Old English Poetry: The Major Latin Texts in Translation.* Cambridge: D. S. Brewer, 1976.

———. *Sources and Analogues of Old English Poetry II: The Major Germanic and Celtic Texts in Translation.* Cambridge: D. S. Brewer, 1983.

Allen, Rosamund, trans. *Brut.* London: Dent, 1992.

———. "Counting Time and Time for Recounting: Narrative Sections: Laȝamon's *Brut.*" *Orality and Literacy in Early Middle English.* ScriptOralia 83. Ed. Herbert Pilch. Tübingen: Gunter Narr Verlag, 1996. 71–92.

———, ed. *King Horn.* New York: Garland Medieval Texts, 1984.

American Heritage Dictionary. 4th ed. Boston: Houghton Mifflin, 2000.

Amodio, Mark C. "Affective Criticism, Oral Poetics, and Beowulf's Fight with the Dragon." *Oral Tradition* 10 (1995): 54–90.

———. "Old English Oral-Formulaic Tradition and Middle-English Verse." *De Gustibus: Essays for Alain Renoir.* Ed. John Miles Foley. New York: Garland, 1992. 1–20.

———. "Tradition, Modernity, and the Emergence of the Self in *Sir Gawain and the Green Knight.*" *Assays: Critical Approaches to Medieval and Renaissance Texts* 8 (1995): 47–68.

———. "Tradition, Performance, and Poetics in Early Middle English Poetry." *Oral Tradition* 15 (2000): 191–214.

———. *Writing the Oral Tradition: Oral Poetics and Literate Culture in Medieval England.* Notre Dame: University of Notre Dame Press, 2004.

Amodio, Mark C., and Katherine O'Brien O'Keeffe, eds. *Unlocking the Wordhord: Anglo-Saxon Studies in Memory of Edward B. Irving, Jr.* Toronto: University of Toronto Press, 2003.

Anderson, Carolyn. "*Gæst,* Gender and Kin in *Beowulf*: Consumption of Boundaries." *Heroic Age* 5 (2001). Online publication.

Anderson, Earl R. *Folk Taxonomies in Early English.* Madison: Rosemont Publishing, 2003.

———. "The Uncarpentered World of Old English Poetry." *Anglo-Saxon England* 20 (1991): 65–80.

Andres, James Mortimer. "Negational Architecture in Old English Poetry." Ph.D. dissertation, University of Pennsylvania, 2001.

Archer, Lucy. *Architecture in Britain and Ireland: 600–1500.* Photographs by Edwin Smith. London: Harvill Press, 1999.

Arnold, C. J. *An Archaeology of the Early Anglo-Saxon Kingdoms.* New ed. London: Routledge, 1997. Orig. 1988.

Arnovick, Leslie K. *Written Reliquaries: The Resonance of Orality in Medieval English Texts.* Pragmatics and Beyond 153. Amsterdam and Philadelphia: John Benjamins Co., 2006.

Attenborough, F. L. , ed. and trans. *The Laws of the Earliest English Kings.* Cambridge: Cambridge University Press, 1922.

Babcock-Abrahams, Barbara. "The Story in the Story: Metanarration in Folk Narrative." *Studia Fennica* 20 (1976): 177–84.

Bachelard, Gaston. *The Poetics of Space.* Trans. Maria Jolas. Boston: Beacon Press, 1964.

Bailey, Richard N. *Viking Age Sculpture in Northern England.* London: Collins, 1980.

Barney, Stephen A. *Word-Hoard: An Introduction to Old English Vocabulary.* 2nd ed. Yale Language Series. New Haven: Yale University Press, 1985. Orig. 1977.

Barrett, Robert W. *Against All England: Regional Identity and Cheshire Writing, 1195–1656.* Notre Dame: University of Notre Dame Press, 2009.

Barron, W. R., and S. C. Weinberg, ed. and trans. *Laȝamon's Arthur.* Harlow, Essex: Longman Group, 1989.

Bately, Janet. "The Literary Prose of King Alfred's Reign: Translation or Transformation." *Old English Prose: Basic Readings.* Ed. Paul Szarmach. New York: SUNY Press, 2000. 3–27.

Battles, Paul. "Of Graves, Caves, and Subterranean Dwellings: *Eorðscræf* and *Eorð-sele* in the *Wife's Lament.*" *Philological Quarterly* 73 (1994): 267–86.

Baudrillard, Jean, and Jean Nouvel. *The Singular Objects of Architecture.* Trans. Robert Bononno. Minneapolis: University of Minnesota Press, 2006.

Baugh, Albert C. "Improvisation in the Middle English Romance." *Proceedings of the American Philosophical Society* 103 (1959): 418–54.

Bauman, Richard. *Verbal Art as Performance*. Prospect Heights, IL: Waveland Press, 1977.

Belanoff, Patricia. "Women's Songs, Women's Language: *Wulf and Eadwacer* and the *Wife's Lament*." *New Readings on Women in Old English Literature*. Ed. Helen Damico and Alexandra Hennessey Olsen. Bloomington: Indiana University Press, 1990. 193–203.

Ben-Amos, Dan. "The Concepts of Genre in Folklore." *Studia Fennica, Review of Finnish Linguistics and Ethnology* 20 (1976): 30–43.

Benson, Larry. *Art and Tradition in* Sir Gawain and the Green Knight. New Brunswick: Rutgers University Press, 1965.

Bessinger, J. B. *A Short Dictionary of Anglo-Saxon Poetry*. Toronto: University of Toronto Press, 1960.

Bessinger, Jess B., and Philip H. Smith. *A Concordance to the Anglo-Saxon Poetic Records*. Ithaca: Cornell University Press, 1978.

Bhattacharya, Prodosh. "An Analogue, and Probable Source, for a Metaphor in Alfred's Preface to the Old English Translation of Augustine's Soliloquies." *Notes and Queries* 45 (1998): 161–63.

Biggam, Carole P. "*Grund* to *Hrof*: Aspects of the Old English Semantics of Building and Architecture." *Lexicology, Semantics, and Lexicography: Selected Papers from the Fourth G. L. Brook Symposium, Manchester, August 1998*. Ed. Julie Coleman and Christian J. Kay. Amsterdam/Philadelphia: John Benjamins, 2000.

Blake, N. F., ed. *The Phoenix*. Old and Middle English Texts. Manchester: Manchester University Press, 1964.

———. "Rhythmical Alliteration." *Modern Philology*. 67 (1969): 118–24.

Bliss, A. J., ed. *Sir Orfeo*. 2nd ed. Oxford: Clarendon Press, 1966.

Boenig, Robert. *Saint and Hero:* Andreas *and Medieval Doctrine*. Lewisburg, PA: Bucknell University Press, 1991.

———, trans. *The Acts of Andrew in the Country of the Cannibals: Translations from the Greek, Latin, and Old English*. Garland Library of Medieval Literature, 70, Series B. New York: Garland, 1991.

Bommesberger, Alfred. "Grendel Enters Heorot." *Notes and Queries* 54.2 (2007): 119–20.

Bosley, Keith. "Introduction." *Kalevala: An Epic Poem after Oral Tradition by Elias Lönnrot*. Oxford: Oxford University Press, 1989. xiii–liv.

Bosworth, Joseph. *An Anglo-Saxon Dictionary*. Ed. and enlarged by T. Northcote Toller. London: Oxford University Press, 1988. Suppl. 1921. Addenda 1972. Online ed. http://beowulf.engl.uky.edu/~kiernan/BT/Bosworth-Toller.htm.

Bowden, Betsy. *Chaucer Aloud: The Varieties of Textual Interpretation*. Philadelphia: University of Pennsylvania Press, 1987.

Bradbury, Nancy Mason. "Literacy, Orality, and the Poetics of Middle English Romance." *Oral Poetics in Middle English Literature*. Ed. Mark C. Amodio. New York: Garland Publishing, 1994. 39–69.

———. *Writing Aloud: Storytelling in Late Medieval England.* Urbana: University of Illinois Press, 1998.

Bradley, S. A. J., trans. *Anglo-Saxon Poetry.* London: Dent, 1982.

Braverman, Richard. "The Narrative Architecture of Rasselas." *The Age of Johnson: A Scholarly Annual* 3 (1990): 91–111.

Bredehoft, Thomas A. *Authors, Audiences, and Old English Verse.* Toronto: University of Toronto Press, 2009.

Bronner, Simon J. "Building Tradition: Control and Authority in Vernacular Architecture." *Vernacular Architecture in the Twenty-first Century: Theory, Education, and Practice.* Ed. Lindsay Asquith and Marcel Vellinga. London: Taylor and Francis, 2006. 23–45.

Brook, G. L., and R. F. Leslie, ed. *Laȝamon: Brut.* 2 vols. Edited from British Museum MS. Cotton Caligula A.ix and British Museum MS. Cotton Otho c. xiii. Oxford: Oxford University Press, 1963.

Brooks, Kenneth R., ed. *Andreas and the Fates of the Apostles.* Oxford: Clarendon Press, 1961.

Brown, Gerard Baldwin. *The Arts in Early England.* London: J. Murray, 1926. Orig. 1903.

Brown, Marjorie A. "The Feast Hall in Anglo Saxon Society." *Food and Eating in Medieval Europe.* Ed. Martha Carlin and Joel T. Rosenthal. London: Hambledon, 1998.

Brown, Michael F. *Who Owns Native Culture?* Cambridge, MA: Harvard University Press, 2003.

Brown, R. Allen. "The Architecture." *The Bayeux Tapestry.* Ed. Frank Stenton. London: Phaidon, 1965.

———. "William of Malmesbury as an Architectural Historian." *Mélanges d'archéologie et d'histoire médiévales en l'honneur du Doyen Michel de Boüard.* Paris: Librairie Droz, 1982. 9–16.

Burke, John. *Roman England.* New York: W. W. Norton, 1983.

Burlin, Robert B. "Gnomic Indirection in *Beowulf.*" *Anglo-Saxon Poetry: Essays in Appreciation for John C. McGalliard.* Ed. Lewis E. Nicholson and Dolores Warwick Frese. Notre Dame: University of Notre Dame Press, 1975. 41–49.

———. *The Old English Advent: A Typological Commentary.* New Haven: Yale University Press, 1968.

Buxton, Richard. "Similes and Other Likenesses." *The Cambridge Companion to Homer.* Ed. Robert Fowler. Cambridge: Cambridge University Press, 2004. 139–55.

Byers, John R. "On the Decorating of Heorot." *PMLA* 80 (1965): 299–300.

Bynum, David. *The Dæmon in the Wood: A Study of Oral Narrative Patterns.* Cambridge, MA: Harvard University Press, 1978.

Cable, Thomas. *The English Alliterative Tradition.* Philadelphia: University of Pennsylvania Press, 1991.

Camargo, Martin. "Oral Traditional Structure in *Sir Gawain and the Green Knight.*" *Comparative Research on Oral Traditions: A Memorial for Milman Parry.* Ed. John Miles Foley. Columbus, OH: Slavica, 1987. 121–37.

Cameron, Malcolm. *Anglo-Saxon Medicine.* Cambridge: Cambridge University Press, 1993.

Campbell, Jackson J., ed. *The Advent Lyrics of the Exeter Book.* Princeton: Princeton University Press, 1959.

Campbell, James, ed. *Ecclesiastical History of the English People.* By Bede. New York: Washington Square Press, 1968.

Carnicelli, T. A., ed. *King Alfred's Version of St. Augustine's Soliloquies.* Cambridge: Cambridge University Press, 1969.

Carruthers, Mary. *The Book of Memory: A Study of Memory in Medieval Culture.* Cambridge: Cambridge University Press, 190.

———. *Craft of Thought: Meditation, Rhetoric, and the Making of Images, 400–1200.* New York: Garland, 1998.

Carruthers, Mary, and Jan M. Ziolkowski, eds. *The Medieval Craft of Memory: An Anthology of Texts and Pictures.* Philadelphia: University of Pennsylvania Press, 2002.

Carter, H. Malcolm. *The Fort of Othona and the Chapel of St. Peter-on-the Wall, Bradwell-on-Sea, Essex.* Hunstanton, Norfolk: St. Peter's Chapel Committee and Witley Press, 1966.

Carter, Thomas, and Elizabeth Collins Cromley. *Invitation to Vernacular Architecture: A Guide to the Study of Ordinary Buildings and Landscapes.* Vernacular Architecture Studies. Knoxville: University of Tennessee Press, 2005.

Carter, Thomas, and Bernard L. Herman. "Introduction." *Perspectives in Vernacular Architecture* 3 (1989): 1–6.

———. "Introduction: Toward a New Architectural History." *Perspectives in Vernacular Architecture* 4 (1991): 1–6.

Carver, M. O. H. "Contemporary Artifacts Illustrated in Late Saxon Manuscripts." *Archaeologia* 108 (1986): 117–46.

———. "Exploring, Explaining, Imagining: Anglo-Saxon Archaeology 1998." *The Archaeology of Anglo-Saxon England.* Ed. Catherine Karkov. New York: Garland, 1999. 25–52.

Chambers Murray Latin-English Dictionary. Ed. William Smith and John Lockwood. Edinburgh: Chambers, 1994.

Chickering, Howell D. "The Literary Magic of 'Wið Færstice.'" *Viator* 2 (1971): 83–104.

Christie, Håkon, Olaf Olsen, Hon. F. S. A., and H. M. Taylor, F. S. A. "The Wooden Church of St. Andrew at Greensted, Essex." *Antiquaries Journal* 59 (1979): 92–112.

Clark, Evelyn. *Cornish Fogous.* London: Methuen, 1961.

Clarke, Catherine A. M. *Literary Landscapes and the Idea of England, 700–1400.* Cambridge: D. S. Brewer, 2006.

Clemoes, Peter. "Style as Criterion for Dating the Composition of *Beowulf*." *The Dating of* Beowulf. Ed. C. Chase. Toronto: University of Toronto Press, 1981. 173–85.

Clifford, James. "Introduction: Partial Truths." *Writing Culture: The Poetics and Politics of Ethnography*. Ed. James Clifford and George E. Marcus. Berkeley: University of California Press, 1986. 1–26.

Clough, Andrea. "The French Element in *Sir Gawain and the Green Knight*." *Neu - philologische Mitteilungen* 86 (1985): 187–96.

Cockcroft, Robert. "Castle Hautdesert: Patchwork or Portrait?" *Neophilologus* 62 (1978): 459–77.

Colgrave, Bertram, and R. A. B. Mynors, eds. *Bede's Ecclesiastical History*. Oxford Medieval Texts. Oxford: Clarendon Press, 1969.

Conybeare, J. J., with W. D. Conybeare, ed. *Illustrations of Anglo-Saxon Poetry*. London: Harding and Leopard, 1826.

Cook, Albert, ed. *The Christ of Cynewulf: A Poem in Three Parts*. New York: AMS, 1973. Orig. 1900.

Cowling, David. *Building the Text: Architecture as Metaphor in Late Medieval and Early Modern France*. Oxford: Clarendon Press, 1998.

Cramp, Rosemary. "The Changing Image, Divine and Human, in Anglo-Saxon Art." *Aedificaia Nova: Studies in Honor of Rosemary Cramp*. Eds. Catherine E. Karkov and Helen Damico. Kalamazoo: Medieval Institute Publications, Western Michigan University, 2008. 3–32.

———. "The Hall in *Beowulf* and Archaeology." *Heroic Poetry in the Anglo-Saxon Period: Studies in Honor of Jess B. Bessinger*. Ed. Helen Damico and John Leyerle. Kalamazoo, MI: Medieval Institute Publications, 1993. 331–46.

———. "Not Why but How: The Contribution of Archaeological Evidence to the Understanding of Anglo-Saxon England." *The Preservation and Transmission of Anglo-Saxon Culture*. Ed. Paul E. Szarmach and Joel T. Rosenthal. Kalamazoo, MI: Medieval Institute Publications, 1997. 271–84.

Crane, Susan. *Insular Romance: Politics, Faith, and Culture in Anglo-Norman and Middle English Literature*. Berkeley: University of California Press, 1986.

Creed, Robert P. "How the *Beowulf* Poet Composed His Poem." *Oral Tradition* 18 (2003): 214–15.

———. "The Remaking of *Beowulf*." *Oral Tradition in Literature*. Ed. John Miles Foley. Columbia: University of Missouri Press, 1986. 136–46.

Davis, R. H. C., and Marjorie Chibnall, ed. and trans. *The* Gesta Gvillelmi *of William of Poitiers*. Oxford: Clarendon Press, 1998.

Day, Mabel. "Introduction." *Sir Gawain and the Green Knight*. Ed. Israel Gollancz. Early English Text Society. London: Oxford University Press, 1940.

de la Bédoyère, Guy. *Architecture in Roman Britain*. Buckinghamshire: Shire, 2000.

———. *The Buildings of Roman Britain*. London: B. T. Batsford, 1991.

Desmond, Marilynn. "The Voice of Exile: Feminist Literary History and the Anonymous Anglo-Saxon Elegy." *Critical Inquiry* 16 (1990): 572–90.

Diaz Vera, Javier E. *The Semantic Architecture of the Old English Verbal Lexicon: A Historical-Lexicographical Proposal*. Amsterdam: Rodopi, 2002.

Doane, A. N. "The Ethnography of Scribal Writing and Anglo-Saxon Poetry: Scribe as Performer." *Oral Tradition* 9 (1994): 420–39.

———. "Heathen Form and Christian Function in *The Wife's Lament*." *Medieval Studies* 28 (1966): 77–91.

———. "Oral Texts, Intertexts, and Intratexts: Editing Old English." *Influence and Intertextuality in Literary History*. Ed. Jay Clayton and Eric Rothstein. Madison: University of Wisconsin Press, 1991. 75–113.

———, ed. *The Saxon Genesis: An Edition of the West Saxon* Genesis B *and the Old Saxon Vatican* Genesis. Madison: University of Wisconsin Press, 1991.

Dobbie, Elliott Van Kirk, ed. *The Anglo-Saxon Minor Poems*. Anglo-Saxon Poetic Records, vol. 6. New York: Columbia University Press, 1942.

Dodwell, C. R. *Anglo-Saxon Art: A New Perspective*. Ithaca: Cornell University Press, 1982.

Donahue, Dennis. "Laȝamon's Ambivalence." *Speculum* 65 (1990): 537–63.

———. *Lawman's* Brut, *An Early Arthurian Poem: A Study of Middle English Formulaic Composition*. Lewiston: Edwin Mellen Press, 1991.

———. "Lawman's Formulaic Themes and the Characterization of King Arthur in the *Brut*." *Orality and Literacy in Early Middle English*. ScriptOralia 83. Ed. Herbert Pilch. Tübingen: Gunter Narr Verlag, 1996. 93–112.

Dronke, Peter. "The Return of Eurydice." *Classica et Mediaevalia* 23 (1962): 198–215.

Drout, Michael. *How Tradition Works: A Meme-Based Cultural Poetics of the Anglo-Saxon Tenth Century*. Tempe: Arizona Center for Medieval and Renaissance Studies, 2006.

Dunleavy, Gareth. "A De Excidio Tradition in the Old English Ruin?" *Philological Quarterly* 38 (1959): 112–118.

Dunning, T. P., and A. J. Bliss, eds. *The Wanderer*. New York: Appleton-Century-Crofts, 1969.

Earl, James W. "Maxims I, Part I." *Neophilologus* 67 (1983): 277–83.

———. *Thinking about* Beowulf. Stanford: Stanford University Press, 1995.

Earle, John. "An Ancient Saxon Poem of a City in Ruins, Supposed to Be Bath." *Proceedings of the Bath Natural History and Antiquities Field Club* 2 (1870–73): 259–70.

———. "The Ruined City." *Academy* 26 (1884): 29.

Eaton, Tim. "Old Ruins, New World." *British Archaeology* 60 (2001). Online.

Eisenstein, Elizabeth L. *The Printing Press as an Agent of Change: Communications and Cultural Transformations in Early-Modern Europe*. 2 vols. Cambridge: Cambridge University Press, 1997.

Eliason, Norman E. "Burning of Heorot." *Speculum* 55 (1980): 73–83.

———. "On 'Wulf and Eadwacer': A Solution to the Critics' Riddle." *Neophilologus* 60 (1976): 130–37.

Elliott, Ralph W. *The Gawain Country.* Leeds Texts and Monographs, n.s., 8. Leeds: University of Leeds School of English, 1984.

———. "Landscape and Geography." *A Companion to the Gawain-Poet.* Woodbridge: Boydell and Brewer, 1997. 105–17.

———. "Sir Gawain in Staffordshire: A Detective Essay in Literary Geography." (London) *Times,* May 21, 1958, 12.

Evans, Angela C. *The Sutton Hoo Ship Burial.* London: Published for the Trustees of the British Museum by British Museum Publications, 1986.

Excell, Stanley P. *Sompting Parish Church: A Brief Guide.* Sompting: Friends of Sompting Church, 1979.

Falk, Oren. "The Son of Orfeo: Kingship and Compromise in a Middle English Romance." *Journal of Medieval and Early Modern Studies* 30 (2000): 247–74.

Fell, Christine. *Women in Anglo-Saxon England and the Impact of 1066.* Bloomington: Indiana University Press, 1984.

Fernie, Eric. *The Architecture of Norman England.* Oxford: Oxford University Press, 2000.

———. *Architecture of the Anglo-Saxons.* New York: Holmes and Meier, 1983.

Field, Rosalind. "The Anglo-Norman Background to Alliterative Romance." *Middle English Alliterative Poetry and Its Literary Background.* Ed. David Lawton. Cambridge: D. S. Brewer, 1982. 54–69.

Fischer, W. "Wanderer v. 25 and v. 6–7." *Anglia* 59 (1935): 299–302.

Fleming, John, Hugh Honour, and Nikolaus Pevsner. *Dictionary of Architecture.* 4th ed. London: Penguin, 1991.

Foley, John Miles. "Genre(s) in the Making: Diction, Audience, and Text in the Old English *Seafarer.*" *Poetics Today* 4 (1983): 683–706.

———. *Homer's Traditional Art.* University Park: Pennsylvania State University Press, 1999.

———. "How Genres Leak in Traditional Verse." *Unlocking the Wordhord: Anglo-Saxon Studies in Memory of Edward B. Irving, Jr.* Ed. Mark C. Amodio and Katherine O'Brien O'Keeffe. Toronto: University of Toronto Press, 2003. 76–108.

———. *How to Read an Oral Poem.* Urbana: University of Illinois Press, 2002.

———. *Immanent Art: From Structure to Meaning in Traditional Oral Epic.* Bloomington: Indiana University Press, 1991.

———. "The Implications of Oral Tradition." *Oral Tradition in the Middle Ages.* Ed. W. F. H. Nicolaisen. Binghamton, NY: Medieval and Renaissance Texts and Studies, 1995. 31–58.

———. "Literary Art and Oral Tradition in Old English and Serbian Poetry." *Anglo-Saxon England* 12 (1983): 183–214.

———. *Oral-Formulaic Theory and Research: An Introduction and Annotated Bibliography.* New York: Garland, 1985.

———, ed. "Oral Literature Today." *HarperCollins World Reader.* Ed. Mary Ann Caws and Christopher Prendergast. New York: HarperCollins, 1994. 2590–2655.

————. "Performance of Homeric Epic." *Didaskalia* 3.3 (1996). http://didaskalia .open.ac.uk/journal.shtml.

————. *The Singer of Tales in Performance.* Bloomington: Indiana University Press, 1995.

————, ed. *Teaching Oral Traditions.* New York: Modern Language Association, 1998.

————. *The Theory of Oral Composition: History and Methodology.* Bloomington: Indiana University Press, 1988.

————. *Traditional Oral Epic: The* Odyssey, Beowulf, *and the Serbo-Croatian Return Song.* Berkeley: University of California Press, 1990.

————, ed. and trans. *The Wedding of Mustajbey's Son Bećirbey.* As performed by Halil Bajgorić. Folklore Fellows' Communications, vol. 283. Helsinki: Academia Scientiarum Fennica, 2004.

Fowler, Peter, and Susan Mills. "Bede's World: A Late-Twentieth-Century Creation of a Medieval Landscape." *The Reconstructed Past.* Ed. John Jameson. Walnut Creek, CA: Altamira Press, 2004. 103–26.

Frankis, P. J. "The Thematic Significance of *enta geweorc* and Related Imagery in *The Wanderer.*" *Anglo-Saxon England* 2 (1973): 253–69.

Frantzen, Allen J. *Desire for Origins: New Language, Old English, and Teaching the Tradition.* New Brunswick: Rutgers University Press, 1990.

French, W. H. "*The Wanderer* 98: 'Wyrmlicum Fah.'" *Modern Language Notes* 8 (1952): 526–29.

Fry, Donald K. "The Cliff of Death in Old English Poetry." *Comparative Research on Oral Traditions: A Memorial for Milman Parry.* Ed. John Miles Foley. Columbus, OH: Slavica, 1985. 213–34.

————. "Wulf and Eadwacer: A Wen Charm." *Chaucer Review* 5 (1971): 247–63.

Fulk, R. D., Robert E. Bjork, and John D. Niles, eds. *Klaeber's* Beowulf. 4th ed. Toronto: University of Toronto Press, 2008.

Garner, Lori Ann. "Anglo-Saxon Charms in Performance." *Oral Tradition* 19 (2004): 20–42.

————. "The Art of Translation in the Old English *Judith.*" *Studia Neophilologica* 73 (2001): 171–83.

————. "Contexts of Interpretation in the Burdens of Middle English Carols." *Neophilologus* 84 (2000): 467–82.

————. "The Old English *Andreas* and the Mermedonian Cityscape." *Essays in Medieval Studies* 24 (2007): 53–63.

————. "Oral Tradition and Genre in Old and Middle English Poetry." Ph.D. dissertation, University of Missouri, 2000.

————. "The Role of Proverbs in Middle English Narrative." *New Directions in Oral Theory.* Ed. Mark C. Amodio. Medieval and Renaissance Texts and Studies. Tempe: Arizona Center for Medieval and Renaissance Studies, 2005. 255–77.

Gem, Richard. "Bishop Wulfstan II and the Romanesque Cathedral Church of Worcester." *Medieval Art and Architecture at Worcester Cathedral.* Ed. G. Popper.

London: British Archaeological Association Conference Transactions, 1978. 15–37.

———. "Towards an Iconography of Anglo-Saxon Architecture." *Journal of the Warburg and Courtauld Institutes* 46 (1983): 1–18.

Gittos, Helen. "Architecture and Liturgy in England, c. 1000: Problems and Possibilities." *The White Mantle of Churches: Architecture, Liturgy, and Art Around the Millennium.* Ed. Nigel Hiscock. International Medieval Research, Art History, vol. 10. Turnhout, Belgium: Brepols, 2003. 91–106.

Glassie, Henry. *Vernacular Architecture.* Bloomington: University of Indiana Press, 2000.

Godden, Malcolm, ed. *Ælfric's Catholic Homilies.* Second Series. Oxford: Early English Text Society, 1979.

Gombrich, E. H. *Art and Illusion: A Study in the Psychology of Pictorial Representation.* Washington, DC: Pantheon Books, 1960.

Gordon, R. K., trans. *Anglo-Saxon Poetry.* New York: Dutton, 1926.

Gradon, P. O. E., ed. *Cynewulf's Elene.* New York: Appleton-Century-Crofts, 1966.

Green, Charles. *Sutton Hoo: The Excavation of a Royal Ship-Burial.* London: Merlin Press, 1968.

Greenfield, Stanley B. "The Formulaic Expression of the Theme of 'Exile' in Anglo-Saxon Poetry." *Speculum* 30 (1955): 200–206.

———. "'Gifstol' and Goldhoard in *Beowulf.*" *Old English Studies in Honor of John C. Pope.* Ed. Robert Burlin and Edward Irving. Toronto: University of Toronto Press, 107–17.

———. "Of Locks and Keys—Line 19 of the O. E. *Christ.*" *Modern Language Notes* 67 (1952): 238–40.

———. "*Min, Sylf,* and Dramatic Voices in *The Seafarer.*" *Journal of English and Germanic Philology* 68 (1969): 212–20.

———. "The Old English Elegies." *Hero and Exile: The Art of Old English Poetry.* Ed. George H. Brown. London: Hambledon Press, 1989. 93–124. Rpt. from *Continuations and Beginnings: Studies in Old English Literature.* Ed. E. G. Stanley. London: Nelson, 1966.

———. "The *Wanderer*: A Reconsideration of Theme and Structure." *Hero and Exile: The Art of Old English Poetry.* Ed. George H. Brown. London: Hambledon Press, 1989. 133–48.

Greensted Church Guidebook. n.p., n.d.

Gretlund, Jan Nordby. "Architexture in Short Stories by Flannery O'Connor and Eudora Welty." *The Art of Brevity.* Ed. P. Winther et al. Columbia: University of South Carolina Press, 2004. 151–61.

Grundy, Lynne, and Jane Roberts. "Shapes in the Landscape: Some Words." *Names, Places, and People: An Onomastic Miscellany in Memory of John McNeal Dodgson.* Ed. Alexander R. Rumble and A. D. Mills. Stamford: Paul Watkins, 1997. 96–110.

Hall, J. R. Clark. "The Building of the Temple in *Exodus*: Design for Typology." *Neophilologus* 59 (1975): 616–21.

———. *A Concise Anglo-Saxon Dictionary.* 4th ed. Toronto: University of Toronto Press, 1960.

Hall, Joseph, ed. *King Horn: A Middle-English Romance.* Oxford: Clarendon Press, 1901. Rpt. 1976.

Harbus, Antonina. "Metaphors of Authority in Alfred's Prefaces." *Neophilologus* 91 (2007): 717–27.

Harding, Christopher, Bill Hines, Richard Ireland, and Philip Rawlings. *Imprisonment in England and Wales: A Concise History.* London: Croom Helm, 1985.

Harris, Joseph, ed. *The Ballad and Oral Literature.* Cambridge, MA: Harvard University Press, 1991.

———. "*Beowulf* as Epic." *Oral Tradition* 15 (2000): 159–69.

———. "A Note on Eorðscræf/Eorðsele and Current Interpretation of *The Wife's Lament.*" *English Studies* 58 (1977): 204–8.

Harrison, Mark. *Anglo-Saxon Thegn.* London: Reed International Books, 1993.

Hart, Andrew. *Earls Barton, All Saints Church: A Brief History and Guide.* Earls Barton: All Saints Church; printed by Addison Print, Northampton, 1997.

Hayles, Katherine N. "Boundary Disputes: Homeostasis, Reflexivity, and the Foundations of Cybernetics." *Virtual Realities and Their Discontents.* Ed. Robert Markley. Baltimore: Johns Hopkins University Press, 1996.

Healey, Antonette diPaolo. *The Old English Vision of St. Paul.* Speculum Anniversary Monographs 2. Cambridge: Cambridge University Press, 1978.

Healey, Antonette diPaolo, et al., eds. *Dictionary of Old English: A to F.* CD-ROM. Toronto: Pontifical Institute of Mediaeval Studies, 2003.

Heaney, Seamus, trans. *Beowulf.* New York: W. W. Norton, 2000.

Hearn, M. F., and M. Thurlby. "Previously Undetected Wooden Ribbed Vaults in Medieval Britain." *Journal of the British Archaeological Association* 150 (1997): 48–58.

Heitz, C. "The Iconography of Architectural Form." *The Anglo-Saxon Church: Papers on History, Architecture, and Archaeology in Honour of Dr. H. M. Taylor.* Ed. L. A. S. Butler and R. K. Morris. London: Council for British Archaeology, 1986. 90–100.

Henderson, Dave. "Tradition and Heroism in the Middle English Romances." *Oral Poetics in Middle English Poetry.* Ed. Mark C. Amodio. Albert Bates Lord Studies in Oral Tradition, vol. 13. New York: Garland, 1994. 89–108.

Herben, Stephen J. "The Ruin." *Modern Language Notes* 54 (1939): 37–39.

Herron, Thomas. "Irish Den of Thieves: Souterrains (and a Crannog?) in Books V and VI of Spenser's *Faerie Queene.*" *Spenser Studies* 14 (2000): 303–17.

Herzman, Ronald B., Graham Drake, and Eve Salisbury, eds. *King Horn. Four Romances of England.* Kalamazoo, MI: Medieval Institute Publications, 1999. www.lib.rochester.edu/camelot/teams/danents.htm.

Hill, Joyce. "Confronting *Germania Latina*: Changing Responses to Old English Biblical Verse." *The Poems of MS Junius 11.* Ed. R. M. Liuzza. New York: Routledge. 1–19.

Hills, Catherine M. "*Beowulf* and Archaeology." *Beowulf Handbook*. Ed. Robert E. Bjork and John D. Niles. Lincoln: University of Nebraska Press, 1997. 291–310.

———. *Origins of the English*. London: Duckworth, 2003.

Hines, John. "*Beowulf* and Archaeology—Revisited." *Aedificaia Nova: Studies in Honor of Rosemary Cramp*. Ed. Catherine E. Karkov and Helen Damico. Kalamazoo: Medieval Institute Publications, Western Michigan University, 2008. 89–105.

Hoagland, Alison K., and Kenneth A. Breisch, eds. "Constructing Image, Identity, and Place." *Perspectives in Vernacular Architecture* 9 (2003): xiii–xvii.

Holan, Jerri. *Norwegian Wood: A Tradition of Building*. New York: Rizzoli, 1990.

Honko, Lauri, ed. *Siri Epic*. 2 vols. Perf. Gopala Naika. Helsinki: Academia Scientiarum Fennica, 1998.

Hope-Taylor, Brian. *Yeavering: an Anglo-British Centre of Early Northumbria*. London: HMSO, 1977.

Hornblower, Simon, and Antony Spawforth, eds. *The Oxford Classical Dictionary*. 3rd ed. rev. Oxford: Oxford University Press, 2003.

Horner, Shari. "En/Closed Subjects: *The Wife's Lament* and the Culture of Early Female Monasticism." *Old English Literature: Critical Essays*. Ed. R. M. Liuzza. New Haven: Yale University Press, 2002. 381–91.

Hough, Carol. "The Riddle of the Wife's Lament, Line 34b." *ANQ* 16 (2003): 5–8.

Howe, Nicholas. "From Bede's World to 'Bede's World.' " *Reading Medieval Culture*. Ed. Robert M. Stein and Sandra Pierson Prior. Notre Dame: University of Notre Dame Press, 2005. 21–44.

———. "The Landscape of Anglo-Saxon England: Inherited, Invented, Imagined." *Inventing Medieval Landscapes: Senses of Place in Western Europe*. Ed. John Howe and Michael Wolfe. Gainesville: University Press of Florida, 2002. 91–112.

———. *Migration and Mythmaking in Anglo-Saxon England*. New Haven: Yale University Press, 1989.

———. *The Old English Catalogue Poems*. Angelistica 23. Copenhagen: Rosekilde and Bagger, 1985.

———. "Rome: Capital of Anglo-Saxon England." *Journal of Medieval and Early Modern Studies* 34 (2004): 147–72.

Huisman, Johannes A. "Generative Classification in Medieval Literature." *Theories of Literary Genre*. Ed. Joseph P. Strelka. University Park: Pennsylvania State University Press, 1978. 123–49.

Hume, Kathryn. "The Concept of the Hall in Old English Poetry." *Anglo-Saxon England* 3 (1974): 63–74.

———. "The 'Ruin Motif' in Old English Poetry." *Anglia: Zeitschrift für Englische Philologie* 94 (1976): 339–60.

Hunter, Michael. "Germanic and Roman Antiquity and the Sense of the Past in Anglo-Saxon England." *Anglo-Saxon England* 3 (1974): 29–50.

Huppé, B. F. "The Wanderer: Theme and Structure." *Journal of English and Germanic Philology* 42 (1943): 516–38.

Hurt, James. "The Texts of *King Horn*." *Journal of the Folklore Institute* 7 (1970): 47–59.

Irvine, Martin. "Medieval Textuality and the Archaeology of Textual Culture." *Speaking Two Languages: Traditional Disciplines and Contemporary Theory in Medieval Studies*. Ed. Allen Frantzen. Albany: SUNY Press, 1991. 181–210.

Irving, Edward Burroughs, Jr. "Heroic Experience in the Old English Riddles." *Old English Shorter Poems: Basic Readings*. Ed. Katherine O'Brien O'Keeffe. New York: Garland, 1994. 199–212.

———, ed. *The Old English Exodus*. New Haven: Yale University Press, 1953.

———. *A Reading of* Beowulf. New Haven: Yale University Press, 1968.

———. *Rereading* Beowulf. Philadelphia: University of Pennsylvania Press, 1992.

Iser, Wolfgang. *The Implied Reader: Patterns of Communication in Prose Fiction from Bunyan to Beckett*. Baltimore: Johns Hopkins University Press, 1978.

———. "Indeterminacy and the Reader's Response in Prose Fiction." *Aspects of Narrative*. Ed. J. Hillis Miller. New York: Columbia University Press, 1971. 1–45.

Jack, George, ed. *Beowulf: A Student Edition*. Oxford: Clarendon, 1994.

Jónsson, Guðni, ed. *Völsunga saga*. Reykjavik: Íslendingasagnaútgáfan, 1981.

Kantrowitz, Joanne Spencer. "The Anglo-Saxon 'Phoenix' and Tradition." *Philological Quarterly* 43 (1964): 1–13.

Karkov, Catherine, ed. *The Archaeology of Anglo-Saxon England*. New York: Garland, 1999.

———. "The Decoration of Early Wooden Architecture in Ireland and Northumbria." *Studies in Insular Art and Archaeology*. American Early Medieval Studies 1. Ed. Catherine Karkov and Robert Farrell. Oxford, OH: Miami University School of Fine Arts, 1991. 27–48.

Kaske, R. E. "Gawain's Green Chapel and the Cave at Wetton Mill." *Medieval Literature and Folklore Studies: Essays in Honor of Francis Lee Utley*. Ed. Jerome Mandel and Bruce A. Rosenberg. New Brunswick: Rutgers University Press, 1970. 111–22.

Keenan, Hugh T. "The Ruin as Babylon." *Tennessee Studies in Literature* 11 (1966): 109–17.

Kelber, Werner. *The Oral and the Written Gospel*. Voices in Performance and Text. Bloomington: Indiana University Press, 1997. Orig. Fortress Press, 1983.

Kendrick, Laura. "Chaucer's *House of Fame* and the French *Palais de Justice*." *Studies in the Age of Chaucer: The Yearbook of the New Chaucer Society* 6 (1984): 121–33.

Kendrick, T. D. *History of the Vikings*. Mineola, NY: Dover, 2004.

Kennedy, C. W. *Old English Elegies.* Princeton: Princeton University Press, 1936.

Ker, N. R., ed. *The Old English Version of the Heptateuch.* London: EETS 160. Rpt. with additions by N. R. Ker 1969. Orig. 1922.

Kerr, Mary, and Nigel Kerr. *Anglo-Saxon Architecture.* Aylesbury, U.K.: Shire, 1983.

———. *A Guide to Anglo-Saxon Sites.* London: Granada, 1982.

Keynes, S., and M. Lapidge, trans. *Asser's* Life of King Alfred *and Other Contemporary Sources.* London: Penguin, 1983.

Klaeber, F., ed. *Beowulf and the Fight at Finnsburg.* 1st ed. Boston: D. C. Heath and Co., 1922.

Klein, Stacy S. "Gender and the Nature of Exile in Old English Elegies." *A Place to Believe In: Locating Medieval Landscapes.* Ed. Clare A. Lees and Gillian R. Overing. University Park: Pennsylvania State University Press, 2006. 113–31.

Kleinschmidt, Harald. "Architecture and the Dating of *Beowulf.*" *Poetica: An International Journal of Linguistic-Literary Studies* 34 (1991): 39–56.

Klinck, Anne, ed. *The Old English Elegies: A Critical Edition and Genre Study.* Montreal: McGill Queen's University Press, 1992.

Kolve, V. A. *Chaucer and the Imagery of Narrative: The First Five Canterbury Tales.* Stanford: Stanford University Press, 1984.

Kramer, Johanna. "'þu eart se weallstan': Architectural Metaphor and Christological Imagery in the Old English *Christ I* and the Book of Kells." *Source of Wisdom: Old English and Early Medieval Latin Studies in Honour of Thomas D. Hill.* Ed. Charles D. Wright, Frederick M. Biggs, and Thomas N. Hall. Toronto: University of Toronto Press, 2007. 90–112.

Krapp, George Philip, ed. *The Junius Manuscript.* Anglo-Saxon Poetic Records, vol. 1. New York: Columbia University Press, 1931.

———. *The Vercelli Book.* Anglo-Saxon Poetic Records. Vol. 2. New York: Columbia University Press, 1932.

Krapp, George Philip, and Elliot Van Kirk Dobbie, eds. *The Exeter Book.* Anglo-Saxon Poetic Records, vol. 3. New York: Columbia University Press, 1936.

Lang, James. "The Imagery of the Franks Casket: Another Approach." *Northumbria's Golden Age.* Ed. Jane Hawkes and Susan Mills. Phoenix Mill: Sutton Publishing, 1999. 247–55.

Lapidge, Michael. "The Anglo-Latin Background." *A New Critical History of Old English Literature.* Ed. Stanley B. Greenfield and Daniel G. Calder. New York: New York University Press, 1986. 5–37.

———. "Cynewulf and the *Passio S. Iulianae.*" *Unlocking the Wordhord: Studies in Memory of Edward B. Irving Jr.* Ed. Mark Amodio and Katherine O'Brien O'Keeffe. Toronto: University of Toronto Press, 2003. 147–71.

Laskaya, Anne, and Eve Salisbury, eds. *Sir Orfeo. The Middle English Breton Lays.* Kalamazoo, MI: Medieval Institute Publications, 1995.

Lee, Alvin. *Gold-hall and Earth Dragon: Beowulf as Metaphor.* Toronto: University of Toronto Press, 1998.

Leech, Roger H. "Impermanent Architecture in the English Colonies of the Eastern Caribbean: New Contexts for Innovation in the Early Modern Atlantic World." *Perspectives in Vernacular Architecture* 10 (2005): 153–67.

Lees, Clare A., and Gillian R. Overing. "Before History, Before Difference: Bodies, Metaphor, and the Church in Anglo-Saxon England." *Yale Journal of Criticism* 11.2 (1998): 315–34.

Lerer, Seth. *Error and the Academic Self: The Scholarly Imagination, Medieval to Modern.* New York: Columbia University Press, 2002.

———. *Literacy and Power in Anglo-Saxon Literature.* Lincoln: University of Nebraska Press, 1991.

Le Saux, Françoise H. M. *Laȝamon's* Brut: *The Poem and Its Sources.* Cambridge: D. S. Brewer, 1989.

Leslie, Roy F. *Three Old English Elegies.* Manchester: University of Manchester Press, 1961.

Liberi Ezrae, Tobiae, Iudith. Biblia Sacra Iuxta Latinam Vulgatam Versionem ad Codicum Fidem. Ordinis Sancti Benedicti, vol. 8. Rome: Typsis Polyglotttis Vaticanis, 1926.

Lionarons, Joyce Tally. "Bodies, Buildings, and Boundaries: Metaphors of Liminality in Old English and Old Norse Literature." *Essays in Medieval Studies* 11 (1994): 43–50.

Liuzza, Roy M., trans. *Beowulf.* Peterborough, ON: Broadview Press, 2000.

———. "*Sir Orfeo:* Sources, Traditions, and the Poetics of Performance." *Journal of Medieval and Renaissance Studies* 21 (1991): 269–84.

———. "The Tower of Babel: *The Wanderer* and the Ruins of History." *Studies in the Literary Imagination* 36 (2003): 1–35.

Longsworth, Robert M. "*Sir Orfeo,* the Minstrel, and the Minstrel's Art." *Studies in Philology* 79 (1982): 1–11.

Loomis, Roger Sherman, and Laura Hibbard Loomis, trans. *Medieval Romances.* New York: McGraw-Hill, 1965.

Lord, Albert. *The Singer of Tales.* Cambridge, MA: Harvard University Press, 1960. Rpt. 2000.

———. "The Theme in Anglo-Saxon Poetry." *The Singer Resumes the Tale.* Ed. Mary Louise Lord. Ithaca: Cornell University Press, 1995. 137–66.

———. "The Theme of the Withdrawn Hero in Serbo-Croatian Oral Epic." *Prilozi za književnost, jezik, istoriju i folklor* 35 (1969): 18–30.

Lucas, Peter. "The Cloud in the Interpretation of the Old English *Exodus.*" *English Studies* 51 (1970): 297–311.

———, ed. *Exodus.* London: Methuen, 1977.

Luyster, Robert. "*The Wife's Lament* in the Context of Scandinavian Myth and Ritual." *Philological Quarterly* 77 (1998): 243–70.

Mackay, Anne. "Narrative Tradition in Early Greek Oral Poetry and Vase Painting." *Oral Tradition* 10 (1995): 282–303.

Magennis, Hugh. *Images of Community in Old English Poetry.* Cambridge: Cambridge University Press, 1996.

Markey, Thomas. "Germanic Terms for Temple and Cult." *Studies for Einar Haugen.* Ed. Nils Hasselmo, Evelyn Firchow-Coleman, and Kaaren Grimstad. The Hague and Paris: Mouton, 1972. 365–78.

Marsden, Barry. *The Early Barrow-Diggers.* Ann Arbor: University of Michigan Press, 1974.

Marsden, Richard. *The Text of the Old Testament in Anglo-Saxon England.* Cambridge Studies in Anglo-Saxon England 15. Cambridge: Cambridge University Press, 1995.

Martin, Richard P. "Similes and Performance." *Written Voices, Spoken Signs: Tradition, Performance, and the Epic Text.* Ed. Egbert Bakker and Ahuvia Kahane. Cambridge, MA: Harvard University Press, 1997. 138–66.

Mattox, Wesley S. "Encirclement and Sacrifice in 'Wulf and Eadwacer.'" *Annuale Mediaevale* 16 (1975): 33–40.

McClendon, Charles B. *The Origins of Medieval Architecture: Building in Europe, A.D. 600–900.* New Haven: Yale University Press, 2005.

McDonald, Dennis Ronald, ed. *Acts of Andrew and the Acts of Andrew and Matthias in the City of the Cannibals.* Atlanta: Scholars Press, 1990.

McDonald, Margaret Read. *Ghost Stories from the Pacific Northwest.* American Storytelling. Little Rock: August House, 1995.

McFayden, N. Lindsay. "Architecture and Alliteration in the Old English *Advent.*" *Language Quarterly* 15.3–4 (1977): 56, 60.

McGillivray, Murray. *Memorization in the Transmission of the Middle English Romances.* Albert Bates Lord Studies in Oral Tradition, 5. New York: Garland, 1990.

Middle English Dictionary. Ed. Frances McSparran et al. Ann Arbor: University of Michigan Press, 2001. Available through University of Michigan Digital Library Service: http://quod.lib.umich.edu/m/med/.

Migne, J. P., ed. *Patrologia Latina.* Vol. 77. Electronic database. Alexandria, VA: Chadwyck Healey, 1996. http://pld.chadwyck.co.uk.

Millns, Tony. "The 'Wanderer' 98: 'Weal Wundrum Heah Wyrmlicum Fah.'" *Review of English Studies* 28 (1977): 431–38.

Mills, Susan. "(Re)Constructing Northumbrian Timber Buildings: The Bede's World Experience." *Northumbria's Golden Age.* Ed. J. Hawkes and S. Mills. Phoenix Mill: Sutton Publishing, 1999. 66–72.

Mitchell, Peta. "Constructing the Architext: Georges Perec's *Life a User's Manual.*" *Mosaic* 37 (2004): 1–16.

Mora, María José. "The Invention of the Old English Elegy." *English Studies* 76 (1995): 129–39.

Morris, Richard, ed. *The Blickling Homilies.* EETS. London: Oxford University Press, 1874–80.

Muir, Bernard J., ed. *The Exeter Anthology of Old English Poetry.* 2 vols. 2nd ed. rev. Exeter: University of Exeter Press, 2000.

Mynors, R. A. B., ed. and trans. *Gesta Regum Anglorum: The History of the English Kings.* By William of Malmesbury. Vol. 1. Completed by R. M. Thomson and M. Winterbottom. Oxford: Clarendon Press, 1998.

Nalbantoğlu, Gülsüm Baydar. "Beyond Lack and Excess: Other Architectures/Other Landscapes." *Journal of Architectural Education* 54 (2000): 20–27.

Nelson, Marie. *Judith, Juliana, and Elene: Three Fighting Saints.* New York: Peter Lang, 1991.

Neuman de Vegvar, Carol. "Reading the Franks Casket: Contexts and Audiences." *Intertexts: Studies in Anglo-Saxon Culture Presented to Paul Szarmach.* Ed. Virginia Blanton and Helene Scheck. Tempe: Arizona Center for Medieval and Renaissance Studies, 2008. 141–59.

Neville, Jennifer. *Representations of the Natural World in Old English Poetry.* Cambridge Studies in Anglo-Saxon England 27. Cambridge: Cambridge University Press, 1999.

Niditch, Susan. *Oral World and Written Word.* Louisville, KY: Westminster John Knox Press, 1996.

Niles, John. "Beowulf's Great Hall." *History Today* 56 (2006): 40–44.

———. *Homo Narrans: The Poetics and Anthropology of Oral Literature.* Philadelphia: University of Pennsylvania Press, 1999.

Niles, John, and Mark Amodio, eds. *Anglo-Scandinavian England: Norse-English Relations in the Period before the Conquest.* Lanham, MD: University Press of America, 1989.

Niles, John, et al., eds. *Beowulf and Lejre.* Medieval and Renaissance Texts and Studies 323. Tempe: Arizona Center for Medieval and Renaissance Studies, 2007.

Niles, Susan A. *The Shape of Inca History: Narrative and Architecture in an Andean Empire.* Iowa City: University of Iowa Press, 1999.

Noble, James. "Laȝamon's 'Ambivalence' Reconsidered." *The Text and Tradition of Laȝamon's* Brut. Ed. Françoise Le Saux. Cambridge: D. S. Brewer, 1994. 171–82.

Noel, William. *The Harley Psalter.* Cambridge: Cambridge University Press, 1995.

North, Richard. *Heathen Gods in Old English Literature.* Cambridge: Cambridge University Press, 1997.

North, Sterling. *Abe Lincoln: Log Cabin to White House.* New York: Random House, 1993. Orig. 1956.

Notopoulos, James A. "Continuity and Interconnexion in Homeric Oral Composition." *Transactions of the American Philological Association* 82 (1951): 81–101.

———. "Parataxis in Homer." *Transactions of the American Philological Association* 80 (1949): 1–23.

O'Brien O'Keeffe, Katherine. "Deaths and Transformations: Thinking through the 'End' of Old English Verse." *New Directions in Oral Theory.* Ed. Mark C. Amodio. Tempe: Medieval and Renaissance Texts and Studies, 2003. 149–78.

———. "The Performing Body on the Oral-Literate Continuum: Old English Poetry." *Teaching Oral Traditions.* Ed. John Miles Foley. New York: Modern Language Association, 1998. 46–58.

———, ed. *Reading Old English Texts.* Cambridge: Cambridge University Press, 1997.

———. *Visible Song: Transitional Literacy in Old English Verse.* Cambridge: Cambridge University Press, 1992.

O'Donnell, Daniel Paul. "Fish and Fowl: Generic Expectations and the Relationship between the Old English *Phoenix* Poem and Lactantius's *De Ave Phoenice.*" *Germania Latina* 4 (2001): 157–71.

Oliver, Lisi. *The Beginnings of English Law.* Toronto: University of Toronto Press, 2002.

Oliver, Paul. *Dwellings: The Vernacular House Worldwide.* Austin: University of Texas Press, 1987.

Olsen, Alexandra H. "Oral Formulaic Research in Old English Studies. Part 1." *Oral Tradition* 1 (1986): 548–606.

———. "Oral Formulaic Research in Old English Studies. Part 2." *Oral Tradition* 3 (1988): 138–90.

Ong, Walter. *Orality and Literacy.* New York: Routledge, 1982.

———. "A Writer's Audience Is Always a Fiction." *PMLA* 90 (1975): 9–21.

Opie, Iona, and Peter Opie. *The Classic Fairy Tales.* New York: Oxford University Press, 1974.

Orchard, Andy. "Oral Tradition." *Reading Old English Texts.* Ed. Katherine O'Brien O'Keeffe. Cambridge: Cambridge University Press, 1997. 101–23.

———. "Reconstructing *The Ruin.*" *Intertexts: Studies in Anglo-Saxon Culture Presented to Paul Szarmach.* Ed. Virginia Blanton and Helene Scheck. Tempe: Arizona Center for Medieval and Renaissance Studies, 2008. 45–67.

O'Toole, Tess. "Siblings and Suitors in the Narrative Architecture of The Tenant of Wildfell Hall." *SEL: Studies in English Literature, 1500–1900* 39 (1999): 715–31.

Ousby, Ian. *Blue Guide, England.* London: A&C Black, 1995.

Overing, Gillian R. "Some Aspects of Metonymy in Old English Poetry." *Old English Shorter Poems: Basic Readings.* Ed. Katherine O'Brien O'Keeffe. New York: Garland, 1994. 85–102.

Overing, Gillian R., and Marijane Osborn. *Landscape of Desire: Partial Stories of the Medieval Scandinavian World.* Minneapolis: University of Minnesota Press, 1994.

Oxford English Dictionary. 20 vols. 2nd ed. New York: Oxford University Press, 1989. Available at www.oed.com.

Page, R. I. *Anglo-Saxon Aptitudes: An Inaugural Lecture Delivered before the University of Cambridge on 6 March 1985.* Cambridge: Cambridge University Press, 1985.

Parks, Ward. "The Oral-Formulaic Theory in Middle English Studies." *Oral Tradition* 1 (1986): 636–94.

———. "The Return Song and a Middle English Romance: *Sir Orfeo,* 'Četić Osmanbey,' 'Djulić Ibrahim,' and the *Odyssey.*" *Southeastern Europe* 10 (1983): 222–41.

Pasternack, Carol Braun. "Anonymous Polyphony and the *Wanderer*'s Textuality." *Anglo-Saxon England* 20 (1991): 99–122.

———. *The Textuality of Old English Poetry.* Cambridge: Cambridge University Press, 1995.

Pearson, Mike, and Michael Shanks. *Theatre/Archaeology.* London: Routledge, 2001.

Perdue, Martin. "Hiding behind Trees and Building Shelter without Walls: Stick and Foliate Structures in the Civil War Landscape." *Perspectives in Vernacular Architecture* 9 (2003): 101–15.

Pickles, Christopher. *Texts and Monuments: A Study of Ten Anglo-Saxon Churches of the Pre-Viking Period.* BAR British Series 277. Oxford: Archaeopress, Publishers of British Archaeological Reports, 1999.

Pocock, Michael, and Hazel Wheeler. "Excavations at Escomb Church, County Durham." *Journal of the British Archaeological Association* 34 (1971): 11–29.

Pollington, Stephen. *The Mead-Hall: The Feasting Tradition in Anglo-Saxon England.* Norfolk, U.K.: Anglo-Saxon Books, 2003.

Pope, John C. "Dramatic Voices in *The Wanderer* and *The Seafarer*." *Franciplegius: Medieval and Linguistic Studies in Honour of F. P. Magoun, Jr.* Ed. J. B. Bessinger and R. P. Creed. New York: New York University Press, 1965. 164–93.

———. "Second Thoughts on the Interpretation of *The Seafarer*." *Anglo-Saxon England* 3 (1974): 75–86.

Pragnell, Hubert. *The Styles of English Architecture.* London: B. T. Batsford, 1984.

Pugh, R. B. *Imprisonment in Medieval England.* Cambridge: Cambridge University Press, 1968.

Quinn, William A., and Audley S. Hall. *Jongleur: A Modified Theory of Oral Improvisation.* Washington, DC: University Press of America, 1982.

Radford, C. A. Ralegh. "The Saxon House: A Review and Some Parallels." *Medieval Archaeology* 1 (1957): 27–56.

Raffel, Burton, and Alexandra H. Olsen, ed. and trans. *Poems and Prose from the Old English.* New Haven: Yale University Press, 1998.

Randall, Dale B. J. "Was the Green Knight a Fiend?" *Studies in Philology* 57 (1960): 479–91.

Reed, Michael. *Landscape of Britain: From the Beginnings to 1914.* London: Routledge, 1990.

Renoir, Alain. "Descriptive Techniques in *Sir Gawain and the Green Knight*." *Orbis Littararum* 13 (1958): 126–32.

———. "*Judith* and the Limits of Poetry." *English Studies* 43 (1962): 144–55.

———. *A Key to Old Poems: The Oral-Formulaic Approach to the Interpretation of West-Germanic Verse.* University Park: Pennsylvania State University Press, 1988.

———. "The Progressive Magnification: An Instance of Psychological Description in *Sir Gawain and the Green Knight*." *Modern Språk* 54 (1960): 245–53.

———. "A Reading Context for *The Wife's Lament*." *Anglo-Saxon Poetry: Essays in Appreciation for John C. McGalliard.* Ed. Lewis E. Nicholson, Dolores Warwick

Frese, and John C. Gerber. Notre Dame: University of Notre Dame Press, 1975. 224–41.

Richards, J. M. *The National Trust Book of English Architecture*. New York: W. W. Norton, 1981.

Richardson, Vicky. *New Vernacular Architecture*. New York: Watson-Guptill Publications, 2001.

Rigby, S. H. *Medieval Grimsby: Growth and Decline*. Hull: University of Hull Press, 1993.

Roberts, Alexander, and James Donaldson, eds. and trans. *The Ante-Nicene Fathers: Translations of the Writings of the Fathers Down to A.D. 325*. Vol. 7. Buffalo: Christian Literature Co., 1886.

Rodwell, Warwick. "Anglo-Saxon Church Building: Aspects of Design and Construction." *The Anglo-Saxon Church*. CBA Research Report No. 60. London: Council for British Archaeology, 1986. 156–75.

Rouse, Robert. "English Identity in *Havelok, Horne Childe*, and *Beues of Hamtoun*." *Cultural Encounters in the Romance of Medieval England*. Rochester: D. S. Brewer, 2005. 69–83.

Rudofsky, Bernard. *Architecture without Architects: A Short Introduction to Non-Pedigreed Architecture*. Albuquerque: University of New Mexico Press, 1964.

Russom, Geoffrey. "A Germanic Concept of Nobility in *The Gifts of Men* and *Beowulf*." *Speculum* 53 (1978): 1–15.

Ryan, Michael. "Sacred Cities?" *Text, Image, Interpretation: Studies in Anglo-Saxon Literature and Its Insular Context in Honour of Éamonn Ó Carragáin*." Ed. Alastair Minnis and Jane Roberts. Turnhout: Brepols, 2007. 515–28.

St. James Church, Selham: A Church Guide. 1998.

Sands, Donald B., ed. *Middle English Verse Romances*. New York: Holt, Rinehart, and Winston, 1966.

Schaefer, Ursula. "*Ceteris Imparibus*: Orality/Literacy and the Establishment of Anglo-Saxon Literate Culture." *The Preservation and Transmission of Anglo-Saxon Culture*. Ed. Paul E. Szarmach and Joel T. Rosenthal. Kalamazoo, MI: Medieval Institute Publications, 1997. 287–311.

———. "Hearing from Books: The Rise of Fictionality in Old English Poetry." *Vox Intexta: Orality and Textuality in the Middle Ages*. Ed. A. N. Doane and Carol Braun Pasternack. Madison: University of Wisconsin Press, 1991. 117–36.

Scott, Felicity. "Underneath Aesthetics and Utility: The Untransposable Fetish of Bernard Rudofsky." *Assemblage* 38 (1999): 58–89.

Serjeantson, Mary S. *A History of Foreign Words in English*. London: Routledge and Kegan Paul, 1935.

Sherratt, Susan. "Archaeological Contexts." *A Companion to Ancient Epic*. Ed. John Miles Foley. London: Blackwell, 2005. 119–41.

Shurtleff, Harold R. *The Log Cabin Myth: A Study of the Early Dwellings of the English Colonists in North America*. Ed. and introd. Samuel Eliot Morison. Cambridge, MA: Harvard University Press, 1939.

Smenton, Letha. "The Heritage of Timber Architecture in Anglo-Saxon Stone Churches." *Gesta* 1 (1963): 8–11.

Smithers, G. V., ed. *Havelok the Dane.* Oxford: Clarendon, 1987.

Stanbury, Sarah. *Seeing the* Gawain-*Poet: Description and the Act of Perception.* Philadelphia: University of Pennsylvania Press, 1991.

Stanley, Eric. "*Staþol*: A Firm Foundation for Imagery." *Text, Image, Interpretation: Studies in Anglo-Saxon Literature and Its Insular Context in Honour of Éamonn Ó Carragáin.* Ed. Alastair Minnis and Jane Roberts. Turnhout: Brepols, 2007. 319–32.

Stanton, Robert. *The Culture of Translation in Anglo-Saxon England.* Cambridge: D. S. Brewer, 2002.

Stevenson, William Henry, ed. *Asser's* Life of King Alfred. Oxford: Clarendon, 1959.

Stewart, Marion. "King Orphius." *Scottish Studies* 17 (1973): 1–16.

Stock, Brian. *The Implications of Literacy: Written Language and Models of Interpretation in the Eleventh and Twelfth Centuries.* Princeton: Princeton University Press, 1983.

———. *Listening for the Text: On the Uses of the Past.* Baltimore: Johns Hopkins University Press, 1990.

Stoll, Robert. *Architecture and Sculpture in Early Britain.* Photographs by Jean Roubier. New York: Viking, 1967.

Strunk, William, Jr., ed. *Juliana.* Boston: Heath and Co., 1904.

Sweet, Henry, ed. *King Alfred's West-Saxon Version of Gregory's Pastoral Care.* London: Early English Text Society, 1958. Orig. 1871.

Swisher, Michael. "Beyond the Hoar Stone." *Neophilologus* 86 (2002): 133–36.

Taylor, Harold McCarter. *St. Wystan's Church, Repton: A Guide and History.* Derby: J. M. Tatler & Son, 1989.

Taylor, Harold McCarter, and Joan Taylor. *Anglo-Saxon Architecture.* 3 vols. Cambridge: Cambridge University Press, 1965.

Tedlock, Dennis, ed. and trans. *Finding the Center.* Lincoln: University of Nebraska Press, 1972.

Thompson, M. W. "The Green Knight's Castle." *Studies in Medieval History Presented to R. Allen Brown.* Woodbridge: Boydell, 1989. 317–25.

———. *The Medieval Hall: The Basis of Secular Domestic Life, 600–1600 A.D.* Aldershot: Scolar Press, 1995.

———. *The Rise of the Castle.* Cambridge: Cambridge University Press, 1991.

Thomson, R. M., with the assistance of M. Winterbottom. *Gesta Pontificum Anglorum: The History of the English Bishops.* By William of Malmesbury. Vol. 2: *Commentary.* Oxford: Clarendon, 2007.

———. *Gesta Regum Anglorum: The History of the English Kings.* By William of Malmesbury. Vol. 2: *General Introduction and Commentary.* Oxford: Clarendon, 1999.

Thorpe, Benjamin, ed. *Ælfric: Sermones Catholici.* 2 vols. Hildesheim: Georg Olms Verlag, 1983.

———. *Ancient Laws and Institutes of England*. London: Eyre & Spottiswoode, 1840.

———. *Codex exoniensis: A Collection of Anglo-Saxon Poetry, from a Manuscript in the Library of the Dean and Chapter of Exeter*. London: Society of Antiquaries of London, 1842. Orig. Oxford University, digitized in 2007.

Thurlby, Malcolm. "Anglo-Saxon Architecture beyond the Millennium: Its Continuity in Norman Building." *The White Mantle of Churches: Architecture, Liturgy, and Art Around the Millennium*. Ed. Nigel Hiscock. International Medieval Research, Art History 10. Turnhout, Belgium: Brepols, 2003. 119–38.

Timmer, B. J., ed. *Judith*. London: Methuen, 1961.

Titon, Jeff Todd. "Text." *Eight Words for the Study of Expressive Culture*. Ed. Burt Feintuch. Urbana: University of Illinois Press, 2003. 69–98.

Toelken, Barre. *The Dynamics of Folklore*. 2nd ed. Logan: University of Utah Press, 1996.

———. *Morning Dew and Roses: Nuance, Metaphor, and Meaning in Folksongs*. Urbana: University of Illinois Press, 1995.

Tolkien, J. R. R. "The Monsters and the Critics." *The Beowulf Poet: A Collection of Critical Essays*. Ed. Donald K. Fry. Englewood Cliffs, NJ: Prentice-Hall, 1968. 8–56. Orig. 1936.

———, ed. *The Old English Exodus*. Oxford: Clarendon, 1981.

Tolkien, J. R. R., and E. V. Gordon, eds. *Sir Gawain and the Green Knight*. 2nd ed. rev. Norman Davis. Oxford: Clarendon, 1967.

Treharne, Elaine. *Old and Middle English, c. 890–1400: An Anthology*. 2nd ed. Malden, MA: Blackwell, 2004.

Trilling, Renée R. *The Aesthetics of Nostalgia: Historical Representation in Old English Verse*. Toronto: University of Toronto Press, 2009.

Trimpi, Wesley. *Muses of One Mind: The Literary Analysis of Experience and Its Continuity*. Princeton: Princeton University Press, 1983.

Turner, Victor. "Process, System, and Symbol: A New Synthesis." *Daedalus* 106 (177): 61–80.

Twomey, Michael W. "Morgan le Fay at Hautdesert." *On Arthurian Women: Essays in Memory of Maureen Fries*. Ed. Bonnie Wheeler and Fiona Tolhurst. Dallas: Scriptorium Press, 2001. 103–19.

Van Dine, Alan. *Uncommon Structures, Unconventional Builders*. New York: Black Dog and Leventhal, 2001. Orig. 1977.

Vance, Mary. *Anglo-Saxon Architecture: A Bibliography of English Language References*. Monticello, IL: Vance Bibliographies, 1982.

Veck, Sonya. "Anglo-Saxon Oral Tradition and *King Horn*." Ph.D. dissertation, University of Denver, 2006.

Walker-Pelkey, Faye. "Frige hwæt in hatte: *The Wife's Lament* as Riddle." *Papers on Language and Literature* 28 (1992): 227–41.

Waterhouse, Ruth. "Spatial Perception and Conceptions in the (Re-)Presenting and (Re-)Constructing of Old English Texts." *Parergon* 9 (1991): 87–102.

Watkin, David. *English Architecture: A Concise History.* London: Thames and Hudson, 1979.

Watkins, Calvert. *How to Kill a Dragon: Aspects of Indo-European Poetics.* Oxford: Oxford University Press, 1995.

Webster, Leslie. "The Iconographic Programme of the Franks Casket." *Northumbria's Golden Age.* Ed. Jane Hawkes and Susan Mills. Phoenix Mill: Sutton Publishing, 1999. 227–46.

———. "Stylistic Aspects of the Franks Casket." *The Vikings.* Ed. R. Farrell. London: Phillimore, 1982. 20–31.

Wehlau, Ruth. *The Riddle of Creation: Metaphor Structures in Old English Poetry.* New York: Peter Lang, 1997.

Wells, Camille. "Introduction." *Perspectives in Vernacular Architecture* 1 (1982): 5–6.

———. "Old Claims and New Demands: Vernacular Architecture Studies Today." *Perspectives in Vernacular Architecture* 2 (1986): 1–10.

Wells, John Edwin. *A Manual of the Writings in Middle English, 1050–1400.* New Haven: Yale University Press, 1916.

Wentersdorf, Karl P. "The *Beowulf*-poet's Vision of Heorot." *Studies in Philology* 104 (2007): 409–26.

———. "Observations on *The Ruin.*" *Medium Ævum* 46 (1977): 171–80.

———. "The Situation of the Narrator in *The Wife's Lament.*" *Speculum* 56 (1981): 492–516.

Weslager, C. A. *The Log Cabin in America: From Pioneer Days to the Present.* New Brunswick, NJ: Rutgers University Press, 1969.

West, Stanley. *West Stow: The Anglo-Saxon Village.* 2 vols. East Anglian Archaeology Reports, nos. 24 and 25. Ipswich: Suffolk County Planning Department, 1985.

West Stow. DVD. Produced by Take One Productions for West Stow Anglo-Saxon Village Trust, 2004. Includes excavation archive and interviews with Stanley West.

Whitehead, M. A., and J. D. Whitehead. *The Saxon Church Escomb.* Escomb, 1975. Rev. 1992.

Whitelock, Dorothy. *The Beginnings of English Society.* Harmondsworth: Penguin, 1952.

Wickham-Crowley, Kelley M. "Looking Forward, Looking Back: Excavating the Field of Anglo-Saxon Archaeology." *The Archaeology of Anglo-Saxon England.* New York: Garland, 1999. 1–24.

Williamson, Craig, trans. *A Feast of Creatures: Anglo-Saxon Riddle Songs.* Philadelphia: University of Pennsylvania Press, 1982.

———, ed. *The Old English Riddles of the Exeter Book.* Chapel Hill: University of North Carolina Press, 1977.

Winterbottom, M., ed. and trans., with the assistance of R. M. Thomson. *Gesta Pontificum Anglorum: The History of the English Bishops.* By William of Malmesbury. Vol. 1: *Text and Translation.* Oxford: Clarendon, 1999.

Wittig, Susan. *Stylistic and Narrative Structures in the Middle English Romances.* Austin: University of Texas Press, 1978.

Wolfreys, J. "Dickensian Architextures or, the City and the Ineffable." *Victorian Identities: Social and Cultural Formations in Nineteenth-Century Literature.* Ed. R. Robbins and J. Wolfreys. Basingstoke: Macmillan, 1996. 199–214.

Woods, Andrew. *Young Abraham Lincoln: Log Cabin President.* Mahwah, NJ: Troll Communications, 1991.

Woolf, Rosemary, ed. *Juliana.* Methuen's Old English Library. London: Methuen, 1955.

Wright, Charles D. *The Irish Tradition in Old English Literature.* Cambridge: Cambridge University Press, 1993.

Yarwood, Doreen. *The Architecture of Britain.* New York: Charles Scribner's Sons, 1976.

Zumthor, Paul. *Toward a Medieval Poetics.* Trans. Philip Bennett. Minneapolis: University of Minnesota Press, 1992. Orig. 1972.

INDEX

LORI ANN GARNER

is assistant professor of English at Rhodes College, Memphis, Tennessee.